Physical Activity and Nutrition Survey and Evaluation for Public Health

Physical Activity and Nutrition Survey and Evaluation for Public Health

Editors

Roberto Pippi
Carmine Giuseppe Fanelli
Matteo Vandoni

MDPI

Basel • Beijing • Wuhan • Barcelona • Belgrade • Novi Sad • Cluj • Manchester

Editors
Roberto Pippi
University of Perugia
Perugia, Italy

Carmine Giuseppe Fanelli
Perugia University School of Medicine
Perugia, Italy

Matteo Vandoni
Università di Pavia
Pavia, Italy

Editorial Office
MDPI
St. Alban-Anlage 66
4052 Basel, Switzerland

This is a reprint of articles from the Special Issue published online in the open access journal *Nutrients* (ISSN 2072-6643) (available at: https://www.mdpi.com/journal/nutrients/special_issues/physical_activity_nutrition_survey_evaluation).

For citation purposes, cite each article independently as indicated on the article page online and as indicated below:

Lastname, A.A.; Lastname, B.B. Article Title. *Journal Name* **Year**, *Volume Number*, Page Range.

ISBN 978-3-0365-9156-8 (Hbk)
ISBN 978-3-0365-9157-5 (PDF)
doi.org/10.3390/books978-3-0365-9157-5

Contents

Roberto Pippi, Matteo Vandoni and Carmine Giuseppe Fanelli
Physical Activity and Nutrition Survey and Evaluation for Public Health
Reprinted from: *Nutrients* **2023**, *15*, 4139, doi:10.3390/nu15194139 1

Bruno Trovato, Justyna Godos, Simone Varrasi, Federico Roggio, Sabrina Castellano and Giuseppe Musumeci
Physical Activity, Sun Exposure, Vitamin D Intake and Perceived Stress in Italian Adults
Reprinted from: *Nutrients* **2023**, *15*, 2301, doi:10.3390/nu15102301 5

Cristian Petri, Matteo Levi Micheli, Pascal Izzicupo, Niccolò Timperanza, Tommaso Lastrucci, Daniele Vanni, et al.
Bioimpedance Patterns and Bioelectrical Impedance Vector Analysis (BIVA) of Body Builders
Reprinted from: *Nutrients* **2023**, *15*, 1606, doi:10.3390/nu15071606 17

Valeria Calcaterra, Giuseppina Bernardelli, Mara Malacarne, Matteo Vandoni, Savina Mannarino, Vittoria Carnevale Pellino, et al.
Effects of Endurance Exercise Intensities on Autonomic and Metabolic Controls in Children with Obesity: A Feasibility Study Employing Online Exercise Training
Reprinted from: *Nutrients* **2023**, *15*, 1054, doi:10.3390/nu15041054 27

Daniel Śliż, Szczepan Wiecha, Jakub S. Gąsior, Przemysław Seweryn Kasiak, Katarzyna Ulaszewska, Marek Postuła, et al.
The Influence of Nutrition and Physical Activity on Exercise Performance after Mild COVID-19 Infection in Endurance Athletes-CESAR Study
Reprinted from: *Nutrients* **2022**, *14*, 5381, doi:10.3390/nu14245381 45

Roberto Pippi, Matteo Vandoni, Matteo Tortorella, Vittorio Bini and Carmine Giuseppe Fanelli
Supervised Exercise in Water: Is It a Viable Alternative in Overweight/Obese People with or without Type 2 Diabetes? A Pilot Study
Reprinted from: *Nutrients* **2022**, *14*, 4963, doi:10.3390/nu14234963 59

Hao-Ting Ke, Chi-Lin Hsieh and Wei-Jen Cheng
Physical Activity, Dietary Behavior, and Body Weight Changes during the COVID-19 Nationwide Level 3 Alert in Taiwan: Results of a Taiwanese Online Survey
Reprinted from: *Nutrients* **2022**, *14*, 4941, doi:10.3390/nu14224941 69

Mario Kasović, Lovro Štefan and Zvonimir Kalčik
Acute Responses to Resistance Training on Body Composition, Muscular Fitness and Flexibility by Sex and Age in Healthy War Veterans Aged 50–80 Years
Reprinted from: *Nutrients* **2022**, *14*, 3436, doi:10.3390/nu14163436 81

Mateusz Grajek, Karolina Krupa-Kotara, Krzysztof Sas-Nowosielski, Ewa Misterska and Joanna Kobza
Prevalence of Orthorexia in Groups of Students with Varied Diets and Physical Activity (Silesia, Poland)
Reprinted from: *Nutrients* **2022**, *14*, 2816, doi:10.3390/nu14142816 91

Luis M. Béjar
Weekend–Weekday Differences in Adherence to the Mediterranean Diet among Spanish University Students
Reprinted from: *Nutrients* **2022**, *14*, 2811, doi:10.3390/nu14142811 107

Valentina Natalucci, Federica Marmondi, Michele Biraghi and Matteo Bonato
The Effectiveness of Wearable Devices in Non-Communicable Diseases to Manage Physical Activity and Nutrition: Where We Are?
Reprinted from: *Nutrients* **2023**, *15*, 913, doi:10.3390/nu15040913 . . . . **131**

Massimiliano Cavallo, Giovanni Morgana, Ivan Dozzani, Alessandro Gatti, Matteo Vandoni, Roberto Pippi, et al.
Unraveling Barriers to a Healthy Lifestyle: Understanding Barriers to Diet and Physical Activity in Patients with Chronic Non-Communicable Diseases
Reprinted from: *Nutrients* **2023**, *15*, 3473, doi:10.3390/nu15153473 . . . . **151**

Elisabet Montero-Sandiego, Rosario Ferrer-Cascales, Nicolás Ruiz-Robledillo, Borja Costa-López, Cristian Alcocer-Bruno and Natalia Albaladejo-Blázquez
Assessment Strategies to Evaluate the Mediterranean Lifestyle: A Systematic Review
Reprinted from: *Nutrients* **2022**, *14*, 4179, doi:10.3390/nu14194179 . . . . **167**

nutrients

Editorial

Physical Activity and Nutrition Survey and Evaluation for Public Health

Roberto Pippi [1,*], Matteo Vandoni [2] and Carmine Giuseppe Fanelli [1]

1 Centro Universitario Ricerca Interdipartimentale Attività Motoria (C.U.R.I.A.Mo.), Department of Medicine and Surgery, University of Perugia, 06126 Perugia, Italy; carmine.fanelli@unipg.it
2 Laboratory of Adapted Motor Activity (LAMA), Department of Public Health, Experimental Medicine and Forensic Science, University of Pavia, 27100 Pavia, Italy; matteo.vandoni@unipv.it
* Correspondence: roberto.pippi@unipg.it

Citation: Pippi, R.; Vandoni, M.; Fanelli, C.G. Physical Activity and Nutrition Survey and Evaluation for Public Health. *Nutrients* **2023**, *15*, 4139. https://doi.org/10.3390/nu15194139

Received: 13 September 2023
Accepted: 18 September 2023
Published: 25 September 2023

Regular physical activity (PA) and healthy nutrition are effective strategies to improve crucial modifiable lifestyle factors that affect health status, both in healthy people and in special populations suffering from metabolic disorders (e.g., obesity and type 2 diabetes, or DM2) or other Non-Communicable Diseases (NCDs) [1]. For this reason, it is mandatory to provide guidance on the proper implementation of a healthy lifestyle by suggesting nutritional medical therapies and prescribing exercise programs to improve people's health. The evaluation of these modifiable lifestyle factors is also a mandatory component of every medical visit or intervention.

In the Nutrients Special Issue "Physical Activity and Nutrition Survey and Evaluation for Public Health" (https://www.mdpi.com/journal/nutrients/special_issues/physical_activity_nutrition_survey_evaluation (accessed on 22 September 2023)), we presented some papers to focus on the importance of evaluation through surveys, tests, or other forms of evaluation in different settings (i.e., sport and clinical practice) to better orient interventions for public health improvement. This Editorial aims to summarize the twelve articles (nine original articles, one review, and two systematic reviews) that are published in this Special Issue.

Among the behavioral patterns linked to people's health is the Mediterranean Lifestyle (MLS), which includes a high adherence to the Mediterranean Diet (MD) and regular physical activity. Montero-Sandiego et al. [2] presented a systematic review of different methodologies and tools to assess the MLS, and the authors identified four indexes (MEDiLIFE-index, MEDI-Lifestyle, Total Lifestyle Index, and MedCOVID-19 Score). As a consensus has not yet been reached on a single instrument to comprehensively and reliably measure the MLS that has proven and adequate psychometric properties. The authors emphasized the need to design an instrument for the general population that includes all dimensions of the MLS.

Continuing on the theme of Mediterranean nutritional habits, Béjar [3] presented their results on the difference between weekly and weekend dietary patterns that emerged from the evaluation of Mediterranean diet habits in a group of 361 students (263 women and 98 men) of the University of Seville (Andalusia, Spain). Using the Electronic 12-h Dietary Recall smartphone application and calculating the adherence to the Mediterranean diet index, the researchers observed that the diet quality of the entire sample of Spanish university students was poor in general, especially on the weekends. For this reason, these results could be used to improve public health campaigns to promote healthy eating among Spanish university students.

In another paper published in this Special Issue, Trovato et al. [4] analyzed the relationship between PA, sun exposure, vitamin D, and perceived stress in a sample of the general Italian population. The authors identified an association between sunshine/vitamin D only in those who are physically active, suggesting that PA is necessary to realize the benefits of sunshine/vitamin D supplementation for stress.

Some studies of this Special Issue focused on various PA and nutrition aspects that need to be considered when we talk about PA evaluation and prescription. Regarding PA and exercise prescription for health, Calcaterra et al. [5] emphasized the importance of the modality and volume of exercise required to obtain benefits. The authors assessed clinical, auxological, hemodynamic (i.e., weight, height, waist circumference, waist-to-height ratio, visceral adiposity index, fasting blood glucose, lipid profile), and lifestyle parameters (i.e., PA levels, etc.) in a group of 35 children (14 females/21 males) with obesity participating in 12 weeks of online exercise training. The participants were allocated into two groups based on the volume of performed exercise (above or below 1200 MET·min/week). The authors concluded that improvement in the volume of the structured exercise was associated with a reduction in the arterial pressure percentile, and that progress in metabolic controls was evident. Moreover, the online exercise training program, when designed and progressively adapted according to individual fitness level, was a successful instrument and alternative to promote health improvements because it is sustainable both economically and organizationally.

Another alternative card to play in the clinical field is proposed by Pippi et al. [6] with an article examining an aquatic exercise program in 93 adults (72 women and 21 men) with obesity and/or DM2. The paper utilized the well-established evaluation model developed by the C.U.R.I.A.Mo. Healthy Lifestyle Institute of Perugia University (Umbria, Italy). This study showed the effectiveness of an aquatic exercise program, supervised by experts such as kinesiologists, in improving body mass index, waist circumference, and blood pressure values in obese adults with and without type 2 diabetes. The authors recommended the usefulness of aquatic exercise in managing patients with metabolic diseases who often present with other health impairments, such as musculoskeletal problems or cardiovascular or rheumatic disease that could contraindicate gym-based exercise.

Petri et al. [7] performed a body composition assessment in a group of 68 participants (41 males aged 30.1 $\pm$ 9.2 years and 27 females aged 32.1 $\pm$ 8.0 years) at the 2021 World Natural Bodybuilding Federation Italian Championships using the vector bioimpedance methodology (BIVA). The study aimed to provide normative references of body composition with the BIVA and to compare BIVA assessments performed on both sides and the upper and lower body. They concluded that BIVA references in bodybuilders could help adjust their training and nutritional programs during the peak week before a competition.

Kasović et al. [8] evaluated the acute effects of a four-week resistance training program on body composition, muscular fitness, and flexibility in 764 Croatian veterans. The participants were subdivided into two groups (50–64 and 65–80 years old). Based on their results which showed that resistance training increased lean mass, muscular fitness, and flexibility and decreased body weight, body mass index, and fat mass across the groups, the authors concluded that even a relatively short resistance training intervention may lead to higher physical fitness levels in men and women aged 50–80 years.

The "lockdown" and social isolation imposed in some world countries during the SARS-CoV-2 virus global health crisis period led to a drastic alteration in lifestyle habits, which was particularly dangerous for people with NCDs. In this Special Issue, two contributions linked to COVID-19 were presented. Ke et al. [9] presented a study that described an online survey result of PA, dietary behavior, and body weight changes during the COVID-19 nationwide lockdown in Taiwan. The results were obtained from the replies of 374 respondents, aged between 20 and 66, and showed a negative impact on all PA levels of participants, with a significant increase in a sedentary lifestyle. However, the authors reported that some good eating habits, including eating fewer snacks or sweets and being less likely to eat as a reward, significantly increased during this period. This may also explain the lack of significant changes in body weight during the lockdown period. Another contribution to determining the training and nutrition plans of professional athletes after infection with COVID-19 was provided by Sliz et al. [10]. The authors described the assessment of the consequences of SARS-CoV-2 virus infection and pandemic restrictions on nutrition and PA among 49 endurance athletes (43 male and 6 female), and its validation through cardiopulmonary exercise testing. This paper underlined the importance for nutritionists considering which eating habits emerge when athletes have limited training opportunities and spend more time at home (i.e., adequate supply of fluids, fruits and vegetables, vitamins, and whole grains), and that trainers should be more aware of body and performance changes after suffering from COVID-19. In addition, another lesson that the COVID-19 era has taught us is the importance of technology. Considering that wearable devices are increasingly popular in the clinical and non-clinical population as a tool for exercise prescription, the monitoring of daily physical activity and nutrition, and health-related parameter management, Natalucci et al. [11] provided a narrative review of the effectiveness of new technologies in physical activity and nutrition. The authors aimed to review the current application of wearable devices in NCDs, highlighting their role in prescribing and monitoring daily PA and dietary habits in a population living with chronic diseases. This study concluded that the benefits obtained from the use of wearable devices are likely to translate into public health and are important tools for the development of prevention plans in everyday life and clinical practice for optimal patient management.

Although proper nutrition and adequate PA are recognized as the most important factors promoting health, the cult of slimness and excessive attention to a healthy lifestyle in the interaction of some factors can sometimes lead to eating disorders. Orthorexia, in particular, is an informally diagnosed condition characterized by an obsessive preoccupation with eating healthily. This condition is frequently associated with high levels of PA to maintain fitness and health in order to achieve the "ideal" body shape that is promoted by mass media. These themes were discussed by Grajek et al. [12] in their paper evaluating the prevalence of orthorexic behaviors in a group of 300 Polish students in terms of their differential health behaviors, such as diet and PA levels. The authors speculated that students who participate intensely in sports may have a significantly higher exposure to orthorexia than those with lower levels of PA, and they confirmed that orthorexia may occur in students with a low BMI index.

Finally, coaches and clinical team professionals caring for the general population or patients with NDC should better understand the various types of barriers people face that prevent them from adhering to a healthy lifestyle. With regard to difficulties for the general population in adhering to PA and healthy nutrition recommendations, Cavallo et al. [13] presented a systematic review to highlight the barriers that patients with chronic-degenerative diseases experience in implementing a healthier diet and an exercise-based therapeutic program. The authors identified barriers for both for exercise and nutrition including lack of time, environmental barriers, health status, and psychological barriers.

Author Contributions: Conceptualization, R.P., M.V. and C.G.F.; writing—original draft preparation and writing—review and editing, R.P., M.V. and C.G.F. All authors have read and agreed to the published version of the manuscript.

Conflicts of Interest: The authors declare no conflict of interest.

References

1. Marmot, M.; Allen, J.; Bell, R.; Bloomer, E.; Goldblatt, P. Consortium for the European Review of Social Determinants of Health and the Health Divide. WHO European review of social determinants of health and the health divide. *Lancet* **2012**, *380*, 1011–1029. [CrossRef] [PubMed]
2. Montero-Sandiego, E.; Ferrer-Cascales, R.; Ruiz-Robledillo, N.; Costa-López, B.; Alcocer-Bruno, C.; Albaladejo-Blázquez, N. Assessment Strategies to Evaluate the Mediterranean Lifestyle: A Systematic Review. *Nutrients* **2022**, *14*, 4179. [CrossRef]
3. Béjar, L.M. Weekend–Weekday Differences in Adherence to the Mediterranean Diet among Spanish University Students. *Nutrients* **2022**, *14*, 2811. [CrossRef] [PubMed]
4. Trovato, B.; Godos, J.; Varrasi, S.; Roggio, F.; Castellano, S.; Musumeci, G. Physical Activity, Sun Exposure, Vitamin D Intake and Perceived Stress in Italian Adults. *Nutrients* **2023**, *15*, 2301. [CrossRef] [PubMed]
5. Calcaterra, V.; Bernardelli, G.; Malacarne, M.; Vandoni, M.; Mannarino, S.; Pellino, V.C.; Larizza, C.; Pagani, M.; Zuccotti, G.; Lucini, D. Effects of Endurance Exercise Intensities on Autonomic and Metabolic Controls in Children with Obesity: A Feasibility Study Employing Online Exercise Training. *Nutrients* **2023**, *15*, 1054. [CrossRef]

6. Pippi, R.; Vandoni, M.; Tortorella, M.; Bini, V.; Fanelli, C.G. Supervised Exercise in Water: Is It a Viable Alternative in Overweight/Obese People with or without Type 2 Diabetes? A Pilot Study. *Nutrients* **2022**, *14*, 4963. [CrossRef]
7. Petri, C.; Micheli, M.L.; Izzicupo, P.; Timperanza, N.; Lastrucci, T.; Vanni, D.; Gulisano, M.; Mascherini, G. Bioimpedance Patterns and Bioelectrical Impedance Vector Analysis (BIVA) of Body Builders. *Nutrients* **2023**, *15*, 1606. [CrossRef] [PubMed]
8. Kasović, M.; Štefan, L.; Kalčik, Z. Acute Responses to Resistance Training on Body Composition, Muscular Fitness and Flexibility by Sex and Age in Healthy War Veterans Aged 50–80 Years. *Nutrients* **2022**, *14*, 3436. [CrossRef] [PubMed]
9. Ke, H.-T.; Hsieh, C.-L.; Cheng, W.-J. Physical Activity, Dietary Behavior, and Body Weight Changes during the COVID-19 Nationwide Level 3 Alert in Taiwan: Results of a Taiwanese Online Survey. *Nutrients* **2022**, *14*, 4941. [CrossRef] [PubMed]
10. Śliż, D.; Wiecha, S.; Gąsior, J.S.; Kasiak, P.S.; Ulaszewska, K.; Postuła, M.; Małek, Ł.A.; Mamcarz, A. The Influence of Nutrition and Physical Activity on Exercise Performance after Mild COVID-19 Infection in Endurance Athletes-CESAR Study. *Nutrients* **2022**, *14*, 5381. [CrossRef] [PubMed]
11. Natalucci, V.; Marmondi, F.; Biraghi, M.; Bonato, M. The Effectiveness of Wearable Devices in Non-Communicable Diseases to Manage Physical Activity and Nutrition: Where We Are? *Nutrients* **2023**, *15*, 913. [CrossRef] [PubMed]
12. Grajek, M.; Krupa-Kotara, K.; Sas-Nowosielski, K.; Misterska, E.; Kobza, J. Prevalence of Orthorexia in Groups of Students with Varied Diets and Physical Activity (Silesia, Poland). *Nutrients* **2022**, *14*, 2816. [CrossRef]
13. Cavallo, M.; Morgana, G.; Dozzani, I.; Gatti, A.; Vandoni, M.; Pippi, R.; Pucci, G.; Vaudo, G.; Fanelli, C.G. Unraveling Barriers to a Healthy Lifestyle: Understanding Barriers to Diet and Physical Activity in Patients with Chronic Non-Communicable Diseases. *Nutrients* **2023**, *15*, 3473. [CrossRef]

nutrients

MDPI

Article

Physical Activity, Sun Exposure, Vitamin D Intake and Perceived Stress in Italian Adults

Bruno Trovato [1], Justyna Godos [2,*], Simone Varrasi [3], Federico Roggio [1,4], Sabrina Castellano [3,†] and Giuseppe Musumeci [1,†]

[1] Department of Biomedical and Biotechnological Sciences, Section of Anatomy, Histology and Movement Science, School of Medicine, University of Catania, Via S. Sofia 97, 95123 Catania, Italy; bruno.trovato@phd.unict.it (B.T.); federico.roggio@unict.it (F.R.); g.musumeci@unict.it (G.M.)
[2] Department of Biomedical and Biotechnological Sciences, University of Catania, 95123 Catania, Italy
[3] Department of Educational Sciences, University of Catania, 95124 Catania, Italy; simonvarra@gmail.com (S.V.); sabrina.castellano@unict.it (S.C.)
[4] Sport and Exercise Sciences Research Unit, Department of Psychology, Educational Science and Human Movement, University of Palermo, Via Giovanni Pascoli 6, 90144 Palermo, Italy
* Correspondence: justyna.godos@gmail.com
† These authors contributed equally to this work.

Abstract: The last decades of global development have, due to rapid urbanization, pressuring entire populations to changes in lifestyle and dietary habits, led to an increase in the prevalence of mental disorders, including stress. This study explored how lifestyle and dietary factors, such as physical activity, sun exposure, and vitamin D intake are related to perceived stress in a Mediterranean-based population. Physical activity level was evaluated using the international physical activity questionnaires (IPAQ), sun exposure was evaluated using the sunlight exposure measurement questionnaire (SEM-Q), and validated food frequency questionnaires (FFQs) were used to assess dietary intakes. The perceived stress of the study participants was evaluated using the perceived stress scale (PSS). Multivariate logistic regression models were used to test for potential associations. In the most adjusted model, an inverse association between physical activity level, sunlight exposure, vitamin D intake, and high perceived stress was found (OR = 0.72, 95% CI: 0.51, 1.00, OR = 0.72, 95% CI: 0.52, 0.99, OR = 0.69, 95% CI: 0.53, 0.89, respectively). However, when stratifying the population by level of physical activity, the retrieved associations with sunlight exposure and dietary vitamin D intake were significant only among those individuals reporting being moderately to highly physically active (OR = 0.16, 95% CI: 0.08, 0.33 and OR = 0.46, 95% CI: 0.28, 0.76, respectively), while results on low physically active participants were null. In conclusion, this study demonstrated that higher dietary intake of vitamin D and sunlight exposure are associated with a lower likelihood of having high perceived stress among physically active individuals.

Keywords: physical activity; vitamin D; sun exposure; perceived stress; mental health; Mediterranean

Citation: Trovato, B.; Godos, J.; Varrasi, S.; Roggio, F.; Castellano, S.; Musumeci, G. Physical Activity, Sun Exposure, Vitamin D Intake and Perceived Stress in Italian Adults. *Nutrients* **2023**, *15*, 2301. https://doi.org/10.3390/nu15102301

Academic Editor: Aamer Sandoo

Received: 31 March 2023
Revised: 3 May 2023
Accepted: 4 May 2023
Published: 13 May 2023

1. Introduction

The first documented definition of stress in literature is the one given by Selye in 1956, defining stress as a psychological response of the body dealing with positive or negative non-specific demands [1]. Since then, researchers throughout the world failed to identify a rigorous definition of stress, providing misleading definitions of it [2]. The World Health Organization (WHO) defines stress as a state of worry or mental tension due to a difficult situation to challenge. Nowadays, stress is regarded as a series of experiences that generate frustration or anxiety due to a perceived threat to one's security or the inability of an individual to cope with it [3]. Exposure to chronic or acute stressors endorses the release of catecholamines and cortisol that are fundamental for the fight-or-flight response [4]. However, when their levels remain high throughout the day, they can negatively affect psychophysiological well-being [4]. Stressful events are often more easily remembered, and there is a correlation between chronic and acute stress and morphological adaptation/alterations of the amygdala. This indicates that stress has the potential to actively modify a biological system [5]. Furthermore, chronic exposure to stress that elicits a maladaptive response can promote dysregulation of the immune system, inducing migraines and increasing the risk of cardiovascular pathologies, depression, and symptoms related to anxiety [6]. Therefore, targeting modifiable risk factors such as dietary habits and physical activity to improve the resilience of a person is fundamental [7].

Physical activity is one of the most useful strategies to manage stress without the risk of harming an individual with pharmacological treatment. The benefits of physical activity for both healthy and pathological people include reduced risk of metabolic [8], musculoskeletal [9], and neurological diseases [10]. Moreover, the positive effects of being physically active, even at levels below that recommended by the WHO, have also been demonstrated for mental health outcomes [11]. A possible beneficial mechanism through which physical activity may exert an action toward mental health (including tension, anger, and depressive feelings) is outdoor practice [12]. Such activity could increase exposure to sunlight, which can improve mood and has a positive association with cognitive function [13]. Moreover, skin exposure to sunlight starts the metabolism of vitamin D, due to the UVB ray that transforms the 7-dehydrocholesterol in pre-vitamin D3, isomerized later into vitamin D3 [14]. Several studies affirmed that deficiency in levels of vitamin D3 are associated with different health-threatening diseases, such as breast cancer [15], cardio-metabolic conditions [16], musculoskeletal pathologies [17,18], depression [19], and sleep disorders [20]. Low levels of vitamin D may also provoke deficits in strength and degeneration of glycolytic muscle fibers, thus reducing physical performance [21]. The only method to improve the levels of vitamin D, other than the exposition to sunlight, is with nutrition. Currently, in Europe, the intake of vitamin D through nutrition is low and its deficiency in the general population is a main concern for the public health system [22]. Considering that vitamin D supplementation can have positive effects in reducing symptoms of depression and anxiety [23], studying its levels in the general population and promoting a correct intake with nutrition is essential to try to manage stress from different points of view. The aim of this study is to understand the impact of physical activity, sunlight exposure, and vitamin D intake with nutrition on levels of perceived stress in a sample derived from the Italian general population.

2. Materials and Methods

2.1. Study Design and Population

The Mediterranean healthy eating, aging, and lifestyles (MEAL) study is an observational study aiming to assess the link between dietary habits, in the context of a cluster of lifestyle behaviors characterizing the Mediterranean basin, and non-communicable diseases. A complete protocol of the MEAL study has been published previously [24]. The cohort and baseline survey was established between 2014–2015 in southern Italy by randomly enrolling a sample of 2044 men and women aged 18 or more years old through the registered records of local general practitioners stratified by sex and 10-year age groups.

For the purpose of providing a specific relative precision of 5% (Type I error, 0.05; Type II error, 0.10), considering an anticipated 70% participation rate, the theoretical sample size was estimated to be 1500 individuals. In brief, a sample of 2405 individuals was invited to participate in the study, out of which 361 individuals declined, leaving 2044 participants as the final sample included, with a response rate of 85%. The aims of the study were exhaustively explained to all of the participants before the acceptance of participation; those who agreed provided a written informed consent. The study procedures were conducted in line with the Declaration of Helsinki (1989) of the World Medical Association. The study protocol has been evaluated and approved by the concerning ethical committee.

2.2. Physical Activity Assessment

The data were collected by trained personnel via face-to-face, computer-assisted interviews. The physical activity level was evaluated using the international physical activity questionnaires (IPAQ) [25]. The IPAQ consists of questions referring to five domains on time dedicated to physical activity in the last week. In brief, individuals are considered as having a "high physical activity level" if performing strenuous physical activity on no less than three days, reaching a minimum total physical activity of no less than 1500 MET minutes/w or ≥seven days of any combination of walking, moderate-intensity or vigorous-intensity activities reaching a minimum total physical activity of no less than 3000 MET minutes/w, while individuals performing ≥three days of vigorous-intensity activity of at least 20 min/d or ≥five days of moderate-intensity activity or walking of at least 30 min/d or ≥five days of any combination of walking, moderate-intensity or vigorous-intensity activities achieving a minimum of at least 600 MET minutes/w are considered as having "moderate physical activity level". Finally, individuals who do not meet the criteria for being highly or moderately physically active are categorized as having a low physical activity level.

2.3. Sun Exposure Assessment

Information on sun exposure was evaluated using the sunlight exposure measurement questionnaire (SEM-Q) [26]. The tool consisted of 6 items investigating the occasions and level of exposure to sunlight through assigning different weights (ranging between 0 and 1) according to sun exposure (i.e., using sunscreen creams, % of body exposed, etc.). The final scoring algorithm was generated by multiplying the time (minutes) spent in the sun by the proportions of different domains and then divided into three groups, defined as low, medium, and high exposure.

2.4. Dietary Assessment

The dietary exposures were assessed through a long and a short version of food frequency questionnaires (FFQs), formerly tested for validity and reliability in Sicilian individuals [27,28]. The intake of seasonal foods was calculated based on the consumption during the time period of their availability and subsequently adjusted by their proportional intake over one year. Dietary intakes of macro- and micronutrients, as well as total energy intake, were determined using food composition tables of the Council for Research in Agriculture and Analysis of Agricultural Economy (CREA) [29]. In detail, the individual food consumption (in mL or g) was calculated for each individual by converting the standard portion sizes and different frequencies of consumption to 24 h intake. After, the databases were screened for average values of the energy content and macro- and micronutrients contained in each food (per 100 mL or g). Lastly, the energy and nutrient intake from foods was calculated by multiplying the content of each variable by the daily consumption of each food. FFQs with missing data or unreliable dietary intakes (<1000 or >6000 kcal/d) were not included in the analyses. Vitamin D data was calculated from dietary intakes (participants were asked to report eventual supplementation).

The quality of an individual's diet was examined by calculating adherence to the Mediterranean diet using a validated literature-based score [30]. In brief, two points were assigned to the highest category of intake of foods typical of the Mediterranean diet (such as vegetables, fruits, legumes, cereals, fish), one point for the middle category, and 0 points for the lowest category of intake. On the contrary, two points were assigned for the lowest category of intake of foods not characteristic of the Mediterranean diet (such as meat and dairy products), one point for the middle category, and 0 points for the highest category of intake. Moderate alcohol intake and regular use of olive oil contributed to the higher adherence. The final score consists of nine food groups with a minimum of 0 points (lowest adherence) and maximum of 18 points (highest adherence), and individuals catalogued in the subsequent tertiles: (i) low, (ii) medium, and (iii) high adherence to the Mediterranean diet [31].

2.5. Covariate Assessment

In addition to dietary data, information on factors potentially associated with the investigated exposures and outcomes was collected. Data on sex, age, marital and educational (the highest educational degree achieved) status, and smoking status were collected. Marital status was catalogued as (i) unmarried/widowed or (ii) married. Educational status was catalogued as (i) low (primary/secondary), (ii) medium (high school), and (iii) high (university). Smoking status was catalogued as (i) non-smoker, (ii) ex-smoker, and (iii) current smoker. Eating habits comprised questions on skipping breakfast, daily snacking, skipping dinner, and out-of-home eating, with answers categorized as (i) always/often and (ii) seldom/never. Finally, body mass index (BMI) was categorized as normal weight (BMI < 25 kg/m^2), overweight (BMI 25 to 29.9 kg/m^2), and obese (BMI $\geq$ 30 kg/m^2) [32].

2.6. Perceived Stress Assessment

The stress symptoms of the study participants were assessed using the perceived stress scale (PSS) [33]. Briefly, the PSS is a 14-item questionnaire used to evaluate perceived stress by examining the level to which situations in an individual's life are perceived as stressful. Each query has five possible answers ranging from zero to four (0 = never, 1 = almost never, 2 = sometimes, 3 = often, and 4 = always). The final score is the sum of the scores of 14 queries and it ranges from 0 (minimum) to 56 (maximum). The sex-specific median value was considered as a cut-off point to define high or low perceived stress.

2.7. Statistical Analysis

After excluding missing entries from tools or data collection, a total of 1728 individuals were included in the analysis. Categorical variables are reported as frequencies of occurrence and percentages, with the Chi-squared test used to assess differences between physical activity levels. Continuous variables are reported as mean and standard deviations (SDs), with the ANOVA test used to test differences between groups. Multivariate logistic regression models were calculated to determine the cross-sectional association between physical activity level, dietary vitamin D intake, sunlight exposure, and perceived stress. Odds ratios (ORs) and 95% confidence intervals (CIs) were estimated for different models adjusted for potential confounders, including background characteristics and Mediterranean diet adherence as a proxy of diet quality. An additional analysis via stratifying the sample by low and medium/high category for each variable of exposure was further investigated to test their influencing role on each other. The reported p values were based on two-sided tests and compared to a significance level of 5%. All the statistical calculations were performed using SPSS 21 (SPSS Inc., Chicago, IL, USA) software.

3. Results

The background characteristics of the study sample by level of physical activity are presented in Table 1. Among individuals reporting higher levels of physical activity, there was a higher proportion of younger men, with a higher educational level and more current smokers than those reporting lower physical activity. Concerning eating habits, among those more physically active, there also was a higher prevalence of individuals reporting daily snacking and out-of-home eating, as well as a higher adherence to the Mediterranean diet.

The distribution of dietary vitamin D intake and sunlight exposure by the level of physical activity is presented in Figure 1. There was a significant difference in the distribution of both variables; interestingly, there was a higher proportion of individuals reporting low vitamin D intake and sunlight exposure in the medium category of physical activity level, while higher vitamin D intake and sunlight exposure was more evident in both low and high physical activity level groups, suggesting no clear trends in the distribution of these variables.

Table 1. Demographic characteristics of the study participants according to physical activity level (*n* = 1728).

	Physical Activity Level			
	Low (*n* = 329)	**Medium (*n* = 856)**	**High (*n* = 543)**	***p*-Value**
Age, mean (SD)	55 (19.23)	47 (17.24)	44 (14.77)	<0.001
Age groups, *n* (%)				<0.001
18–34	36 (20.0)	51 (22.9)	132 (29.5)	
35–49	36 (20.0)	54 (24.2)	174 (38.8)	
50–64	40 (22.2)	77 (34.5)	105 (23.4)	
65+	68 (37.8)	41 (18.4)	37 (8.3)	
Sex, *n* (%)				<0.001
Men	102 (31.0)	338 (39.5)	285 (52.5)	
Women	227 (69.0)	518 (60.5)	258 (47.5)	
Smoking status, *n* (%)				0.002
Never	213 (64.7)	527 (61.6)	340 (62.6)	
Current	76 (23.1)	195 (22.8)	155 (28.5)	
Former	40 (12.2)	134 (15.7)	48 (8.8)	
BMI categories, *n* (%)				<0.001
Normal weight	101 (35.1)	390 (49.6)	269 (51.8)	
Overweight	101 (35.1)	270 (34.3)	192 (37.0)	
Obese	86 (29.9)	127 (16.1)	58 (11.2)	
Educational level, *n* (%)				<0.001
Low	185 (56.2)	228 (26.6)	153 (28.2)	
Medium	79 (24.0)	327 (38.2)	264 (48.6)	
High	65 (19.8)	301 (35.2)	126 (23.2)	
Marital status, *n* (%)				0.177
Unmarried/widowed	127 (38.6)	362 (42.3)	204 (37.6)	
Married	202 (61.4)	494 (57.7)	339 (62.4)	
Eating habits, *n* (%)				
Skipping breakfast	71 (21.6)	197 (23.0)	148 (27.3)	0.098
Daily snacking	230 (69.9)	693 (81.0)	401 (73.8)	<0.001
Skipping dinner	13 (4.0)	64 (7.5)	36 (6.6)	0.089
Out of home eating	97 (29.5)	479 (56.0)	340 (62.6)	<0.001
Mediterranean diet adherence, *n* (%)				0.009
Low	185 (56.2)	494 (57.7)	264 (48.6)	
Medium	117 (35.6)	288 (33.6)	212 (39.0)	
High	27 (8.2)	74 (8.6)	67 (12.3)	

Table 2 presents the results of the logistic regression analyses assessing the association between the variables of interest and perceived stress. After adjusting for potential confounding factors (including diet quality assessed as higher adherence to the Mediterranean diet), individuals in the highest group of physical activity level (OR = 0.72, 95% CI: 0.51, 1.00), sunlight exposure (OR = 0.72, 95% CI: 0.52, 0.99), and vitamin D intake (OR = 0.69, 95% CI: 0.53, 0.89) were less likely to report perceived stress compared to those in the lowest groups; similar findings were retrieved for the medium category of physical activity level and sunlight exposure (Table 2).

The stratification by low and medium/high category of each variable of exposure to test their influencing role on each other is presented in Figure 2. Interestingly, neither vitamin D intake nor sunlight exposure was significantly associated with perceived stress in the low physical activity group, while individuals reporting medium-to-high physical activity levels and being in the highest category of exposure for both vitamin D intake and sunlight exposure were associated with lower odds of having perceived stress (OR = 0.67, 95% CI: 0.44, 1.01 and OR = 0.77, 95% CI: 0.61, 0.98, respectively; Figure 2). Similarly, when considering low exposure to dietary vitamin D and sunlight exposure, there were no evidence associations for the other variables, while in individuals with higher vitamin D intake there was a significant association of both high physical activity and high sunlight exposure (OR = 0.68, 95% CI: 0.50, 0.93 and OR = 0.75, 95% CI: 0.60, 0.94, respectively); as additionally, individuals with higher sunlight exposure had a significant association of both high physical activity and high vitamin D intake with lower likelihood of having perceived stress (OR = 0.64, 95% CI: 0.42, 0.95 and OR = 0.52, 95% CI: 0.30, 0.92, respectively; Figure 2).

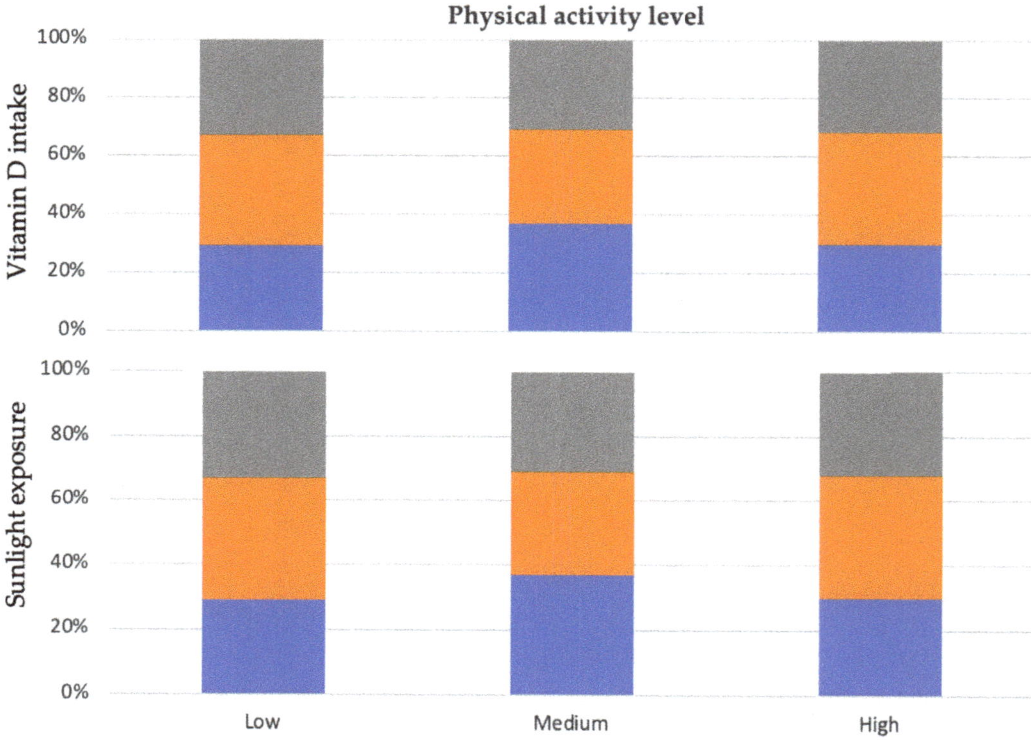

	Physical activity level			
	Low	Medium	High	*P-value*
Vitamin D intake, n (%)				0.019
Low	96 (29.2)	316 (36.9)	162 (29.8)	
Medium	125 (38.0)	276 (32.2)	209 (38.5)	
High	108 (32.8)	264 (30.8)	172 (31.7)	
Sun exposure, n (%)				<0.001
Low	149 (45.3)	633 (73.9)	95 (17.5)	
Medium	53 (16.1)	200 (23.4)	278 (51.2)	
High	127 (38.6)	23 (2.7)	170 (31.3)	

Figure 1. Distribution of dietary vitamin D intake, sunlight exposure, and physical activity level in the study sample (n = 1728). Gray color identifies low category, orange color identifies medium, and blue color identifies high category of vitamin D intake and sunlight exposure.

Table 2. Odds ratios (ORs) and 95% confidence intervals (CIs) of the association between physical activity level, sunlight exposure, vitamin D intake, and perceived stress.

	Perceived Stress, OR (95% CI)		
	Low	Medium	High
Physical activity level			
Unadjusted	1	0.68 (0.51, 0.91)	0.80 (0.60, 1.08)
Model 1 *	1	0.65 (0.47, 0.89)	0.73 (0.53, 1.02)
Model 2 **	1	0.64 (0.46, 0.88)	0.72 (0.51, 1.00)
Vitamin D intake			
Unadjusted	1	0.90 (0.71, 1.14)	0.81 (0.64, 1.02)
Model 1 *	1	0.82 (0.64, 1.05)	0.72 (0.56, 0.94)
Model 2 **	1	0.80 (0.63, 1.03)	0.69 (0.53, 0.89)
Sun exposure			
Unadjusted	1	0.81 (0.63, 1.02)	0.74 (0.55, 1.00)
Model 1 *	1	0.76 (0.59, 0.99)	0.73 (0.53, 1.01)
Model 2 **	1	0.76 (0.59, 0.98)	0.72 (0.52, 0.99)

* Multivariate model 1 was adjusted for BMI (normal, overweight, obese), sex, educational status (low, medium, high), smoking status (never, current, former), age (continuous, years), eating habits (skipping breakfast, daily snacking, skipping dinner, out of home eating), marital status (unmarried/widowed, married). ** Multivariate model 2 was further adjusted for adherence to the Mediterranean diet.

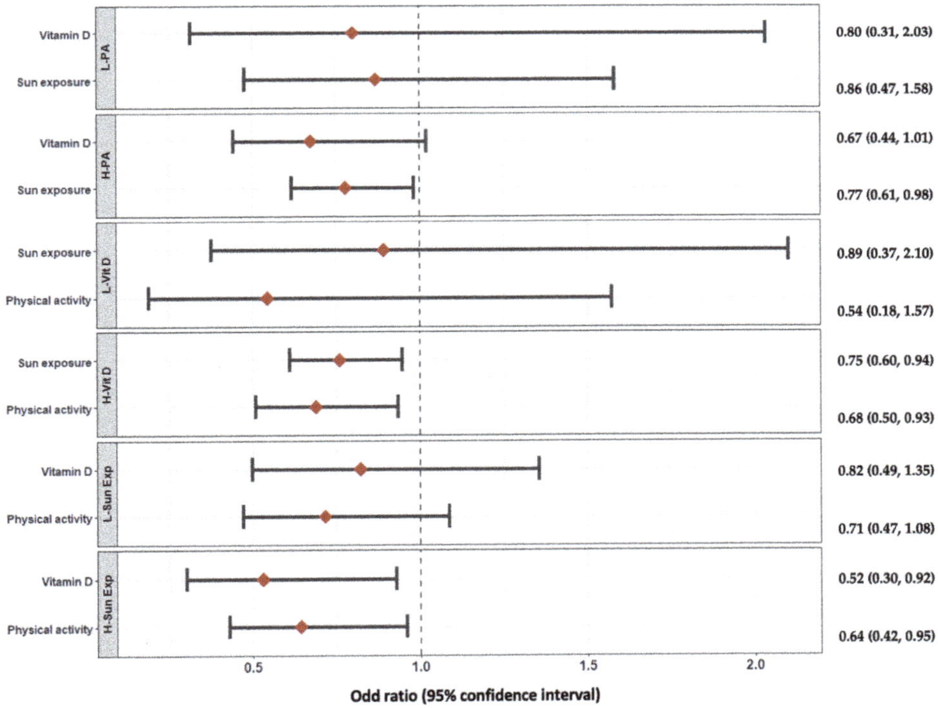

Figure 2. Odds ratio (ORs) and 95% confidence intervals (CIs) of the association between difference level of exposure to physical activity, vitamin D intake, and sunlight exposure and perceived stress. Multivariate model was adjusted for BMI (normal, overweight, obese), sex, educational status (low, medium, high), smoking status (never, current, former), age (continuous, years), eating habits (skipping breakfast, daily snacking, skipping dinner, out of home eating), marital status (unmarried/widowed, married), and adherence to the Mediterranean diet. L-PA, low physical activity; H-PA, high physical activity; L-Vit D, low vitamin D intake; H-Vit D, high vitamin D intake; L-Sun Exp, low sunlight exposure; H-Sun Exp, high sunlight exposure.

4. Discussion

In this study, the association between physical activity level, sunlight exposure, dietary vitamin D intake, and perceived stress levels was investigated in a sample of Italian adults. An inverse association between all the variables of exposure and perceived stress was found. However, when stratifying the population by level of physical activity, vitamin D intake, and sunlight exposure, the retrieved associations of each variable with perceived stress were significant only among individuals with higher exposure to the others, suggesting a strict relation between them.

Physical activity has been positively associated with the reduction of musculoskeletal [34] and major non-communicable diseases [35,36]; furthermore, mental conditions [37] can benefit from its regular and tailored practice. Previous studies reported substantial benefits of physical activity on psychological conditions, such as burnout [38,39], anxiety [40,41], or depression [42]. Concerning perceived stress, a previous study conducted on a sample of 537 college students showed that vigorous and moderate physical activity were inversely associated with perceived stress [43]. In line with our results, similar findings have also been reported in intervention studies. A meta-analysis of 13 randomized controlled trials showed that exercise in evidence-based treatments for individuals with stress or anxiety disorders was able to improve symptoms [44].

The stress reduction related to an increase in physical activity detected in our sample could be explained through several mechanisms. Physical activity promotes the secretion of β-Endorphin, a hormone that can positively influence mood states [45]. Moreover, some physical activity can be performed outdoors, thus increasing exposure to sunlight. There is consistent evidence from the scientific literature that performing physical activity outdoors has a higher positive impact on mood and mental well-being compared to indoor activities, possibly related to exposure to sunlight [12,46]. Additionally, in the present study, we found that sun exposure was associated with lower perceived stress, and that the association was significant among individuals with moderate-to-high physical activity levels. In line with our findings, in a study conducted on 948 Korean adults, people with less exposure to sunlight had significantly higher levels of perceived stress than those who were more exposed to sunlight [47]. Mechanistically, it has been hypothesized that mood regulation by the light needs a pathway independent of the suprachiasmatic nucleus that links intrinsically photosensitive retinal ganglion cells to the perihabenular nucleus, which is a mood regulator [48]. Furthermore, sunlight is fundamental for vitamin D metabolism, with UVB rays transforming 7-dehydrocholesterol to pre-vitamin D3, then isomerizing into vitamin D [14]: the positive effects of sunlight on stress could be explained by enhancement in vitamin D levels. We further found that also higher intake of vitamin D was inversely associated with perceived stress, especially in individuals reporting moderate-to-high physical activity levels. A previous investigation conducted on Northern American adults showed that those having lower serum 25(OH)D concentrations had poorer mental health and psychosocial stress compared to those with higher concentrations of serum 25(OH)D [49]. In fact, vitamin D receptors (VDR) and their activating enzymes are present in various regions of the human brain and 25(OH)D can reach the central nervous system by crossing the blood–brain barrier, indicating that it could potentially have autocrine-paracrine functions within the human brain [50]. VDR and 1a-hydroxylase have been found to be distributed in the human brain, both in glial cells and neurons, in a layer-specific pattern, especially in the hypothalamus and neurons within the substantia nigra [50]. Stress activates the hypothalamic–pituitary–adrenal axis (HPA) [51], which functions in connection with the autonomic nervous system and the immune system in managing the hormonal and inflammatory responses to stress [52]. The HPA activation promotes the release of corticotropin-releasing hormone in the hypothalamus and the secretion of adrenocorticotropin from the pituitary cells, mediating adaptive responses that are necessary for survival [52]. However, chronic stress may elicit harmful changes that can bring an alteration of the HPA fostering long-term pathological alterations [53]. It was shown that one of the metabolites of vitamin D,1,25-dihydroxyvitamin D3 has neuroprotective effects, upregulating neurotrophin-3 and neurotrophin-4 [54], and nerve growth factors [55] that can be found in the hippocampus and neocortex. Furthermore, vitamin D influences inflammatory pathways that have been associated with depression [56] by activating anti-inflammatory pathways through VDR-mediated gene transcription and downregulating autoimmune mechanisms that produce proinflammatory cytokines [54,57]. These underlying physiological mechanisms could explain our findings of an inverse association between lower levels of perceived stress in people with higher vitamin D intake.

To the best of our knowledge, this is the first study that analyzes the association between physical activity, sun exposure, vitamin D, and perceived stress in a sample of the general Italian population. Nonetheless, despite the novelty of this study, the results may be subjected to some limitations. Considering the cross-sectional nature of the analysis, the reverse causation cannot be ruled out. Another limitation concerns the dietary assessment method, as the use of FFQs may potentially under- or overestimate food intake due to recall bias. Additionally, despite adjusting for multiple confounding factors, the results may have been influenced by unmeasured variables. Another limitation may be related to the lack of information on whether individuals are primarily engaged in indoor or outdoor sports and, thus, directly exposed to more or less sunlight. The PSS is a good screening tool to assess the prevalence of stress symptoms in large sample sizes; however, it may not be deemed as a clinical evaluation, and thus may over- or underestimate the outcome prevalence. Finally, the findings of this study may not be generalizable to other populations as several factors may affect the intensity of sun exposure, including but not limited to solar zenith angle, altitude, or skin type.

5. Conclusions

In conclusion, the results of this study highlight that higher sun exposure and dietary intake of vitamin D are associated with a lower likelihood of having high perceived stress among physically active individuals.

Author Contributions: Conceptualization, methodology and formal analysis, J.G. and S.C.; writing—original draft preparation, B.T., J.G., S.V., S.C. and G.M.; writing—review and editing, B.T., J.G., S.V., F.R., S.C. and G.M. All authors have read and agreed to the published version of the manuscript.

Funding: J.G. was supported by the co-financing of the European Union—FSE-REACT-EU, PON Research and Innovation 2014–2020 DM1062/2021; CUP: E65F21002560001.

Institutional Review Board Statement: The study was conducted in accordance with the Declaration of Helsinki, and approved by the Institutional Review Board (or Ethics Committee) of CE Catania 2 (protocol code 802/23 December 2014).

Informed Consent Statement: Informed consent was obtained from all subjects involved in the study.

Data Availability Statement: The data that support the findings of this study are available upon reasonable request.

Conflicts of Interest: The authors declare no conflict of interest.

References

1. Selye, H. *The Stress of Life*; McGraw-Hill: New York, NY, USA, 1956.
2. Del Giudice, M.; Buck, C.L.; Chaby, L.E.; Gormally, B.M.; Taff, C.C.; Thawley, C.J.; Vitousek, M.N.; Wada, H. What is stress? A systems perspective. *Integr. Comp. Biol.* **2018**, *58*, 1019–1032. [CrossRef]
3. McEwen, B.S. In pursuit of resilience: Stress, epigenetics, and brain plasticity. *Ann. N. Y. Acad. Sci.* **2016**, *1373*, 56–64. [CrossRef]
4. Noushad, S.; Ahmed, S.; Ansari, B.; Mustafa, U.-H.; Saleem, Y.; Hazrat, H. Physiological biomarkers of chronic stress: A systematic review. *Int. J. Health Sci. (Qassim)* **2021**, *15*, 46–59.
5. Olsen, L.R.; Mortensen, E.L.; Bech, P. Prevalence of major depression and stress indicators in the Danish general population. *Acta Psychiatr. Scand.* **2004**, *109*, 96–103. [CrossRef]
6. Moritz, B.; Schmitz, A.E.; Rodrigues, A.L.S.; Dafre, A.L.; Cunha, M.P. The role of vitamin C in stress-related disorders. *J. Nutr. Biochem.* **2020**, *85*, 108459. [CrossRef] [PubMed]
7. Godos, J.; Currenti, W.; Angelino, D.; Mena, P.; Castellano, S.; Caraci, F.; Galvano, F.; Del Rio, D.; Ferri, R.; Grosso, G. Diet and mental health: Review of the recent updates on molecular mechanisms. *Antioxidants* **2020**, *9*, 346. [CrossRef]

8. Liang, M.; Pan, Y.; Zhong, T.; Zeng, Y.; Cheng, A.S.K. Effects of aerobic, resistance, and combined exercise on metabolic syndrome parameters and cardiovascular risk factors: A systematic review and network meta-analysis. *Rev. Cardiovasc. Med.* **2021**, *22*, 1523–1533. [CrossRef] [PubMed]
9. Fransen, M.; McConnell, S.; Harmer, A.R.; Van der Esch, M.; Simic, M.; Bennell, K.L. Exercise for osteoarthritis of the knee: A Cochrane systematic review. *Br. J. Sports Med.* **2015**, *49*, 1554–1557. [CrossRef]
10. Abou, L.; Alluri, A.; Fliflet, A.; Du, Y.; Rice, L.A. Effectiveness of Physical Therapy Interventions in Reducing Fear of Falling Among Individuals with Neurologic Diseases: A Systematic Review and Meta-analysis. *Arch. Phys. Med. Rehabil.* **2021**, *102*, 132–154. [CrossRef]
11. Pearce, M.; Garcia, L.; Abbas, A.; Strain, T.; Schuch, F.B.; Golubic, R.; Kelly, P.; Khan, S.; Utukuri, M.; Laird, Y.; et al. Association between Physical Activity and Risk of Depression: A Systematic Review and Meta-analysis. *JAMA Psychiatry* **2022**, *79*, 550–559. [CrossRef] [PubMed]
12. Thompson Coon, J.; Boddy, K.; Stein, K.; Whear, R.; Barton, J.; Depledge, M.H. Does participating in physical activity in outdoor natural environments have a greater effect on physical and mental wellbeing than physical activity indoors? A systematic review. *Environ. Sci. Technol.* **2011**, *45*, 1761–1772. [CrossRef]
13. Kent, S.T.; McClure, L.A.; Crosson, W.L.; Arnett, D.K.; Wadley, V.G.; Sathiakumar, N. Effect of sunlight exposure on cognitive function among depressed and non-depressed participants: A REGARDS cross-sectional study. *Environ. Health* **2009**, *8*, 34. [CrossRef] [PubMed]
14. Wacker, M.; Holick, M.F. Sunlight and vitamin D: A global perspective for health. *Dermato-Endocrinology* **2013**, *5*, 51–108. [CrossRef]
15. Hossain, S.; Beydoun, M.A.; Beydoun, H.A.; Chen, X.; Zonderman, A.B.; Wood, R.J. Vitamin D and breast cancer: A systematic review and meta-analysis of observational studies. *Clin. Nutr. ESPEN* **2019**, *30*, 170–184. [CrossRef] [PubMed]
16. Valer-Martinez, A.; Martinez, J.A.; Sayon-Orea, C.; Galvano, F.; Grosso, G.; Bes-Rastrollo, M. Vitamin D and Cardio-Metabolic Risk Factors in Overweight Adults: An Overview of the Evidence. *Curr. Pharm. Des.* **2019**, *25*, 2407–2420. [CrossRef]
17. Wang, H.; Chen, W.; Li, D.; Yin, X.; Zhang, X.; Olsen, N.; Zheng, S.G. Vitamin D and chronic diseases. *Aging Dis.* **2017**, *8*, 346–353. [CrossRef] [PubMed]
18. Li, S.; Xi, C.; Li, L.; Long, Z.; Zhang, N.; Yin, H.; Xie, K.; Wu, Z.; Tian, J.; Wang, F.; et al. Comparisons of different vitamin D supplementation for prevention of osteoporotic fractures: A Bayesian network meta-analysis and meta-regression of randomised controlled trials. *Int. J. Food Sci. Nutr.* **2021**, *72*, 518–528. [CrossRef]
19. Li, H.; Sun, D.; Wang, A.; Pan, H.; Feng, W.; Ng, C.H.; Ungvari, G.S.; Tao, L.; Li, X.; Wang, W.; et al. Serum 25-Hydroxyvitamin D Levels and Depression in Older Adults: A Dose-Response Meta-Analysis of Prospective Cohort Studies. *Am. J. Geriatr. Psychiatry* **2019**, *27*, 1192–1202. [CrossRef]
20. Gao, Q.; Kou, T.; Zhuang, B.; Ren, Y.; Dong, X.; Wang, Q. The Association between Vitamin D Deficiency and Sleep Disorders: A Systematic Review and Meta-Analysis. *Nutrients* **2018**, *10*, 1395. [CrossRef]
21. Książek, A.; Zagrodna, A.; Słowińska-Lisowska, M. Vitamin D, Skeletal Muscle Function and Athletic Performance in Athletes-A Narrative Review. *Nutrients* **2019**, *11*, 1800. [CrossRef] [PubMed]
22. Cashman, K.D.; Dowling, K.G.; Škrabáková, Z.; Gonzalez-Gross, M.; Valtueña, J.; De Henauw, S.; Moreno, L.; Damsgaard, C.T.; Michaelsen, K.F.; Mølgaard, C.; et al. Vitamin D deficiency in Europe: Pandemic? *Am. J. Clin. Nutr.* **2016**, *103*, 1033–1044. [CrossRef] [PubMed]
23. Casseb, G.A.S.; Kaster, M.P.; Rodrigues, A.L.S. Potential role of vitamin D for the management of depression and anxiety. *CNS Drugs* **2019**, *33*, 619–637. [CrossRef] [PubMed]
24. Grosso, G.; Marventano, S.; D'Urso, M.; Mistretta, A.; Galvano, F. The Mediterranean healthy eating, ageing, and lifestyle (MEAL) study: Rationale and study design. *Int. J. Food Sci. Nutr.* **2017**, *68*, 577–586. [CrossRef] [PubMed]
25. Craig, C.L.; Marshall, A.L.; Sjöström, M.; Bauman, A.E.; Booth, M.L.; Ainsworth, B.E.; Pratt, M.; Ekelund, U.; Yngve, A.; Sallis, J.F.; et al. International physical activity questionnaire: 12-country reliability and validity. *Med. Sci. Sports Exerc.* **2003**, *35*, 1381–1395. [CrossRef] [PubMed]
26. Humayun, Q.; Iqbal, R.; Azam, I.; Khan, A.H.; Siddiqui, A.R.; Baig-Ansari, N. Development and validation of sunlight exposure measurement questionnaire (SEM-Q) for use in adult population residing in Pakistan. *BMC Public Health* **2012**, *12*, 421. [CrossRef] [PubMed]
27. Marventano, S.; Mistretta, A.; Platania, A.; Galvano, F.; Grosso, G. Reliability and relative validity of a food frequency questionnaire for Italian adults living in Sicily, Southern Italy. *Int. J. Food Sci. Nutr.* **2016**, *67*, 857–864. [CrossRef]
28. Buscemi, S.; Rosafio, G.; Vasto, S.; Massenti, F.M.; Grosso, G.; Galvano, F.; Rini, N.; Barile, A.M.; Maniaci, V.; Cosentino, L.; et al. Validation of a food frequency questionnaire for use in Italian adults living in Sicily. *Int. J. Food Sci. Nutr.* **2015**, *66*, 426–438. [CrossRef]
29. Tabelle Composizione Degli Alimenti CREA. Available online: https://www.crea.gov.it/-/tabella-di-composizione-degli-alimenti (accessed on 12 May 2021).
30. Marventano, S.; Godos, J.; Platania, A.; Galvano, F.; Mistretta, A.; Grosso, G. Mediterranean diet adherence in the Mediterranean healthy eating, aging and lifestyle (MEAL) study cohort. *Int. J. Food Sci. Nutr.* **2018**, *69*, 100–107. [CrossRef]
31. Godos, J.; Castellano, S.; Marranzano, M. Adherence to a Mediterranean Dietary Pattern Is Associated with Higher Quality of Life in a Cohort of Italian Adults. *Nutrients* **2019**, *11*, 981. [CrossRef]

32. Mistretta, A.; Marventano, S.; Platania, A.; Godos, J.; Galvano, F.; Grosso, G. Metabolic profile of the Mediterranean healthy Eating, Lifestyle and Aging (MEAL) study cohort. *Med. J. Nutr. Metab.* **2017**, *10*, 131–140. [CrossRef]
33. Cohen, S.; Kamarck, T.; Mermelstein, R. A global measure of perceived stress. *J. Health Soc. Behav.* **1983**, *24*, 385–396. [CrossRef]
34. Hagen, K.B.; Dagfinrud, H.; Moe, R.H.; Østerås, N.; Kjeken, I.; Grotle, M.; Smedslund, G. Exercise therapy for bone and muscle health: An overview of systematic reviews. *BMC Med.* **2012**, *10*, 167. [CrossRef]
35. Warburton, D.E.R.; Bredin, S.S.D. Health benefits of physical activity: A systematic review of current systematic reviews. *Curr. Opin. Cardiol.* **2017**, *32*, 541–556. [CrossRef] [PubMed]
36. Sbert, P.R.; López González, Á.A.; Fe, B.R.; Fe, N.R.; Bote, S.A.; Manent, J.I.R. Influence of physical activity, the Mediterranean diet and sociodemographic variables on the values of different cardiovascular risk scales. *Med. J. Nutr. Metab.* **2022**, *15*, 273–284. [CrossRef]
37. Schuch, F.B.; Vancampfort, D. Physical activity, exercise, and mental disorders: It is time to move on. *Trends Psychiatry Psychother.* **2021**, *43*, 177–184. [CrossRef]
38. Naczenski, L.M.; de Vries, J.D.; van Hooff, M.L.M.; Kompier, M.A.J. Systematic review of the association between physical activity and burnout. *J. Occup. Health* **2017**, *59*, 477–494. [CrossRef] [PubMed]
39. Ochentel, O.; Humphrey, C.; Pfeifer, K. Efficacy of Exercise Therapy in Persons with Burnout. A Systematic Review and Meta-Analysis. *J. Sports Sci. Med.* **2018**, *17*, 475–484.
40. Carter, T.; Pascoe, M.; Bastounis, A.; Morres, I.D.; Callaghan, P.; Parker, A.G. The effect of physical activity on anxiety in children and young people: A systematic review and meta-analysis. *J. Affect. Disord.* **2021**, *285*, 10–21. [CrossRef] [PubMed]
41. Kandola, A.; Stubbs, B. Exercise and Anxiety. *Adv. Exp. Med. Biol.* **2020**, *1228*, 345–352. [CrossRef] [PubMed]
42. Bailey, A.P.; Hetrick, S.E.; Rosenbaum, S.; Purcell, R.; Parker, A.G. Treating depression with physical activity in adolescents and young adults: A systematic review and meta-analysis of randomised controlled trials. *Psychol. Med.* **2018**, *48*, 1068–1083. [CrossRef] [PubMed]
43. Bhuiyan, N.; Kang, J.H.; Papalia, Z.; Bopp, C.M.; Bopp, M.; Mama, S.K. Assessing the stress-buffering effects of social support for exercise on physical activity, sitting time, and blood lipid profiles. *J. Am. Coll. Health* **2022**, *70*, 1563–1569. [CrossRef] [PubMed]
44. Ramos-Sanchez, C.P.; Schuch, F.B.; Seedat, S.; Louw, Q.A.; Stubbs, B.; Rosenbaum, S.; Firth, J.; van Winkel, R.; Vancampfort, D. The anxiolytic effects of exercise for people with anxiety and related disorders: An update of the available meta-analytic evidence. *Psychiatry Res.* **2021**, *302*, 114046. [CrossRef] [PubMed]
45. Dinas, P.C.; Koutedakis, Y.; Flouris, A.D. Effects of exercise and physical activity on depression. *Ir. J. Med. Sci.* **2011**, *180*, 319–325. [CrossRef]
46. Puett, R.; Teas, J.; España-Romero, V.; Artero, E.G.; Lee, D.; Baruth, M.; Sui, X.; Montresor-López, J.; Blair, S.N. Physical activity: Does environment make a difference for tension, stress, emotional outlook, and perceptions of health status? *J. Phys. Act. Health* **2014**, *11*, 1503–1511. [CrossRef]
47. Hwang, H.-J.; Choi, Y.-J.; Hong, D. The Association between Self-Rated Health Status, Psychosocial Stress, Eating Behaviors, and Food Intake According to the Level of Sunlight Exposure in Korean Adults. *Int. J. Environ. Res. Public Health* **2022**, *20*, 262. [CrossRef]
48. Fernandez, D.C.; Fogerson, P.M.; Lazzerini Ospri, L.; Thomsen, M.B.; Layne, R.M.; Severin, D.; Zhan, J.; Singer, J.H.; Kirkwood, A.; Zhao, H.; et al. Light Affects Mood and Learning through Distinct Retina-Brain Pathways. *Cell* **2018**, *175*, 71–84.e18. [CrossRef]
49. Chen, L.; Zhu, H.; Harshfield, G.A.; Treiber, F.A.; Pollock, J.S.; Pollock, D.; Okereke, O.I.; Su, S.; Dong, Y. Serum 25-Hydroxyvitamin D Concentrations Are Associated with Mental Health and Psychosocial Stress in Young Adults. *Nutrients* **2020**, *12*, 1938. [CrossRef] [PubMed]
50. Eyles, D.W.; Smith, S.; Kinobe, R.; Hewison, M.; McGrath, J.J. Distribution of the vitamin D receptor and 1 alpha-hydroxylase in human brain. *J. Chem. Neuroanat.* **2005**, *29*, 21–30. [CrossRef]
51. Saper, C.B.; Lowell, B.B. The hypothalamus. *Curr. Biol.* **2014**, *24*, R1111–R1116. [CrossRef] [PubMed]
52. Leistner, C.; Menke, A. Hypothalamic-pituitary-adrenal axis and stress. *Handb. Clin. Neurol.* **2020**, *175*, 55–64. [CrossRef]
53. de Kloet, E.R.; Joëls, M.; Holsboer, F. Stress and the brain: From adaptation to disease. *Nat. Rev. Neurosci.* **2005**, *6*, 463–475. [CrossRef] [PubMed]
54. Neveu, I.; Naveilhan, P.; Baudet, C.; Brachet, P.; Metsis, M. 1,25-dihydroxyvitamin D3 regulates NT-3, NT-4 but not BDNF mRNA in astrocytes. *Neuroreport* **1994**, *6*, 124–126. [CrossRef] [PubMed]
55. Neveu, I.; Naveilhan, P.; Jehan, F.; Baudet, C.; Wion, D.; De Luca, H.F.; Brachet, P. 1,25-dihydroxyvitamin D3 regulates the synthesis of nerve growth factor in primary cultures of glial cells. *Brain Res. Mol. Brain Res.* **1994**, *24*, 70–76. [CrossRef]
56. Dowlati, Y.; Herrmann, N.; Swardfager, W.; Liu, H.; Sham, L.; Reim, E.K.; Lanctôt, K.L. A meta-analysis of cytokines in major depression. *Biol. Psychiatry* **2010**, *67*, 446–457. [CrossRef] [PubMed]
57. Alroy, I.; Towers, T.L.; Freedman, L.P. Transcriptional repression of the interleukin-2 gene by vitamin D3: Direct inhibition of NFATp/AP-1 complex formation by a nuclear hormone receptor. *Mol. Cell. Biol.* **1995**, *15*, 5789–5799. [CrossRef]

nutrients MDPI

Article

Bioimpedance Patterns and Bioelectrical Impedance Vector Analysis (BIVA) of Body Builders

Cristian Petri [1], Matteo Levi Micheli [2], Pascal Izzicupo [3,*], Niccolò Timperanza [2], Tommaso Lastrucci [2], Daniele Vanni [2], Massimo Gulisano [2] and Gabriele Mascherini [2]

1 Department of Sport and Informatics, Section of Physical Education and Sport, Pablo de Olavide University, 41013 Sevilla, Spain; cpet2@alu.upo.es
2 Exercise Science Laboratory Applied to Medicine "Mario Marella", Department of Experimental and Clinical Medicine, University of Florence, 50134 Florence, Italy; matteo.levimicheli@unifi.it (M.L.M.); niccolo.timperanza@stud.unifi.it (N.T.); tommaso.lastrucci@stud.unifi.it (T.L.); danielevanni88@gmail.com (D.V.); massimo.gulisano@unifi.it (M.G.); gabriele.mascherini@unifi.it (G.M.)
3 Department of Medicine and Aging Sciences, University "G. D'Annunzio" of Chieti-Pescara, Via L. Polacchi, 11, 66100 Chieti, Italy
* Correspondence: pascal.izzicupo@unich.it

Abstract: Bodybuilders are athletes characterized by high muscle mass. During competitions, the evaluation is performed based on aesthetic parameters. The study aims to provide normative references of body composition with the vector bioimpedance methodology (BIVA). A second aim is to compare BIVA assessments performed on both sides and the upper and lower body. A group of 68 elite bodybuilders (41 males aged 30.1 ± 9.2 years and 27 females aged 32.1 ± 8.0 years) was enrolled. A BIVA assessment was performed the day before the 2021 World Natural Bodybuilding Federation Italian Championships. As a result, male and female bodybuilders ranked to the left in the BIVA ellipse relative to the general population. Furthermore, unlike females, males also ranked lower than the general athletic population. In addition, in the symmetry assessment, males show a significantly greater upper body than the lower, right, and left parts, while in women, this is observed for the lower part of the body. The differences in the results obtained between males and females can be attributed to the different patterns of endocrine production between the sexes and the different criteria used by the juries to attribute the final score during the competitions. Therefore, BIVA references in bodybuilders could help adjust the training and nutritional program during the peak week before a competition.

Keywords: body composition; bodybuilding; muscle mass; muscle hypertrophy

Citation: Petri, C.; Micheli, M.L.; Izzicupo, P.; Timperanza, N.; Lastrucci, T.; Vanni, D.; Gulisano, M.; Mascherini, G. Bioimpedance Patterns and Bioelectrical Impedance Vector Analysis (BIVA) of Body Builders. *Nutrients* **2023**, *15*, 1606. https://doi.org/10.3390/nu15071606

Academic Editors: David C. Nieman and Alessandro Sartorio

Received: 7 March 2023
Revised: 24 March 2023
Accepted: 24 March 2023
Published: 25 March 2023

1. Introduction

Body composition assessment is currently a part of functional assessment in sportspeople, allowing the monitoring of athletes' nutritional and health status and checking the state of physical fitness. The study of the relationship between body composition and sports performance is a growing research area in sports science. In particular, some sports, such as gymnastics and running, have a gravitational component; therefore, reduced fat mass values can favor success in competitions. Alternatively, many combat sports are weight-classified; therefore, athletes must stay within a specific range of body mass. Finally, sports characterized by expressions of strength and/or speed, such as sprints in athletics or weightlifting, benefit from the presence of large muscle masses. However, in some competitions, success is attributed based on the aesthetic characteristics of the participants. In this context, monitoring body composition has become fundamental, and in aesthetic sports can provide additional and helpful information [1].

Bodybuilding is an aesthetic sport, and a prerequisite for a successful bodybuilder is to have the expected muscular morphology [2]. Specifically, bodybuilding is a combined aesthetic and weight-class sport in which physical appearance, muscular mass, symmetry, shape, and definition are the evaluation parameters with specific references based on the category in which each athlete competes [3]. Therefore, the goal of a bodybuilder is to attain maximal body muscle by focusing on hypertrophy training and, in preparation for a competition, striving for excellent muscular definition [4].

Among the methods developed to assess body composition, bioelectrical impedance analysis (BIA) has long been an easy and viable technique for obtaining qualitative and quantitative assessment in bodybuilders. However, the studies predominantly used the conventional BIA evaluation, which studies and describes the different body tissues (mainly fat-free and fat-mass) [5]. This approach has some limitations, including sensitivity to hydration status, potential inaccuracy of predictive equation when applied to populations with different characteristics, and a minimum standard error of estimation, even when the equation is accurate [6,7].

An innovative use of BIA consists of evaluating the raw bioelectrical parameters, such as resistance (R), reactance (Xc), and phase angle (PhA) through bioelectrical impedance vector analysis (BIVA) that allows the evaluation of the vector position compared with population-specific tolerance ellipses [8]. Furthermore, studying bioelectrical properties in athletes made it possible to create specific references helpful in monitoring body composition during the competitive season [9]. Recently, studies have investigated the positioning within the ellipse of the R-Xc graph of specific sports populations within the athlete's population, in particular, the bioelectrical characteristics of soccer players [10], cyclists [11], handball players [12], synchronized swimmers [13], and rowers [14] have been studied. Furthermore, side-by-side differences in bioelectrical parameters have been found to be more pronounced in tennis players than in the general population, suggesting this method can be useful to identify body asymmetries in those sports with unilateral loading [15].

The study through the BIVA assessment of bodybuilders could increase the knowledge of the body composition of these athletes, providing specific positioning within the R-Xc graph, given the high muscularity associated with low levels of fat mass that characterize this particular study population. This study hypothesizes that bodybuilders have a position far to the left within the R-Xc graph, with a high phase angle (PhA). Therefore, this study aims to perform a BIVA assessment on a sample of bodybuilders to provide the population-specific tolerance ellipses. A secondary aim of this study is to compare BIVA assessments performed on both sides and on the upper and lower body (hand to hand and foot to foot, respectively). We hypothesize that male and female bodybuilders will show different BIVA patterns according to the sexual dimorphism in body masses distribution.

2. Materials and Methods

2.1. Participants

During the Italian championships 2021 of the World Natural Bodybuilding Federation, athletes were required to participate voluntarily in the study. The inclusion criteria were (1) to be a member of the World Natural Bodybuilding Federation Italy, (2) to be over 18 years old, (3) to have finished at least sixth in the final ranking, (4) to not use drugs that can induce muscle hypertrophy, and (5) be of white ethnicity.

A group of 64 elite bodybuilders (37 males aged 30.1 $\pm$ 9.2 yrs with body mass index = 24.5 $\pm$ 1.5 kg/m^2 and 27 females aged 32.1 $\pm$ 8.0 yrs with body mass index = 19.8 $\pm$ 1.3 kg/m^2) was enrolled in the study after receiving written informed consent. The categories in which the male participated were: eleven subjects in Classic Physique, sixteen in Man Physique, and fourteen in Bodybuilding. At the same time, eight females participated in the Figure and nineteen in the Bikini. The study was carried out in conformity with the ethical standards in the 1975 Declaration of Helsinki.

2.2. Procedures

The recruitment and evaluation of the participants were conducted on the morning of the day before the competition; therefore, during the peak week [2], the athletes showed their optimal body composition (i.e., the lowest fat mass and the highest muscle mass). Weight was measured to the nearest 0.1 kg and height to 0.5 cm (Seca GmbH & Co., Hamburg, Germany). Body mass index (BMI) was then calculated as weight divided by height^2 (W/H, expressed as kg/m^2).

Whole-body BIVA is the body tissues' opposition to the flow of an electric current. It is the vector sum of the resistance (R, Ω)—the major resistance to the current through intracellular and extracellular ionic fluids—and the reactance (Xc, Ω)—the additional opposition due to the capacitive elements such as cell membranes, tissue interfaces, and non-ionic substances. The raw bioimpedance parameters R, Xc, and Phase Angle (PhA, calculated as the arc tangent of Xc/R $\times$ 180°/π) were obtained using a phase-sensitive segmental bioelectrical analyzer (BIA 101 BIVA PRO, Akern, Florence, Italy) with a current of 250 μA at a single frequency of 50 kHz. It was calibrated every morning using a calibration circuit procedure of known impedance (R = 380 Ohm, XC = 47 Ohm, 1% error) supplied by the manufacturer. After cleaning the skin with isotropy alcohol, four low intrinsic impedance adhesive electrodes (Biatrodes Akern Srl, Florence, Italy) were placed on the hand's back and the other four electrodes on the neck of the corresponding feet, respecting the standard protocol [16]. The proximal hand electrode was between the radial and ulnar styloid processes, and the distal hand electrode was positioned in the center of the third proximal phalanx. The proximal foot electrode was placed directly between the medial and lateral malleoli at the ankle, and the distal foot electrode was proximal to the second and third metatarsophalangeal joints. Therefore, through this procedure, with a single impedance measurement, it was possible to collect all the data to evaluate both the whole body and the body side evaluation.

The whole body BIVA assessment uses R and Xc parameters, standardized for the subject height to remove the effect of conductor length, producing a vector plotted in an R-Xc graph. Vector length indicates the hydration status from fluid overload (reduced R, short vector) to dehydration (increased R, longer vector), and lateral migration of the vector due to low or high Xc indicates a decrease or increase in mass dielectric (membranes and tissue interfaces) of soft tissues. The individual vector can be ranked on the R-Xc point graph against tolerance ellipses representing 50%, 75%, and 95%, according to the values of a reference population [17].

The body sides BIVA assessment was performed on the right side (hand to foot right side), left side (hand to foot left side), upper side (hand to hand), and lower side (foot to foot) of the body with the subjects in a supine position with their arms and legs abducted. The evaluation parameters were:

- resistance/height and reactance/height for the upper body (R/hup and Xc/hup);
- resistance/height and reactance/height for the upper body (R/hlo and Xc/hlo);
- resistance/height and reactance/height for the right side of the body (R/hrt and Xc/hrt);
- resistance/height and reactance/height for the left side of the body(R/hlt and Xc/hlt) [14].

In order to verify muscle mass through raw bioelectrical values, the Levi Muscle Index, defined as LMI = (PhA $\times$ H)/R, was calculated [18]. BIA measurements were all taken by the same-trained investigator to avoid inter-observer errors.

2.3. Statistical Analysis

The normality of the data was verified by applying the Shapiro–Wilk test and descriptive statistics were calculated for each independent variable, as reported in Table 1. The bioelectrical impedance variables followed the Gaussian distribution. Differences between the BIVA modalities for the raw bioelectrical parameters were evaluated through the analysis of variance with repeated measures (RM-ANOVA) on the within-subject factor (right side, left side, upper side, and lower side). The Bonferroni–Holm method was used for the post hoc test, and the sphericity was corrected using the Greenhouse–Geisser method when the condition of equal variance was violated. Each participant was plotted in the tolerance ellipses (50%, 75%, and 95%) of the Italian reference population of the same sex [19]. A two-sample Hotelling's T^2 test was used to determine the BIA vector differences concerning the reference population [19] and the athletic population [20] and for BIVA modalities (right and left side, upper and lower body) comparisons. The Mahalanobis' test calculated distances between ellipses [21]. A *p*-value < 0.05 was considered significant. IBM SPSS 23.0 (SPSS, Chicago, IL, USA) was used for statistical calculations, and BIVA software [21] was used for plotting and comparing the bioelectrical parameters, as well as for computing the tolerance ellipses (50%, 75%, and 95%) of the investigated sample.

3. Results

Table 1 describes the general and anthropometric characteristics of the sample for both sexes.

Table 1. General and anthropometric characteristics of the sample for both sexes.

Variable	Mean ± SD	Min–Max	Mean ± SD	Min–Max
Age (years)	30.1 ± 9.2	19.0–54.0	32.1 ± 8.0	20.0–48.0
Body mass (kg)	72.8 ± 6.8	59.8–90.6	53.7 ± 5.5	40.7–63.0
Height (cm)	172.2 ± 5.9	162.8–190.0	164.6 ± 7.0	149.0–179.0
Body mass index (km/m^2)	24.5 ± 1.5	21.2–29.2	19.8 ± 1.3	17.9–22.6

The BIVA point graph indicates that male natural bodybuilders mainly fell outside the 75% percentile (Figure 1a). Furthermore, most bodybuilders fell in the lower left quadrant area to the left of the impedance vector, as previously indicated by Campa for the athletic population [20]. Male bodybuilders were statistically different compared with the general male population [19] and athletic reference [20]. Specifically, they fell more to the left than the general population ($T^2 < 168.8$; D = 2.14; $p < 0.001$) and to the left and down than the athletic population ($T^2 < 17.7$; D = 0.95; $p < 0.001$) (Figure 1b) and their specific the 50%, 75%, and 95% tolerance ellipses are represented in Figure 1c. On the other hand, female bodybuilders compared with the general female population [18] and athletic reference [20] fell to the left of the general population ($T^2 < 67.3$; D = 1.64; $p < 0.001$) but did not differ from the athletic population ($T^2 < 1.9$; D = 0.27; $p < 0.40$) (Figure 1d,e). The specific 50%, 75%, and 95% tolerance ellipses of female natural bodybuilders are represented in Figure 1f. The LMI value of male bodybuilders is 3.7 ± 0.6, while for female bodybuilders, it is 2.3 ± 0.4.

Bioelectrical characteristics of both sexes, for the right and left sides and the upper and lower body, are shown in Figure 2. Significant differences for both sexes were found for R/h (males: $F(1.3, 45.4) = 18.0$, $p < 0.001$, *partial eta squared* = 0.33; females: $F(1.3, 34.2) = 30.6$, $p < 0.001$, *partial eta squared* = 0.54) and Xc/h (males: $F(1.2, 43.2) = 30.8$, $p < 0.001$, *partial eta squared* = 0.461; females: $F(1.3, 32.8) = 10.5$, $p < 0.001$, *partial eta squared* = 0.29). Post hoc analysis showed that in males, the R/h of the upper body significantly differed from the R/h of the lower body ($p < 0.02$), right ($p < 0.001$), and left ($p < 0.001$) sides, respectively. Similarly, the Xc/h of the upper body significantly differed from the Xc/h of the lower body ($p < 0.01$), right ($p < 0.001$), and left ($p < 0.001$) sides, respectively. Furthermore, the Xc/h of the lower body was significantly different from the left side ($p < 0.005$) (Figure 2a). On the other hand, in females, the R/h of the lower body significantly differed from the R/h of the upper body ($p < 0.001$), right ($p < 0.001$), and left ($p < 0.001$) sides, respectively. In comparison, the Xc/h of the lower body significantly differed from the Xc/h of the upper body ($p < 0.004$), right ($p < 0.001$), and left ($p < 0.001$) sides, respectively (Figure 2b). No differences were found in PA for both sexes.

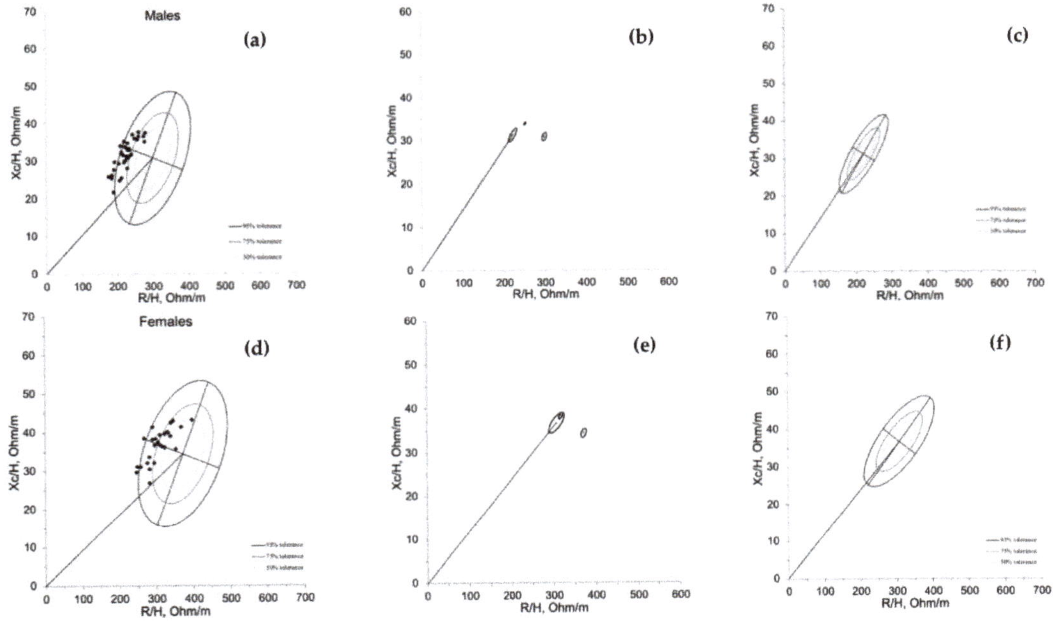

Figure 1. Whole-body BIVA graph of male and female natural bodybuilders. Caption: (**a**) Whole-body BIVA point graph of the male bodybuilders plotted on the tolerance ellipses of the athletic reference. (**b**) Whole-body BIVA mean graph for the whole-body mean impedance vectors of the male bodybuilders and the athletic and general reference population. (**c**) Specific 50%, 75%, and 95% tolerance ellipses of male natural body builders. (**d**) Whole-body BIVA point graph of the female bodybuilders plotted on the tolerance ellipses of the athletic reference. (**e**) Whole-body BIVA mean graph for the whole-body mean impedance vectors of the female bodybuilders and the athletic and general reference population. (**f**) Specific 50%, 75%, and 95% tolerance ellipses of female natural body builders.

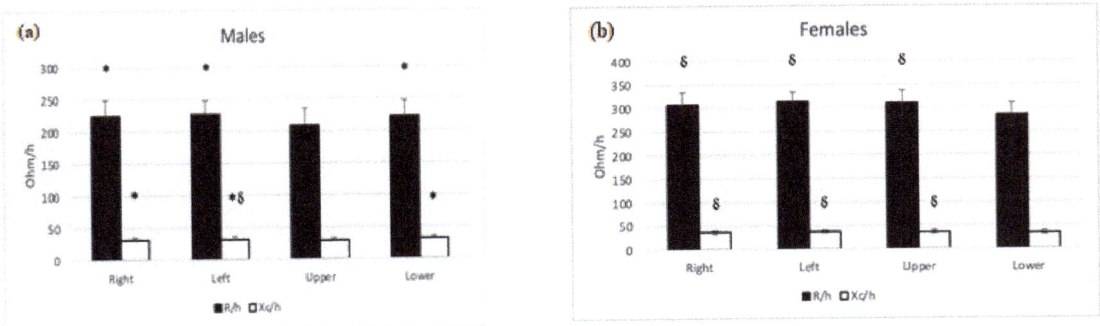

Figure 2. Bioelectrical characteristics of the sample for both sexes, for right and left sides and upper and lower body. (**a**) males. (**b**) females. caption: R/h = resistance/height; Xc/h = reactance/height. * Significantly different from the corresponding upper body bioelectrical parameter; § Significantly different from the corresponding lower body bioelectrical parameter.

Figure 3a compares the BIVA vectors assessed on the right and left sides and on the upper and lower body in males. The Hotelling's T^2 test indicates that the upper body bioelectrical vector was significantly shorter than the corresponding vectors assessed on the right (T^2= 76.6; F = 38.8; D = 1.44; $p < 0.001$) and left (T^2 = 76.6; F = 38.8; D = 1.44;

$p < 0.001$) sides. Figure 3b compares the BIVA vectors assessed on the right and left sides and on the upper and lower body in females. The Hotelling's T^2 test indicates that the lower body bioelectrical vector was significantly shorter than the corresponding vectors assessed on the right ($T^2 = 76.6$; F = 38.8; D = 1.44; $p < 0.001$) and left ($T^2 = 76.6$; F = 38.8; D = 1.44; $p < 0.001$) sides, and upper body ($T^2 = 76.6$; F = 38.8; D = 1.44; $p < 0.001$).

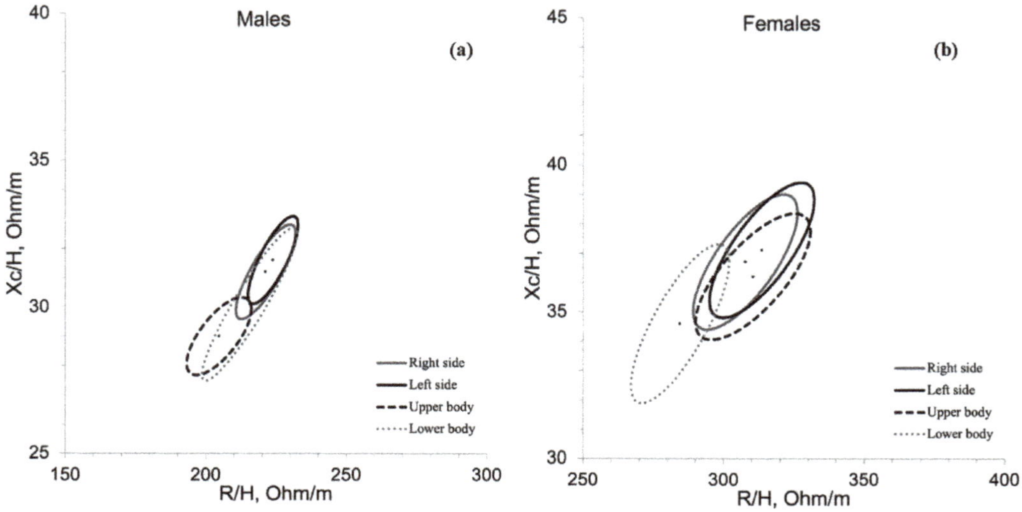

Figure 3. Bioelectrical characteristics of the sample for both sexes, for right and left sides and upper and lower body. Caption: (**a**) BIVA vectors of the right and left sides and on the upper and lower body in males. (**b**) BIVA vectors of the right and left sides and on the upper and lower body in females.

4. Discussion

This study has two aims: (1) to provide for the first time the population-specific tolerance ellipses for BIVA assessment in bodybuilders, and (2) to compare bioelectrical parameters of the upper, lower, right, and left sides.

The hypothesis of the first aim has been verified, as the body structure, endowed with high muscularity, places the study sample in the left quadrant of the ellipse. In detail, male bodybuilders differ from the general population and athletes in being more left-leaning [19] and, therefore, with higher PhA. However, they also rank lower in BIVA ellipses than athletes: they take a higher water content to increase muscle mass due to higher hydration status. The results of the female bodybuilders report differences compared to the general population that is superimposable to the male counterpart [19]. On the other hand, no differences are described concerning the population of athletes. The sample of female athletes described by Campa et al. [20] showed a higher body mass index than the female bodybuilders of this study. Therefore, it is possible to speculate about the search for a slimmer shape by female bodybuilders, probably to have advantages in the judging phase based on the aesthetic character of the competition.

Generally, in peak week, bodybuilders increase aerobic exercise in their training program [22] and re-modulate the carbohydrate loading to increase muscle glycogen storage [23,24] due to the imminence of competition. In particular, a reduction in carbohydrates from 5.3 to 3.8 g/kg/day has been described in the transition from the non-competitive to the competitive phase [25]. However, reducing carbohydrates of this magnitude close to the competition should only happen briefly to avoid muscle loss [26]. Furthermore, approaching the competitive phase, a 5–6% reduction in body fat mass is sought; therefore, the total energy intake is reduced, and proteins and fats are modulated [27]. Increasing the protein content during diets with energy deficit regimes allows the maintenance of muscle mass. Therefore, on average, bodybuilders close to competition are advised to maintain protein values up to 3.1 g/kg of lean body weight during severe calorie restriction [28]. Fat intake is generally the lowest of the three macronutrients and, like carbohydrates, reduces over time in favor of protein maintenance [29]. The optimal strategy of combining training and nutrition for the peak week has yet to be established [29]. Peak week goals are to maximize the volume of muscle mass with the most defined aspect. Therefore, maintaining resistance training levels and increasing protein intake is an established procedure. However, the increase in aerobic exercise [27] for greater muscle definition may lead to a depletion of muscle glycogen with a consequent reduction in the volume of muscle masses. At the same time, the reduction in carbohydrate intake could have the same effect as the reduction in muscle volume due to the reduced fluid recall exerted by the lower muscle glycogen content [24].

The study's second aim was to analyze the different BIVA patterns based on the upper, lower, right, and left body sides. Currently, there are few studies targeting BIVA by body segments. Unfortunately, this paucity in the literature may not allow an appropriate comparison with the results of the present study because the other studies used tools with different work frequencies [30] or did not show all vector impedance parameters [31]. A recent study indicates that BIA discriminated more pronounced asymmetries of bioelectrical parameters in tennis players than in the general population, suggesting this method can be useful in assessing the body characteristics of athletes competing in sports with a dominance of unilateral loading [15]. Thus, the authors believe that evaluating the single body side could be a new direction of study in an aesthetic discipline where symmetry and proportion are reported as a parameter of judgment for the final score between the right and left and between the upper and lower sides. The results of the present study show that the upper body is more relevant in males (Figure 3a). In contrast, the lower body is more relevant for female bodybuilders (Figure 3b): this could be due to the greater muscle mass expressed in different body parts between the sexes. In addition, male and female hormone action differences play a decisive role in final body composition outcomes [32].

The study of body composition using bioimpedance recently has a new orientation toward the vector evaluation of raw bioelectrical parameters: this has promoted the possibility of independent evaluation from formulas in which sex, age, weight, and ethnicity are parameters of these predictive equations [6]. Furthermore, the elaborations of the reference ellipses for different sporting and non-sporting populations were followed. In this context, providing bodybuilders' BIVA references for the first time will be helpful for (1) comparison with athletes from other sports given the muscularity that characterizes this specific sports population; (2) providing training feedback to bodybuilders themselves; therefore, they can adjust the combination of nutrition and training to reach their optimal level. In this context, the evaluation of muscle mass using the Levi Muscle Index (LMI), a new parameter based on raw bioelectrical parameters, is also useful. In detail, the male bodybuilders in this study show higher values than male elite soccer players (3.7 ± 0.6 vs. 3.08 ± 0.35, respectively) [18].

Some studies [14,33,34] link bioelectrical parameters, mainly phase angle [35], with sports performance. However, the physical performance of bodybuilders would not be directly related to the probability of victory, as the aesthetic nature characterizes bodybuilding. Therefore, morphological aspects influence the final score more than higher strength values.

Currently, the bioimpedance assessment performed on some specific body areas does not have a single denomination. Instead, there are simultaneously terms such as "regional," "segmental," and "district," which in some cases are used as synonyms, but each has its specific meaning. Therefore, greater homogeneity in the terminology of this specific area is advisable to ensure correct scientific progress in this field of research.

Future directions of study could be:

1. increase the sample size of bodybuilders in the BIVA study, which would make it possible to provide both normative reference values for this specific population and a left

border of the ellipse in the R-Xc graph of the sports population that are more reliable from a statistical point of view.

2. Deepen the evaluation of body sides in sports where symmetry is a parameter that can determine success in a competition. This could be done by increasing the number of bodybuilders evaluated and by carrying out symmetry assessments on both large body areas (e.g., upper–lower or right–left sides) and small body areas (e.g., right–left tight or right–left arm) and then using the localized impedance measurement technique.

Strengths and Limitations of the Study

This study has strengths. The first is the sample size, which aligns with the studies on larger numbers of bodybuilders. Second, the enrolled athletes participated in the national championship and were all enrolled as competitive athletes, unlike some studies of amateur athletes. Thirdly, it is the first study to perform total bioelectrical and body side assessment on bodybuilders.

However, this research is not without its limitations. First, the subjects are from the same country; therefore, the results may only be generalizable to some athletes worldwide with different ethnicity. Secondly, the muscle mass values recorded in the present study's sample may be lower than in other studies (the BMI value falls within the normal weight range). However, the authors have chosen this federation to avoid drug use that could compromise the reliability of the physiological hypertrophic response. Third, enrolled athletes fall into different categories, following different metrics that could influence training goals; however, this heterogeneity could also provide a broader picture of possible responses to bodybuilding practice.

5. Conclusions

In summary, this study provided, for the first time, the BIVA ellipses for the athletic bodybuilder population. In addition, the high muscularity that characterizes these athletes allows us to provide the hypothetical left margin of the BIVA ellipse of the general athletic population and therefore have a reference.

Furthermore, this study highlights asymmetries between the upper and lower body in both sexes. This aspect could compromise the competition result, as the symmetry, intended not only between the right and left sides, is part of the judgment parameters for the final score.

Author Contributions: Conceptualization, M.L.M. and G.M.; methodology, M.L.M. and D.V.; software, P.I.; validation, G.M. and M.L.M.; formal analysis, P.I.; investigation, D.V., N.T. and T.L.; data curation, D.V., N.T. and T.L.; writing—original draft preparation, G.M. and C.P.; visualization, M.L.M. and D.V.; supervision, M.L.M. and M.G. All authors have read and agreed to the published version of the manuscript.

Funding: This research received no external funding.

Institutional Review Board Statement: The study was conducted in accordance with the Declaration of Helsinki. Ethical review and approval were waived for this study because this research is part of an international project entitled "The International Bio-impedance Analysis Multi-center Collaboration project" which the first published article is Campa F, Thomas DM, Watts K, Clark N, Baller D, Morin T, Toselli S, Koury JC, Melchiorri G, Andreoli A, Mascherini G, Petri C, Sardinha LB, Silva AM. Reference Percentiles for Bioelectrical Phase Angle in Athletes. Biology (Basel). 8 February 2022; 11 (2): 264. doi: 10.3390/biology11020264.

Informed Consent Statement: Informed consent was obtained from all subjects involved in the study.

Data Availability Statement: Data can be obtained from Gabriele Mascherini on a reasonable request gabriele.mascherini@unifi.it.

Acknowledgments: The authors express their gratitude to all the participants involved in this study.

Conflicts of Interest: The authors declare no conflict of interest.

References

1. Ackland, T.R.; Lohman, T.G.; Sundgot-Borgen, J.; Maughan, R.J.; Meyer, N.L.; Stewart, A.D.; Müller, W. Current status of body composition assessment in sport: Review and position statement on behalf of the ad hoc research working group on body composition health and performance, under the auspices of the I.O.C. Medical Commission. *Sport. Med.* **2012**, *42*, 227–249. [CrossRef]
2. Alves, R.C.; Prestes, J.; Enes, A.; de Moraes, W.M.A.; Trindade, T.B.; de Salles, B.F.; Aragon, A.A.; Souza-Junior, T.P. Training Programs Designed for Muscle Hypertrophy in Bodybuilders: A Narrative Review. *Sports* **2020**, *8*, 149. [CrossRef] [PubMed]
3. Barnman, M.M.; Hunter, G.R.; Newton, L.E.; Roney, R.K.; Khaled, M.A. Changes in body composition, diet and strength of bodybuilders during the 12 weeks prior to competition. *J. Sport. Med. Phys. Fit.* **1993**, *33*, 383–391.
4. Katch, V.L.; Katch, F.I.; Moffatt, R.; Gittleson, M. Muscolar development and lean body weight in body builders and weight lifters. *Med. Sci. Sport. Exerc.* **1980**, *12*, 340–344. [CrossRef]
5. Huygens, W.; Claessens, A.L.; Thomis, M.; Loos, R.; Van Langendonck, L.; Peeters, M.; Philippaerts, R.; Meynaerts, E.; Vlietinck, R.; Beunen, G. Body composition estimations by BIA versus anthropometric equations in body builders and other power athletes. *J. Sport. Med. Phys. Fit.* **2002**, *42*, 45–55.
6. Ward, L.C. Bioelectrical impedance analysis for body composition assessment: Reflections on accuracy, clinical utility, and standardisation. *Eur. J. Clin. Nutr.* **2019**, *73*, 194–199. [CrossRef] [PubMed]
7. Coratella, G.; Campa, F.; Matias, C.N.; Toselli, S.; Koury, J.C.; Andreoli, A.; Sardinha, L.S.B.; Silva, A.M. Generalized bioelectric impedance-based equations underestimate body fluids in athletes. *Scand. J. Med. Sci. Sport.* **2021**, *31*, 2123–2132. [CrossRef]
8. Castizo-Olier, J.; Irurtia, A.; Jemni, M.; Carrasco-Marginet, M.; Fernández-García, R.; Rodríguez, F.A. Bioelectrical impedance vector analysis (BIVA) in sport and exercise: Systematic review and future perspectives. *PLoS ONE* **2018**, *13*, e0197957. [CrossRef]
9. Campa, F.; Toselli, S.; Mazzilli, M.; Gobbo, L.A.; Coratella, G. Assessment of Body Composition in Athletes: A Narrative Review of Available Methods with Special Reference to Quantitative and Qualitative Bioimpedance Analysis. *Nutrients* **2021**, *13*, 1620. [CrossRef]
10. Micheli, M.L.; Pagani, L.; Marella, M.; Gulisano, M.; Piccoli, A.; Angelini, F.; Burtscher, M.; Gatterer, H. Bioimpedance and impedance vector patterns as predictors of league level in male soccer players. *Int. J. Sport. Physiol. Perform.* **2014**, *9*, 532–539. [CrossRef]
11. Giorgi, A.; Vicini, M.; Pollastri, L.; Lombardi, E.; Magni, E.; Andreazzoli, A.; Orsini, M.; Bonifazi, M.; Lukaski, H.; Gatterer, H. Bioimpedance patterns and bioelectrical impedance vector analysis (BIVA) of road cyclists. *J. Sport. Sci.* **2018**, *36*, 2608–2613. [CrossRef]
12. Di Credico, A.; Gaggi, G.; Vamvakis, A.; Serafini, S.; Ghinassi, B.; Di Baldassarre, A.; Izzicupo, P. Bioelectrical Impedance Vector Analysis of Young Elite Team Handball Players. *Int. J. Environ. Res. Public Health* **2021**, *18*, 12972. [CrossRef] [PubMed]
13. Carrasco-Marginet, M.; Castizo-Olier, J.; Rodríguez-Zamora, L.; Iglesias, X.; Rodríguez, F.A.; Chaverri, D.; Brotons, D.; Irurtia, A. Bioelectrical impedance vector analysis (BIVA) for measuring the hydration status in young elite synchronized swimmers. *PLoS ONE* **2017**, *12*, e0178819. [CrossRef] [PubMed]
14. Campa, F.; Mascherini, G.; Polara, G.; Chiodo, D.; Stefani, L. Association of regional bioelectrical phase angle with physical performance: A pilot study in elite rowers. *Muscles Ligaments Tendons J.* **2021**, *11*, 449–456. [CrossRef]
15. D'Hondt, J.; Chapelle, L.; Droogenbroeck, L.V.; Aerenhouts, D.; Clarys, P.; D'Hondt, E. Bioelectrical impedance analysis as a means of quantifying upper and lower limb asymmetry in youth elite tennis players: An explorative study. *Eur. J. Sport Sci.* **2022**, *22*, 1343–1354. [CrossRef] [PubMed]
16. Kyle, U.G.; Bosaeus, I.; De Lorenzo, A.D.; Deurenberg, P.; Elia, M.; Gómez, J.M.; Heitmann, B.L.; Kent-Smith, L.; Melchior, J.-C.; Pirlich, M.; et al. Bioelectrical impedance analysis—Part II: Utilization in clinical practice. *Clin. Nutr.* **2004**, *23*, 1430–1453. [CrossRef] [PubMed]
17. Lukaski, H.C.; Piccoli, A. Bioelectrical impedance vector analysis for assessment of hydration in physiological states and clinical conditions. In *Handbook of Anthropometry*; Preedy, V., Ed.; Springer: New York, NY, USA, 2012; pp. 287–305.
18. Levi Micheli, M.; Cannataro, R.; Gulisano, M.; Mascherini, G. Proposal of a New Parameter for Evaluating Muscle Mass in Footballers through Bioimpedance Analysis. *Biology* **2022**, *11*, 1182. [CrossRef]
19. Piccoli, A.; Rossi, B.; Pillon, L.; Bucciante, G. A new method for monitoring body fluid variation by bioimpedance analysis: The RXc graph. *Kidney Int.* **1994**, *46*, 534–539. [CrossRef]
20. Campa, F.; Matias, C.; Gatterer, H.; Toselli, S.; Koury, J.C.; Andreoli, A.; Melchiorri, G.; Sardinha, L.B.; Silva, A.M. Classic Bioelectrical Impedance Vector Reference Values for Assessing Body Composition in Male and Female Athletes. *Int. J. Environ. Res. Public Health* **2019**, *16*, 5066. [CrossRef]
21. Piccoli, A.; Pastori, G. *BIVA Software*; Department of Medical and Surgical Sciences, University of Padova: Padova, Italy, 2002.
22. Mitchell, L.; Slater, G.; Hackett, D.; Johnson, N.; O'connor, H. Physiological implications of preparing for a natural male bodybuilding competition. *Eur. J. Sport Sci.* **2018**, *18*, 619–629. [CrossRef]
23. Schoenfeld, B.J.; Alto, A.; Grgic, J.; Tinsley, G.; Haun, C.T.; Campbell, B.I.; Escalante, G.; Sonmez, G.T.; Cote, G.; Francis, A.; et al. Alterations in Body Composition, Resting Metabolic Rate, Muscular Strength, and Eating Behavior in Response to Natural Bodybuilding Competition Preparation: A Case Study. *J. Strength Cond. Res.* **2020**, *34*, 3124–3138. [CrossRef] [PubMed]

24. de Moraes, W.M.A.M.; de Almeida, F.N.; Dos Santos, L.E.A.; Cavalcante, K.D.G.; Santos, H.O.; Navalta, J.W.; Prestes, J. Carbohydrate Loading Practice in Bodybuilders: Effects on Muscle Thickness, Photo Silhouette Scores, Mood States and Gastrointestinal Symptoms. *J. Sport. Sci. Med.* **2019**, *18*, 772–779.
25. Spendlove, J.; Mitchell, L.; Gifford, J.; Hackett, D.; Slater, G.; Cobley, S.; O'Connor, H. Dietary Intake of Competitive Bodybuilders. *Sport. Med.* **2015**, *45*, 1041–1063. [CrossRef]
26. Robinson, S.L.; Lambeth-Mansell, A.; Gillibrand, G.; Smith-Ryan, A.; Bannock, L. A nutrition and conditioning intervention for natural bodybuilding contest preparation: Case study. *J. Int. Soc. Sport. Nutr.* **2015**, *12*, 20. [CrossRef] [PubMed]
27. Bauer, P.; Majisik, A.; Mitter, B.; Csapo, R.; Tschan, H.; Hume, P.; Martínez-Rodríguez, A.; Makivic, B. Body Composition of Competitive Bodybuilders: A Systematic Review of Published Data and Recommendations for Future Work. *J. Strength Cond. Res.* **2023**, *37*, 726–732. [CrossRef]
28. Helms, E.R.; Zinn, C.; Rowlands, D.S.; Brown, S.R. A systematic review of dietaryprotein during caloric restriction in resistance trained lean athletes: A casefor higher intakes. *Int. J. Sport Nutr. Exerc. Metab.* **2014**, *24*, 127–138. [CrossRef]
29. Chappell, A.J.; Simper, T.; Barker, M.E. Nutritional strategies of high level natural bodybuilders during competition preparation. *J. Int. Soc. Sport. Nutr.* **2018**, *15*, 4. [CrossRef]
30. Tinsley, G.M.; Harty, P.S.; Moore, M.L.; Grgic, J.; Silva, A.M.; Sardinha, L.B. Changes in total and segmental bioelectrical resistance are correlated with whole-body and segmental changes in lean soft tissue following a resistance training intervention. *J. Int. Soc. Sport. Nutr.* **2019**, *16*, 58. [CrossRef]
31. Marra, M.; Da Prat, B.; Montagnese, C.; Caldara, A.; Sammarco, R.; Pasanisi, F.; Corsetti, R. Segmental bioimpedance analysis in professional cyclists during a three week stage race. *Physiol. Meas.* **2016**, *37*, 1035. [CrossRef]
32. Mascherini, G.; Castizo-Olier, J.; Irurtia, A.; Petri, C.; Galanti, G. Differences between the sexes in athletes' body composition and lower limb bioimpedance values. *Muscles Ligaments Tendons J.* **2018**, *7*, 573–581. [CrossRef]
33. Hetherington-Rauth, M.; Leu, C.G.; Júdice, P.B.; Correia, I.R.; Magalhães, J.P.; Sardinha, L.B. Whole body and regional phase angle as indicators of muscular performance in athletes. *Eur. J. Sport Sci.* **2021**, *21*, 1684–1692. [CrossRef] [PubMed]
34. Bongiovanni, T.; Rossi, A.; Iaia, F.M.; Alberti, G.; Pasta, G.; Trecroci, A. Association of phase angle and appendicular upper and lower body lean soft tissue with physical performance in young elite soccer players: A pilot study. *J. Sport. Med. Phys. Fit.* **2022**, *62*, 1015–1022. [CrossRef] [PubMed]
35. Campa, F.; Thomas, D.M.; Watts, K.; Clark, N.; Baller, D.; Morin, T.; Toselli, S.; Koury, J.C.; Melchiorri, G.; Andreoli, A.; et al. Reference Percentiles for Bioelectrical Phase Angle in Athletes. *Biology* **2022**, *11*, 264. [CrossRef] [PubMed]

nutrients

MDPI

Article

Effects of Endurance Exercise Intensities on Autonomic and Metabolic Controls in Children with Obesity: A Feasibility Study Employing Online Exercise Training

Valeria Calcaterra [1,2], Giuseppina Bernardelli [3,4], Mara Malacarne [5], Matteo Vandoni [6], Savina Mannarino [7], Vittoria Carnevale Pellino [6,8], Cristiana Larizza [9], Massimo Pagani [3], Gianvincenzo Zuccotti [1,10] and Daniela Lucini [3,5,*]

1 Pediatric Unit, Pediatric Department, Buzzi Children's Hospital, 20154 Milan, Italy
2 Department of Internal Medicine, University of Pavia, 27100 Pavia, Italy
3 Exercise Medicine Unit, Istituto Auxologico Italiano, IRCCS, 20135 Milan, Italy
4 DISCCO Department, University of Milan, 20122 Milan, Italy
5 BIOMETRA Department, University of Milan, 20129 Milan, Italy
6 Laboratory of Adapted Motor Activity (LAMA), Department of Public Health, Experimental Medicine and Forensic Science, University of Pavia, 27100 Pavia, Italy
7 Pediatric Cardiology Unit, Pediatric Department, Buzzi Children's Hospital, 20154 Milan, Italy
8 Department of Industrial Engineering, University of Rome Tor Vergata, 00133 Rome, Italy
9 Department of Electrical, Computer and Biomedical Engineering, University of Pavia, 27100 Pavia, Italy
10 Department of Biomedical and Clinical Science, University of Milano, 20157 Milan, Italy
* Correspondence: daniela.lucini@unimi.it

Abstract: Exercise is one of the major determinants of a healthy lifestyle, which is particularly important in childhood and serves as a powerful preventive tool. On the other hand, obesity and arterial hypertension rates are increasing in children, representing a huge risk for developing major cardiovascular and metabolic diseases in adult life. Of fundamental importance is the modality and volume of exercise required to obtain benefits. In this feasibility study, we considered a group of obese children, studied before and after a 12-week online exercise training program, and subdivided the participants into two groups considering the volume of exercise performed (above or below 1200 MET·min/week). This threshold level was applied in two different ways: subdivision A considered the total weekly physical activity volume (considering both time spent walking for at least 10 min consecutively and time spent performing structured exercise) and subdivision B considered only the weekly volume of structured exercise. We assessed autonomic and metabolic control and auxological and lifestyle parameters. We observed that the improved volume of structured exercise was associated with reduced arterial pressure percentile only in subdivision B and an improvement in markers of vagal and metabolic control was evident. Moreover, the 12-week online exercise training program, defined considering individual fitness level and progressively adapted as the goal was reached, proved to be sustainable from an economical and organizational point of view.

Keywords: exercise intensity; training; autonomic nervous system; heart rate variability; metabolic control; children; online exercise training; obesity

Citation: Calcaterra, V.; Bernardelli, G.; Malacarne, M.; Vandoni, M.; Mannarino, S.; Pellino, V.C.; Larizza, C.; Pagani, M.; Zuccotti, G.; Lucini, D. Effects of Endurance Exercise Intensities on Autonomic and Metabolic Controls in Children with Obesity: A Feasibility Study Employing Online Exercise Training. *Nutrients* **2023**, *15*, 1054. https://doi.org/10.3390/nu15041054

Academic Editor: Aloys Berg

Received: 20 January 2023
Revised: 9 February 2023
Accepted: 16 February 2023
Published: 20 February 2023

1. Introduction

Childhood and youth are ideally the best periods in life to instill healthy behaviors [1], thereby fostering wellbeing and preventing chronic non-communicable diseases (CNCD). On the other hand, overweight, obesity, and the prevalence of hypertension are increasing, particularly in the initial phases of life [2,3], thus determining a dramatic increase in the risk of diseases such as diabetes, coronary artery disease, and cancer [3,4]. Unhealthy lifestyles, such as poor nutrition and sedentariness, contribute to this phenomenon. Additionally, recent data show that obesity [5] and an unhealthy lifestyle, in particular sedentariness [6], are linked to poor prognosis in COVID-19 patients, thus expanding the role of lifestyle in determining health status further to CNCD.

Physical activity is one of the major determinants of a healthy lifestyle, in addition to healthy nutrition, not smoking, good sleep hygiene, and the capability to manage stress [7,8]. Regular physical activity is particularly important in childhood and youth as it grants immediate (improvement of wellbeing, scholastic performance, social relationships [9], etc.), and long-term benefits (prevention/treatment of many diseases), and it may be considered a sustainable tool [10] for the individual and environment. On the other hand, epidemiological data from the USA show that only 28.3% of youth aged 6 to 11 years are active for ≥60 min every day of the week, thus meeting more recent guideline recommendations [3,11–13], and this decreases to 16.5% of youth aged 12 to 17 years [4]. European Commission data show that 32.4% of Italian children aged 8–9 years are estimated to meet sufficient physical activity levels (considering WHO guidelines), and this percentage decreases to 11.9% of children aged 11 years old and further decreases to 6.8% of children aged 15 years old [14].

International guidelines [11–13] indicate that children and adolescents should perform moderate-to-vigorous intensity, mostly aerobic, physical activity at least an average of 60 min every day of the week and that vigorous-intensity aerobic activities, as well as activities that strengthen muscle and bone, should be incorporated at least 3 days a week. A recent paper [15] reported that a minimum of 20 min/day of vigorous endurance exercise may be best for maximizing cardiorespiratory fitness in adolescence, a parameter that a growing body of epidemiological and clinical evidence [16] considers to be a potentially strong predictor of mortality, showing that the intensity of endurance exercise may be a determinant of the beneficial effect of exercise programs.

Recent data on the association between walking pace and telomere length [17] (a parameter associated with chronic diseases and proposed as a marker of biological age) underlined the importance of exercise intensity, showing that only brisk walkers had significantly longer telomeres than slow walkers.

An exercise program, and a lifestyle program in general, may be considered efficacious only if it leads to an improvement of the underlying pathogenetic mechanisms that determine a disease or risk of developing a disease. The mechanisms that are potentially improved by exercise are multifarious and complex, ranging from improved immunological and metabolic profiles to an improvement in hemodynamics [1,4,7,8,11,16,18]. An amelioration in cardiac autonomic regulation (CAR, autonomic control of cardiovascular system) may also play an additional, but little recognized, beneficial role [19], generating a "risk factor gap" above and beyond usual treatments. Several chronic diseases, such as arterial hypertension and diabetes, are characterized in adulthood [20,21] and also in childhood and adolescence [22,23] by autonomic nervous system (ANS) impairment, which may be reversed by exercise training and/or healthy nutrition programs [10,22,24–27].

The literature is particularly rich with scientific data demonstrating that exercise may positively interfere with many mechanisms underlying chronic diseases, rendering it a well-recognized preventive and therapeutic tool [1,4,7,8,11,16,18,22,24–28]. However, the implementation of efficacious exercise programs is less defined [7,8,12,29]. Generally, programs that group children together, such as school-based programs or participation in team sports [12], are considered more effective than home-based exercise programs, since they also foster socialization and play an educational role. On the other hand, these approaches may present some economical and organizational barriers [30,31], such as the need for transportation to the gym or sports field, lack of parental support, cost, and family time management. These barriers may have a particular impact on families of low socio-economical level or in a country, such as Italy, where time spent at school is limited. Moreover, other important barriers, such as lack of skills, motivation, enjoinment, and peer support, as well as feeling shy about physical activity in public [31,32], need to be accounted for in the case of obese children and adolescents. Home-based exercise intervention programs may help in overcoming some of these barriers [33–35]. As previously reported [36], remote physical activity programs may provide a valuable strategy for fostering compliance with physical activity guidelines, representing an opportunity for pediatric subjects with obesity to stay healthy. On the other hand, their effectiveness may vary [12,33,37] according to the level of support granted by exercise professionals and the level of personalization of the proposed program.

The goal of this feasibility study was to verify the effectiveness on cardiac autonomic regulation and metabolic parameters of a supervised, home-based exercise program specifically designed to meet obese children's needs and be enjoyable and sustainable from an economical and organizational point of view in order to facilitate acceptance and compliance. In particular, we assessed the autonomic and metabolic effects considering the volume of physical activity actually performed by children.

2. Materials and Methods

We consecutively enrolled 35 Caucasian children and adolescents (14 females/21 males) admitted to our pediatric outpatient clinic for obesity by their general practitioner or by their primary care pediatric consultant between March 2021 and December 2021. We studied them before (T0) and after (T1) a 12-week online exercise training protocol.

To be included in our study, the children must have been aged between 8 and 13 years, have a body mass index (BMI) z-score ≥ 2 (according to World Health Organization [38]), and have Italian language competency. The exclusion criteria were: known secondary obesity conditions, no comprehension of Italian language, cardiovascular and respiratory chronic diseases, orthopedic problems, and absolute contraindications to practicing physical activity.

This study was approved by the institutional ethics committee (Milano Area 1 protocol number 2020/ST/298, approval date 2 December 2020) and conducted in accordance with the Helsinki Declaration of 1975, as revised in 2008.Written consent was obtained by all participants or their responsible guardians once they were well informed about the study.

2.1. Clinical Evaluations

All children underwent the following assessments.

2.1.1. Clinical, Auxological, and Hemodynamic Assessment

In all patients, weight, height, waist circumference (WC), pubertal stage according to Marshall and Tanner [39,40], BMI, waist-to-height ratio (WHtR) [41], triponderal mass index [42], and visceral adiposity index (VAI) [43] were considered as adiposity indexes related to cardiometabolic risk [44]. A basal musculoskeletal assessment was employed in order to exclude the presence of musculoskeletal limitations to the exercise program. Weight was measured with patients not wearing shoes and in light clothing, standing upright in the center of the scale platform (Seca, Hamburg, Germany), facing the recorder, hands at the sides, and looking straight ahead. Standing height was measured using a Harpenden stadiometer (Holtain Ltd., Cross-well, Crymych, UK) with a fixed vertical backboard and adjustable headpiece [44].

WC was performed in the horizontal plane midway between the lowest ribs and iliac crest, using a flexible inch tape [44].

BMI was calculated as body weight (kilograms) divided by height (meters squared) and was transformed into BMI z-scores using WHO reference values [38].

Other adiposity indexes were calculated as follows [42,43]:

$$\text{WHtR} = \text{WC}/\text{Ht}$$

$$\text{TMI} = \text{weight (kg)}/\text{height (m)}^3$$

$$\text{VAI}$$

$$\text{Male} = [\text{WC}/(39.68 + (1.88 \times \text{BMI}))] \times (\text{TG}/1.03) \times (1.31/\text{HDL-C});$$

$$\text{Female} = [\text{WC}/(36.58 + (1.89 \times \text{BMI}))] \times (\text{TG}/0.81) \times (1.52/\text{HDL-C})$$

Pubertal stages according to Tanner were classified as follows: prepubertal stage 1 = Tanner 1; middle puberty stage 2 = Tanner 2–3; and late puberty stage 3 = Tanner 4–5 [39,40].

Systolic arterial pressure (SAP) and diastolic arterial pressure (DAP) were measured twice, in the supine position, using an electronic mercury sphygmomanometer (A & D Medical, Tokyo, Japan) with an appropriately sized cuff on the right arm after 5 min of rest [45]; the second measurement was used for analysis. We determined the blood pressure percentile for each child, following recent guidelines [46–48]. Moreover, every child underwent a basal electrocardiogram and echocardiogram in order to verify the absence of main cardiac diseases that might contraindicate or limit exercise training, particularly at high intensities.

2.1.2. Metabolic Assessment

A blood sample for the evaluation of fasting blood glucose (FBG), total cholesterol (TOT Cho), high-density lipoprotein (HDL C) cholesterol, triglycerides (TG), and insulin was obtained in fasting state between 8:30 and 9:00 a.m. and analyzed the same morning by standard methods (Advia XPT, Siemens Healthcare). As a surrogate of insulin resistance (IR), we considered the homeostasis model assessment (HOMA-IR) calculated as insulin resistance = (insulin × glucose)/22.5 [49] and the triglyceride and glucose (TyG) index was calculated as ln[fasting triglycerides (mg/dL) × fasting plasma glucose (mg/dL)/2]) [50].

2.1.3. Lifestyle Assessment

An ad hoc questionnaire was employed to quantify lifestyle [51–55]:

- Nutrition was assessed using the American Heart Association Healthy Diet Score (AHA score) [8], taking into consideration fruit/vegetables, fish, sweetened beverages, whole grain, and sodium consumption (assessment of the latter was adapted to Italian eating habits) [55].
- The lifestyle questionnaire inquired also about hours of sleep/day, hours of sedentariness/week, and perceptions of quality of sleep, health, and school performance (assessed using evaluation scales from 0 ('worst quality') to 10 ('best quality') for each measure).
- Physical activity (total activity volume) was assessed by a modified version of the commonly employed short version of the International Physical Activity Questionnaire (IPAQ) [52,53], which focuses on intensity (nominally estimated in metabolic equivalents (METs) according to the type of activity) and duration (in min) of physical activity. We decided to employ this questionnaire, even if it was designed for adults, because it has the advantage of furnishing a numeric parameter of exercise volume (expressed in METs) capable of reflecting the total exercise volume.

We considered the following levels: brisk walking (≈3.3 METs), other activities of moderate intensity (≈4.0 METs), and activities of vigorous intensity (≈8.0 METs).

In accordance with current guidelines [11,12], these levels were used to assess the weekly exercise volume, using the following equations:

- (METsTOT) Total weekly physical activity volume [MET·min/week] = (3.3 × minutes of brisk walking × days of brisk walking) + (4.0 × minutes of other moderate intensity activity × days of other moderate intensity activities) + (8.0 × minutes of vigorous intensity activity × days of vigorous intensity activity).
- (METsMV) Weekly physical activity volume calculated only considering other activities of moderate intensity and activities of vigorous intensity [MET·min/week] = (4.0 × minutes of other moderate intensity activity × days of other moderate intensity activities) + (8.0 × minutes of vigorous intensity activity × days of vigorous intensity activity). METsMV may be considered as the total weekly volume of structured exercise.

The population of our study was subdivided into two groups: those reaching the physical activity goals suggested by the latest guidelines [11,12], corresponding to at least an average of 60 min/day of moderate-to-vigorous intensity, mostly aerobic, physical activity (above 1200 MET·min/week, and those who did not reach the physical activity goals (below 1200 MET·min/week. Accordingly, we considered the physical activity volume reached at the end of the training.

The threshold level of 1200 MET·min/week was obtained in two different ways:

- Subdivision A considered the total weekly physical activity volume (METsTOT), i.e., considering both time spent walking (at least for 10 min consecutively) and time spent performing structured exercise (other moderate intensity activities and vigorous intensity activities)
- Subdivision B considered only the weekly volume of structured exercise (METsMV) (only other moderate intensity activities and vigorous intensity activities).

The results considering these two different subdivisions are reported respectively in Tables 1 and 2.

Table 1. Summary of descriptive data of the study population subdivided into two groups considering total volume of physical activity (METsTOT) (Subdivision A).

Indices	Groups		Significance		
	Group 1 n = 12	Group 2 n = 23			
	Below 1200 METs	Above 1200 METs	Between Groups	Between T0–T1	Interaction
	Median (Percentile 25°; 75°)	Median (Percentile 25°; 75°)			
HR T0 [b/min]	90.76 (83.38; 97.48)	82.15 (75.67; 85.90)	0.283	0.843	0.163
HR T1	90.80 (78.83; 95.34)	83.52 (77.86; 95.90)			
RR T0 [msec]	661.20 (615.73; 719.99)	730.38 (698.48; 792.92)	0.186	0.898	0.289
RR T1	660.93 (629.34; 761.20)	718.41 (625.64; 770.63)			
RRTP T0 [msec^2]	2015.38 (700.66; 4175.22)	2070.68 (1174.64; 4358.51)	0.726	0.694	0.604
RRTP T1	1941.73 (1036.30; 2996.04)	1974.04 (880.01; 3978.67)			
RRLFa T0 [msec^2]	278.57 (152.21; 1536.34)	569.95 (324.55; 1064.11)	0.613	0.911	0.795
RRLFa T1	414.05 (246.20; 1126.03)	679.74 (218.92; 1833.57)			
RRHFa T0 [msec^2]	565.22 (124.40; 1610.27)	600.91 (198.91; 1718.47)	0.917	0.423	0.331
RRHFa T1	461.04 (252.52; 1177.21)	630.36 (235.87; 1128.62)			
RRLFnu T0 [nu]	30.66 (25.04; 48.65)	46.38 (31.23; 55.80)	0.267	0.264	0.727
RRLFnu T1	41.86 (34.10; 44.14)	41.52 (33.52; 65.68)			
RRHFnu T0 [nu]	52.41 (37.54; 61.06)	46.00 (28.39; 59.02)	0.808	0.310	0.367
RRHFnu T1	47.47 (32.09; 56.59)	43.79 (28.31; 57.69)			
RRLF/HF T0 [.]	0.58 (0.41; 1.30)	1.01 (0.46; 2.27)	0.299	0.660	0.691
RRLF/HF T1	0.91 (0.55; 1.46)	0.95 (0.59; 2.32)			
SAPpc T0 [%]	78.00 (35.50; 87.00)	80.00 (63.00; 92.00)	0.058	0.464	0.895
SAPpc T1	58.50 (49.50; 65.00)	80.00 (51.00; 93.00)			
DAPpc T0 [%]	75.00 (56.00; 92.00)	71.00 (59.00; 95.00)	0.348	0.376	0.068
DAPpc T1	61.50 (42.50; 84.50)	78.00 (59.00; 91.00)			
AHA score T0 [.]	1.50 (1.00; 2.50)	2.00 (1.00; 3.00)	0.157	0.180	0.180
AHA score T1	2.00 (1.00; 2.50)	3.00 (2.00; 3.00)			
Hours of sleep T0 [h/day]	8.00 (8.00; 9.00)	8.50 (8.00; 9.00)	0.156	0.208	0.402
Hours of sleep T1	9.00 (7.00; 9.00)	9.00 (8.00; 9.00)			
Quality of Sleep T0 [.]	8.50 (6.00; 10.00)	10.00 (8.00; 10.00)	**0.020**	0.351	0.829
Quality of SleepT1	8.50 (4.50; 9.50)	9.00 (9.00; 10.00)			
Health T0 [.]	7.00 (6.00; 9.00)	8.00 (6.00; 10.00)	**0.051**	0.215	0.215
Health T1	6.50 (5.00; 9.00)	8.00 (6.00; 9.00)			
School Performance T0 [.]	8.00 (7.00; 10.00)	9.00 (7.00; 10.00)	0.450	0.215	0.907
School Performance T1	8.50 (7.00; 9.00)	8.00 (7.00; 9.00)			

Table 1. *Cont.*

Indices	Groups		Significance		
	Group 1 n = 12	**Group 2 n = 23**			
	Below 1200 METs	**Above 1200 METs**	**Between Groups**	**Between T0–T1**	**Interaction**
	Median (Percentile 25°; 75°)	**Median (Percentile 25°; 75°)**			
Sedentariness T0 [h/week]	68.00 (61.00; 82;00)	56.00 (49.00; 68.00)	**0.038**	0.229	0.775
Sedentariness T1	66.50 (52.00; 84.50)	61.00 (28; 68.00)			
METsMV T0 [MET·min/week]	240.00 (0.00; 880.00)	480.00 (0.00; 720.00)	0.056	0.119	0.117
METsMV T1	480.00 (330.00; 670.00)	960.00 (720.00; 1800.00)			
METsTOT T0 [MET·min/week]	361.50 (153.00; 966.25)	918.00 (495.00; 1635.00)	**0.000**	**0.008**	**0.030**
METsTOT T1	752.25 (538.50; 960.50)	1860.00 (1395.00; 2580.00)			
BMI z-score T0 [.]	2.13 (1.65; 2.52)	2.04 (1.84; 2.41)	0.678	**0.004**	0.200
BMI z-score T1	2.00 (1.35; 2.54)	1.97 (1.82; 2.49)			
WHtR T0 [.]	0.59 (0.57; 0.62)	0.59 (0.57; 0.64)	0.702	0.223	0.142
WHtR T1	0.58 (0.54; 0.60)	0.58 (0.55; 0.60)			
FBG T0 [mg/dL]	89.50 (87.00; 91.50)	87.00 (85.00; 95.00)	0.638	0.683	0.406
FBG T1	93.00 (86.50; 99.00)	89.00 (85.00; 95.00)			
Insulin T0 [mg/dL]	17.55 (11.25; 25.85)	17.40 (13.14; 30.70)	0.343	0.515	0.375
Insulin T1	15.40 (8.80; 30.75)	18.00 (12.00; 30.10)			
HOMA-IR T0 [.]	3.97 (2.50; 5.59)	3.87 (2.76; 6.64)	0.354	0.596	0.363
HOMA-IR T1	3.78 (1.86; 7.02)	3.78 (2.77; 5.72)			
TG T0 [mg/dL]	93.00 (64.50; 117.50)	113.00 (73.00; 150.00)	0.281	0.886	0.331
TG T1	91.00 (60.00; 119.00)	110.00 (65.00; 148.00)			
TOT Chol T0 [mg/dL]	149.00 (123.00; 156.00)	170.00 (150.00; 190.00)	**0.048**	0.314	0.068
TOT Chol T1	143.00 (129.00; 183.00)	167.00 (144.00; 172.00)			
HDL C T0 [mg/dL]	47.00 (37.00; 53.50)	45.00 (41.00; 50.00)	0.990	0.427	0.567
HDL C T1	49.00 (43.00; 52.00)	47.00 (40.00; 50.00)			
TMI T0 [.]	19.13 (18.17; 21.30)	18.64 (17.24; 20.53)	0.637	**0.000**	0.160
TMI T1	18.62 (17.47; 20.91)	18.32 (16.72; 19.68)			
VAI T0 [.]	3.33 (1.60; 4.90)	3.30 (1.58; 4.96)	0.330	0.137	0.392
VAI T1	3.01 (2.01; 4.53)	4.46 (2.48; 5.58)			
TyG T0 [.]	8.26 (8.01; 8.54)	8.56 (7.90; 8.82)	0.523	0.722	0.306
TyG T1	8.35 (7.94; 8.47)	8.47 (7.93; 8.80)			
6MWT T0 [m]	464.00 (427.00; 540.00)	472.00 (438.00; 504.00)	0.596	**0.000**	0.122
6MWT T1	516.00 (482.00. 560.00)	540.00 (500.00; 574.00)			
PAQ-C score T0 [.]	1.92 (1.74; 2.17)	1.97 (1.57; 2.30)	0.840	**0.043**	0.858
PAQ-C score T1	2.39 (1.90; 2.53)	2.25 (1.77; 2.69)			
IFIS score T0 [.]	3.40 (3.20; 4.20)	3.00 (2.80; 3.80)	0.159	0.543	0.653
IFIS score T1	3.80 (3.20; 4.00)	3.40 (2.80; 4.00)			

Abbreviations: T0 = before intervention; T1 = after intervention; HR = heart rate; RR= RR interval; RRTP = RR total power (RR interval variance); LF = low frequency component of RR variability; HF = high frequency component of RR variability; nu = normalized unit; LF/HF = RRLF on RRHF ratio; SAPpc = percentile of systolic arterial pressure; DAPpc = percentile of diastolic arterial pressure; AHA score = American Heart Association Nutrition Score; METsTOT = total weekly physical activity volume; METsMV = weekly physical activity volume calculated only considering other activities of moderate intensity and activities of vigorous intensity volume (i.e., volume of structured exercise); BMI= body mass index; WHtR = waist-to-height ratio; FBG = fasting blood glucose; HOMA-IR = homeostasis model assessment—insulin resistance; TG = triglycerides; TOT Chol = total cholesterol; HDL C = HDL cholesterol; TMI = triponderal mass index; VAI = visceral adiposity index; TyG = triglyceride and glucose index; 6MWT = 6-min walk test; PAQ-C = physical activity questionnaire—children; IFIS = international fitness scale; [.] = arbitrary units. Significant values are evidenced in bold.

Table 2. Summary of descriptive data of the study population subdivided into two groups considering weekly volume of structured exercise (METsMV) (Subdivision B).

Indices	Groups		Significance		
	Below 1200 METs	Above 1200 METs	Between Groups	Between T0–T1	Interaction
	Median (Percentile 25°; 75°)	Median (Percentile 25°; 75°)			
HR T0 [b/min]	86.61 (81.86; 95.46)	77.07 (73.44; 83.37)	0.139	0.555	0.344
HR T1	89.55 (80.08; 95.83)	80.87 (68.25; 94.11)			
RR T0 [msec]	692.84 (628.57; 732.96)	778.47 (719.76; 816.99)	0.062	0.721	0.675
RR T1	670.07 (626.13; 749.24)	741.94 (637.58; 879.14)			
RRTP T0 [msec^2]	1602.01 (775.36; 3131.09)	3215.74 (2070.68; 4532.33)	0.686	0.996	0.552
RRTP T1	1711.46 (1036.30; 2996.04)	2342.19 (815.39; 4338.19)			
RRLFa.T0 [msec^2]	392.29 (165.69; 1052.10)	952.41 (465.37; 1154.68)	0.995	0.740	0.702
RRLFa T1	498.63 (246.86; 1390.14)	679.74 (138.87; 1833.57)			
RRHFa. T0 [msec^2]	551.61 (158.16; 1360.03)	773.98 (269.76; 2289.90)	0.754	0.942	0.266
RRHFa T1	474.34 (252.52; 1092.48)	777.43 (235.87; 1485.89)			
RRLFnu T0 [nu]	44.24 (27.10; 51.30)	48.20 (26.04; 69.70)	0.947	0.735	0.063
RRLFnu.T1	42.13 (34.23; 57.47)	34.69 (22.89; 67.94)			
RRHFnu T0 [nu]	49.16 (40.03; 59.66)	49.43 (20.20; 67.22)	0.651	0.952	**0.032**
RRHFnu. T1	42.55 (32.09; 55.36)	55.05 (27.20; 70.76)			
RRLF/HF T0 [.]	0.87 (0.48; 1.29)	0.98 (0.44; 3.53)	0.450	0.546	**0.015**
RRLF/HF T1	1.09 (0.59; 1.68)	0.60 (0.32; 2.58)			
SAPpc T0 [%]	77.00 (46.00; 87)	86.00 (65.00; 94.00)	0.315	0.243	0.197
SAPpc T1	64.5 (56.00; 91.00)	83.00 (50.00; 92.00)			
DAPpc T0 [%]	75.00 (60.00; 92.00)	65.00 (58.00; 95.00)	0.987	0.864	0.768
DAPpc T1	79.5 (49.5; 90.5)	76.00 (55.00; 89.00)			
AHA score T0 [.]	1.00 (1.00; 2.00)	2.00 (2.00; 3.00)	**0.019**	**0.045**	0.359
AHA score T1	2.00 (1.00; 3.00)	3.00 (2.00; 4.00)			
Hours of sleep T0 [h]	8.5 (8.00; 9.00)	8.00 (8.00; 9.00)	0.507	0.575	0.141
Hours of sleep.T1	8.00 (7.50; 9.00)	9.00 (8.00; 9.00)			
Quality of Sleep T0 [.]	9.00 (8.00; 10.00)	10.00 (8.00;1 0.00)	0.233	0.414	0.935
Quality of Sleep T1	9.00 (7.00; 10.00)	9.00 (9.00; 10.00)			
Health T0 [.]	8.00 (6.00; 10.00)	7.00 (6.00; 9.00)	0.744	0.703	0.229
Health T1	8.00 (5.50; 9.00)	7.00 (6.00; 9.00)			
School Performance T0 [.]	9.00 (7.00; 10.00)	8.00 (7.00; 10.00)	0.921	0.160	0.560
School Performance T1	8.00 (7.00; 9.00)	8.00 (6.00; 9.00)			
Sedentariness T0 [h/week]	66.00 (56.00; 78.50)	53.00 (48.00; 56.00)	**0.010**	0.162	0.708
Sedentariness T1	63.00 (52.00; 79.50)	54.00 (26.00; 67.00)			
METsMV T0 [MET·min/week]	240.00 (0.00; 480.00)	720.00 (0.00;1 680.00)	**0.000**	**0.002**	**0.007**
METsMV T1	600.00 (480.00; 720.00)	1800 (1200.00; 2080.00)			
METsTOT T0 [MET·min/week]	648.75 (268.50; 1333.00)	819.00 (0.00; 1920.00)	**0.012**	**0.000**	**0.012**
METsTOT T1	1207.50 (752.25; 1644.00)	2493.00 (1860.00; 2773.00)			
BMI z-score T0 [.]	2.11 (1.91; 2.38)	1.99 (1.69; 2.55)	0.885	**0.033**	0.282
BMI z-score T1	1.99 (1.63; 2.35)	1.90 (1.58; 2.52)			
WHtR T0 [.]	0.59 (0.57; 0.63)	0.59 (0.56; 0.64)	0.647	0.848	0.142
WHtR T1	0.57 (0.56; 0.60)	0.59 (0.55; 0.63)			
FBG T0 [mg/dL]	89.00 (86.00; 92.50)	87.00 (86.00; 96.00)	0.708	0.939	0.594
FBG T1	90.00 (85.50; 96.00)	88.00 (87.00; 96.00)			
Insulin T0 [mg/dL]	16.80 (11.75; 23.80)	18.00 (13.14; 35.00)	0.420	0.088	0.061
Insulin T1	16.00 (10.24; 30.15)	18.20 (14.80; 30.10)			
HOMA-IR T0 [.]	3.80 (2.51; 5.36)	3.87 (2.76; 7.78)	0.372	0.103	**0.053**
HOMA-IR T1	3.75 (2.22; 6.46)	4.27 (3.22; 5.72)			
TG T0 [mg/dL]	96.00 (69.50; 122.50)	121.00 (62.00; 169.00)	0.362	0.876	0.991
TG T1	91.00 (63.00; 120.00)	112.00 (75.00; 156.00)			
TOT Chol T0 [mg/dL]	156.00 (139.00; 187.00)	165.00 (150.00; 190.00)	0.782	**0.048**	0.199
TOT Chol T1	155.50 (133.00; 176.00)	151.00 (144.00; 168.00)			

Table 2. *Cont.*

Indices	Groups		Significance		
	Below 1200 METs	Above 1200 METs	Between Groups	Between T0–T1	Interaction
	Median (Percentile 25°; 75°)	Median (Percentile 25°; 75°)			
HDL C T0 [mg/dL]	47.50 (40.50; 55.50)	43.00 (39.00; 48.00)	0.390	0.445	0.675
HDL C T1	48.00 (43.00; 52.00)	46.00 (39.00; 48.00)			
TMI T0 [.]	19.08 (18.30; 21.03)	17.58 (17.15; 19.93)	0.285	**0.003**	0.760
TMI T1	19.07 (17.69; 20.91)	17.48 (16.38; 19.68)			
VAI T0 [.]	3.26 (1.79; 4.85)	3.42 (1.51; 5.53)	0.611	**0.012**	**0.048**
VAI T1	3.61 (2.07; 4.73)	5.34 (2.65; 5.85)			
TyG T0 [.]	8.35 (7.99; 8.66)	8.58 (7.88; 8.97)	0.454	0.998	0.938
TyG T1	8.35 (7.92; 8.62)	8.61 (8.09; 8.84)			
6MWT T0 [m]	464.00 (432.00; 509.00)	490.00 (440.00; 509.00)	0.532	**0.000**	0.263
6MWT T1	520.00 (492.00; 560.00)	564.00 (520.00; 580.00)			
PAQ-C score T0 [.]	1.97 (1.73; 2.17)	1.84 (1.57; 2.39)	0.895	**0.046**	0.731
PAQ-C score T1	2.30 (1.77; 2.53)	2.25 (1.81; 2.69)			
IFIS score T0 [.]	3.00 (2.80; 3.60)	3.20 (3.00; 4.20)	0.693	0.578	0.214
IFIS score T1	3.60 (3.20; 4.00)	3.40 (2.80; 4.00)			

Abbreviations: T0 = before intervention; T1 = after intervention; HR = heart rate; RR = RR interval; RRTP = RR total power (RR interval variance); LF = low frequency component of RR variability; HF = high frequency component of RR variability; nu = normalized unit; LF/HF = RRLF on RRHF ratio; SAPpc = percentile of systolic arterial pressure; DAPpc = percentile of diastolic arterial pressure; AHA score = American Heart Association Nutrition Score; METsTOT = total weekly physical activity volume; METsMV = weekly physical activity volume calculated only considering other activities of moderate intensity and activities of vigorous intensity volume (i.e., volume of structured exercise); BMI= body mass index; WHtR = waist-to-height ratio; FBG = fasting blood glucose; HOMA-IR = homeostasis model assessment—insulin resistance; TG = triglycerides; TOT Chol = total cholesterol; HDL C = HDL cholesterol; TMI = triponderal mass index; VAI = visceral adiposity index; TyG = triglyceride and glucose index; 6MWT = 6-min walk test; PAQ-C = physical activity questionnaire—children; IFIS = international fitness scale; [.] = arbitrary units. Significant values are evidenced in bold.

We considered these two different subdivisions in order to unveil the possible different effects associated with structured exercise (generally of higher intensity) or with physical activities of less intensity, such as walking.

All children were equipped with an activity tracker (Fitbit Charge 2 ©, Fitbit Inc, San Francisco, CA, USA) to monitor their heart rate during the day and during the supervised training sessions.

2.1.4. Physical Fitness (PF) Assessment

Prior to starting the training program, all the children were tested for cardiovascular fitness, as follows:

- Six-minute walk test (6MWT). This field test is considered a valid and reliable tool for measuring PF in children and is widespread, has inexpensive equipment, and is easy to administer in a clinical setting [56]. The 6MWT was performed according to international administration guidelines [57]. The children were instructed by the trainers to walk the greatest distance possible while maintaining their own pace. Standardized encouragement and information about the remaining time were given to the children every minute; for example, "you are doing well" or "keep up the good work" [58]. Children were permitted to stop (if required) during the test but were instructed to resume walking once able and the covered distance was registered in meters. Test-retest reliability was undertaken, and the intraclass correlation coefficient (95% confidence interval) was calculated as 0.94 (0.89–0.96).
- After an adequate recovery time, children were interviewed by the same investigator to assess perceived physical fitness and physical activity level, respectively, using the International Fitness Enjoyment Scale (IFIS) and Physical Activity Questionnaire for Older Children (PAQ-C) questionnaires.

- The International Fitness Enjoyment Scale (IFIS) questionnaire is a self-reported, easy, and rapid fitness scale previously validated in several European countries and languages. It describes physical fitness as an indicator of physical competence [59]. The IFIS is composed of a 5-point Likert scale (from 1 'very poor' to 5 'very good'), with questions focused on five areas of fitness: general fitness, cardiorespiratory, strength, speed-agility, and flexibility. The IFIS has high validity and moderate-to-good reliability (average weighted Kappa: 0.70 and 0.59) for school-aged children.
- The Physical Activity Questionnaire for Older Children (PAQ-C) evaluates the weekly amount of physical activity reported by children. This questionnaire was verified to be adequate for school-aged children (approximate ages between 8 and 14). The PAQ-C is recognized as a valid and reliable measurement of general physical activity level from childhood to adolescence. The PAQ-C utilizes cues such as break time at school and evening physical activity to ameliorate the recall ability of children. The PAQ-C is cost- and time-efficient, simple to administer, and displays normal distribution properties. The PAQ-C is shown to have good reliability and an intraclass correlation (ICC) = 0.96 [60].

2.1.5. Cardiac Autonomic Regulation (CAR) Assessment

On the day of autonomic evaluation, all subjects arrived at the clinic avoiding caffeinated beverages since awakening as well as heavy physical exercise in the preceding 24 h. Recordings were performed between 04:00 am and 06:00 pm in an air conditioned, quiet room. After a preliminary 10-min rest period in the supine position, electrocardiogram (ECG) and respiratory activity (piezoelectric belt) were continuously recorded over a minimum 5-min period using a two-way radiotelemetry system (Marazza, Monza Italy). Subsequently, subjects were asked to stand up unaided and remain in the upright position for 5 min, during which recordings were maintained. Data were acquired with a PC at 250 samples/second using a custom built software tool (HeartScope) that automatically provided a series of indices describing heart rate variability (HRV) in the time domain: RR interval (in msec) and RR interval variability (RRTP) (assessed as total power, i.e., variance, in msec^2), taken as simple classifiers typical of vagal control [21,61,62]. A series of indices were also provided in the frequency domain: autoregressive spectral components both in the low frequency (LF, center frequency $\approx$ 0.1 Hz) and high frequency (HF, centered with respiration, $\approx$0.25 Hz) (assessed in msec^2 as well as in normalized units [nu]) and markers of prevalent sympathetic and vagal activities, indicating sinoatrial node function [21,62].

Based on all of these assessments before starting the training, a medical exercise prescription defining the modality, intensity, duration, frequency, and progression of exercise was created for each participant, who were individually followed by exercise physiologists using a Zoom online platform.

2.2. Exercise Training Protocol

Children performed a 12-week online training program supervised by two sport specialists using the Zoom online platform (California, USA). The training protocol consisted of three 60-min sessions per week, over 12 weeks, for a total of 36 sessions. Each session was streamed in real-time using the Zoom platform, which allowed live interaction among the instructors and children. Two sport specialists supervised every training session, which usually consisted of different typology and intensity of exercises, defined considering individual fitness levels and progressively adapted as each individual reached the goal. In detail, all sessions were divided into three sub-sessions: an initial warm-up of approximately 5 min to ensure the correct preparation of the children for the subsequent exercises, the main training that consisted of a combination of aerobic and muscular routines for approximately 50 min, and a final part of cool down of approximately 5 min to ensure the return of the body to the rest condition. The exercise physiologist recorded that the training session was actually performed by the child. All the proposed exercises were playful and recreative activities; for example, we proposed motor and active fabulation, dancing to music, imitation games, circuit training in a playful way, playing with small objects such as balls, books, pencils, and paper, and paths through the furniture. The activities started from low intensity and progressed through the training to moderate and high intensities with values of maximum heart rate ranging from 50% to 80%, as calculated using the Tanaka equation [63] after clinical verification that no cardiovascular contraindications were present for the execution of vigorous exercise. Shorter bouts of yoga and mindfulness were proposed as cool-down activities [64]. The main goal of the intervention was to administer a simple and enjoyable online training sessions with interaction and adaptable loads that were affordable and sustainable for families and had no cost or transportation difficulties. Starting 30 min from the beginning of the session, the trainers acquired the children's heart rates in order to control the intensity of the training using the Fitbit Charge 2 © (Fitbit Inc, San Francisco, CA, USA).

To better comply with the guidelines [11,12] recommending 60 min of moderate-to-vigorous exercise per day for children and adolescents, we provided a dedicated YouTube channel "LAMA Junior" with adapted exercise routines for days without supervised training [34]. See Figure 1.

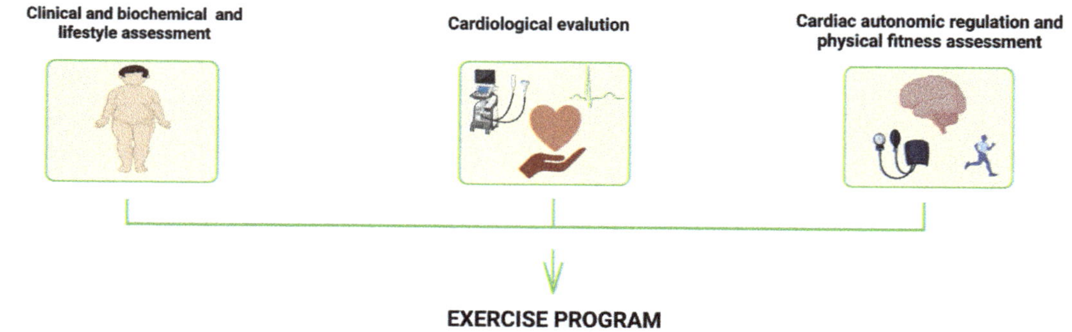

	I Month	II Month	III Month
Supervised (3 times/week)	1) 30' of aerobic and playful exercises. Attention to the technique of the movements. Active breaks. 2) 30' of home-strength and playful exercises 3) 30' of mixed training with playful exercises	1) 35' of aerobic and playful exercises. Attention to the technique of the movements. Active breaks. 2) 35' of home-strength and playful exercises 3) 35' of mixed training with playful exercises	1) 30' of aerobic and playful exercises. Active breaks. 15' of home-strength exercises. 2) 30' of home-strength and playful exercises and 15' of aerobic exercises. 3) 45' of mixed training with playful exercises
Each session lasted from 45' to 60' and was composed by a 10' of initial warm-up and 5' of final stretching.			
Unsupervised (3 times/week)	1) Online video on Youtube (LAMA Junior channel) 2) Home-based plays 3) Outdoor activities and team sports	1) Online video on Youtube (LAMA Junior channel) 2) Home-based plays 3) Outdoor activities and team sports	1) Online video on Youtube (LAMA Junior channel) 2) Home-based plays 3) Outdoor activities and team sports
Each session lasted from 45' to 60' and was recorded on a diary.			

Figure 1. Exercise program.

Throughout the exercise program, patients were asked to maintain a healthy diet but no standard modifications were made.

2.3. Statistical Analysis

Data are presented as the median (25–75 percentile). The significance of differences was assessed with repeated measures GLM (General Linear Model), considering group and intervention as factors. Differences in pubertal stage between T0 and T1 were assessed using the Chi-squared test. Bivariate Pearson's correlation analysis was employed with two-tailed significance.

Computations were performed using IBM SPSS Statistics for Windows, version 27 (IBM Corp., Armonk, NY, USA) with a PC (DELL). A value of $p < 0.05$ was taken as the threshold for statistical significance.

3. Results

Throughout the program period, no significant changes in pubertal stage were noted. (Stage 1 = 19 vs. 17, Stage 2 = 6 vs. 8, Stage 3 = 10 vs. 10, $p = 0.82$).

As specified in the methods, we subdivided the population into two groups: those reaching the physical activity goals suggested by the latest guidelines (corresponding to at least an average of 60 min/day of moderate-to-vigorous intensity, mostly aerobic, physical activity, i.e., above 1200 MET·min/week) and those who did not reach the physical activity goals (i.e., below 1200 MET·min/week).

Table 1 reports the results of subdivision A considering the total weekly physical activity volume (METsTOT) (i.e., both time spent walking and time spent performing structured exercise), while Table 2 reports the results of subdivision B considering only the weekly volume of structured exercise (METsMV). The tables report data before (T0) and after (T1) exercise intervention.

3.1. Clinical, Auxological, Hemodynamical and Metabolic Data

Subdivision A showed that significant differences were present between conditions in clinical auxological parameters (BMI z-score $p = 0.004$ and TMI $p < 0.001$) and between groups in metabolic parameters (total cholesterol $p = 0.048$). No significant differences were noted regarding systolic arterial pressure, diastolic arterial pressure percentile, and heart rate. Similarly, there was no difference in autonomic parameters for RRV.

Subdivision B showed significant differences between conditions in clinical auxological parameters (BMI z-score $p = 0.033$, TMI $p = 0.003$, and VAI $p = 0.012$) and metabolic parameters (total cholesterol $p = 0.048$), with an interaction for HOMA-IR ($p = 0.05$) and VAI ($p = 0.048$). No significant differences were noted regarding systolic arterial pressure, diastolic arterial pressure percentile, and heart rate. Borderline significance was noted in RR interval ($p = 0.062$).

3.2. Lifestyle Data

No significant differences were noted in subdivisions A and B regarding hours sleep/day and school performance. Quality of sleep and health perceptions were slightly different between groups in subdivision A. Hours of sedentariness/week was slightly different between groups in subdivisions A and B. The AHA score (quality of nutrition index) was slightly different between groups only in subdivision B, and it improved after training. As expected, the volume of performed physical activity was significantly increased after intervention in both subdivisions A and B ($p = 0.008$ and $p < 0.001$, respectively). Interestingly, in both subdivisions, the subjects who performed higher volumes of physical activity after intervention were also characterized by higher volumes of physical activity before intervention ($p < 0.001$ and $p = 0.012$, respectively), with significant interaction ($p = 0.030$ and $p = 0.012$, respectively), suggesting that the increase was significantly higher in group 2 for both subdivisions.

3.3. Physical Fitness Assessment Data

The covered distance of 6MWT and PAQ-C score were significantly increased after intervention in groups 1 and 2, for both subdivisions A and B. No significant differences between groups or conditions were observed in the IFIS score for both subdivisions A and B.

3.4. Cardiac Autonomic Regulation Data

No significant differences between groups or condition were observed in any of the autonomic variables in subdivision A.

Subdivision B unveiled an interaction effect in RRHFnu (marker of prevalent vagal modulation of the sinoatrial node) and LF/HF ratio, being slightly increased only in those subjects who performed higher volumes of structured exercise.

Table 3 reports the Pearson's correlations among changes (Δ) between T0 and T1 for the major variables. Notably, ΔMETsTOT was correlated, as expected, with ΔRRTP (change in total variance of heart rate variability), while ΔMETsMV was significantly correlated not only with ΔRRTP but also with ΔRR (change in RR interval) and ΔHFnu. Moreover, ΔMETsMV was significantly correlated (r = −0.400, p = 0.017) with Δ SAPpc (change in percentile of systolic arterial pressure), suggesting that only structured exercise was associated with a reduction of the percentile of SAP. Additionally, ΔRRTP and ΔRR were significantly correlated with ΔSAPpc.

Table 3. Pearson's correlations among changes between T0 and T1 of main variables.

	Δ METsTOT	Δ METsMV	Δ RR	Δ RRTP	Δ RRLFnu	Δ RRHFnu	Δ LF/HF	Δ SAPpc
Δ METsMV	**0.844 **** **0.000**							
Δ RR	0.227 0.189	**0.423 *** **0.011**						
Δ RRTP	**0.405 *** **0.016**	**0.509 **** **0.002**	**0.686 **** **0.000**					
Δ RRLFnu	−0.117 0.504	−0.204 0.239	−0.086 0.622	−0.012 0.946				
Δ RRHFnu	0.216 0.213	**0.335 *** **0.049**	0.061 0.729	0.088 0.617	**−0.872 **** **0.000**			
Δ LF/HF	−0.137 0.433	−0.238 0.168	−0.004 0.983	0.069 0.692	**0.721 **** **0.000**	**0.716 **** **0.000**		
Δ SAPpc	−0.136 0.436	**−0.400 *** **0.017**	**−0.512 **** **0.002**	**−0.368 *** **0.030**	0.214 0.217	−0.187 0.281	0.061 0.729	
Δ BMI z-score	−0.088 0.617	−0.008 0.963	−0.189 0.278	−0.243 0.160	0.099 0.572	−0.103 0.555	−0.079 0.654	0.094 0.590

Abbreviations: Δ = change between T0 and T1; METsTOT = total weekly physical activity volume; METsMV = weekly physical activity volume calculated only considering other activities of moderate intensity and activities of vigorous intensity volume (i.e., volume of structured exercise); RR = RR interval; RRTP = RR total power (RR interval variance); LF = low frequency component of RR variability; HF = high frequency component of RR variability; nu= normalized unit; LF/HF= RRLF on RRHF ratio; SAPpc= percentile of systolic arterial pressure. BMI= body mass index. Significant values are evidenced in bold. **: correlation is significant at the 0.01 level (2-tailed). *: correlation is significant at the 0.05 level (2-tailed).

4. Discussion

In this feasibility study, we observed that only the improvement in the volume of structured exercise was associated with the reduction in arterial pressure percentile and improvement of markers of vagal control in obese children. Moreover, structured exercise improved the auxological and metabolic parameters. The increase in volume of structured exercise was obtained through a 12-week exercise training protocol delivered online by exercise physiologists [34,54], using an individualized exercise prescription that was progressively adapted as each individual reached their goal and was specifically designed to meet the needs of obese children and their families, while being economically and organizationally sustainable.

The beneficial effects of exercise are well reported in the literature and exercise is now considered a mandatory preventive and therapeutic strategy in all CNCD, particularly in youth [11–13], as underlined in the introduction. Of fundamental importance is the dose/volume of physical activity required to obtain such benefits. While international guidelines [11–13] clearly indicate the volume of required physical activity and the need to perform moderate and vigorous exercise at a young age, their practical translation into everyday life is sometimes less specific. Simply walking or practicing sports, without paying attention to the volume and particularly the intensity of exercise, is considered efficacious. This phenomenon is well emblemized by the importance given to the number of steps walked every day [65] independent of the speed of walking. On the contrary, the literature shows that the benefits of endurance exercise are also linked to the level of cardiorespiratory fitness [15,16] in children and that only brisk walkers had significantly longer telomeres than slow walkers among adults [17], thereby showing a direct correlation between exercise intensity and longevity. In this paper, we observed that only the volume of exercise due to structured moderate-to-vigorous intensity exercise was associated with improved cardiac autonomic control, reduced systolic arterial pressure, and improved auxologic and metabolic parameters. Of particular interest is the reduction in the HOMA-IR index, which suggested reduced insulin resistance after training, confirming the relevant influence of different types of exercise on insulin resistance [66]. In contrast, we observed only a slight change in the auxologic parameters, such as BMI z-score and TMI, considering that the MET count also included METs linked to simple walking for more than 10 min.

The data in our study, albeit preliminary, suggest that only structured exercise was capable of inducing an improvement in autonomic and metabolic control. Of particular interest is the observation that the change in the SAP percentile with training was associated with the change in structured exercise volume and changes in ANS variable markers of vagal control. Arterial hypertension is a condition that characterizes childhood obesity [2,3,6] and increases the risk of major cardiovascular disease over the lifespan. Many studies have demonstrated that exercise is a powerful tool to prevent/treat arterial hypertension and obesity [11–13]. The data in the current study corroborate previous observations in which improved autonomic cardiac regulation was among the benefits of exercise in the management of hypertension and obesity [10,22,24–27].

Another interesting point to discuss is the methodology employed to help children with obesity become physically active. Participation in team sports or programs that generally group children together are considered more effective, but they may present some practical barriers (economical, organizational, and psychological), as reported in the introduction. In this paper, we observed that a home-based, online exercise training program could overcome, albeit in part, these barriers, and could be enjoyable and sustainable from an economical and organizational point of view, thus facilitating acceptance and compliance of children and their families. This observation was corroborated by 86% of children in our study remaining in the program after completing the final evaluations.

In addition, the possibility of starting exercise at home, thus avoiding interaction with peers while improving their physical performance, may result in an improvement of self-efficacy [67] and, consequently, motivate obese children to exercise in a different environment close to their peers. A fundamental characteristic of the employed protocol [34] was the balance between the possibility of being delivered online and tailoring the proposed modality/intensity of exercises to the child's needs, preferences, and reached goals [54]. An individualized clinical assessment and exercise prescription was essential to the achievement of this goal, which required exercise physiologists to interact online with children, design enjoyable exercises, and adjust the program during the training period. In contrast [12,37,68], home-base exercise programs that were not tailored to individual needs showed poor or no efficacy in previous studies.

In this observational study, we also observed that children with obesity who significantly increased their exercise volume through the intervention program were already characterized by higher exercise volumes and less sedentary hours (considering both subdivisions) before starting the intervention program. This finding suggests that other factors, in addition to the methodology employed in the exercise program, need to be considered, such as psychological and social conditions [9,67]. Although we do not have data to support this hypothesis, we observed that the group of children who actually increased their exercise volume in subdivision A were characterized before the intervention by slightly higher health and quality of sleep perceptions.

Throughout the exercise program, children with obesity were asked to maintain a healthy diet but no standard modifications were made. Nevertheless, the group of subjects who significantly increased the volume of structured exercise was also characterized by a higher AHA score, suggesting an improvement in the quality of nutrition. Further supporting the hypothesis expressed in the previous paragraph, we also observed that this group was characterized by better AHA scores before the intervention.

Some limitations of this study must be acknowledged. First, this study was an observational feasibility study and the group size was small, thus limiting the interpretative value of the results. Additionally, we did not consider a control group (subjects studied before and after sham intervention). Nevertheless, we observed in other studies that sham interventions did not induce modifications of the autonomic nervous system per se [69,70], corroborating the idea that the observed changes were attributable to functional remodeling. Second, only 19 children (54.29%) wore the activity tracker both during the day and during the training sessions and were considered for the specific analysis. Interestingly, we observed a significant correlation ($r = 0.445$, $p = 0.049$) between the total steps recorded by the tracker and the total volume of structured exercise (METsMV), while no significant correlation ($r = 0.235$, $p = 0.3.19$) was observed with the total volume of physical activity (METsTOT). Third, the children's diets were not standardized, allowing for a potential bias. Moreover, we did not have data regarding immunological control (another main control system that plays an important role in cardiometabolic conditions) and psychological and social aspects. These are important factors to consider when studying the effects of intervention programs in subjects with obesity. In addition, the intervention lasted only 12 weeks and we do not have data regarding the long-lasting effects of our model. Therefore, in view of the small number of subjects and overall feasibility of the design, generalizing the results is not possible.

5. Conclusions

In conclusion, this study showed the feasibility of an online exercise program as a practical tool to improve cardiac autonomic control and hemodynamic, metabolic, and auxological parameters in a group of children with obesity, rendering it a valuable strategy for fostering compliance with physical activity guidelines and providing an opportunity for pediatric subjects with obesity to stay healthy, thus managing the increased risk of CNCD. Moreover, by guaranteeing that an adequate level of exercise intensity was reached, this study underlines the importance of structured exercise in obtaining significant health benefits. The benefits of exercise overcome those of "simple" weight reduction (which in this study was present when considering subdivision A), which are also linked to improvements in important endocrine and autonomic control mechanisms (which in this study was evident when considering subdivision B). In addition, the ability of exercise to affect control mechanisms, particularly cardiac autonomic control, seems only to be evident if exercise reaches an adequate intensity, i.e., even at the same exercise volume (1200 METs), the effect may differ depending on the intensity of the exercise performed. With this in mind, we have to consider that this was a feasibility study. Therefore, the capability of the exercise program to affect CAR and its economical/organizational sustainability must be verified. On the basis of the present observations, larger and longer lasting studies aimed at confirming these preliminary satisfactory data seem justified.

Author Contributions: Conceptualization, D.L., V.C. and M.V.; methodology, D.L., M.P., M.V., V.C.P., V.C. and G.Z.; software, D.L., M.P., M.V. and C.L.; formal analysis, D.L., G.B. and M.M.; investigation, D.L., G.B., M.M., V.C.P., V.C. and S.M.; resources, D.L., G.Z., M.V., D.L., M.M. and G.B.; writing—original draft preparation, D.L. and M.P.; writing—review and editing, D.L., G.B., M.M., M.V., V.C.P., V.C., S.M., C.L., G.Z. and M.P.; supervision, D.L., V.C., G.Z. and M.V.; project administration, M.V. and D.L.; funding acquisition, D.L. and G.Z. All authors have read and agreed to the published version of the manuscript.

Funding: This research was partially funded by the Italian Ministry of Health.

Institutional Review Board Statement: This study were approved by the institutional ethics committee (Milano Area 2 proto-col number 2020/ST/298, approval date 2 December 2020).

Informed Consent Statement: Written consent was obtained by all participants or their responsible guardians once they were well informed about the study.

Data Availability Statement: Data will be available on justified request. We have not yet uploaded the data because they are part of an ongoing study on the effects of exercise in children and other papers may be prepared using them.

Acknowledgments: We thank Fitbit Inc., San Francisco, CA, USA to have furnished activity trackers (Fitbit Charge 2 ©).

Conflicts of Interest: The authors declare no conflict of interest.

References

1. Turco, J.V.; Inal-Veith, A.; Fuster, V. Cardiovascular health promotion: An issue that can no longer wait. *J. Am. Coll. Cardiol.* **2018**, *72*, 908–913. [CrossRef] [PubMed]
2. Song, P.; Zhang, Y.; Yu, J.; Zha, M.; Zhu, Y.; Rahimi, K.; Rudan, I. Global Prevalence of Hypertension in Children: A Systematic Review and Meta-analysis. *JAMA Pediatr.* **2019**, *173*, 1154–1163. [CrossRef]
3. Hampl, S.E.; Hassink, S.G.; Skinner, A.C.; Armstrong, S.C.; Barlow, S.E.; Bolling, C.F.; Avila Edwards, K.C.; Eneli, I.; Hamre, R.; Joseph, M.M.; et al. Clinical Practice Guideline for the Evaluation and Treatment of Children and Adolescents With Obesity. *Pediatrics* **2023**, *151*, e2022060640. [CrossRef] [PubMed]
4. Tsao, C.W.; Aday, A.W.; Almarzooq, Z.I.; Alonso, A.; Beaton, A.Z.; Bittencourt, M.S.; Boehme, A.K.; Buxton, A.E.; Carson, A.P.; Commodore-Mensah, Y.; et al. Heart Disease and Stroke Statistics—2022 Update: A Report From the American Heart Association. *Circulation* **2022**, *145*, e153–e639. [CrossRef] [PubMed]
5. Gao, M.; Wang, Q.; Piernas, C.; Astbury, N.M.; Jebb, S.A.; Holmes, M.V.; Aveyard, P. Associations between body composition, fat distribution and metabolic consequences of excess adiposity with severe COVID-19 outcomes: Observational study and Mendelian randomisation analysis. *Int. J. Obes.* **2022**, *46*, 943–950. [CrossRef] [PubMed]
6. Sallis, R.; Young, D.R.; Tartof, S.Y.; Sallis, J.F.; Sall, J.; Li, Q.; Smith, G.N.; Cohen, D.A. Physical inactivity is associated with a higher risk for severe COVID-19 outcomes: A study in 48 440 adult patients. *Br. J. Sports Med.* **2021**, *55*, 1099–1105. [CrossRef] [PubMed]
7. Artinian, N.T.; Fletcher, G.F.; Mozaffarian, D.; Kris-Etherton, P.; Van Horn, L.; Lichtenstein, A.H.; Kumanyika, S.; Kraus, W.E.; Fleg, J.L.; Redeker, N.S.; et al. Interventions to Promote Physical Activity and Dietary Lifestyle Changes for Cardiovascular Risk Factor Reduction in Adults: A scientific statement from the American Heart Association. *Circulation* **2010**, *122*, 406–441. [CrossRef]
8. Lloyd-Jones, D.M.; Hong, Y.; Labarthe, D.; Mozaffarian, D.; Appel, L.J.; Van Horn, L.; Greenlund, K.; Daniels, S.; Nichol, G.; Tomaselli, G.F.; et al. Defining and setting national goals for cardiovascular health promotion and disease reduction: The American heart association's strategic impact goal through 2020 and beyond. *Circulation* **2010**, *121*, 586–613. [CrossRef]
9. Centers for Disease Control and Prevention. *The Association Between School-Based Physical Activity, Including Physical Education, and Academic Performance*; US Department of Health and Human Services: Atlanta, GA, USA, 2010.
10. Jackson, T.; Dixon, J. The New Zealand Resource Management Act: An exercise in delivering sustainable development through an ecological modernisation agenda. *Environ. Plan. B Plan. Des.* **2007**, *34*, 107–120. [CrossRef]
11. Chaput, J.-P.; Willumsen, J.; Bull, F.; Chou, R.; Ekelund, U.; Firth, J.; Jago, R.; Ortega, F.B.; Katzmarzyk, P.T. 2020 WHO guidelines on physical activity and sedentary behaviour for children and adolescents aged 5–17 years: Summary of the evidence. *Int. J. Behav. Nutr. Phys. Act.* **2020**, *17*, 141. [CrossRef]
12. Wyszyńska, J.; Ring-Dimitriou, S.; Thivel, D.; Weghuber, D.; Hadjipanayis, A.; Grossman, Z.; Ross-Russell, R.; Dereń, K.; Mazur, A. Physical Activity in the Prevention of Childhood Obesity: The Position of the European Childhood Obesity Group and the European Academy of Pediatrics. *Front. Pediatr.* **2020**, *8*, 662. [CrossRef] [PubMed]
13. Steinberger, J.; Daniels, S.R.; Hagberg, N.; Isasi, C.R.; Kelly, A.S.; Lloyd-Jones, D.; Pate, R.R.; Pratt, C.; Shay, C.M.; Towbin, J.A.; et al. Cardiovascular Health Promotion in Children: Challenges and Opportunities for 2020 and Beyond: A Scientific Statement From the American Heart Association. *Circulation* **2016**, *134*, e236–e255. [CrossRef] [PubMed]
14. Available online: https://www.euro.who.int/__data/assets/pdf_file/0009/513756/Physical-activity-2021-Italy-eng.pdf (accessed on 12 January 2023).
15. Burden, S.J.; Weedon, B.D.; Turner, A.; Whaymand, L.; Meaney, A.; Dawes, H.; Jones, A. Intensity and Duration of Physical Activity and Cardiorespiratory Fitness. *Pediatrics* **2022**, *150*, e2021056003. [CrossRef]
16. Ross, R.; Blair, S.N.; Arena, R.; Church, T.S.; Despres, J.P.; Franklin, B.A.; Haskell, W.L.; Kaminsky, L.A.; Levine, B.D.; Lavie, C.J.; et al. Importance of Assessing Cardiorespiratory Fitness in Clinical Practice: A Case for Fitness as a Clinical Vital Sign: A Scientific Statement from the American Heart Association. *Circulation* **2016**, *134*, e653–e699. [CrossRef]

17. Dempsey, P.C.; Musicha, C.; Rowlands, A.V.; Davies, M.; Khunti, K.; Razieh, C.; Timmins, I.; Zaccardi, F.; Codd, V.; Nelson, C.P.; et al. Investigation of a UK biobank cohort reveals causal associations of self-reported walking pace with telomere length. *Commun. Biol.* **2022**, *5*, 381. [CrossRef] [PubMed]
18. Fiuza-Luces, C.; Santos-Lozano, A.; Joyner, M.; Carrera-Bastos, P.; Picazo, O.; Zugaza, J.L.; Izquierdo, M.; Ruilope, L.M.; Lucia, A. Exercise benefits in cardiovascular disease: Beyond attenuation of traditional risk factors. *Nat. Rev. Cardiol.* **2018**, *15*, 731–743. [CrossRef]
19. Joyner, M.J.; Green, D.J. Exercise protects the cardiovascular system: Effects beyond traditional risk factors. *J. Physiol.* **2009**, *587*, 5551–5558. [CrossRef] [PubMed]
20. Esler, M.; Rumantir, M.; Wiesner, G.; Kaye, D.; Hastings, J.; Lambert, G. Sympathetic nervous system and insulin resistance: From obesity to diabetes. *Am. J. Hypertens.* **2001**, *14*, S304–S309. [CrossRef]
21. Lucini, D.; Mela, G.S.; Malliani, A.; Pagani, M. Impairment in cardiac autonomic regulation preceding arterial hypertension in humans: Insights from spectral analysis of beat-by-beat cardiovascular variability. *Circulation* **2002**, *106*, 2673–2679. [CrossRef]
22. Lucini, D.; Zuccotti, G.; Malacarne, M.; Scaramuzza, A.; Riboni, S.; Palombo, C.; Pagani, M. Early Progression of the Autonomic Dysfunction Observed in Pediatric Type 1 Diabetes Mellitus. *Hypertension* **2009**, *54*, 987–994. [CrossRef]
23. Calcaterra, V.; Palombo, C.; Malacarne, M.; Pagani, M.; Federico, G.; Kozakova, M.; Zuccotti, G.; Lucini, D. Interaction between Autonomic Regulation, Adiposity Indexes and Metabolic Profile in Children and Adolescents with Overweight and Obesity. *Children* **2021**, *8*, 686. [CrossRef] [PubMed]
24. Grassi, G.; Seravalle, G.; Colombo, M.; Bolla, G.; Cattaneo, B.M.; Cavagnini, F.; Mancia, G. Body Weight Reduction, Sympathetic Nerve Traffic, and Arterial Baroreflex in Obese Normotensive Humans. *Circulation* **1998**, *97*, 2037–2042. [CrossRef] [PubMed]
25. Soares-Miranda, L.; Sattelmair, J.; Chaves, P.; Duncan, G.E.; Siscovick, D.S.; Stein, P.K.; Mozaffarian, D. Physical Activity and Heart Rate Variability in Older Adults: The Cardiovascular Health Study. *Circulation* **2014**, *129*, 2100–2110. [CrossRef] [PubMed]
26. Lucini, D.; Milani, R.V.; Costantino, G.; Lavie, C.J.; Porta, A.; Pagani, M. Effects of cardiac rehabilitation and exercise training on autonomic regulation in patients with coronary artery disease. *Am. Heart J.* **2002**, *143*, 977–983. [CrossRef]
27. Lucini, D.; Zuccotti, G.V.; Scaramuzza, A.; Malacarne, M.; Gervasi, F.; Pagani, M. Exercise might improve cardiovascular autonomic regulation in adolescents with type 1 diabetes. *Acta Diabetol.* **2012**, *50*, 341–349. [CrossRef]
28. Calcaterra, V.; Vandoni, M.; Rossi, V.; Berardo, C.; Grazi, R.; Cordaro, E.; Tranfaglia, V.; Pellino, V.C.; Cereda, C.; Zuccotti, G. Use of Physical Activity and Exercise to Reduce Inflammation in Children and Adolescents with Obesity. *Int. J. Environ. Res. Public Health* **2022**, *19*, 6908. [CrossRef]
29. Lucini, D.; Pagani, M. Exercise Prescription to Foster Health and Well-Being: A Behavioral Approach to Transform Barriers into Opportunities. *Int. J. Environ. Res. Public Health* **2021**, *18*, 968. [CrossRef]
30. Abu-Omar, K.; Messing, S.; Sarkadi-Nagy, E.; Kovács, V.A.; Kaposvari, C.; Brukało, K.; Hassapidou, M.; Janssen, D.; Sandu, P.; Tecklenburg, E.; et al. Barriers, facilitators and capacities for childhood obesity prevention in 12 European Union Member States: Results of a policy-maker survey. *Public Health Panor.* **2018**, *4*, 360–367.
31. Shahsanai, A.; Bahreynian, M.; Fallah, Z.; Hovsepian, S.; Kelishadi, R. Perceived barriers to healthy lifestyle from the parental perspective of overweight and obese students. *J. Educ. Health Promot.* **2019**, *8*, 79. [CrossRef]
32. Zabinski, M.F.; Saelens, B.E.; Stein, R.; Hayden-Wade, H.A.; Wilfley, D.E. Overweight Children's Barriers to and Support for Physical Activity. *Obes. Res.* **2003**, *11*, 238–246. [CrossRef]
33. Kirwan, M.; Chiu, C.L.; Laing, T.; Chowdhury, N.; Gwynne, K. A Web-Delivered, Clinician-Led Group Exercise Intervention for Older Adults with Type 2 Diabetes: Single-Arm Pre-Post Intervention. *J. Med. Internet Res.* **2022**, *24*, e39800. [CrossRef] [PubMed]
34. Calcaterra, V.; Iafusco, D.; Pellino, V.C.; Mameli, C.; Tornese, G.; Chianese, A.; Cascella, C.; Macedoni, M.; Redaelli, F.; Zuccotti, G.; et al. "CoVidentary": An online exercise training program to reduce sedentary behaviours in children with type 1 diabetes during the COVID-19 pandemic. *J. Clin. Transl. Endocrinol.* **2021**, *25*, 100261. [CrossRef] [PubMed]
35. Calcaterra, V.; Verduci, E.; Vandoni, M.; Rossi, V.; Di Profio, E.; Pellino, V.C.; Tranfaglia, V.; Pascuzzi, M.C.; Borsani, B.; Bosetti, A.; et al. Telehealth: A Useful Tool for the Management of Nutrition and Exercise Programs in Pediatric Obesity in the COVID-19 Era. *Nutrients* **2021**, *13*, 3689. [CrossRef] [PubMed]
36. Vandoni, M.; Pellino, V.C.; Gatti, A.; Lucini, D.; Mannarino, S.; Larizza, C.; Rossi, V.; Tranfaglia, V.; Pirazzi, A.; Biino, V.; et al. Effects of an Online Supervised Exercise Training in Children with Obesity during the COVID-19 Pandemic. *Int. J. Environ. Res. Public Health* **2022**, *19*, 9421. [CrossRef] [PubMed]
37. Showell, N.N.; Fawole, O.; Segal, J.; Wilson, R.F.; Cheskin, L.J.; Bleich, S.N.; Wu, Y.; Lau, B.; Wang, Y. A Systematic Review of Home-Based Childhood Obesity Prevention Studies. *Pediatrics* **2013**, *132*, e193–e200. [CrossRef]
38. Available online: https://www.who.int/tools/child-growth-standards (accessed on 12 January 2023).
39. Marshall, W.A.; Tanner, J.M. Variations in the Pattern of Pubertal Changes in Boys. *Arch. Dis. Child.* **1970**, *45*, 13–23. [CrossRef]
40. Marshall, W.A.; Tanner, J.M. Variations in pattern of pubertal changes in girls. *Arch. Dis. Child.* **1969**, *44*, 291–303. [CrossRef]
41. Maffeis, C.; Banzato, C.; Talamini, G.; Obesity Study Group of the Italian Society of Pediatric Endocrinology and Diabetology. Waist-to-Height Ratio, a Useful Index to Identify High Metabolic Risk in Overweight Children. *J. Pediatr.* **2008**, *152*, 207–213. [CrossRef]
42. Ramírez-Vélez, R.; Correa-Bautista, J.E.; Carrillo, H.A.; González-Jiménez, E.; Schmidt-RioValle, J.; Correa-Rodríguez, M.; García-Hermoso, A.; González-Ruíz, K. Tri-Ponderal Mass Index vs. Fat Mass/Height3 as a Screening Tool for Metabolic Syndrome Prediction in Colombian Children and Young People. *Nutrients* **2018**, *10*, 412. [CrossRef]

43. Mameli, C.; Krakauer, N.Y.; Krakauer, J.C.; Bosetti, A.; Ferrari, C.M.; Moiana, N.; Schneider, L.; Borsani, B.; Genoni, T.; Zuccotti, G. The association between a body shape index and cardiovascular risk in overweight and obese children and adolescents. *PLoS ONE* **2018**, *13*, e0190426. [CrossRef]
44. Calcaterra, V.; Verduci, E.; Schneider, L.; Cena, H.; De Silvestri, A.; Vizzuso, S.; Vinci, F.; Mameli, C.; Zuccotti, G. Sex-Specific Differences in the Relationship between Insulin Resistance and Adiposity Indexes in Children and Adolescents with Obesity. *Children* **2021**, *8*, 449. [CrossRef] [PubMed]
45. National High Blood Pressure Education Program Working Group on High Blood Pressure in Children and Adolescents. The fourth report on the diagnosis, evaluation, and treatment of high blood pressure in children and adolescents. *Pediatrics* **2004**, *114*, 555–576. [CrossRef]
46. Rosner, B.; Cook, N.; Portman, R.; Daniels, S.; Falkner, B. Determination of Blood Pressure Percentiles in Normal-Weight Children: Some Methodological Issues. *Am. J. Epidemiol.* **2008**, *167*, 653–666. [CrossRef] [PubMed]
47. Flynn, J.T.; Kaelber, D.C.; Baker-Smith, C.M.; Blowey, D.; Carroll, A.E.; Daniels, S.R.; De Ferranti, S.D.; Dionne, J.M.; Falkner, B.; Flinn, S.K.; et al. Clinical Practice Guideline for Screening and Management of High Blood Pressure in Children and Adolescents. *Pediatrics* **2017**, *140*, e20171904. [CrossRef]
48. Available online: https://www.bcm.edu/bodycomplab/BPappZjs/BPvAgeAPPz.html (accessed on 12 January 2023).
49. Matthews, D.R.; Hosker, J.P.; Rudenski, A.S.; Naylor, B.A.; Treacher, D.F.; Turner, R.C. Homeostasis model assessment: Insulin resistance and β-cell function from fasting plasma glucose and insulin concentrations in man. *Diabetologia* **1985**, *28*, 412–419. [CrossRef]
50. Vieira-Ribeiro, S.A.; Fonseca, P.C.; Andreoli, C.S.; Ribeiro, A.Q.; Hermsdorff, H.H.; Pereira, P.F.; Priore, S.E.; Franceschini, S.C. The TyG index cutoff point and its association with body adiposity and lifestyle in children. *J. Pediatr.* **2019**, *95*, 217–223. [CrossRef]
51. Lucini, D.; Solaro, N.; Lesma, A.; Gillet, V.B.; Pagani, M.; Dickerson, J.; Ivannikov, M. Health Promotion in the Workplace: Assessing Stress and Lifestyle with an Intranet Tool. *J. Med. Internet Res.* **2011**, *13*, e88. [CrossRef]
52. Craig, C.L.; Marshall, A.L.; Sjöström, M.; Bauman, A.E.; Booth, M.L.; Ainsworth, B.E.; Pratt, M.; Ekelund, U.L.; Yngve, A.; Sallis, J.F.; et al. International Physical Activity Questionnaire: 12-Country Reliability and Validity. *Med. Sci. Sports Exerc.* **2003**, *35*, 1381–1395. [CrossRef]
53. Minetto, M.A.; Motta, G.; Gorji, N.E.; Lucini, D.; Biolo, G.; Pigozzi, F.; Portincasa, P.; Maffiuletti, N.A. Reproducibility and validity of the Italian version of the International Physical Activity Questionnaire in obese and diabetic patients. *J. Endocrinol. Investig.* **2017**, *41*, 343–349. [CrossRef]
54. Lucini, D.; Pagani, E.; Capria, F.; Galliano, M.; Marchese, M.; Cribellati, S. Evidence of Better Psychological Profile in Working Population Meeting Current Physical Activity Recommendations. *Int. J. Environ. Res. Public Health* **2021**, *18*, 8991. [CrossRef]
55. Lucini, D.; Zanuso, S.; Blair, S.; Pagani, M. A simple healthy lifestyle index as a proxy of wellness: A proof of concept. *Acta Diabetol.* **2014**, *52*, 81–89. [CrossRef] [PubMed]
56. Ruiz, J.R.; Castro-Pinero, J.; Espana-Romero, V.; Artero, E.G.; Ortega, F.B.; Cuenca, M.M.; Jimenez-Pavon, D.; Chillon, P.; Girela-Rejon, M.J.; Mora, J.; et al. Field-based fitness assessment in young people: The ALPHA health-related fitness test battery for children and adolescents. *Br. J. Sports Med.* **2011**, *45*, 518–524. [CrossRef]
57. Holland, A.E.; Spruit, M.A.; Troosters, T.; Puhan, M.A.; Pepin, V.; Saey, D.; McCormack, M.C.; Carlin, B.W.; Sciurba, F.C.; Pitta, F.; et al. An official European Respiratory Society/American Thoracic Society technical standard: Field walking tests in chronic respiratory disease. *Eur. Respir. J.* **2014**, *44*, 1428–1446. [CrossRef] [PubMed]
58. Vandoni, M.; Correale, L.; Puci, M.V.; Galvani, C.; Codella, R.; Togni, F.; La Torre, A.; Casolo, F.; Passi, A.; Orizio, C.; et al. Six minute walk distance and reference values in healthy Italian children: A cross-sectional study. *PLoS ONE* **2018**, *13*, e0205792. [CrossRef]
59. Ortega, F.B.; Ruiz, J.R.; España-Romero, V.; Vicente-Rodriguez, G.; Martínez-Gómez, D.; Manios, Y.; Béghin, L.; Molnar, D.; Widhalm, K.; Moreno, L.A.; et al. The International Fitness Scale (IFIS): Usefulness of self-reported fitness in youth. *Int. J. Epidemiol.* **2011**, *40*, 701–711. [CrossRef] [PubMed]
60. Benítez-Porres, J.; López-Fernández, I.; Raya, J.F.; Carnero, S.; Alvero-Cruz, J.R.; Carnero, E. Reliability and Validity of the PAQ-C Questionnaire to Assess Physical Activity in Children. *J. Sch. Heal.* **2016**, *86*, 677–685. [CrossRef]
61. La Rovere, M.T.; Bigger, J.T., Jr.; Marcus, F.I.; Mortara, A.; Schwartz, P.J. Baroreflex sensitivity and heart-rate variability in prediction of total cardiac mortality after myocardial infarction. *Lancet* **1998**, *351*, 478–484. [CrossRef]
62. Solaro, N.; Pagani, M.; Lucini, D. Altered Cardiac Autonomic Regulation in Overweight and Obese Subjects: The Role of Age-and-Gender-Adjusted Statistical Indicators of Heart Rate Variability and Cardiac Baroreflex. *Front. Physiol.* **2021**, *11*, 567312. [CrossRef]
63. Cicone, Z.S.; Holmes, C.J.; Fedewa, M.V.; MacDonald, H.V.; Esco, M.R. Age-Based Prediction of Maximal Heart Rate in Children and Adolescents: A Systematic Review and Meta-Analysis. *Res. Q. Exerc. Sport* **2019**, *90*, 417–428. [CrossRef]
64. Calcaterra, V.; Vandoni, M.; Pellino, V.C.; Cena, H. Special Attention to Diet and Physical Activity in Children and Adolescents With Obesity During the Coronavirus Disease-2019 Pandemic. *Front. Pediatr.* **2020**, *8*, 407. [CrossRef]
65. Paluch, A.E.; Bajpai, S.; Bassett, D.R.; Carnethon, M.R.; Ekelund, U.; Evenson, K.R.; Galuska, D.A.; Jefferis, B.J.; Kraus, W.E.; Lee, I.M.; et al. Daily steps and all-cause mortality: A meta-analysis of 15 international cohorts. *Lancet Public Health* **2022**, *7*, e219–e228. [CrossRef] [PubMed]

66. Calcaterra, V.; Verduci, E.; Vandoni, M.; Rossi, V.; Fiore, G.; Massini, G.; Berardo, C.; Gatti, A.; Baldassarre, P.; Bianchi, A.; et al. The Effect of Healthy Lifestyle Strategies on the Management of Insulin Resistance in Children and Adolescents with Obesity: A Narrative Review. *Nutrients* **2022**, *14*, 4692. [CrossRef] [PubMed]
67. Han, S.-S.; Li, B.; Wang, G.-X.; Ke, Y.-Z.; Meng, S.-Q.; Li, Y.-X.; Cui, Z.-L.; Tong, W.-X. Physical Fitness, Exercise Behaviors, and Sense of Self-Efficacy Among College Students: A Descriptive Correlational Study. *Front. Psychol.* **2022**, *13*, 932014. [CrossRef] [PubMed]
68. Pamungkas, R.A.; Chamroonsawasdi, K. Home-Based Interventions to Treat and Prevent Childhood Obesity: A Systematic Review and Meta-Analysis. *Behav. Sci.* **2019**, *9*, 38. [CrossRef] [PubMed]
69. Lucini, D.; Malacarne, M.; Solaro, N.; Busin, S.; Pagani, M. Complementary medicine for the management of chronic stress: Superiority of active versus passive techniques. *J. Hypertens.* **2009**, *27*, 2421–2428. [CrossRef]
70. Lucini, D.; Riva, S.; Pizzinelli, P.; Pagani, M. Stress management at the worksite: Reversal of symptoms profile and cardiovascular dysregulation. *Hypertension* **2007**, *49*, 291–297. [CrossRef]

nutrients MDPI

Article

The Influence of Nutrition and Physical Activity on Exercise Performance after Mild COVID-19 Infection in Endurance Athletes-CESAR Study

Daniel Śliż [1,2,*], Szczepan Wiecha [3,*], Jakub S. Gąsior [4], Przemysław Seweryn Kasiak [5], Katarzyna Ulaszewska [5], Marek Postuła [6], Łukasz A. Małek [7] and Artur Mamcarz [1]

1 3rd Department of Internal Medicine and Cardiology, Medical University of Warsaw, 04-749 Warsaw, Poland
2 School of Public Health, Postgraduate Medical Education Center, 01-813 Warsaw, Poland
3 Department of Physical Education and Health, Faculty in Biala Podlaska, Jozef Pilsudski University of Physical Education in Warsaw, 21-500 Biala Podlaska, Poland
4 Department of Pediatric Cardiology and General Pediatrics, Medical University of Warsaw, 02-091 Warsaw, Poland
5 Students' Scientific Group of Lifestyle Medicine, 3rd Department of Internal Medicine and Cardiology, Medical University of Warsaw, 04-749 Warsaw, Poland
6 Center for Preclinical Research and Technology CEPT, Department of Experimental and Clinical Pharmacology, Medical University of Warsaw, 02-097 Warsaw, Poland
7 Department of Epidemiology, Cardiovascular Disease Prevention and Health Promotion, National Institute of Cardiology, 04-635 Warsaw, Poland
* Correspondence: sliz.daniel@gmail.com (D.Ś.); szczepan.wiecha@awf.edu.pl (S.W.)

Citation: Śliż, D.; Wiecha, S.; Gąsior, J.S.; Kasiak, P.S.; Ulaszewska, K.; Postuła, M.; Małek, Ł.A.; Mamcarz, A. The Influence of Nutrition and Physical Activity on Exercise Performance after Mild COVID-19 Infection in Endurance Athletes-CESAR Study. *Nutrients* **2022**, *14*, 5381. https://doi.org/10.3390/nu14245381

Academic Editors: Roberto Pippi, Carmine G. Fanelli and Matteo Vandoni

Received: 30 November 2022
Accepted: 16 December 2022
Published: 18 December 2022

Abstract: COVID-19 and imposed restrictions are linked with numerous health consequences, especially among endurance athletes (EA). Unfavorable changes in physical activity and nutrition may affect later sports and competition performance. The aims of this study were: (1) to assess the impact of COVID-19 infection and pandemic restrictions on the nutrition and physical activity of EAs and (2) to compare them with the results of cardiopulmonary exercise testing (CPET). In total, 49 EAs (n_{male} = 43, n_{female} = 6, mean age = 39.9 ± 7.8 year., height = 178.4 ± 6.8 cm, weight = 76.3 ± 10.4 kg; BMI = 24.0 ± 2.6 $kg \cdot m^{-2}$) underwent pre- and post-COVID-19 CPET and fulfilled the dietary and physical activity survey. COVID-19 infection significantly deteriorated CPET performance. There was a reduction in oxygen uptake and in heart rate post-COVID-19 (both $p < 0.001$). Consuming processed meat and replacing meat with plant-based protein affected blood lactate concentration ($p = 0.035$). Fat-free mass was linked with consuming unsaturated fatty acids ($p = 0.031$). Adding salt to meals influenced maximal speed/power ($p = 0.024$) and breathing frequency ($p = 0.033$). Dietary and Fitness Practitioners and Medical Professionals should be aware of possible COVID-19 infection and pandemic consequences among EA. The results of this study are a helpful guideline to properly adjust the treatment, nutrition, and training of EA.

Keywords: COVID-19; endurance athletes; nutrition; diet; physical activity; sport performance; cardiopulmonary exercise test; health promotion; lifestyle interventions; exercise

1. Introduction

As reported by the World Health Organization, the coronavirus disease-2019 (COVID-19) pandemic has affected the lives of all humanity due to its rapid spread and high mortality rate (https://covid19.who.int (accessed on: 22 November 2022)). Despite the passage of time, a fully effective method of preventing and treating COVID-19 infection has not been found [1]. In addition, a large part of the population remains reluctant to be vaccinated [2], and full vaccination does not completely protect against COVID-19 complications, especially those affecting the circulatory and respiratory systems [3]. A mounting problem for caregivers is the high mutation ability of the virus, which can take various forms [4]. Mutations consist of changes in proteins' structure and modification of bonds. Due to the unpredictability of the directions of changes, an effective approach to limit spreading and provide sufficient protection in public places is a matter of vital importance.

The period of the pandemic has negatively affected the lifestyle of people around the world. Many people have experienced adverse lifestyle changes [5]. One of the key aspects is changes in physical activity and amount of sitting time [6]. An important aspect related to imposed restrictions is their negative impact on nutrition [7], which may have very serious consequences in the future, such as being overweight, weakening of physical capacity, and civilization diseases [8]. Physical activity and nutrition are both important factors influencing immunity. A potentially better prognosis with COVID-19 infection is achieved by patients consuming more fiber and plants. Such a diet has a positive effect on the gut microflora [9].

The lockdown has affected the performance and lifestyle of professional athletes [10], which may affect later performance in sports. Being ill with COVID-19 has also reduced the number of training days in this population [11], even though athletes are not considered to be at high risk of severe infection and pass it mainly mildly [12]. Studies show that the pandemic has also affected the nutrition of athletes. For example, adverse changes such as increased caloric intake and decreased fruit intake were shown in a group of Rugby players [13]. Moreover, eating disorders associated with mental health deterioration have been noticed among young athletes during the pandemic [14], another study described that the pandemic could have a negative impact on people with eating disorders [15].

COVID-19 disease through multifactorial pathological mechanisms may be accompanied by acute cardiovascular conditions, such as myocarditis, acute myocardial infarction, and cardiomyopathy [16]. The infection may have a long-term negative impact on systemic health status, including the respiratory system due to the risk of respiratory failure, pulmonary thromboembolism, pulmonary embolism, and pneumonia [17]. Due to frequent long-term abnormal lung function, fatigue, shortness of breath, chest pain, and coughing, the disease can be severe for athletes or physically active people [18]. In one study, it was described that post-COVID-19 patients examined by cardiopulmonary exercise testing (CPET) show breathing and decreased peripheral oxygen extraction or decrease in maximum oxygen uptake (VO_{2max}) [19].

CPET is a test that can be performed on a treadmill or cycle ergometer and is used to assess aerobic capacity. Is a useful tool to assess progress and plan training [20]. There is a study that shows that the use of CPET as a test to determine persistent symptoms of COVID-19 infection can be helpful in testing endurance athletes [21]. Another study found that patients with persistent dyspnea post-COVID-19 have decreased VO_{2max} as well as present circulatory exercise limitations [22]. An interesting aspect is the influence of nutrition on performance results. For example, a paper comparing a ketogenic diet to a well-balanced diet shows that in the second case even with reduced caloric intake increases in endurance could be achieved [23]. Another study shows that severe deficiencies of micro- and macronutrients such as folic acid and vitamin B12 cause anemia and reduce the performance of endurance work [24]. Thus, paying attention to nutrition among endurance athletes remains a highly important aspect.

We stipulate that previous COVID-19 infections, even with a mild course, paired with imposed restrictions and overall shifts in public life negatively influenced lifestyle and physical performance among endurance athletes. We also hypothesize that those changes are linked together. The aims of this study were: (1) to assess dietary habits, nutrition, and physical activity with their changes caused by mild COVID-19 infection and imposed restrictions, (2) to measure differences in physical performance caused by mild COVID-19 infection, and (3) to compare changes in both areas together and find whether they are correlated.

2. Materials and Methods

2.1. Study Design

This was a prospective study using data from CPET performed between June 2021 and December 2022. Procedures were conducted in the Tertiary Care Sports Diagnostics Clinic SportsLab (SportsLab, Warsaw, Poland). Participants underwent double CPET pre- and post-COVID-19 infection and had to fulfill a health-assessing questionnaire.

The study group comprised amateur and professional endurance athletes. Inclusion criteria were: (1) CPET performed at the Sportslab Clinic no earlier than 3 years before COVID-19 infection, (2) previous COVID-19 infection (documented by a PCR mRNA test or a positive antigen test) in a period of 14 days to 6 months prior to re-test of CPET, (3) mild course of COVID-19 infection (mandatory no hospitalization), (4) completing each part of the questionnaire, (5) declared lack of actual long-lasting COVID-19 infection consequences, (6) current negative PCR test for COVID-19. The health status of the participants, based on the declared information, was assessed by a medical professional in internal medicine or cardiology before post-COVID-19 CPET. Exclusion criteria were: (1) any respiratory diseases (COPD, poorly controlled bronchial asthma, blood saturation <95%), (2) any cardiovascular diseases (cardiac arrhythmias in the ECG, myocardial ischemia, prolongation of the QT interval in the ECG, structural disorders of the heart in echocardiography, decompensated hypertension with blood pressure >160/100 mmHg), (3) neurological and psychiatric conditions, (4) musculoskeletal disorders, and (5) significant deviations in CBC (leukocytosis >10,000$\cdot$mm^{-3}, anemia with HB levels <10 g$\cdot$dL^{-1}). The flowchart of study procedures is presented in Figure 1.

Each athlete underwent CPET on the same modality pre- and post-COVID-19 infection because each modality was previously linked with different performance results [25]. During the post-COVID-19 CPET, athletes received a questionnaire covering selected areas of general health assessment.

2.2. Survey Tool

Subjects fulfilled a questionnaire assessing general health and lifestyle during the CPET post-COVID-19 infection. A validated questionnaire from the PaLS study (Pandemic against LifeStyle project) was used [26–28]. The questions covered 3 general areas: demographic information and infection course, diet and eating habits, and physical activity.

Physical activity was rated by the International Physical Activity Questionnaire- Short Form. This part examines three levels of activity: low-, moderate- and vigorous-intensity. Additional questions relate to the period of sitting every day calculated in minutes and hours. Questions related to diet and eating habits were prepared based on Polish National Institute of Public Health recommendations (https://www.pzh.gov.pl/; accessed on 13 November 2022). EAs were asked about the ingredients included in their diet and the intake of particular nutrients (i.e., vegetables and fruits, milk and dairy, processed meat, animal fats and trans fatty acids, sweetened drinks and fruit juices, salt). Moreover, we included questions about eating behaviors (i.e., eating in front of the screen, reading labels of the products, and number of meals pre- and post-COVID-19 pandemic). EAs chose one of the following responses: once a week and less often, 2–3 times a week, most days of the week, every day. "Dietary product" was defined as a food included in the diet (not a dietary supplement) and "Dietary habit" was defined as the habitual decision of individuals regarding what foods they eat. Participants received information about the definition of the above-mentioned terms at the beginning of the survey. Their proper understanding was a mandatory requirement. Demographic and infection-related questions were the author's questions and assessed, among others, primary sports discipline, sports competition experience, long-lasting COVID-19 consequences, etc.

An additional original question was added to each assessed area, in which respondents rated the impact of the COVID-19 pandemic and previous infection on a given part of their lifestyle or health via a −5/0/+5 scale. Negative (−5/−1) values represented a negative impact, 0 indicated no impact, and +1/+5 values a represented positive impact (values were adjusted for impact strength).

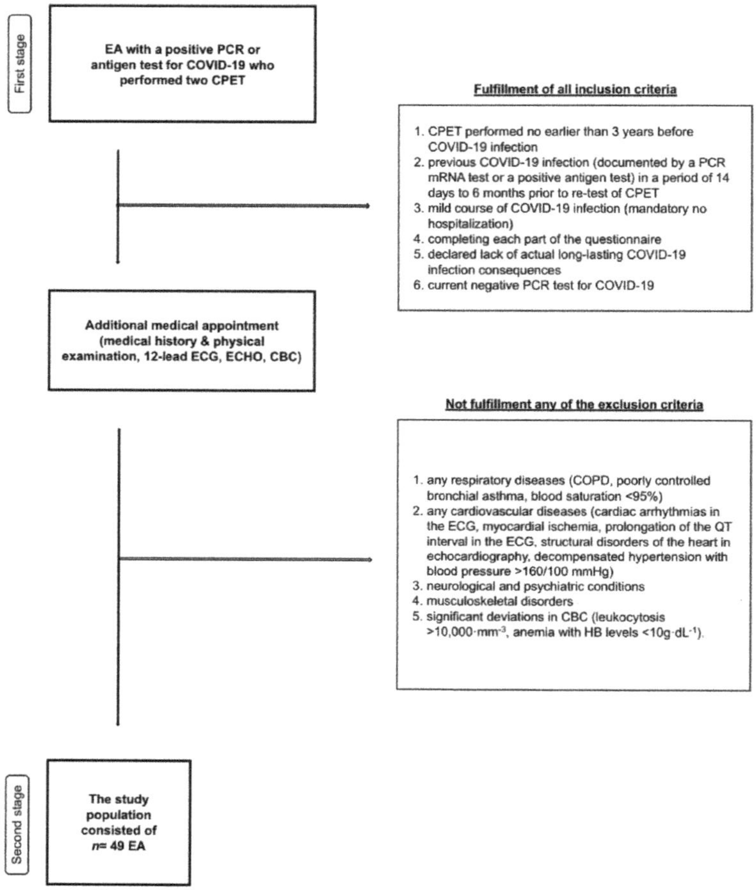

Figure 1. Study procedure. Abbreviations: EA, endurance athlete; PCR, polymerase chain reaction; COVID-19, coronavirus disease 2019; CPET, cardiopulmonary exercise test; ECG, 12-lead electrocardiogram; ECHO, echocardiography examination; CBC, complete blood count; COPD, Chronic obstructive pulmonary disease.

2.3. CPET and Somatic Measurements

Body composition was assessed using the Tanita device (Tanita, MC 718, Japan) before each of the double CPETs. Multifrequencies of 5 kHz/50 kHz/250 kHz were used. Body composition analysis and CPET were conducted under the same environmental conditions: ventilated room, an ambient temperature of 20–22 degrees Celsius, and humidity between 40 and 60%. Participants received information on how to properly prepare a few days before the stress test: (1) eat a high-carbohydrate energy meal 2–3 h before, (2) stay hydrated with isotonic sports drinks, (3) avoid intense physical exercise a few days before the test, and (4) be familiar with the test protocol and exercise characteristics on a mechanical treadmill or stationary cycle ergometer.

Cycle CPET was performed on the Cyclus ergometer (RBM elektronik-automation GmbH, Leipzig, Germany). Running CPET was performed on the Cosmos treadmill (h/p/Cosmos quasar, Germany). Cardio-pulmonary measurements were obtained via a

Cosmed Quark CPET device (Rome, Italy). Exercises began with a 3–5-min warm-up. It consisted of slow running or walking at a conversational pace (between 7–12 km·h^{-1}) or pedaling without resistance. The initial load was individually adjusted for each participant. The speed was then increased every 2 min by 1 km·h^{-1} (constant inclination of 1%), while the load was increased every 2 min by 20 Watts for females and 30 Watts for males. The test was considered terminated if: (1) the participant declared further inability to continue the effort or (2) the VO_{2max} plateau was reached (no increase in the curve of oxygen uptake with increasing exercise intensity). Athletes were encouraged to continue CPET and achieve the best possible result by their supervisor.

The following somatic parameters were measured: weight, height, body fat percentage (BF), fat mass (FM), and fat-free mass (FFM). The following exercise parameters were measured: speed (S) for treadmill or power (P) for cycle ergometry, relative oxygen uptake (VO_2), absolute oxygen uptake (VO_{2a}), heart rate (HR), pulmonary ventilation (VE), breathing frequency (f_R), and blood lactate concentration (Lac). Each exercise variable was measured at anaerobic threshold (AT), respiratory compensation point (RCP), and maximal exertion. CPET indices were obtained using the breath-by-breath method and a Hans Rudolph V2 Mask (Hans Rudolph Inc, Shawnee, Kansas). VO_{2max} was calculated as the average value of the 10 s period immediately preceding the termination, while HR was considered as the highest value during the stress test. Blood for Lac was collected: (1) before the test, (2) after each increase in intensity, and (3) 3 min after exercise. A 20 µL blood sample was taken each time. The first few drops were drained into a cotton swab before collecting the proper sample. A Super GL2 analyzer (Müller Gerätebau GmbH, Freital, Germany) was used for the analysis, which was calibrated for each participant.

AT was evaluated after meeting the following parameters: (1) the VE/VO_2 plot was rising with a constant plot of VE/VCO_2 and (2) the end-tidal partial pressure of oxygen increased at a constant end-tidal partial pressure of carbon dioxide. RCP was evaluated after meeting the following parameters: (1) the VE/VCO_2 plot had reached its lowest value and started to increase, (2) the decline in the end-tidal partial pressure of carbon dioxide had begun after maximal exertion, (3) there was a rapid increase in VE (2nd deflection), and (4) there was an increase in VCO_2 relative to VO_2 (these variables lost their linear relationship) [29].

2.4. Ethics

The athletes were tested in accordance with the Declaration of Helsinki. The study protocol was approved by the Bioethics Committee of the Medical University of Warsaw (approval no. KB/50/21 from 19th April 2021). The subjects had to give written consent to participate in the study, published obtained results in the scientific literature and were informed about the potential risks and nuisances related to the procedures. Personal data has been anonymized and does not allow for the identification of the subjects.

2.5. Statistical Analysis

Basic data are presented as mean with standard deviation (SD) for continuous variables and numbers (n) with percentage (%) for categorical variables. The data are presented in accordance with APA guidelines (https://apastyle.apa.org/; accessed on 26 November 2022). Normal distribution was assessed using the Shapiro–Wilk test. Between-group differences comparing data from in vivo CPET with declared results from questionnaires were analyzed with Kruskal–Wallis rang's ANOVA. Differences between CPET and somatic measurements were obtained from Student's t-test for independent variables.

The total sample size was determined using the G*Power program (version 3.1.9.2; Düsseldorf, Germany). The significance level was set at p = 0.05. The total number of people required is the minimum effective value.

The basic analyses were performed using Excel software (Microsoft Corporation, Washington, USA), and the advanced statistics were conducted in the STATISTICA software (version 13.3, StatSoft Polska Sp. z o.o., Kraków, Poland) and SPSS software (version 28; IBM SPSS, Chicago, IL, USA).

3. Results

3.1. Basic Population Data

In total, 49 endurance athletes who were referred for CPET and received a survey were included in the study. The baseline description is presented in Table 1. The cohort was 43 (87.8%) males and six (12.2%) females. The average age was 39.9 ± 7.8 years. A total of 31 (62.8 %) endurance athletes completed CPET on the treadmill and 18 (37.7%) on the cycle ergometer. The interval between CPETs was 591.7 ± 282.2 days, while the interval between pre-COVID-19 CPET and negative PCR (indicated as the end of the infection) was 436.4 ± 290.4 and the interval between post-COVID-19 CPET and negative PCR was 155.3 ± 82.52. Twenty (40.8%) athletes declared themselves runners, 14 (28.6%) cyclists, and the remaining 15 (30.6%) declared other disciplines (triathlon, football, and martial arts) as their primary sport. Training experience was 1–2 years for four (8.2%) athletes, 3–5 years for 14 (28.6%) athletes, 6–10 years for 19 (38.8%) athletes and 12 (21.3%) athletes declared >10 years of training experience. COVID-19 infection resulted in waived competition for 23 (46.9%) participants. On a 0–5 scale subjects declared their overall health as 4.8 ± 0.5 before infection and as 4.1 ± 0.5 after. Ten (20.4%) participants suffered from long-lasting COVID-19 consequences for >14 days.

Table 1. Participants' characteristics.

Variable		Males (n = 43)	Females (n = 6)
Age (years)		40.7 ± 7.0	38.1 ± 6.4
Height (cm)		178.5 ± 6.8	178.4 ± 6.9
CPET modality	Treadmill	25 (51.0%)	4 (8.2%)
	Cycle ergometer	16 (32.7%)	2 (4.1%)
Primary sport discipline	Running	16 (32.7%)	4 (8.2%)
	Cycling	13 (26.5%)	1 (2.0%)
	Other	14 (28.6%)	1 (2.0%)
Waived competition due to COVID-19 infection	Yes	21 (42.9%)	2 (4.1%)
	No	23 (46.9%)	4 (8.2%)
	Pre-COVID-19	Post-COVID-19	p-value
Weight (kg)	76.6 ± 10.0	76.7 ± 10.9	0.951
BMI (kg·m^{-2})	24.0 ± 2.5	24.0 ± 2.7	0.931
FFM (kg)	63.4 ± 7.6	63.5 ± 8.0	0.774
BF (%)	17.1 ± 4.7	16.9 ± 5.1	0.604
FATM (kg)	13.3 ± 4.7	13.2 ± 5.2	0.848

Abbreviations: COVID-19, coronavirus disease 2019; BMI, body mass index; FFM, fat-free mass; BF, body fat; FATM, fat mass. Data are presented as means with standard derivations (±) for continuous variables and numbers with percentages (%) for categorical variables.

3.2. CPET Characteristics

We found significant differences between CPET performance conducted pre- and post-\COVID-19 infection. The most significant differences were noted for VO_2 at AT, RCP, and maximum (each $p < 0.001$). The mean VO_2 before infection was 35.0 ± 6.4 mL·kg·min^{-1}, 43.9 ± 7.3 mL·kg·min^{-1}, and 47.8 ± 7.8 mL·kg·min^{-1}, respectively, for AT, RCP, and maximal. Meanwhile, post-infection values were 32.4 ± 5.9 mL·kg·min^{-1}, 40.5 ± 6.6 mL·kg·min^{-1}, and 45.0 ± 7.0 mL·kg·min^{-1}, respectively, for AT, RCP, and maximal. In HR measurements there was also an aggravation at AT and RCP (both $p < 0.001$). The peak HR before infection was 145.1 ± 10.8 bpm for AT and 168.8 ± 9.0 bpm for RCP. Post-infection values were 141.1 ± 10.0 bpm for AT and 165.1 ± 9.7 bpm for RCP. Lac_{max} and VE only deteriorated for RCP. Their precise values are presented in Table 2.

Table 2. Differences in CPET performance before and after COVID-19 infection.

Variable	Pre-COVID-19	Post-COVID-19	*p*-Value
VO_{2AT} (mL·kg·min^{-1})	35.0 ± 6.5	32.4 ± 6.0	<0.001
VO_{2Ata} (mL·min^{-1})	2650.0 ± 470.9	2446.1 ± 400.3	<0.001
HR_{AT} (beats·min^{-1})	145.1 ± 10.9	141.1 ± 10.1	0.001
VE_{AT} (L·min^{-1})	70.8 ± 18.7	68.1 ± 14.7	0.090
S_{AT} (km·h^{-1})	11.4 ± 1.4	11.1 ± 1.3	0.044
P_{AT} (Watts)	162.8 ± 25.9	154.8 ± 25.9	0.066
f_{RAT} (breaths·min^{-1})	32.1 ± 9.0	32.1 ± 8.1	0.706
Lac_{AT} (mmol·L^{-1})	2.0 ± 0.9	2.1 ± 0.9	0.630
VO_{2RCP} (mL·kg·min^{-1})	43.9 ± 7.4	40.5 ± 6.7	<0.001
VO_{2RCPa} (mL·min^{-1})	3324.3 ± 512.9	3063.7 ± 440.1	<0.001
HR_{RCP} (beats·min^{-1})	168.8 ± 9.2	165.1 ± 9.8	<0.001
VE_{RCP} (L·min^{-1})	106.8 ± 21.7	98.9 ± 18.3	<0.001
S_{RCP} (km·h^{-1})	14.3 ± 1.9	13.8 ± 1.5	<0.001
P_{RCP} (Watts)	245.2 ± 42.0	232.2 ± 39.7	0.061
f_{RRCP} (breaths·min^{-1})	41.3 ± 8.7	40.1 ± 8.9	0.876
Lac_{RCP} (mmol·L^{-1})	4.9 ± 1.4	4.3 ± 1.1	0.013
VO_{2max} (mL·kg·min^{-1})	47.8 ± 8.0	45.0 ± 7.1	<0.001
VO_{2maxa} (mL·min^{-1})	3623.5 ± 552.1	3406.0 ± 474.5	<0.001
HR_{max} (beats·min^{-1})	180.8 ± 10.1	179.8 ± 10.0	0.273
VE_{max} (L·min^{-1})	143.0 ± 26.9	138.50 ± 23.9	0.068
S_{max} (km·h^{-1})	16.6 ± 1.6	16.4 ± 1.7	0.264
P_{max} (Watts)	310.0 ± 37.2	312.2 ± 49.1	0.811
f_{Rmax} (breaths·min^{-1})	58.9 ± 14.4	57.3 ± 11.0	0.959
Lac_{max} (mmol·L^{-1})	9.7 ± 2.3	9.6 ± 2.4	0.880

Abbreviations: COVID-19, coronavirus disease 2019; VO_{2AT}, oxygen uptake at the anaerobic threshold; VO_{2ATa}, absolute oxygen uptake at the anaerobic threshold; HR_{AT}, heart rate at the anaerobic threshold; VE_{AT}, pulmonary ventilation at the anaerobic threshold; S_{AT}, speed at the anaerobic threshold; P_{AT}, power at the anaerobic threshold; f_{RAT}, breathing frequency at the anaerobic threshold; VO_{2RCP}, oxygen uptake at the respiratory compensation point; VO_{2RCPa} absolute oxygen uptake at the respiratory compensation point; HR_{RCP}, heart rate at the respiratory compensation point; VE_{RCP} pulmonary ventilation at the respiratory compensation point; S_{RCP}, speed at the respiratory compensation point; P_{AT}, power at the respiratory compensation point; f_{RRCP}, breathing frequency at the respiratory compensation point; Lac_{RCP}, blood lactate concentration at the respiratory compensation point; VO_{2max}, maximal oxygen uptake; VO_{2maxa}, absolute maximal oxygen uptake; HR_{max}, maximal heart rate; VE_{max}, maximal pulmonary ventilation; S_{max}, maximal speed, P_{max}, maximal power; f_{Rmax}, maximal breathing frequency; Lac_{max}, maximal blood lactate concentration. Data are presented as means with standard derivations (±). Speed is presented for treadmill CPET (n = 29) and power is presented for cycle ergometer CPET (n = 18).

3.3. Nutrition and Eating Habits

Descriptive results of the survey along with mean rangs have been presented in Table 3. Participants received information about the definition of "Dietary product" and "Dietary habit" at the beginning of the survey. Due to a high number of possible combinations, only significant results (with $p < 0.05$) have been shown. A Kruskal–Wallis H-test showed significant differences between the frequency of particular dietary products, eating habits, and CPET scores. Precise results are presented in Table 4. Consuming products containing processed meat significantly affected Lac_{max} [H(3) = 8.9; p = 0.030]. The highest Lac_{max} was noted for participants who chose "Majority of days within a week" compared to other responses (mean rang= 20.1). However, replacing meat with protein-rich plant products such as nuts and legumes influenced both Lac_{max} [H(3) = 8.6; p = 0.035] and maximal HR [H(3) = 8.6; p = 0.036]. Athletes who again selected "Majority of days within a week" had the highest Lac_{max} (mean rang= 19.2) and HR_{max} (mean rang= 32.4). It is worth mentioning that FFM was linked with consuming products that are sources of unsaturated fatty acids [H(3) = 8.9; p = 0.031]. Adding salt to meals influenced maximal speed or power [H(3) = 9.4; p = 0.024] and f_R at RCP [H(3) = 13.7; p = 0.033].

Table 3. Nutrition and dietary habits of participants.

Question	Frequency				Lack of Answer
	Once a Week or Less Often	2–3 Times per Week	Majority of Days Within a Week	Every Day	
	N (%)	*N* (%)	*N* (%)	*N* (%)	*N* (%)
Consuming more meals per day than before the pandemic (including snacking)	32 (65.3%)	7 (14.3%)	7 (14.3%)	0 (0.0%)	3 (6.1%)
Consuming less than 3 servings of wholegrain products daily (less than 90 g/day)	20 (40.8%)	18 (36.7%)	6 (12.2%)	2 (4.1%)	3 (6.1%)
Consuming less than 400 g vegetables and fruits	22 (44.9)	11 (22.5%)	11 (22.5%)	2 (4.1%)	3 (6.122%)
Consuming less than 2 glasses of unsweetened milk or other dairy products daily	24 (49.0%)	9 (18.4%)	8 (16.3%)	5 (10.2%)	3 (6.1%)
Consuming products containing processed meat, (such as sausages, ham, frankfurters, etc.)	20 (40.8%) 10.9 for Lac_{max}	15 (30.6%) 16.6 for Lac_{max}	8 (16.3%)20.1 for Lac_{max}	2 (4.1%)4.5 for Lac_{max}	4 (8.2%)
Replacing meat with protein-rich plant products such as nuts and legumes: beans, chickpeas, soy, lentils, fava beans, peas	17 (34.7%) 19.1 for HR_{max} 10.9 for Lac_{max}	14 (28.6%) 27.3 for HR_{max} 18.1 for Lac_{max}	8 (16.3%)32.4 for HR_{max}19.2 for Lac_{max}	7 (14.3%)16.3 for HR_{max}7.1 for Lac_{max}	3 (6.1%)
Consuming products that aresources of animal fats or trans fatty acids present in products, such as pastries, candy bars, salty snacks, and fast-food products	24 (49.00%)	12 (24.5%)	7 (14.3%)	2 (4.1%)	4 (8.2%)
Consuming products that are sources of unsaturated fatty acids, such as canola oil, olive oil, or fish	9 (18.4%) 35.2 for FFM	20 (40.8%) 19.6 for FFM	11 (22.5%)21.1 for FFM	6 (12.2%)23.4 for FFM	3 (6.1%)
Drinking sweetened beverages or fruit juices instead of water	40 (81.6%)	5 (10.2%)	2 (4.1%)	0 (0.0%)	2 (4.1%)
Adding salt to meals	27 (55.1%) 26.7 for S_{max}/P_{max} 21.0 for f_{RRCP}	9 (18.4%) 25.2 for S_{max}/P_{max} 37.7 for f_{RRCP}	6 (12.2%)17.5 for S_{max}/P_{max}20.5 for f_{RRCP}	4 (8.2%)7.1 for S_{max}/P_{max}13.0 for f_{RRCP}	3 (6.1%)
Consuming meals while looking at the screen of a TV, computer, or other device	21 (32.9%)	12 (24.5%)	9 (18.4%)	4 (8.2%)	3 (6.1%)
Paying attention to labels of chosen products during shopping, taking into account ingredients, amount of calories, etc.	10 (20.4%)	6 (12.2%)	11 (22.4%)	19 (38.8%)	3 (6.1%)
Self-assessed impact of COVID-19 pandemic and imposed restrictions on nutrition and dietary habits [in −5/0/+5 scale]	0.09 ± 1.43				0 (0.0%)

Abbreviations: COVID-19, coronavirus disease 2019; na, Lac_{max}, maximal blood lactate concentration; HR_{max}, maximal heart rate; f_{RRCP}, breathing frequency at the respiratory compensation point; S_{max}, maximal speed; P_{max}, maximal power. Data are presented as numbers (N) with percentages (%) of the whole population and in the −5/0/+5 scale question data are presented as means with standard deviations (±). The mean rang has been added only for significant differences (p < 0.05) between a particular group and CPET performance. The mean rang was calculated by the Kruskal–Wallis H-test.

Table 4. Relationships between nutrition, dietary habits, and CPET performance.

CPET Variable	Survey Question	*p*-Value
Lac_{max}	How often did you eat processed meat products?	0.030
HR_{max}	How often did you replace meat with plant-based protein products?	0.036
Lac_{max}	How often did you replace meat with plant-based protein products?	0.035
FFM	How often unsaturated fats were the main source of fat in your diet?	0.031
S_{max}/P_{max}	How often did you add salt to your meals?	0.024
f_{RRCP}	How often did you add salt to your meals?	0.033

Abbreviations: Lac_{max}, maximal blood lactate concentration; HR_{max}, maximal heart rate; FFM, fat-free mass; S_{max}, maximal speed; P_{max}, maximal power; f_{RRCP}, breathing frequency at the respiratory compensation point. Due to a high number of possible combinations, only significant results (with $p < 0.05$) have been shown.

3.4. Physical Activity

Declared results of physical activity questions are presented in Table 5. There were not any significant differences (each $p > 0.05$) between the frequency of selected answers in the International Physical Activity Questionnaire—Short Form and CPET performance.

Table 5. Results of physical activity questions.

Type of Activity	Amount	Median (IQR)
Vigorous physical activity	Days/week	3 (2.8–5)
	Minutes/week	60 (43.8–90)
Moderate physical activity	Days/week	3 (2–4.3)
	Minutes/week	50 (30–90)
Walking	Days/week	6.5 (4–7)
	Minutes/week	40 (20–60)
Sitting time	Hours/day	8 (5–9.3)
Weekly running distance (question only for runners)		25 (0–50)
Weekly cycling distance (question for cyclists)		70 (3.75–200)
Self-assessed fitness level in pre-COVID-19 [in 0–10 scale]		8 (6–9)
Self-assessed fitness level post-COVID-19 [in 0–10 scale]		6 (4.8–8)
Self-assessed impact of COVID-19 pandemic and imposed restrictions on fitness level [in −5/0/+5 scale]		−1 (−3–0)

Abbreviations: IQR, interquartile range; COVID-19, coronavirus disease 2019. Data are presented as medians with the interquartile range due to their non-normal distribution.

4. Discussion

The detrimental effect of COVID-19 infection on nutrition and eating habits and CPET results in the group of endurance athletes was shown. The main findings were: (1) among changes in eating habits, the most commonly reported were drinking sweetened drinks and fruit juices instead of water, more salting of food, and consumption of more meals per day compared to the pre-pandemic time; (2) post-COVID-19 status influenced outcomes of CPET such as VO_2 at AT, RCP, and maximum, as well as HR at AT and RCP (each $p < 0.001$); (3) eating habits during the pandemic influenced the achieved results of CPET, e.g., Lac_{max} increased in people who more often consumed products containing processed meat and Lac_{max} and HR_{max} were affected by replacing meat with protein-rich plant products such as nuts and legumes.

There are studies describing the impact of COVID-19 on CPET scores and the physical performance of patients. One study shows that post-COVID-19 people had a reduced VO_2 score compared to the control group, and they also showed more respiratory failure

(VE/VCO_2) [30]. This means that this study, like our study, did not achieve the expected result at peak exercise, which may be due to the long-term effects of the disease on the cardiovascular or respiratory systems [31]. In a study in a sample of elite swimmers that compared CPET results in athletes who had the infection and athletes who did not have the disease, no evidence of the effect of the disease on the variability of results was found [32]. A similar study on volleyball players showed results typical of detraining, but without access to the patient's results before the onset of the disease, it is difficult to assess [33]. The conclusions differ from our results, but the reason for this may be the different course of the disease and its impact on healthy people, especially athletes who are not considered to be at risk [34]. The next study assessed the exercise capacity of mildly symptomatic patients using an ergometer, comparing the results before and after contracting COVID-19. Slight differences in MET and VO_{2peak} results were noted [35]; median VO_{2max} in the cited study was 21,857 pre-COVID-19 and 21,699 post-COVID-19, while in our study pre-COVID-19 it was 3623.47 and post-COVID-19, 3406.00 ($ml \cdot kg \cdot min^{-1}$), which proves that athletes, despite the disease, have a greater capacity than other patients. Another study claims that symptomatic patients with the post-COVID-19 syndrome were more likely to show lower main VO_{2peak}, less likely to reach the AT, and symptoms of the syndrome worsened during examinations [36]. In patients with long-term symptoms after infection, 55% had reduced pVO_{2peak} in CPET, and 31% had reduced pVO_{2peak} secondary to limitation and muscular impairment [37]. The data from these studies are worrying because they show the long-term impact on patients' health. Reduced performance deteriorates the quality of life of any patient, especially professional athletes. It was recognized that VO_{2max} could be used as a clinical tool for estimating the severity of COVID-19 infection [38]. It turns out that the VO_2 result can also be a good predictor of mortality in patients with SARS-CoV-2 [37]; therefore, the use of the CPET test in our work reliably showed the impact of COVID-19 on the health and performance of patients. The probable explanation why we observed the decrease in HR among the EAs may be due to age-related changes in the cardiovascular system [39]. Although some time had elapsed between both CPETs, time-related impact is justified. It is worth noting here that Komici et al. observed a change in forced expiratory volume in one second examined in spirometry in EAs who had survived COVID-19 [40].

There is no doubt that proper nutrition is one of the most important components of human health and life. Professional athletes in their daily diet care for the building of muscles, but also for the proper development of other tissues (such as the vascular system and central nervous system) [41] and providing the right amount of energy to the body. Adequate nutrition for endurance athletes is difficult because it depends on many factors, such as the amount and type of training, time to competition, and type of exercise performed [42]. Even more so, the period of the COVID-19 pandemic and disease did not contribute positively to the improvement of nutrition [28]. Evidence supports that high carbohydrate intake provides muscle glycogen stores and prevents hypoglycemia [43], and there is debate about fluid intake as water poisoning has occurred in the ultra-resistant environment [44].

We recommend further similar studies that include analysis adjusted with participants' competition results. It is worth mentioning that one study conducted on Olympic athletes did not affect the results achieved during the competition [45], but more research should be performed to deeply investigate those findings. Many competitions were canceled during the pandemic and EAs had no chance to face them. Returning to competition after a long break should be well thought out [46]. Moreover, other competitions had to be adapted to the new circumstances. In the case of a long-term break from training, it is worth using rehabilitation aimed at improving respiratory efficiency. In addition to physical preparation, mental and dietary preparation are also important [47,48]. Thus, EAs during and after illness require special attention to their mood and nutrition.

Our respondents found that more frequent consumption of processed meat increases Lac_{max}, which is not desired by professional athletes [49]. Excessive consumption of processed meat can even be carcinogenic [50]. As described in the Results, it was pointed out that up to 59.2% of participants eat processed meat more than two times per week. In a study that investigated the effect of a plant-based diet on cardiovascular disease, it turned out to be positive because it lowered blood pressure, HR, and insulin levels [51]. Furthermore, our respondents, who were more likely to use plant-based protein products, had an aggravation in HR and Lac_{max}. Among studies examining the effect of unsaturated fats on health, one of them showed that the consumption of such fats is associated with a reduction in the risk of cardiovascular disease, and also increases the share of lean body mass [52], and this was also achieved by the athletes in our survey. Another study in mice showed that eating unsaturated fats compared to saturated fats provides more energy and endurance [53]. Excessive salt added to food can have long-term effects such as the risk of high blood pressure, stroke, kidney, and heart disease [54]. There are studies that show health problems in athletes who consume too little and too much sodium, and salt should be replaced after exercise, remembering to hydrate reasonably [55]. These and other aspects of nutrition are very important for professional athletes due to their impact on body structure and endurance, so it is important to take care of meals even in the case of illness and the COVID-19 pandemic. A proper diet introduced after recovering from COVID-19 can reduce the long-term effects of the disease [56]. However, the explanation of the physiological basis of the obtained results is beyond the scope of this paper. Thus, we recommend it for further research.

Limitations

Probably due to the small sample size and structure of questions, we did not observe any significance in the results of the physical activity questionnaire. The limitation of our questionnaire is the possibility that the physical activity and nutrition of the respondents changed during the pandemic; in addition, they may not remember their old habits. There was a relatively long period of time between the two CPET tests, so this may have influenced the changes in parameters. We are aware of the existing limitations, therefore we recommend carefully evaluating the results.

5. Conclusions

EAs require special professional care to be ready for sports competitions. Training loads and nutrition status, especially considering the period after infection, should be carefully adjusted. The results of this study may be used in determining the training and nutrition plans of professional athletes. Nutritionists should consider what eating habits emerge when athletes have limited training opportunities and spend more time at home. It is important to remember the adequate supply of fluids, fruits and vegetables, vitamins, and whole grains. Thanks to these results, doctors and trainers will be more aware of how performance and the body changes after suffering from COVID-19. Gradual adaptation of EAs to loads after a break in training is crucial to staying in shape and avoiding injury. Rehabilitation may also be required in the event of greater damage to health and condition. This will allow them to choose the right treatment and tests to avoid long-term complications. Each EA should be treated individually and comprehensive care should be implemented to facilitate recovery.

Author Contributions: Conceptualization, D.Ś. and S.W.; methodology, D.Ś. and P.S.K.; validation, D.Ś. and S.W.; formal analysis, D.Ś., J.S.G. and P.S.K.; investigation, D.Ś., S.W. and A.M.; resources, D.Ś. and S.W.; data curation, D.Ś., S.W., P.S.K., K.U., M.P. and Ł.A.M.; writing—original draft preparation, D.Ś., P.S.K. and K.U.; writing—review and editing, D.Ś., S.W., J.S.G., P.S.K. and K.U.; visualization, D.Ś., S.W., J.S.G. and P.S.K.; supervision, D.Ś., S.W. and A.M.; project administration, D.Ś., S.W. and A.M.; funding acquisition, D.Ś. All authors have read and agreed to the published version of the manuscript.

Funding: This research was funded by the affiliated university—the Medical University of Warsaw (2022/EL12489).

Institutional Review Board Statement: This study was conducted in accordance with the Declaration of Helsinki and approved by the Institutional Review Board of the Medical University of Warsaw (approval no. KB/50/21 from 19 April 2021).

Informed Consent Statement: Written informed consent was obtained from the patients to publish this paper.

Data Availability Statement: The data presented in this study are available on request from the corresponding author. The data are not publicly available due to not obtaining consent from respondents to publish the data.

Conflicts of Interest: The authors declare no conflict of interest.

References

1. Tsang, H.F.; Chan, L.W.C.; Cho, W.C.S.; Yu, A.C.S.; Yim, A.K.Y.; Chan, A.K.C.; Ng, L.P.W.; Wong, Y.K.E.; Pei, X.M.; Li, M.J.W.; et al. An update on COVID-19 pandemic: The epidemiology, pathogenesis, prevention and treatment strategies. *Expert Rev. Anti Infect. Ther.* **2021**, *19*, 877–888. [CrossRef] [PubMed]
2. Ulaszewska, K.; Jodczyk, A.M.; Dlugolecki, P.; Emerla, S.; Stanska, W.; Kasiak, P.S.; Gasior, J.S.; Parol, D.; Mamcarz, A.; Sliz, D. Factors Associated with Willingness to Receive a COVID-19 Vaccine in Adult Polish Population-A Cross-Sectional Survey. *Vaccines* **2022**, *10*, 1715. [CrossRef]
3. Fiolet, T.; Kherabi, Y.; MacDonald, C.J.; Ghosn, J.; Peiffer-Smadja, N. Comparing COVID-19 vaccines for their characteristics, efficacy and effectiveness against SARS-CoV-2 and variants of concern: A narrative review. *Clin. Microbiol. Infect.* **2022**, *28*, 202–221. [CrossRef] [PubMed]
4. Thakur, V.; Bhola, S.; Thakur, P.; Patel, S.K.S.; Kulshrestha, S.; Ratho, R.K.; Kumar, P. Waves and variants of SARS-CoV-2: Understanding the causes and effect of the COVID-19 catastrophe. *Infection* **2022**, *50*, 309–325. [CrossRef] [PubMed]
5. Balanzá-Martínez, V.; Kapczinski, F.; de Azevedo Cardoso, T.; Atienza-Carbonell, B.; Rosa, A.R.; Mota, J.C.; De Boni, R.B. The assessment of lifestyle changes during the COVID-19 pandemic using a multidimensional scale. *Rev. Psiquiatr. Salud. Ment.* **2021**, *14*, 16–26. [CrossRef] [PubMed]
6. Romero-Blanco, C.; Rodríguez-Almagro, J.; Onieva-Zafra, M.D.; Parra-Fernández, M.L.; Prado-Laguna, M.D.C.; Hernández-Martínez, A. Physical Activity and Sedentary Lifestyle in University Students: Changes during Confinement Due to the COVID-19 Pandemic. *Int. J. Environ. Res. Public Health* **2020**, *17*, 6567. [CrossRef] [PubMed]
7. Di Renzo, L.; Gualtieri, P.; Pivari, F.; Soldati, L.; Attinà, A.; Cinelli, G.; Leggeri, C.; Caparello, G.; Barrea, L.; Scerbo, F.; et al. Eating habits and lifestyle changes during COVID-19 lockdown: An Italian survey. *J. Transl. Med.* **2020**, *18*, 229. [CrossRef] [PubMed]
8. Santos, L. The impact of nutrition and lifestyle modification on health. *Eur. J. Intern. Med.* **2022**, *97*, 18–25. [CrossRef] [PubMed]
9. Rishi, P.; Thakur, K.; Vij, S.; Rishi, L.; Singh, A.; Kaur, I.P.; Patel, S.K.S.; Lee, J.K.; Kalia, V.C. Diet, Gut Microbiota and COVID-19. *Indian J. Microbiol.* **2020**, *60*, 420–429. [CrossRef]
10. Fikenzer, S.; Fikenzer, K.; Laufs, U.; Falz, R.; Pietrek, H.; Hepp, P. Impact of COVID-19 lockdown on endurance capacity of elite handball players. *J. Sports Med. Phys. Fit.* **2021**, *61*, 977–982. [CrossRef]
11. Krzywański, J.; Mikulski, T.; Krysztofiak, H.; Pokrywka, A.; Sobierajski, T.; Młyńczak, M.; Piechuta, A.; Kuchar, E. Vaccine versus infection—COVID-19-related loss of training time in elite athletes. *J. Sci. Med. Sport* **2022**, *25*, 950–959. [CrossRef]
12. Gervasi, S.F.; Pengue, L.; Damato, L.; Monti, R.; Pradella, S.; Pirronti, T.; Bartoloni, A.; Epifani, F.; Saggese, A.; Cuccaro, F.; et al. Is extensive cardiopulmonary screening useful in athletes with previous asymptomatic or mild SARS-CoV-2 infection? *Br. J. Sports Med.* **2021**, *55*, 54–61. [CrossRef]
13. Roberts, C.; Gill, N.; Sims, S. The Influence of COVID-19 Lockdown Restrictions on Perceived Nutrition Habits in Rugby Union Players. *Front. Nutr.* **2020**, *7*, 589737. [CrossRef] [PubMed]
14. Firoozjah, M.H.; Shahrbanian, S.; Homayouni, A.; Hower, H. Comparison of eating disorders symptoms and body image between individual and team sport adolescent athletes during the COVID-19 pandemic. *J. Eat. Disord.* **2022**, *10*, 119. [CrossRef] [PubMed]
15. Kasiak, P.S.; Adamczyk, N.; Jodczyk, A.M.; Kaproń, A.; Lisowska, A.; Mamcarz, A.; Śliż, D. COVID-19 Pandemic Consequences among Individuals with Eating Disorders on a Clinical Sample in Poland-A Cross-Sectional Study. *Int. J. Environ. Res. Public Health* **2022**, *19*, 8484. [CrossRef]
16. Abdel Moneim, A.; Radwan, M.A.; Yousef, A.I. COVID-19 and cardiovascular disease: Manifestations, pathophysiology, vaccination, and long-term implication. *Curr. Med. Res. Opin.* **2022**, *38*, 1071–1079. [CrossRef] [PubMed]
17. Silva Andrade, B.; Siqueira, S.; de Assis Soares, W.R.; de Souza Rangel, F.; Santos, N.O.; Dos Santos Freitas, A.; Ribeiro da Silveira, P.; Tiwari, S.; Alzahrani, K.J.; Góes-Neto, A.; et al. Long-COVID and Post-COVID Health Complications: An Up-to-Date Review on Clinical Conditions and Their Possible Molecular Mechanisms. *Viruses* **2021**, *13*, 700. [CrossRef]
18. Sanchez-Ramirez, D.C.; Normand, K.; Zhaoyun, Y.; Torres-Castro, R. Long-Term Impact of COVID-19: A Systematic Review of the Literature and Meta-Analysis. *Biomedicines* **2021**, *9*, 900. [CrossRef]
19. Naeije, R.; Caravita, S. CPET for Long COVID-19. *JACC Heart Fail.* **2022**, *10*, 214–215. [CrossRef]

20. Wiecha, S.; Price, S.; Cieśliński, I.; Kasiak, P.S.; Tota, Ł.; Ambroży, T.; Śliż, D. Transferability of Cardiopulmonary Parameters between Treadmill and Cycle Ergometer Testing in Male Triathletes-Prediction Formulae. *Int. J. Environ. Res. Public Health* **2022**, *19*, 1830. [CrossRef]
21. Moulson, N.; Gustus, S.K.; Scirica, C.; Petek, B.J.; Vanatta, C.; Churchill, T.W.; Guseh, J.S.; Baggish, A.; Wasfy, M.M. Diagnostic evaluation and cardiopulmonary exercise test findings in young athletes with persistent symptoms following COVID-19. *Br. J. Sports Med.* **2022**, *56*, 927–932. [CrossRef] [PubMed]
22. Mancini, D.M.; Brunjes, D.L.; Lala, A.; Trivieri, M.G.; Contreras, J.P.; Natelson, B.H. Use of Cardiopulmonary Stress Testing for Patients With Unexplained Dyspnea Post-Coronavirus Disease. *JACC Heart Fail.* **2021**, *9*, 927–937. [CrossRef] [PubMed]
23. Kysel, P.; Haluzíková, D.; Doležalová, R.P.; Laňková, I.; Lacinová, Z.; Kasperová, B.J.; Trnovská, J.; Hrádková, V.; Mráz, M.; Vilikus, Z.; et al. The Influence of Cyclical Ketogenic Reduction Diet vs. Nutritionally Balanced Reduction Diet on Body Composition, Strength, and Endurance Performance in Healthy Young Males: A Randomized Controlled Trial. *Nutrients* **2020**, *12*, 2832. [CrossRef] [PubMed]
24. Lukaski, H.C. Vitamin and mineral status: Effects on physical performance. *Nutrition* **2004**, *20*, 632–644. [CrossRef] [PubMed]
25. Price, S.; Wiecha, S.; Cieśliński, I.; Śliż, D.; Kasiak, P.S.; Lach, J.; Gruba, G.; Kowalski, T.; Mamcarz, A. Differences between Treadmill and Cycle Ergometer Cardiopulmonary Exercise Testing Results in Triathletes and Their Association with Body Composition and Body Mass Index. *Int. J. Environ. Res. Public Health* **2022**, *19*, 3557. [CrossRef] [PubMed]
26. Gruba, G.; Kasiak, P.S.; Gębarowska, J.; Adamczyk, N.; Sikora, Z.; Jodczyk, A.M.; Mamcarz, A.; Śliż, D. PaLS Study of Sleep Deprivation and Mental Health Consequences of the COVID-19 Pandemic among University Students: A Cross-Sectional Survey. *Int. J. Environ. Res. Public Health* **2021**, *18*, 9581. [CrossRef]
27. Jodczyk, A.M.; Gruba, G.; Sikora, Z.; Kasiak, P.S.; Gębarowska, J.; Adamczyk, N.; Mamcarz, A.; Śliż, D. PaLS Study: How Has the COVID-19 Pandemic Influenced Physical Activity and Nutrition? Observations a Year after the Outbreak of the Pandemic. *Int. J. Environ. Res. Public Health* **2021**, *18*, 9632. [CrossRef]
28. Jodczyk, A.M.; Kasiak, P.S.; Adamczyk, N.; Gebarowska, J.; Sikora, Z.; Gruba, G.; Mamcarz, A.; Sliz, D. PaLS Study: Tobacco, Alcohol and Drugs Usage among Polish University Students in the Context of Stress Caused by the COVID-19 Pandemic. *Int. J. Environ. Res. Public Health* **2022**, *19*, 1261. [CrossRef]
29. Beaver, W.L.; Wasserman, K.; Whipp, B.J. A new method for detecting anaerobic threshold by gas exchange. *J. Appl Physiol (1985)* **1986**, *60*, 2020–2027. [CrossRef]
30. Singh, I.; Joseph, P.; Heerdt, P.M.; Cullinan, M.; Lutchmansingh, D.D.; Gulati, M.; Possick, J.D.; Systrom, D.M.; Waxman, A.B. Persistent Exertional Intolerance After COVID-19: Insights From Invasive Cardiopulmonary Exercise Testing. *Chest* **2022**, *161*, 54–63. [CrossRef]
31. Mercier, J.; Grosbois, J.M.; Préfaut, C. Interpreting exercise tests. *Rev. Pneumol Clin.* **1997**, *53*, 289–296. [PubMed]
32. Milovancev, A.; Avakumovic, J.; Lakicevic, N.; Stajer, V.; Korovljev, D.; Todorovic, N.; Bianco, A.; Maksimovic, N.; Ostojic, S.; Drid, P. Cardiorespiratory Fitness in Volleyball Athletes Following a COVID-19 Infection: A Cross-Sectional Study. *Int. J. Environ. Res. Public Health* **2021**, *18*, 4059. [CrossRef] [PubMed]
33. Mazzucco, G.A.; Torres-Castro, R.; Intelangelo, L.; Vila Ortiz, B.; Lista-Paz, A. Does COVID-19 Affect the Exercise Capacity of Non-hospitalized Patients? *Cureus* **2021**, *13*, e18135. [CrossRef] [PubMed]
34. Goergen, J.; Bavishi, A.; Eimer, M.; Zielinski, A.R. COVID-19: The Risk to Athletes. *Curr. Treat. Options Cardiovasc. Med.* **2021**, *23*, 68. [CrossRef]
35. Cassar, M.P.; Tunnicliffe, E.M.; Petousi, N.; Lewandowski, A.J.; Xie, C.; Mahmod, M.; Samat, A.H.A.; Evans, R.A.; Brightling, C.E.; Ho, L.P.; et al. Symptom Persistence Despite Improvement in Cardiopulmonary Health—Insights from longitudinal CMR, CPET and lung function testing post-COVID-19. *EClinicalMedicine* **2021**, *41*, 101159. [CrossRef]
36. Barbagelata, L.; Masson, W.; Iglesias, D.; Lillo, E.; Migone, J.F.; Orazi, M.L.; Maritano Furcada, J. Cardiopulmonary Exercise Testing in Patients with Post-COVID-19 Syndrome. *Med. Clin.* **2022**, *159*, 6–11. [CrossRef] [PubMed]
37. Oliynyk, O.V.; Rorat, M.; Barg, W. Oxygen metabolism markers as predictors of mortality in severe COVID-19. *Int. J. Infect. Dis.* **2021**, *103*, 452–456. [CrossRef]
38. Ahmed, I. COVID-19—Does exercise prescription and maximal oxygen uptake (VO(2) max) have a role in risk-stratifying patients? *Clin. Med.* **2020**, *20*, 282–284. [CrossRef]
39. Pal, R.; Singh, S.N.; Chatterjee, A.; Saha, M. Age-related changes in cardiovascular system, autonomic functions, and levels of BDNF of healthy active males: Role of yogic practice. *Age* **2014**, *36*, 9683. [CrossRef]
40. Komici, K.; Bianco, A.; Perrotta, F.; Dello Iacono, A.; Bencivenga, L.; D'Agnano, V.; Rocca, A.; Bianco, A.; Rengo, G.; Guerra, G. Clinical Characteristics, Exercise Capacity and Pulmonary Function in Post-COVID-19 Competitive Athletes. *J. Clin. Med.* **2021**, *10*, 3053. [CrossRef]
41. Jeukendrup, A.E. Periodized Nutrition for Athletes. *Sports Med.* **2017**, *47*, 51–63. [CrossRef] [PubMed]
42. Maughan, R.J. Nutritional aspects of endurance exercise in humans. *Proc. Nutr. Soc.* **1994**, *53*, 181–188. [CrossRef] [PubMed]
43. Maughan, R.J.; Greenhaff, P.L.; Leiper, J.B.; Ball, D.; Lambert, C.P.; Gleeson, M. Diet composition and the performance of high-intensity exercise. *J. Sports Sci.* **1997**, *15*, 265–275. [CrossRef] [PubMed]
44. Peters, E.M. Nutritional aspects in ultra-endurance exercise. *Curr. Opin. Clin. Nutr. Metab. Care* **2003**, *6*, 427–434. [CrossRef] [PubMed]

45. Csulak, E.; Petrov, Á.; Kováts, T.; Tokodi, M.; Lakatos, B.; Kovács, A.; Staub, L.; Suhai, F.I.; Szabó, E.L.; Dohy, Z.; et al. The Impact of COVID-19 on the Preparation for the Tokyo Olympics: A Comprehensive Performance Assessment of Top Swimmers. *Int. J. Environ. Res. Public Health* **2021**, *18*, 9770. [CrossRef]
46. Lodi, E.; Scavone, A.; Carollo, A.; Guicciardi, C.; Reggianini, L.; Savino, G.; Modena, M.G. Return to sport after the COVID-19 pandemic. How to behave? *G. Ital. Cardiol.* **2020**, *21*, 514–522. [CrossRef]
47. Dove, J.; Gage, A.; Kriz, P.; Tabaddor, R.R.; Owens, B.D. COVID-19 and Review of Current Recommendations for Return to Athletic Play. *Rhode Isl. Med. J.* **2020**, *103*, 15–20.
48. Haddad, M.; Abbes, Z.; Mujika, I.; Chamari, K. Impact of COVID-19 on Swimming Training: Practical Recommendations during Home Confinement/Isolation. *Int. J. Environ. Res. Public Health* **2021**, *18*, 4767. [CrossRef]
49. Heuberger, J.; Gal, P.; Stuurman, F.E.; de Muinck Keizer, W.A.S.; Mejia Miranda, Y.; Cohen, A.F. Repeatability and predictive value of lactate threshold concepts in endurance sports. *PLoS ONE* **2018**, *13*, e0206846. [CrossRef]
50. González, N.; Marquès, M.; Nadal, M.; Domingo, J.L. Meat consumption: Which are the current global risks? A review of recent (2010-2020) evidences. *Food Res. Int.* **2020**, *137*, 109341. [CrossRef]
51. Najjar, R.S.; Moore, C.E.; Montgomery, B.D. A defined, plant-based diet utilized in an outpatient cardiovascular clinic effectively treats hypercholesterolemia and hypertension and reduces medications. *Clin. Cardiol* **2018**, *41*, 307–313. [CrossRef] [PubMed]
52. Monnard, C.R.; Dulloo, A.G. Polyunsaturated fatty acids as modulators of fat mass and lean mass in human body composition regulation and cardiometabolic health. *Obes. Rev.* **2021**, *22* (Suppl. 2), e13197. [CrossRef] [PubMed]
53. Zhang, G.; Shirai, N.; Suzuki, H. Relationship between the effect of dietary fat on swimming endurance and energy metabolism in aged mice. *Ann. Nutr. Metab.* **2011**, *58*, 282–289. [CrossRef] [PubMed]
54. Rust, P.; Ekmekcioglu, C. Impact of Salt Intake on the Pathogenesis and Treatment of Hypertension. *Adv. Exp. Med. Biol.* **2017**, *956*, 61–84. [CrossRef]
55. Veniamakis, E.; Kaplanis, G.; Voulgaris, P.; Nikolaidis, P.T. Effects of Sodium Intake on Health and Performance in Endurance and Ultra-Endurance Sports. *Int. J. Environ. Res. Public Health* **2022**, *19*, 3651. [CrossRef]
56. Barrea, L.; Grant, W.B.; Frias-Toral, E.; Vetrani, C.; Verde, L.; de Alteriis, G.; Docimo, A.; Savastano, S.; Colao, A.; Muscogiuri, G. Dietary Recommendations for Post-COVID-19 Syndrome. *Nutrients* **2022**, *14*, 1305. [CrossRef]

nutrients

MDPI

Article

Supervised Exercise in Water: Is It a Viable Alternative in Overweight/Obese People with or without Type 2 Diabetes? A Pilot Study

Roberto Pippi [1,*], Matteo Vandoni [2], Matteo Tortorella [3], Vittorio Bini [4] and Carmine Giuseppe Fanelli [1]

1 Healthy Lifestyle Institute, C.U.R.I.A.Mo. (Centro Universitario Ricerca Interdipartimentale Attività Motoria), Department of Medicine and Surgery, University of Perugia, Via G. Bambagioni, 19, 06126 Perugia, Italy
2 Laboratory of Adapted Motor Activity (LAMA), Department of Public Health, Experimental Medicine and Forensic Science, University of Pavia, 27100 Pavia, Italy
3 Guy's and St Thomas' NHS Foundation Trust, Great Maze Pond, London SE1 9RT, UK
4 Department of Medicine and Surgery, University of Perugia, Via Gambuli, 1, 06132 Perugia, Italy
* Correspondence: roberto.pippi@unipg.it

Abstract: The study of the effects of a water-based exercise program in overweight/obese people with or without type 2 diabetes is a topic of relatively recent interest. This type of exercise presents some advantages in reducing the risk of injury or trauma, and it can be a valuable therapeutic card to play for sedentary or physically inactive patients who have chronic metabolic diseases. This work aims to make a contribution showing the effects of a water-based exercise intervention, supervised by graduates in sports sciences, in a group of overweight/obese people with or without type 2 diabetes. In total, 93 adults (age 60.59 ± 10.44 years), including 72 women (age 60.19 ± 10.97 years) and 21 men (age 61.95 ± 8.48 years), were recruited to follow a water-based exercise program (2 sessions/week, for 12 weeks) at the C.U.R.I.A.Mo. Healthy Lifestyle Institute of Perugia University. Results showed an improvement in body mass index (−0.90 ± 1.56, $p = 0.001$), waist circumference (−4.32 ± 6.03, $p < 0.001$), and systolic (−7.78 ± 13.37, $p = 0.001$) and diastolic (−6.30 ± 10.91, $p = 0.001$) blood pressure. The supervised water-based intervention was useful in managing patients with metabolic diseases who often present with other health impairments, such as musculoskeletal problems or cardiovascular or rheumatic disease that could contraindicate gym-based exercise.

Keywords: exercise; overweight/obesity; type 2 diabetes; water-based exercise

Citation: Pippi, R.; Vandoni, M.; Tortorella, M.; Bini, V.; Fanelli, C.G. Supervised Exercise in Water: Is It a Viable Alternative in Overweight/Obese People with or without Type 2 Diabetes? A Pilot Study. *Nutrients* **2022**, *14*, 4963. https://doi.org/10.3390/nu14234963

Academic Editor: Hirofumi Tanaka

Received: 10 November 2022
Accepted: 20 November 2022
Published: 23 November 2022

1. Introduction

Type 2 diabetes (DM2) is an ever-increasing, noncommunicable disease usually associated with overweight, obesity, and a sedentary lifestyle. The beneficial effects of physical activity and exercise in people with overweight/obesity with or without DM2 are well documented by solid evidence [1–4]. Guidelines from the World Health Organization (WHO) [5], the American College of Sports Medicine (ACSM) [6], and the American Diabetes Association (ADA) [7], as well as Italian national standards of care [8], state that adult people should be engaged in at least 150–300 min per week of moderate aerobic physical activity or at least 75–150 min of vigorous aerobic physical activity, or an equivalent combination, in addition to muscle-strengthening activities on two or more days per week [5]) to obtain substantial health benefits. Despite this, many people are sedentary or physically inactive (people who do not engage in at least 150 min per week of MVPA are defined as inactive by WHO), with increased health risks [9]. Physical activity level and sedentary behaviors affect people's health status [10], especially people with obesity and DM2 [11], who frequently are also affected by one or more osteoarticular or micro- or macroangiopathic complications.

In water-based exercise, the effect of body weight is limited due to the partial weight support the water provides. This in turn reduces weight-bearing stress on skeletal joints [12].

As a result, people with overweight/obesity can more easily engage in water-based exercise rather than ground-based exercise, which can cause more physical discomfort due to the effect of gravity [13]. By reducing the risk of injury or trauma, aquatic exercise can be a valuable therapeutic card to play in place of total weight-bearing exercises or aerobic activity, such as walking on land [14], which patients are less likely to enjoy and, in some cases, are associated with greater risk of injury or long-term disability. According to Bonifazi (2005), water-based exercise is a "type of activity that includes performing exercises to improve muscle tone and joint mobility" [15].

Although some authors have highlighted how physical activities practiced in water are useful in managing patients with health impairments such as musculoskeletal damage, cardiovascular diseases, and rheumatic and metabolic diseases [16–21], the effect of a water-based exercise intervention on health has not been comprehensively studied in people with overweight or obesity with or without DM2. In particular, the efficacy in weight reduction and metabolic improvements is not clear/well documented.

For these reasons, this work aims to show the effects of a water-based supervised exercise intervention on weight management and metabolic panel in overweight/obese people with or without DM2.

2. Materials and Methods

2.1. Participants

Among 1464 patients enrolled between January 2010 and February 2014 in the C.U.R.I.-A.Mo. trial a total sample (Figure 1) of 93 adults (mean age of 60.59 $\pm$ 10.44 years), including 72 women (age 60.19 $\pm$ 10.97 years) and 21 men (age 61.95 $\pm$ 8.48 years), was recruited to follow a multidisciplinary intervention at the C.U.R.I.A.Mo. Healthy Lifestyle Institute of Perugia University. The intervention included educational classes with endocrinologists and nutritionists as well as a water-based exercise program (2 sessions/week, for 12 weeks). Particularly at the beginning, the exercise program entailed water-based drills which were aimed to improve both patients' relationship with water and their swimming technique [22].

Inclusion criteria were: age between 37 and 78 years; BMI $\geq$ 25 kg/m^2; the presence of musculoskeletal disorders or other health conditions that could contraindicate gym exercise or Nordic walking activities. The exclusion criteria were: the presence of clinical conditions that could seriously reduce life expectancy or ability to participate in the study; no written informed consent to study participation. According to these criteria, this study involved 90 adults (mean age of 60.86 $\pm$ 9.50 years), including 69 women (age 60.52 $\pm$ 9.82 years) and 21 men (age 61.95 $\pm$ 8.48 years). Furthermore, a selection was performed to include only participants (n = 38 overweight/obese people, of which n = 20 with diabetes and 18 without diabetes) with baseline (T0) and follow-up (T1) data on every measured variable. Finally, we studied a small group of participants (n = 23 overweight/obese people, of which n = 13 with diabetes and 10 without diabetes) who presented all data for anthropometric and clinical variables at T0, T1, and T2.

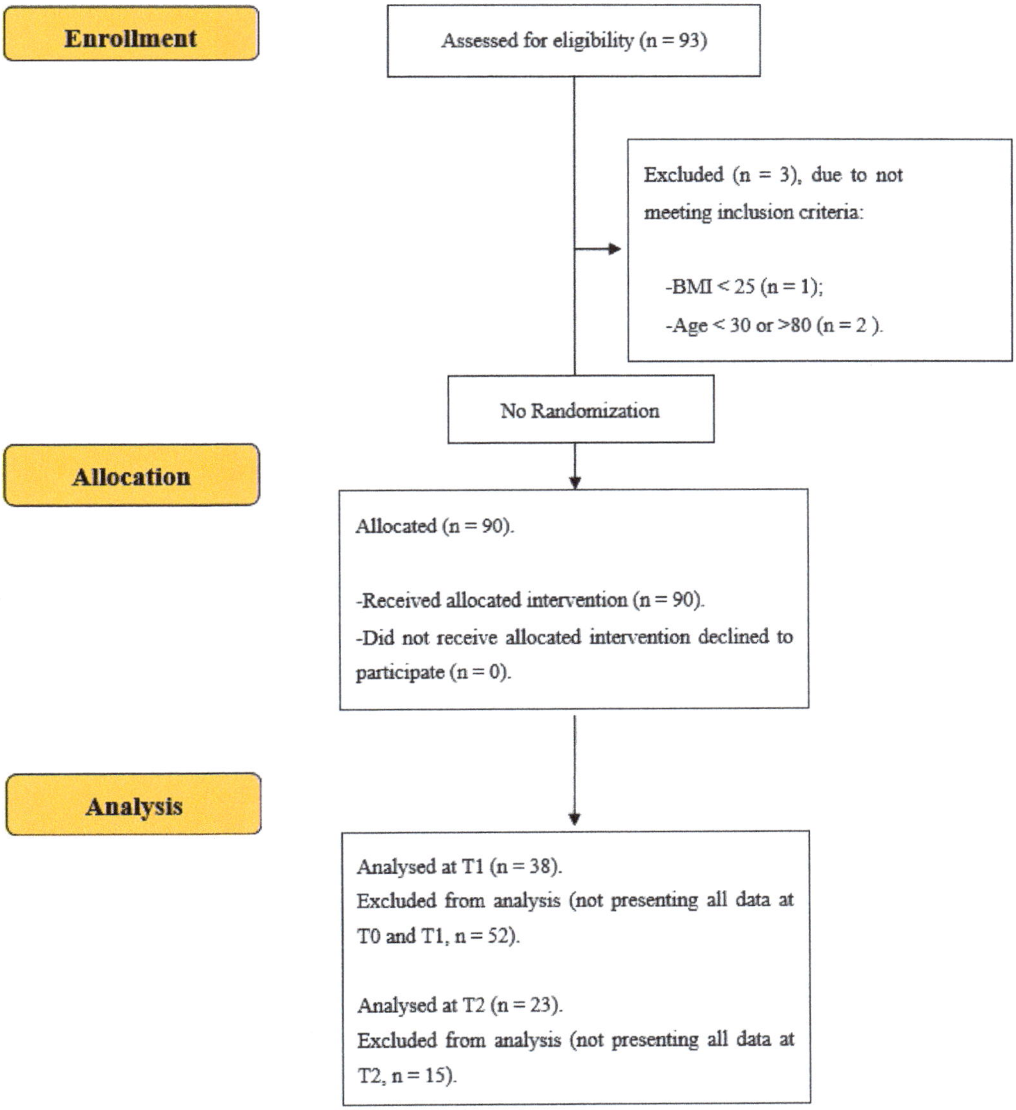

Figure 1. CONSORT flow diagram (adapted from CONSORT 2010 flow diagram).

2.2. Study Design

This is anuncontrolled pilot study involving a subsample of subjects who participated in the C.U.R.I.A.Mo. (Centro Universitario di Ricerca Interdipartimentale Attività Motoria) trial [22]. The C.U.R.I.A.Mo. trial has been registered in the Australian New Zealand Clinical Trials Registry (a Primary Registry in the WHO registry network) with the number ACTRN12611000255987. Anthropometric and clinical as well as other haematobiochemical variables were assessed at the beginning (T0), and after three months (T1) of the water-based exercise program using a quasiexperimental study design. For a small group of participants (n = 23, those patients who have adhered to all the follow-up visits foreseen by the C.U.R.I.A.Mo. program), data after one year (T2) from the end of the intensive period of activity are also available.

2.3. The C.U.R.I.A.Mo. Clinical Model

All the participants have been assessed through the C.U.R.I.A.Mo. evaluation model composed of some clinical steps: (1) a clinical examination, conducted by an endocrinologist, to exclude the existence of any clinical conditions that could contraindicate the exercise and to prescribe blood sample tests according to national standards of care [8]; (2) a brief motivational interview, conducted by a psychologist, to assess participants psychological status; (3) a nutritional assessment conducted to assess the nutritional habits of the participants; (4) a water-based exercise intervention consisting of three-month repeated cycles of water exercises, as specified below.

2.4. The Exercise Intervention

The exercise program was a water-based exercise intervention in a 25 m swimming pool lane. The protocol consisted of a 12-week water-based exercise program of two sessions per week lasting fifty (50) minutes each.

Each session was composed of an initial warm-up of twenty (20) minutes, in which each patient performed light water-based movements and some breathing exercises. The warm-up procedures were adapted to each participant's skill level and involved swimming unaided or with aids (noodles, floating belts). Each participant was asked to start slowly and increase exercise intensity subjectively to a moderate intensity during which, ideally, they could still talk to each other.

The second part of the session was resistance-oriented and based on upper and lower limb exercises lasting fifteen (15) minutes. During this section, upper and lower limbs were exercised through water-resistance movements. Those participants that showed improvement through the weeks had extra resistance added by introducing floating dumbbells for the upper limbs and noodles for the lower limbs.

After the resistance section, a cool-down of ten (10) minutes and some light stretching for five (5) minutes were provided. During the cool-down, each participant was required to execute some light and continuous water exercise at a lower intensity than the warm-up. Stretching was executed in the water and involved mainly upper and lower limbs.

After the first follow-up medical visit, we offered the patients the opportunity to repeat the three-month cycle of water-based exercise.

2.5. Clinical Assessments

Before (T0) starting, at the end of the three-month exercise program (T1) and after one year (T2), all the participants underwent a clinical assessment of anthropometric and clinical variables, as follows:

2.5.1. Anthropometric Variables

Anthropometric measurements of weight, body mass index (BMI), and waist circumference (WC) were collected. Weight was assessed using a Tanita body composition analyzer BC-420MA (Tokyo, Japan), and BMI was calculated as weight (kg)/height (m)^2. According to the World Health Organization and the International Diabetes Federation (IDF) tips [23], WC was measured in the horizontal plane midway between the lowest ribs and the iliac crest, using the ergonomic circumference measuring tape Seca® 201 model.

2.5.2. Clinical Variables

Systolic (SBP) and diastolic (DBP) blood pressure and blood sample variables, such as fasting blood glucose, glycated hemoglobin (HbA1c), total cholesterol, high-density lipoprotein (HDL) cholesterol, low-density lipoprotein (LDL) cholesterol, triglycerides, and uric acid were also collected.

Systolic blood pressure (SBP) and diastolic blood pressure (DBP) values were measured three times during the first medical visit with one minute between consecutive measurements 5 min of sitting at rest using an upper arm blood pressure monitor (UM-101 mercury-free sphygmomanometer, A&D Medical, Naples, Italy) on the right upper arm using a size-appropriate cuff.

Biochemical blood test variables were collected from tests performed by patients in routine clinical practice.

2.6. Statistical Analysis

Descriptive analyses in terms of means, standard deviations, or percentages were computed for each investigated variable at baseline (T0). Participants' data were then split into two subgroups according to the pathological condition diagnosed by the endocrinologist (overweight/obesity with or without DM2), and an unpaired t-test was conducted to compare all variables at baseline (please see Table S1). To evaluate the effects of the water-based exercise program, parameters at baseline and after three months of exercise intervention were compared through a t-test for paired samples (Table 1). Delta (Δ) changes (T1-T0) are presented as means ± standard deviations. Moreover, to evaluate the effects of water-based exercise programs over a longer period (1 year), parameters at baseline, after 3 (T1), and after 12 months (T2) were compared through a linear mixed model repeated measures analysis of variance in a small group of participants (n = 23) who presented all data for anthropometric and clinical variables collected both before and after the intervention. Means ± standard errors for all data and delta changes (using a method of multiple testing correction with Bonferroni adjustment) were presented (Table 2). p-value < 0.05 was indicated as statistically significant. Finally, to study the delta changes trend of declining, we calculated the B coefficient with SE for all the variables using linear regression with time as the independent variable. All analyses were performed with IBM SPSS® version 25.0 (IBM Corp. Released 2013. IBM SPSS Statistics for Windows, Version 22.0. Armonk, NY, USA: IBM Corp.).

Table 1. Anthropometric, blood pressure, and blood chemistry parameters values at baseline (T0) in the entire sample (n = 38), overweight/obese with diabetes (n = 20), and overweight/obese without diabetes (n = 18) subjects. Results are presented as mean ± standard deviation. Statistical significance was set for p values ≤ 0.05.

Variables	All			Overweight/Obese with Diabetes			Overweight/Obese without Diabetes		
	T0	Δ Test-T (T1 vs. T0)	p	T0	Δ Test-T (T1 vs. T0)	p	T0	Δ Test-T (T1 vs. T0)	p
Weight (kg)	65.96 ± 47.62	−2.61 ± 7.79	0.013	72.59 ± 46.99	−4.16 ± 10.45	0.037	58.87 ± 48.08	−1.00 ± 2.71	0.057
BMI (kg/m^2)	36.77 ± 6.21	−0.90 ± 1.56	0.001	37.44 ± 7.25	1.24 ± 1.8	0.008	36.03 ± 4.89	−0.54 ± 1.22	0.075
WC (cm)	115.82 ± 12.89	−4.32 ± 6.03	<0.001	118.85 ± 15.63	5.55 ± 5.69	<0.001	112.44 ± 8.11	−2.94 ± 6.25	0.062
SBP (mmhg)	136.08 ± 11.85	−7.78 ± 13.37	0.001	136.75 ± 13.11	−8.0 ± 15.08	0.028	135.29 ± 10.53	−7.53 ± 11.48	0.016
DBP (mmhg)	81.89 ± 7.67	−6.30 ± 10.91	0.001	82.5 ± 7.86	9.15 ± 11.18	0.002	81.18 ± 7.61	−2.94 ± 9.85	0.236
Fasting blood glucose (mg/dL)	108.95 ± 30.37	−1.49 ± 20.91	0.668	122.1 ± 36.09	1.10 ± 27.48	0.860	94.33 ± 11.02	−4.53 ± 8.29	0.039
HbA1c (%)	6.36 ± 1.22	−0.28 ± 0.85	0.074	6.91 ± 1.46	−0.33 ± 1.08	0.206	5.78 ± 0.48	−0.22 ± 0.41	0.083
Total cholesterol (mg/dL)	211 ± 51.41	−8.00 ± 35.43	0.184	197.70 ± 57.34	−5.26 ± 36.89	0.542	225.78 ± 40.48	−11.06 ± 34.59	0.206
HDL (mg/dL)	49.45 ± 9.79	1.00 ± 9.93	0.550	49.25 ± 10.65	0.47 ± 11.76	0.863	49.67 ± 9.04	1.59 ± 7.71	0.408
LDL cholesterol (mg/dL)	132.41 ± 42.30	−8.55 ± 27.67	0.072	114.72 ± 43.62	−2.34 ± 26.68	0.707	152.07 ± 31.48	−15.49 ± 6.76	0.036
Triglycerides (mg/dL)	152.68 ± 82.58	−8.62 ± 53.19	0.331	169.65 ± 92.95	−17.05 ± 63.27	0.243	133.83 ± 66.88	1.29 ± 37.66	0.889
Uric acid (mg/dL)	5.64 ± 1.36	−0.10 ± 0.78	0.510	5.71 ± 1.44	0.02 ± 0.77	0.942	5.58 ± 1.33	−0.22 ± 0.80	0.349

Legend: BMI = body mass index; WC = waist circumference; SBP = systolic blood pressure; DBP = diastolic blood pressure; HbA1c = glycosylated haemoglobin; Hdl = high-density lipoprotein; LDL = low-density lipoprotein.

Table 2. Anthropometric, blood pressure, and blood chemistry parameters values at baseline (T0) and after 3 months (T1) and 12 months (T2) post-intervention. Results are presented as mean ± standard errors (SE) in n = 23 subjects. Statistical significance was set for p values ≤ 0.05.

Variables	T0	T1 (3 Months)	T2 (12 Months)	p	B	SE	Delta Changes					
							T1 vs. T0	p	T2 vs. T0	p	T2 vs. T1	p
Weight (kg)	58.70 ± 7.14	55.57 ± 7.00	52.06 ± 7.13	0.023	−1.517	2.382	−3.12 ± 1.21	0.038	−6.64 ± 3.05	0.103	−3.52 ± 2.83	0.659
BMI (kg/m^2)	37.27 ± 1.18	35.98 ± 1.19	36.1 ± 1.17	0.020	−0.585	0.827	−1.28 ± 0.34	0.003	−1.17 ± 0.58	0.169	0.11 ± 0.51	1.000
WC (cm)	117.22 ± 2.28	111.52 ± 2.35	110.09 ± 2.32	<0.001	−3.727	2.563	−5.70 ± 0.97	<0.001	−7.13 ± 1.06	<0.001	−1.43 ± 0.56	0.050
SBP (mmhg)	135.95 ± 2.20	129.14 ± 2.82	126.48 ± 2.37	0.013	−4.435	1.604	−6.81 ± 3.32	0.160	−9.48 ± 3.24	0.025	−2.67 ± 2.86	1.000
DBP (mmhg)	82.62 ± 1.68	77 ± 1.61	76.71 ± 1.24	0.019	−2.952	1.095	−5.62 ± 2.66	0.141	−5.90 ± 1.99	0.023	−0.29 ± 2.05	1.000
Fasting blood glucose (mg/dL)	117.83 ± 6.85	114.78 ± 6.47	120.57 ± 9.11	0.500	−0.955	4.877	−3.04 ± 4.18	1.000	2.74 ± 5.88	1.000	5.78 ± 4.39	0.604
HbA1c (%)	6.63 ± 0.32	6.24 ± 0.22	6.30 ± 0.23	0.099	−0.167	0.186	−0.40 ± 0.21	0.234	−0.33 ± 0.21	0.395	0.06 ± 0.06	0.894
Total cholesterol (mg/dL)	222.75 ± 11.46	208.92 ± 8.76	201.17 ± 8.79	0.013	−10.457	7.086	−13.83 ± 7.30	0.212	−21.58 ± 7.42	0.024	−7.75 ± 4.24	0.242
HDL (mg/dL)	48.29 ± 1.97	49.12 ± 2.45	49.17 ± 2.52	0.097	0.587	1.690	0.83 ± 2.23	1.000	0.88 ± 2.43	1.000	0.04 ± 2.05	1.000
LDL (mg/dL)	140.34 ± 9.98	129.38 ± 7.73	123.97 ± 7.39	0.024	−7.848	6.153	−10.96 ± 5.87	0.224	−16.38 ± 6.39	0.052	−5.42 ± 3.28	0.336
Triglycerides (mg/dL)	171.42 ± 19.35	152.04 ± 18.17	139.96 ± 11.40	0.066	−16.522	12.212	−19.38 ± 11.96	0.357	−31.46 ± 14.96	0.140	−12.08 ± 12.47	1.000
Uric acid (mg/dL)	5.49 ± 0.33	5.37 ± 0.30	5.55 ± 0.24	0.612	0.031	0.201	−0.12 ± 0.21	1.000	0.06 ± 0.16	1.000	0.18 ± 0.16	0.866

Legend: BMI = body mass index; WC = waist circumference; SBP = systolic blood pressure; DBP = diastolic blood pressure; HbA1c = glycosylated haemoglobin; Hdl = high-density lipoprotein; LDL = low-density lipoprotein.

3. Results

3.1. Baseline Results

Anthropometric and clinical variables values did not show statistically significant differences between overweight/obesity with or without DM2 at baseline (please see Table S1), except for fasting blood glucose (p = 0.003), HbA1c (p = 0.004), and LDL cholesterol (p = 0.005).

3.2. Follow-Up Results

At the first follow up (T1), statistically significant improvements in weight (p = 0.013) and BMI (p = 0.001) and reductions in WC (p < 0.001), SBP (p = 0.001), and DBP (p = 0.001) were observed in the entire sample (Table 1). Clinical effects, although not statistically significant, were observed in the differential values of blood sample variables such as fasting blood glucose (−1.49 mg/dL), HbA1c (−0.28%), total cholesterol (−8.00 mg/dL), HDL (+1 mg/dL), LDL cholesterol (−8.55 mg/dL), triglycerides (−8.62 mg/dL), and uric acid (−0.10 mg/dL). In the overweight/obese with diabetes, data showed statistically significant variations in weight (p = 0.037) and BMI (p = 0.008) and reductions in WC (p < 0.001), SBP (p = 0.028), and DBP (p = 0.002), while in patients without diabetes, we observed reductions in SBP (p = 0.016) and fasting blood glucose (p = 0.039).

Data analyzed from all patients with an available one-year (T2) follow-up evaluation (n = 23, 1 male and 22 female, mean age 58.78 ± 9.17 years) confirmed a statistically significant change (Table 2) in the following outcomes: weight (p = 0.023), BMI (p = 0.020), WC (p < 0.001), SBP (p = 0.013), and DBP (p = 0.019). Furthermore, the time factor effect was observed in total cholesterol (p = 0.013) and LDL (p = 0.024).

4. Discussion

This study aimed to show the effects of a water-based exercise program of 24 biweekly sessions on some anthropometric (i.e., weight, BMI, and WC) and clinical (i.e., SBP and DBP, lipids, and glycemic variables) outcomes in a group of overweight/obese adults with and without DM2. Preliminary results showed an improvement in BMI, WC, SBP, and DBP in all the participants that exercised for 12 weeks.

Previously, contrasting results were obtained in similar water-based exercise programs. A Tanaka's review article [24] reported that few studied have addressed the effects of swimming exercise on bodyweight and them stated no changes in weight [25,26]. Recent studies conducted by Rezaeipour et al. [27] and Cugusi et al. [2] observed a significant reduction in weight and BMI, as we observed in this study. Conversely, Rezaeipour, M. (2020) [28] reported that pool workouts are ineffective in terms of weight loss and changes in body composition, as also stated by Gubiani et al. [29]. In an epidemiological study, other authors [30] observed that regular physical activity (including swimming exercise) is associated with an attenuation of weight regain over a middle–long period (10 years). Interestingly, our study results showed that weight reduction was observed not only after a short period of a water-based exercise program but also after 1 year (respectively, −3.12 kg and −6.64 kg).

Previous studies showed contrasting metabolic effects of water-based exercise training. Some authors evaluated anthropometric and cardiometabolic parameters in women [31,32] and adult men with obesity and DM2 [2]. While the first observed no significant improvements in body weight and body composition, Cugusi et al. showed a significant improvement in the cardiovascular system and metabolic profile (body weight, WC, BMI, and blood pressure improvements). Some authors [33–35] have studied the impact of regular exercise on lipid and lipoprotein plasma levels, especially HDL, as the main tool for reducing the risk of cardiovascular diseases. Other authors [36] have specifically studied the effects of water exercise on blood lipid outcomes. Rezaeipour et al. [33] found that there was not a significant alteration of blood lipid parameters, and we did not observe a statistically significant improvement in total cholesterol, HDL, LDL cholesterol, and triglycerides ($p > 0.005$), after the intensive phase of the exercise program (12 weeks). These results could probably be due to the short period of observation and nutritional habits. In fact, at T2 (Table 2) data seems to show encouraging results regarding lipid control.

Water-based exercise effects on blood pressure were assessed in previous studies. A recent meta-analysis [37] reported that water-based exercise had positive effects on BP values. Particularly, SBP decrease was estimated equal to −8.4 mmHg, while DBP decrease was estimated equal to −3.3 mmHg. After three months of water-based exercise in our sample, we found a lower improvement in SBP (−7.78 mmHg), but a higher improvement of DBP (−6.30 mmHg). Although Delevatti et al. [38] concluded that "aerobic training in an aquatic environment provides effects similar to aerobic training in a dry-land environment in patients with type 2 diabetes", the result of the present study seems to be promising compared to previous studies conducted in small samples of people with overweight/obesity who exercised for three months in a gym-based program [39].

Certainly, this study has some limitations. First, we did not include a control group that could have better clarified the extent of the results; the original C.U.R.I.A.Mo. intervention model did not foresee it. Second, we enrolled only a small group of participants. This was due mainly to technical and methodological reasons. It was possible to provide access to the pool for only a small number of patients for each exercise group. Both for the limited space available and for the need to guarantee personalized supervision of the activity, we decided to set up groups no larger than five participants each. Additionally, a water exercise-based program encountered various critical issues in the adherence of patients, who have reported difficulties related to the time necessary to carry out activities in the water (i.e., long preparation times due for example to the fact of having to dry the hair, etc.). Furthermore, many key measures (i.e., waist circumference, blood pressure) were derived using manual methods subject to investigator bias, even if measurements at T0 and T1 were always conducted by the same operator to minimize operator variability and all operators were specifically trained in accordance with standard measurement procedures. Additionally, in this study, we did not show data referring to nutritional habits and pharmacological treatment. In future studies, an analysis of eating habits should be carried out together with insights into the drugs taken, given that these components are relevant in this type of patient with metabolic diseases. Our results showed that in a relatively short period of educational training it is possible to obtain positive effects which have a significant impact on people's health. Reductions in anthropometric (such as BMI and WC) and clinical (such as blood pressure and cholesterol) variables values are linked to obesity and cardiovascular risks [40]. These aspects are particularly important for people with health conditions for whom weight-bearing exercise is contraindicated or for the elderly [41,42].

5. Conclusions

The supervised water-based intervention was effective in improving weight, BMI, waist circumference, and blood pressure. Although it showed lower results on short-term glucometabolic control, this type of exercise practiced in water was useful in managing patients with health problems—i.e., musculoskeletal problems, cardiovascular disease, rheumatic and metabolic diseases—that could contraindicate gym-based exercises. Longer periods of intervention and observation, which may involve larger numbers of participants, are desirable for future research.

Supplementary Materials: The following supporting information can be downloaded at: https://www.mdpi.com/article/10.3390/nu14234963/s1, Table S1: Anthropometric, blood pressure, and blood chemistry parameters values at baseline (T0) in all the sample (n = 38), over-weight/obese with diabetes (n = 20) and over-weight/obese without diabetes (n = 18) subjects.

Author Contributions: Conceptualization, R.P., M.V. and M.T.; data curation, R.P., V.B., M.V. and M.T.; formal analysis, R.P. and V.B.; funding acquisition: C.G.F.; investigation, R.P., M.T. and C.G.F.; methodology, R.P., M.V. and C.G.F.; project administration, R.P. and C.G.F.; software, R.P., M.T. and V.B.; supervision, M.V. and C.G.F.; writing—original draft, R.P., M.V. and M.T.; writing—review and editing, R.P., M.V., M.T., V.B. and C.G.F. All authors have read and agreed to the published version of the manuscript.

Funding: This research received no external funding.

Institutional Review Board Statement: C.U.R.I.A.Mo. project has been registered in the Australian New Zealand Clinical Trials Registry (a Primary Registry in the WHO registry network) with the number ACTRN12611000255987. Moreover, the study was conducted in compliance with the guidelines in the Declaration of Helsinki.

Informed Consent Statement: Written informed consent was obtained from all subjects involved in the study.

Data Availability Statement: The datasets used during the current study are available from the corresponding author upon reasonable request.

Conflicts of Interest: The authors declare no conflict of interest.

References

1. Shawahna, R.; Batta, A.; Asa'ad, M.; Jomaah, M.; Abdelhaq, I. Exercise as a complementary medicine intervention in type 2 diabetes mellitus: A systematic review with narrative and qualitative synthesis of evidence. *Diabetes Metab. Syndr.* **2021**, *15*, 273–286. [CrossRef] [PubMed]
2. Cugusi, L.; Cadeddu, C.; Nocco, S.; Orrù, F.; Bandino, S.; Deidda, M.; Caria, A.; Bassareo, P.P.; Piras, A.; Cabras, S.; et al. Effects of an aquatic-based exercise program to improve cardiometabolic profile, quality of life, and physical activity levels in men with type 2 diabetes mellitus. *Pm&R* **2015**, *7*, 141–148. [CrossRef]
3. Heberle, I.; de Barcelos, G.T.; Silveira, L.M.P.; Costa, R.R.; Gerage, A.M.; Delevatti, R.S. Effects of aerobic training with and without progression on blood pressure in patients with type 2 diabetes: A systematic review with meta-analyses and meta-regressions. *Diabetes Res. Clin. Pract.* **2021**, *171*, 108581. [CrossRef] [PubMed]
4. Sbroma Tomaro, E.; Pippi, R.; Reginato, E.; Aiello, C.; Buratta, L.; Mazzeschi, C.; Perrone, C.; Ranucci, C.; Tirimagni, A.; Russo, A.; et al. Intensive lifestyle intervention is particularly advantageous in poorly controlled type 2 diabetes. *Nutr. Metab. Cardiovasc. Dis.* **2017**, *27*, 688–694. [CrossRef]

5. Bull, F.C.; Al-Ansari, S.S.; Biddle, S.; Borodulin, K.; Buman, M.P.; Cardon, G.; Carty, C.; Chaput, J.-P.; Chastin, S.; Chou, R.; et al. World Health Organization 2020 Guidelines on Physical Activity and Sedentary Behaviour. *Br. J. Sports Med.* **2020**, *54*, 1451–1462. [CrossRef]
6. Colberg, S.R.; Albright, A.L.; Blissmer, B.J.; Braun, B.; Chasan-Taber, L.; Fernhall, B.; Regensteiner, J.G.; Rubin, R.R.; Sigal, R.J. Exercise and type 2 diabetes: American College of Sports Medicine and the American Diabetes Association: Joint position statement. Exercise and type 2 diabetes. *Med. Sci. Sports Exerc.* **2010**, *42*, 2282–2303. [CrossRef]
7. American Diabetes Association Professional Practice Committee. 5. Facilitating Behavior Change and Well-being to Improve Health Outcomes: Standards of Medical Care in Diabetes—2022. *Diabetes Care* **2022**, *45*, S60–S82. [CrossRef]
8. Italian Standards for Diabetes Mellitus 2018. Available online: http://aemmedi.it/wp-content/uploads/2009/06/AMD-Standard-unico1.pdf (accessed on 8 October 2022).
9. Guo, C.; Zhou, Q.; Zhang, D.; Qin, P.; Li, Q.; Tian, G.; Liu, D.; Chen, X.; Liu, L.; Liu, F.; et al. Association of total sedentary behaviour and television viewing with risk of overweight/obesity, type 2 diabetes and hypertension: A dose–response meta-analysis. *Diabetes Obes. Metab.* **2020**, *22*, 79–90. [CrossRef]
10. Whipple, M.O.; Regensteiner, J.G.; Bergouignan, A. Is Being Physically Active Enough to Be Metabolically Healthy? The Key Role of Sedentary Behavior. *Diabetes Care* **2021**, *44*, 17–19. [CrossRef]
11. Nakanishi, S.; Hirukawa, H.; Shimoda, M.; Tatsumi, F.; Kohara, K.; Obata, A.; Okauchi, S.; Katakura, Y.; Sanada, J.; Fushimi, Y.; et al. Impact of physical activity and sedentary time on glycated hemoglobin levels and body composition: Cross-sectional study using outpatient clinical data of Japanese patients with type 2 diabetes. *J. Diabetes Investig.* **2020**, *11*, 633–639. [CrossRef]
12. Ruoti, R.G.; Troup, J.T.; Berger, R.A. The effects of nonswimming water exercises on older adults. *J. Orthop. Sports Phys. Ther.* **1994**, *19*, 140–145. [CrossRef] [PubMed]
13. Bocalini, D.S.; Serra, A.J.; Murad, N.; Levy, R.F. Water-versus land-based exercise effects on physical fitness in older women. *Geriatr. Gerontol. Int.* **2008**, *8*, 265–271. [CrossRef] [PubMed]
14. Dong, R.; Wu, Y.; Xu, S.; Zhang, L.; Ying, J.; Jin, H.; Wang, P.; Xiao, L.; Tong, P. Is aquatic exercise more effective than land-based exercise for knee osteoarthritis? *Medicine* **2018**, *97*, e13823. [CrossRef] [PubMed]
15. Bonifazi, M. *Federazione Italiana Nuoto. Il Fitness in Acqua*; Multimedia Sport Service: Milano, Italy, 2005.
16. Raimondi, P.; Vincenzini, O. *Teoria, Metodologia e Didattica del Movimento*; Margiacchi Galeno Editrice: Perugia, Italy, 2003.
17. Bartels, E.M.; Lund, H.; Hagen, K.B.; Dagfinrud, H.; Christensen, R.; Danneskiold-Samsøe, B. Aquatic exercise for the treatment of knee and hip osteoarthritis. *Cochrane Database Syst. Rev.* **2007**, *4*, CD005523. [CrossRef]
18. Becker, B.E. Aquatic Therapy: Scientific Foundations and Clinical Rehabilitation Applications. *Pm&R* **2009**, *1*, 859–872. [CrossRef]
19. Kim, I.S.; Chung, S.H.; Park, Y.J.; Kang, H.Y. The effectiveness of an aquarobic exercise program for patients with osteoarthritis. *Appl. Nurs. Res.* **2012**, *25*, 181–189. [CrossRef]
20. Scheer, A.S.; Naylor, L.H.; Gan, S.K.; Charlesworth, J.; Benjanuvatra, N.; Green, D.J.; Maiorana, A.J. The Effects of Water-based Exercise Training in People with Type 2 Diabetes. *Med. Sci. Sports Exerc.* **2020**, *52*, 417–424. [CrossRef]
21. van den Ende, C.H.; Breedveld, F.C.; le Cessie, S.; Dijkmans, B.A.; de Mug, A.W.; Hazes, J.M. Effect of intensive exercise on patients with active rheumatoid arthritis: A randomised clinical trial. *Ann. Rheum. Dis.* **2000**, *59*, 615–621. [CrossRef]
22. De Feo, P.; Fatone, C.; Burani, P.; Piana, N.; Pazzagli, C.; Battistini, D.; Capezzali, D.; Pippi, R.; Chipi, B.; Mazzeschi, C. An innovative model for changing the lifestyles of persons with obesity and/or Type 2 diabetes mellitus. *J. Endocrinol. Investig.* **2011**, *34*, e349–e354.
23. Ma, W.Y.; Yang, C.Y.; Shih, S.R.; Hsieh, H.J.; Hung, C.S.; Chiu, F.C.; Lin, M.S.; Liu, P.H.; Hua, C.H.; Hsein, Y.C.; et al. Measurement of Waist Circumference: Midabdominal or iliac crest? *Diabetes Care* **2013**, *36*, 1660–1666. [CrossRef]
24. Tanaka, H. Swimming Exercise. *Sports Med.* **2009**, *39*, 377–387. [CrossRef] [PubMed]
25. Gwinup, G. Weight loss without dietary restriction: Efficacy of different forms of aerobic exercise. *Am. J. Sports Med.* **1987**, *15*, 275–279. [CrossRef] [PubMed]
26. Kasch, F.W. Physiological changes with swimming and running during two years of training. *Scand. J. Sports Sci.* **1981**, *3*, 23–26.
27. Rezaeipour, M. Effects of two water-based exercise programs on body weight and blood lipid parameters in elderly obese males with a sedentary lifestyle. *Diabetes Metab. Syndr.* **2021**, *15*, 102194. [CrossRef]
28. Rezaeipour, M. Investigation of Pool Workouts on Weight, Body Composition, Resting Energy Expenditure, and Quality of Life among Sedentary Obese Older Women. *Montenegrin J. Sports Sci. Med.* **2020**, *9*, 67–72. [CrossRef]
29. Gubiani, G.L.; Pires Neto, C.S.; Petroski, É.L.; Lopes, A.d.S. Efeitos da hidroginástica sobre indicadores antropométricos de mulheres entre 60 e 80 anos de idade. *Rev. Bras. Cineantropometria Desempenho Hum.* **2001**, *3*, 34–41. Available online: https://periodicos.ufsc.br/index.php/rbcdh/article/view/3982/16864 (accessed on 8 October 2022).
30. Littman, A.J.; Kristal, A.R.; White, E. Effects of physical activity intensity, frequency, and activity type on 10-y weight change in middle-aged men and women. *Int. J. Obes.* **2005**, *29*, 524–533. [CrossRef] [PubMed]
31. Penaforte, F.; Calhau, R.; Mota, G.R.; Chiarello, P.G. Impact of short-term water exercise programs on weight, body composition, metabolic profile and quality of life of obese women. *J. Hum. Sport Exerc.* **2015**, *10*, 915–926. [CrossRef]
32. Charmas, M.; Gromisz, W. Effect of 12-week swimming training on body composition in young women. *Int. J. Environ. Res. Public Health* **2019**, *16*, 346. [CrossRef]
33. Rezaeipour, M.; Apanasenko, G. Effects of Waterobics Programs on Body Mass, Body Composition, and Coronary Risk Profile of Sedentary Obese Middle-aged Women. *Women's Health Bull.* **2019**, *6*, 13–17. [CrossRef]

34. Russo, A.; Pirisinu, I.; Vacca, C.; Reginato, E.; Tomaro, E.S.; Pippi, R.; Aiello, C.; Talesa, V.N.; De Feo, P.; Romani, R. An intensive lifestyle intervention reduces circulating oxidised low-density lipoprotein and increases human paraoxonase activity in obese subjects. *Obes. Res. Clin. Pract.* **2018**, *12*, 108–114. [CrossRef] [PubMed]
35. Marini, E.; Mariani, P.G.; Ministrini, S.; Pippi, R.; Aiello, C.; Reginato, E.; Siepi, D.; Innocente, S.; Lombardini, R.; Paltriccia, R.; et al. Combined aerobic and resistance training improves microcirculation in metabolic syndrome. *J. Sports Med. Phys. Fit.* **2019**, *59*, 1571–1576. [CrossRef] [PubMed]
36. Igarashi, Y.; Nogami, Y. Response of Lipids and Lipoproteins to Regular Aquatic Endurance Exercise: A Meta-Analysis of Randomized Controlled Trials. *J. Atheroscler. Thromb.* **2019**, *26*, 14–30. [CrossRef] [PubMed]
37. Igarashi, Y.; Nogami, Y. The effect of regular aquatic exercise on blood pressure: A meta-analysis of randomized controlled trials. *Eur. J. Prev. Cardiol.* **2018**, *25*, 190–199. [CrossRef] [PubMed]
38. Delevatti, R.S.; Kanitz, A.C.; Alberton, C.L.; Marson, E.C.; Lisboa, S.C.; Pinho, C.D.; Lovatel, G.A.; Korb, A.; Bertoldi, K.; Macedo, R.C.; et al. Glucose control can be similarly improved after aquatic or dry-land aerobic training in patients with type 2 diabetes: A randomized clinical trial. *J. Sci. Med. Sport* **2016**, *19*, 688–693. [CrossRef]
39. Pippi, R.; Bini, V.; Reginato, E.; Aiello, C.; Fanelli, C. Are three months multidisciplinary lifestyle intervention enough to get benefits on blood pressure in overweight/obese adults? *Phys. Act. Rev.* **2021**, *9*, 40–53. [CrossRef]
40. Zhu, Z.; Yan, W.; Yu, Q.; Wu, P.; Bigambo, F.M.; Chen, J. Association between Exercise and Blood Pressure in Hypertensive Residents: A Meta-Analysis. *Evid. Based Complement. Altern. Med.* **2022**, *2022*, 2453805. [CrossRef]
41. Bergamin, M.; Zanuso, S.; Alvar, B.A.; Ermolao, A.; Zaccaria, M. Is water-based exercise training sufficient to improve physical fitness in the elderly? *Eur. Rev. Aging Phys. Act.* **2012**, *9*, 129–141. [CrossRef]
42. Nelson, M.E.; Rejeski, W.J.; Blair, S.N.; Duncan, P.W.; Judge, J.O.; King, A.C.; Macera, C.A.; Castaneda-Sceppa, C. Physical activity and public health in older adults: Recommendation from the American College of Sports Medicine and the American Heart Association. *Circulation* **2007**, *116*, 1094–1105. [CrossRef]

nutrients

MDPI

Article

Physical Activity, Dietary Behavior, and Body Weight Changes during the COVID-19 Nationwide Level 3 Alert in Taiwan: Results of a Taiwanese Online Survey

Hao-Ting Ke [1], Chi-Lin Hsieh [2] and Wei-Jen Cheng [1,3,4,*]

1 Center for Traditional Chinese Medicine, Chang Gung Memorial Hospital, Taoyuan 333, Taiwan
2 Department of Internal Medicine, Chang Gung Memorial Hospital, Taoyuan 333, Taiwan
3 Graduate Institute of Clinical Medical Sciences, College of Medicine, Chang Gung University, Taoyuan 333, Taiwan
4 School of Traditional Chinese Medicine, Chang Gung University, Taoyuan 333, Taiwan
* Correspondence: misterarren@gmail.com; Tel.: +886-3-3196200 (ext. 2625)

Abstract: This cross-sectional study aimed to explore the influence of the COVID-19 pandemic on physical activity (PA) and dietary habits, and their impact on body weight changes during the Level 3 alert period that resulted in the lockdown in Taiwan. The study was conducted between 1 July 2021 and 15 July 2021, using a Google Forms online survey platform. Personal data, anthropometric information, PA information, and dietary habit information were collected before and during the alert period. Exactly 374 respondents, aged between 20 and 66, were included in the study. The results indicate that the lockdown during the alert period negatively impacted all levels of PA, including vigorous and moderate activities and walking. Additionally, respondents showed a sedentary lifestyle, with an increased daily sitting time of 22%. However, body weight and dietary behavior were not significantly affected, and some dietary questions achieved significant differences, including eating three meals less regularly, among others. During the pandemic, exercise was still one of the most important ways to maintain health; therefore, we hope to bring more attention to the prevention of sedentary lifestyles and dietary abnormalities in Taiwan during a pandemic.

Keywords: COVID-19; physical activity; eating habits; lifestyle; bodyweight

Citation: Ke, H.-T.; Hsieh, C.-L.; Cheng, W.-J. Physical Activity, Dietary Behavior, and Body Weight Changes during the COVID-19 Nationwide Level 3 Alert in Taiwan: Results of a Taiwanese Online Survey. *Nutrients* **2022**, *14*, 4941. https://doi.org/10.3390/nu14224941

Academic Editors: Roberto Pippi, Carmine G. Fanelli and Matteo Vandoni

Received: 20 October 2022
Accepted: 18 November 2022
Published: 21 November 2022

1. Introduction

Coronavirus disease 2019, or COVID-19, is a novel coronavirus caused by severe acute respiratory syndrome coronavirus 2 (SARS-CoV-2) [1,2]. Since the first case reported in Wuhan, China, in December 2019, COVID-19 has affected more than 60 countries worldwide, with over 6000 cases and 106 deaths, only two months after the outbreak [3]. Despite its proximity to and its dense economic activities with China, Taiwan took rapid responses and quickly instituted specific approaches for a containment strategy and resource allocation to control the outbreak [4–6]. Thus, there were only 443 cases and seven deaths as of 7 June 2020. However, on 19 May 2021, due to the surge in the number of indigenous cases and the increasing number of deaths, Taiwan's Central Epidemic Command Center (CECC) raised the COVID-19 alert to Level 3 nationwide. The control measures of Level 3 alerts include mandatory wearing of masks in public; closing entertainment venues; banning physical activities in open spaces, gyms, and sports centers; and food vendors offering only takeout services [7]. While these restrictions helped to reduce the rate of infection, such limitations have led to numerous behavioral changes, such as social distancing and prolonged homestay, which caused negative effects by reducing physical activity (PA) and restricting access to many forms of exercise (e.g., closed civil sports centers and gyms, restrictions on walking distance, and insufficient space for exercise at home) [8–10]. Exercise is one of the most important risk factors for major disease morbidity. Multiple studies in humans and animals have demonstrated that regular exercise is positively linked to immune function [11]. Additionally, the benefits of exercise may reduce the COVID-19 fatality rate due to its positive effect on COVID-19-related comorbidities (e.g., cardiovascular disease, hypertension, type-2 diabetes, and obesity) [12].

In addition to limiting access to PA, banning indoor dining and limiting the number of people in supermarkets and grocery stores may change eating habits because it is less easy to obtain food than usual. Additionally, limited access to fresh food can have a negative effect on overall health both physically and mentally [13]. Combined with a structural barrier to maintaining a physically active lifestyle during the lockdown period, impaired nutritional habits could produce a state of positive energy balance, in which caloric intake exceeds energy expenditure, which can cause weight gain due to increased body fat [10]. Therefore, this study aimed to investigate the effect of the COVID-19 pandemic on physical activity and dietary behavior, and to further understand the relationship between physical activity, dietary behavior, and changes in body weight during the COVID-19 nationwide Level 3 alert period in Taiwan.

2. Materials and Methods

2.1. Study Design

This cross-sectional study investigated the changes in physical activity and dietary habits, and their impact on body weight during the COVID-19 pandemic in Taiwan.

2.2. Participants

Participants were recruited through social media platforms, including Facebook™ (Meta Platforms Inc., Menlo Park, CA, USA), WhatsApp™ (Meta Platforms Inc.), Instagram™ (Meta Platforms Inc.), and Line™ Corporation, Tokyo, Japan). We included people older than 20 years who were living in Taiwan during the nationwide Level 3 COVID-19 alert period. All participants were fully informed about the study requirements, and that the results could be used for research purposes. Each participant could answer only once. They could withdraw their participation in the survey at any point before submission, and incomplete responses could not be saved. To maintain and protect the confidentiality of participants, their personal information and data were anonymized.

2.3. Survey Development and Privacy

The questionnaire was administered during the nationwide Level 3 COVID-19 alert period in Taiwan, using the Google Forms® online survey platform. A link to the survey was shared on social media (Facebook™, WhatsApp™, Instagram™, and Line™). Participants completed the questionnaire directly connected to the Google platform, and the final database was downloaded as a Microsoft Excel spreadsheet.

This study was approved by the Institutional Review Board (IRB) of the Chang Gung Medical Foundation. As participation was voluntary and survey responses were anonymous, the IRB waived the need for informed consent.

2.4. Survey Questionnaires

The questionnaire included three sections with 46 questions: (1) personal data (including gender, age, level of education, marital status, and employment status) and anthropometric information (including height and weight); (2) physical activity information, using the Taiwanese version of the International Physical Activity Questionnaire Short Form (IPAQ-SF) [14]; and (3) dietary habit information, using the Diet Behavior Questionnaire from Health Promotion Administration, Ministry of Health and Welfare, Taiwan (HPA-MOHW) [15]. This was a self-report survey that asked participants to recall information regarding body weight, physical activity, and dietary habits before the Level 3 alert was launched (19 May 2021) and over the past 7 days. No actual measurements were taken. The entire questionnaire was completely anonymous and the respondents provided replies for both timeframes in one survey.

2.4.1. Sociodemographic Characteristics

Information on age, sex, level of education, marital status, employment status, height, and weight before and during the Level 3 alert was collected.

2.4.2. Physical Activity Levels

Changes in physical activity levels due to Level 3 alerts were identified using the Taiwanese version of the IPAQ-SF. The CVI of the IPAQ-Taiwan version was higher than 0.9, indicating good content validity. The retest reliability was 0.67 and the concurrent validity was 0.63, which was similar to other language versions, and it can be used as a tool to compare the physical activity levels of people around the world [16]. According to the official IPAQ-SF guidelines, data from the IPAQ-SF were summed within each category, including vigorous activity (V), moderate activity (M), and walking (W), to estimate the total amount of time engaged in PA per week [17,18]. Moderate activities are defined as walking with more than five kilograms of weight on one's back (carrying children or heavy items), more laborious household tasks, tai chi, etc. Vigorous activities refer to weight training, hiking, long-distance running, playing ball, aerobic dance or riding a spinning bike, etc. The questionnaire referred to the PA of the last 7 days, and each activity had to take at least 10 min to be included. The respondents' total weekly PA was estimated in metabolic equivalents of tasks performed in minutes per week (MET-min/week). This was calculated by multiplying three parameters: the MET value of an activity, the duration of the activity (in minutes), and the number of times the activity was carried out (V = 8 METs, M = 4 METs, W = 3.3 METs). We then added the MET minutes achieved in each category to obtain the total MET minutes of PA per week. The time spent sitting was also recorded in the questionnaire in order to assess sedentary behavior.

2.4.3. Dietary Habits Information

The impact of Level 3 alerts on dietary habits was assessed using the Diet Behavior Questionnaire from the HPA-MOHW. This is an online survey sourced from "Overcoming Obesity: A Weight Loss Guide" published by the National Health Service, Ministry of Health and Welfare in 1997 [15]. The questionnaire had 12 questions, namely "Q1. Eating three meals regularly", "Q2. No snacks or sweets", "Q3. Eat slowly and chew carefully", "Q4. No sugary drinks", "Q5. Avoid high-fat foods", "Q6. Eat fruits every day", "Q7. Eat green vegetables every day", "Q8. Eat late-night snacks", "Q9. Eat while watching TV or reading books", "Q10. Emotional eating behavior", "Q11. Eat as a reward", and "Q12. Eat only when hungry".

The response choices and the designated scores for the first seven questions were as follows: "Always" = 3; "Most of the time" = 2; "Sometimes" = 1; "Never" = 0. The response choices and the designated scores for the eighth to twelfth questions were as follows: "Always" = 0; "Most of the time" = 1; "Sometimes" = 2; "Never" = 3. The total score of this questionnaire corresponded to the sum of the scores in the 12 questions ranging from 0 to 36, where "0~12" represents very unhealthy dietary behavior, "13~20" represents fine dietary behavior, "21~30" represents good dietary behavior, and "31~36" represents very healthy dietary behavior.

2.5. Data Analysis

Descriptive statistics were used to determine the demographic and personal characteristics and anthropometric parameters of the study sample. Data are represented as numbers and percentages (n (%)) for categorical variables or as mean and standard deviation (M $\pm$ SD) for continuous variables. To calculate the significant differences in responses before and during the Level 3 alert period, paired-sample t-tests were used.

To determine the magnitude of the change in the score, Cohen's d_s was calculated as the effect size for the comparison between two means. This was interpreted as 0.2 to be considered a "small" effect size, 0.5 for a "medium" effect size, and 0.8 for a "large" effect size. All of the statistical analyses were performed using GraphPad Prism 9.4.1 and Microsoft Excel 2019. The significance level was set at $p < 0.05$.

3. Results

3.1. General Characteristics of the Participants

The nationwide Level 3 COVID-19 alert in Taiwan began on 19 May 2021, and lasted until 27 July 2021. The web survey was launched on 1 July 2021, and was concluded on 15 July 2021. In total, the data of 374 respondents (243 female and 131 male participants) aged between 20 and 66 years were analyzed, with four of the original 378 respondents excluded due to missing data.

Overall, 65.0% of the participants were female. The general characteristics, including education level, marital status, and employment status, are presented in Table 1.

Table 1. Participant characteristics.

		n	%
Gender			
	Male	131	35.0%
	Female	243	65.0%
Age (years)	20–29	175	46.8%
	30–39	56	15.0%
	40–49	72	19.3%
	50–59	55	14.7%
	60–69	16	4.3%
Level of education			
	Graduate school or above	83	22.2%
	University	266	71.1%
	Senior/vocational high school	23	6.1%
	Junior high school or below	2	0.5%
Marital status			
	Single	171	45.7%
	Married/partnership	195	52.1%
	Divorced/widowed	8	2.1%
Employment status			
	Employed	244	65.2%
	Self-employed	27	7.2%
	Unemployed	27	7.2%
	Student	58	15.5%
	Retired	17	4.5%
	Unable to work	1	0.3%

3.2. Anthropometrics Information before and during the Level 3 Alert Period

Table 2 presents the changes in body weight. The results indicated no significant differences in body weight before and during the Level 3 alert period.

Table 2. Body weight changes before and during the Level 3 alert period.

	Before Level 3 Alert	During Level 3 Alert	*n*	Difference (%)	Student *t*	
					T	*p*
Female	58.04 ± 11.10	58.15 ± 11.13	243	0.12 (0.2%)	0.9794	0.3284
Male	73.95 ± 11.41	73.89 ± 11.26	131	−0.06 (−0.08%)	0.2504	0.8027

3.3. *Physical Activity Level Changes during the Level 3 Alert Period*

The responses to the physical activity questionnaire recorded before and during the Level 3 alerts are shown in Table 3. There was a significant decrease in all of the physical activity levels. The effect of the COVID-19 Level 3 alert on different gender and age groups for all of the PA MET values are shown in Tables 4 and 5. All gender and age groups, except for 60–69 years, showed significant differences.

Table 3. Effect of the COVID-19 Level 3 alert on the physical activity level.

		Before Level 3 Alert (n = 374)	During Level 3 Alert (n = 374)	Difference (%)	Student t: t	Student t: p	Cohen's d_s
Vigorous activity (V)	times/week	1.63 ± 1.54	1.01 ± 1.52	−0.62 (−38.0%)	8.23	<0.001	0.409
	mins/time	37.66 ± 36.47	19.33 ± 29.25	−18.33 (−48.7%)	10.47	<0.001	0.555
	MET values	780.32 ± 1008.97	410.05 ± 744.12	−370.3 (−47.5%)	8.05	<0.001	0.418
Moderate activity (M)	times/week	1.59 ± 1.53	1.30 ± 1.47	−0.28 (−17.6%)	3.92	<0.001	0.187
	mins/time	30.28 ± 31.15	22.38 ± 26.19	−7.90 (−26.1%)	5.07	<0.001	0.275
	MET values	290.21 ± 401.87	211.60 ± 339.71	−78.61 (−27.0%)	4.67	<0.001	0.212
Walking (W)	times/week	3.32 ± 1.80	2.02 ± 1.85	−1.30 (−39.2%)	14.18	<0.001	0.713
	mins/time	40.99 ± 37.64	25.83 ± 32.48	−15.16 (−37.0%)	8.71	<0.001	0.432
	MET values	555.49 ± 624.22	286.94 ± 498.24	−268.5 (−48.3%)	9.59	<0.001	0.476
All physical activities	MET values	1626.02 ± 1527.25	908.60 ± 1198.23	−717.4 (−44.1%)	10.80	<0.001	0.523
Sitting	hours/day	5.8 ± 3.0	7.1 ± 3.5	1.29 (22.2%)	6.82	<0.001	−0.399

Table 4. Effects of COVID-19 Level 3 alert on gender for all of the PA MET values.

All PA MET Values						
Gender	Before Level 3 Alert	During Level 3 Alert	Difference (%)	Student t: t	Student t: p	Cohen's d_s
Female (n = 243)	1313.12 ± 1237.23	756.95 ± 953.36	−556.2 (−42.4%)	7.71	<0.001	0.505
Male (n = 131)	2206.43 ± 1822.22	1189.90 ± 1518.16	−1017.0 (−46.1%)	7.78	<0.001	0.606

Table 5. Effects of the COVID-19 Level 3 alert on different age groups for all of the PA MET values.

All PA MET Values						
Age	Before Level 3 Alert	During Level 3 Alert	Difference (%)	Student t: t	Student t: p	Cohen's d_s
20–29 y (n = 175)	1876.02 ± 1719.73	967.84 ± 1241.66	−908.2 (−48.4%)	8.41	<0.001	0.605
30–39 y (n = 56)	1297.47 ± 1197.62	820.31 ± 1316.14	−477.2 (−36.8%)	2.84	0.0062	0.380
40–49 y (n = 72)	1314.69 ± 1120.53	733.63 ± 1055.70	−581.1 (−44.2%)	5.02	<0.001	0.536
50–59 y (n = 55)	1550.75 ± 1652.85	923.48 ± 1167.27	−627.3 (−40.4%)	3.76	<0.001	0.441
60–69 y (n = 16)	1680.47 ± 1047.75	1291.78 ± 975.70	−388.7 (−20.1%)	1.99	0.0642	0.397

The number of times/week of vigorous activity decreased by 38.0% during the Level 3 alert, compared with before ($p < 0.001$, $d = 0.409$) and the number of minutes/time decreased by 48.7% ($p < 0.001$, $d = 0.555$). In addition, the MET values of vigorous activity were 47.5% lower during the Level 3 alert period compared with before ($p < 0.001$, $d = 0.418$). As for moderate activity, the number of times/week and minutes/time decreased by 17.6% ($p < 0.001$, $d = 0.187$) and 26.1% ($p < 0.001$, $d = 0.275$), respectively, compared with before. In addition, the MET values of the moderate activity were 27.0% lower during the Level 3 alerts ($p < 0.001$, $d = 0.212$). As for walking, the number of times/week and minutes/time during the Level 3 alerts, compared with before, decreased by 39.2% ($p < 0.001$, $d = 0.713$) and 37% ($p < 0.001$, $d = 0.432$), respectively. Additionally, the MET values of walking were 48.3% lower during the Level 3 alerts ($p < 0.001$, $d = 0.476$). Overall, the MET values of all PA were 44.1% lower during the Level 3 alerts ($p < 0.001$, $d = 0.523$). In terms of the effects of the COVID-19 Level 3 alert on different gender and age groups, male participants and those aged 20–29 years were impacted the most, as their PA MET values were 46.1% ($p < 0.001$, $d = 0.606$) and 48.4% ($p < 0.001$, $d = 0.605$) lower during the Level 3 alerts, respectively. Regarding the hours of sitting per day, the results increased by 22.2% during the Level 3 alert period ($p < 0.001$, d = -0.399).

3.4. Dietary Behavior Changes during the Level 3 Alert Period

3.4.1. Total Score of Diet Behavior Questionnaire

With regard to the dietary behavior status, no significant difference was observed between the total scores of the dietary behavior results during the Level 3 alert compared to before (Table 6). The subgroups of the dietary behavior status before and during the Level 3 alert period are presented in Table 7.

Table 6. Participants' total scores of dietary behavior before and during the Level 3 alert period.

	Total Scores	Difference (%)	Student *t*	
			t	*p*
Before Level 3 alert	20.94 ± 5.42	−0.02 (0.1%)	0.657	0.5
During Level 3 alert	20.92 ± 5.76			

Table 7. Subgroups of dietary behavior status before and during the Level 3 alert period.

Total Scores (Dietary Behavior Status)	Before Level 3 Alert	During Level 3 Alert
0~12 (Very unhealthy)	23	31
13~20 (Fine)	147	152
21~30 (Good)	190	170
31~36 (Very healthy)	14	21

"0~12" represents a very unhealthy dietary behavior, "13~20" represents a fine dietary behavior, "21~30" represents a good dietary behavior, and "31~36" represents a very healthy dietary behavior.

3.4.2. Score of Each Dietary Question

The recorded scores in each response to the dietary behavior questionnaire before and during the alert period are shown in Figure 1. The Q1 score (eat three meals regularly) decreased significantly during the period ($t = 2.528$, $p = 0.0119$, $d = 0.17$). The Q2 score (no snacks or sweets) increased significantly during the period ($t = 3.054$, $p = 0.0024$, $d = -0.19$), and the Q11 score (eat as reward) was significantly higher during the period ($t = 2.192$, $p = 0.0290$, $d = -0.14$). As for the remaining questions, no significant difference was found before and during the alert period.

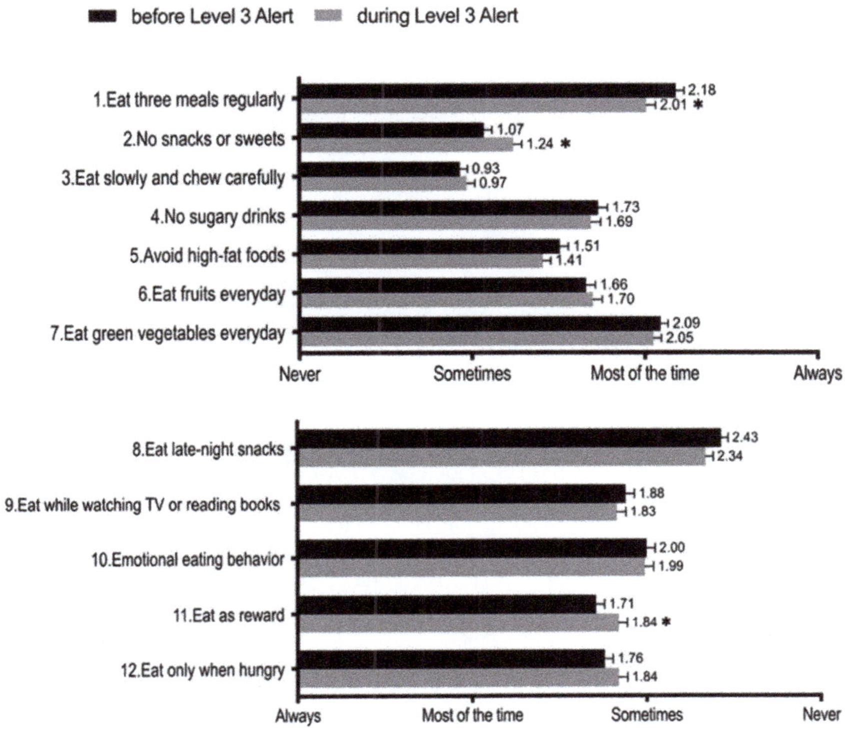

Figure 1. Participants' scores in response to the related diet behavior questions. * Significant differences between "before" and "during" the COVID-19 Level 3 alert period.

4. Discussion

Different studies and surveys that have been conducted worldwide suggest that the COVID-19 lockdown affected the population's daily lifestyle [19–23]. This cross-sectional study provides information regarding the impact of the COVID-19 lockdown on body weight, physical activity, and dietary behavior changes among Taiwanese residents during the Level 3 alert period. There were 374 replies, and the female respondents were about twice the number of males; 81.1% of the respondents were 20–49 years; 93.3% of the respondents were educated to college degree or above. According to a report on the age structure of the Taiwanese population in 2020 [24], the percentage of the population aged 20–49 years was about 52.5%. Statistics from Taiwan's Ministry of the Interior, Department of Statistics showed that 47.3% of citizens aged over 15 years had a college degree or above by the end of 2020 [25]. Those aged 25–29 years had the highest percentage (81.42%) of people with a college degree or above, and 63.90% had a college degree. Our demographic data did show some bias toward younger populations and higher education levels. A review study comparing Facebook™ recruitment of participants with traditional recruitment methods showed an over representation of females, young adults, and people with higher education levels and incomes [26], which was similar to our survey population.

The findings from the online survey confirmed that the COVID-19 Level 3 alert negatively affected all levels of PA, including vigorous and moderate activity, and walking, as was initially expected. Furthermore, we found that respondents had a sedentary lifestyle with an increased daily sitting time of 22%. While the effect size for most values was small to medium, a 39.2% reduction in the number of times per week on walking, a 48.7% reduction in the number of minutes per week on vigorous activity, and a 44.1% reduction in MET minutes per week on overall PA were medium to large. This result is consistent with recent studies, indicating that COVID-19 home confinement could greatly impact activities in life, including participation in sports activities and PA engagement [19]. We also saw a 46.1% reduction and 48.4% reduction in MET values on overall PA in the male group and the group aged 20–29 years, respectively, showing that these groups were impacted the most. This result is consistent with a study from Bangladesh [27], which showed that the prevalence of physical inactivity during the COVID-19 pandemic was significantly higher among young adults compared with other groups. A possible explanation could be the closure of schools, which led to a lack of physical education courses, meaning that young adults were more prone to spend more time on the internet and electronic devices, leading to a decrease in all levels of PA. In terms of gender, it is traditionally believed that females tend to have more household chores compared with males. More time spent at home during the Level 3 alert could have led to more housework, which could be one possible reason why females showed less of a decrease in overall PA MET values than males. Yet, our results are inconsistent with those of previous studies conducted in Taiwan on investigating exercise behavior during the COVID-19 pandemic. In this study, the results showed that most Taiwanese maintained their exercise frequency, duration, or intensity during the COVID-19 pandemic, with only 20% of individuals decreasing their exercise frequency [28]. However, it is worth noting that the study was conducted from 7 April to 13 May 2020, and the COVID-19 Level 3 alert in Taiwan was not launched at that time. Although Taiwan did not have a large-scale lockdown compared with other parts of the world, Level 3 alert restrictions, such as shutting most business and public places, banning group gatherings and physical activities in open spaces, gyms, and sports centers, may still have created a barrier to maintaining exercise behavior among Taiwanese individuals [7]. While public life restrictions associated with the pandemic were usually of a limited duration, some studies have shown that even a short-term increase in physical inactivity and sedentary behavior can have significant adverse effects [29]. For example, 14 days of step reduction can lead to insulin resistance as well as increased central and liver fat and dyslipidemia, while reducing cardiorespiratory fitness [30]. In another study, 5 days of bed rest was seen to lead to a significant decrease in endothelial function, increased arterial stiffness, and elevated diastolic blood pressure [31]. Although most of these changes are reversible by a resumption of habitual physical activity in younger individuals, this is less true for the elderly and for individuals with metabolic disease [32]. Therefore, identifying ways to maintain or even enhance PA during the confinement periods seems to be of the utmost importance.

Before the COVID-19 pandemic, insufficient physical activity had already been recognized as a public health problem globally. Out of 168 countries, 27.5% of adults do not achieve the levels of physical activity necessary for good health [33]. Home confinement created a structural barrier to maintaining a physically active lifestyle; with a drastic drop in PA and exercise levels, while dietary behaviors remain unchanged or fail to counteract this inactivity lifestyle, leading to a positive energy balance that will gradually cause weight gain [10,34]. However, no significant changes in body weight were observed in our study, inconsistent with a previous study showing an increase in self-reported body weight among obese patients. Even when adjusted for physical activity, age, and gender, the habit of taking snacks remained a risk factor [35]. Additionally, another study showed weight gain between 0.5 and 1.8 kg (±2.8 kg) after just 2 months of quarantine, and risk factors included increased eating in response to sight and smell, emotional eating, and increased snacking frequency [36,37]. Contrary to our expectations, there was no significant difference between the total scores of dietary behavior during and before the COVID-19 Level 3 alert period in our study. However, some dietary questions achieved a significant difference, including eating three meals less regularly, eating fewer snacks or sweets, and being less likely to eat as a reward. The negative changes in regular eating can be attributed to remote work from home and distance learning. When work and study activities were shifted to home, the lack of a clear routine of time and space caused a free work schedule, thus leading to irregular meals. Some good eating habits, including eating fewer snacks or sweets and being less likely to eat as a reward, were significantly increased during this period. A possible explanation for this could be the differences in living habits between Taiwan and Western countries. Owing to the popularity of the Internet, consumer electronics (cell phones, TVs, PCs, play devices, etc.), developed delivery services, and online shopping in Taiwan, it is easy to purchase food and daily necessities, thus reducing anxiety and stress from the shortage of supplies. In addition, Taiwanese people tend to believe that one should eat healthier before and after receiving COVID vaccines. A healthy diet prevents hyper-inflammation and might help to protect against inflammation from virus infections [38]. The concept of a health regimen based on traditional Chinese medicine is deeply rooted in the minds of the Taiwanese people, which could be a possible explanation for why they consumed fewer snacks during the COVID pandemic.

Our study had several limitations. First, the sample size was small and mostly comprised of females, aged 20–59 years, and individuals with a higher education levels, which may not be representative of the population. Second, the data were collected through a web-based survey, which might have limited the participation of certain groups (e.g., groups that do not have Internet access or who do not use the Internet often). However, the Internet use rate among Taiwanese people aged 12 years and above reached 83.0% in 2020 [39], suggesting high Internet usage by the Taiwanese. Moreover, the Internet use rate was over 90% among those aged below 55 years, 86.2% among those aged 55–59 years, and 72.8% among those aged 60–64 years, but only 42.7% among those aged 65 years and above, which could explain our respondents' age distribution. Third, because of the cross-sectional design of the study and the use of a self-report questionnaire, the existence of recall bias cannot be ruled out, which may have resulted in an over or underestimation of the results. However, the IPAQ is an international tool for the assessment of PA and time spent sitting, and is widely used because of its simplicity and inexpensiveness, and its validity and reliability have been proven in numerous studies [40–42]. Fourth, we asked participants to recall their body weight, physical activity, and dietary habits before the Level 3 alert was launched (19 May 2021); however, we did not clarify the length of the recall period, meaning that it could be any amount of time before the alert. Additionally, the body weight was self-reported, so the data might not be accurate. However, it is very common for patients in Taiwan to measure their blood pressure as well as height and weight before visiting a clinic or hospital, and it is also common to have a weight scale at home. Therefore, it should not be too difficult to measure one's body weight at home.

5. Conclusions

The results of this cross-sectional study indicate that the lockdown period during the COVID-19 Level 3 alert had a negative impact on all PA levels of Taiwanese adults, with a significant increase in sitting time, leading to a more sedentary lifestyle. However, body weight and dietary behavior were not significantly affected, probably because the changes in PA level could not be reflected in weight changes over such a short period. Furthermore, the body composition was not measured; therefore, we could not determine the relative variation in total fat and skeletal muscle mass proportion. In addition, eating three meals irregularly could be attributed to remote work from home and distance learning during the Level 3 alert period, which is a bad eating habit that can easily lead to obesity. Nevertheless, some good eating habits, including eating fewer snacks or sweets and being less likely to eat as a reward, were significantly increased during this period. This may also explain the lack of significant changes in body weight during the lockdown period.

During the pandemic, exercise is still one of the most important ways to effectively maintain health [2]. Government health organizations should be aware that reducing the possibility of performing PA during Level 3 alerts might have negative consequences on the health status of the population. According to the American College of Sports Medicine, 150–300 min of moderate-intensity aerobic exercise and two sessions of resistance exercise per week are recommended to maintain a healthy body [43]. Although adverse effects on short-term physical inactivity are reversible by habitual PA in younger individuals, this is less true for the elderly. Therefore, it is important to identify ways to enhance PA during confinement periods.

Author Contributions: Conceptualization, H.-T.K.; methodology, H.-T.K. and C.-L.H.; validation, H.-T.K., C.-L.H. and W.-J.C.; investigation, H.-T.K. and C.-L.H.; data curation, H.-T.K.; writing—original draft preparation, H.-T.K.; writing—review and editing, H.-T.K., C.-L.H. and W.-J.C.; visualization, H.-T.K.; supervision, H.-T.K., C.-L.H. and W.-J.C. All authors have read and agreed to the published version of the manuscript.

Funding: This research was supported by grants from the Chang Gung Memorial Hospital (CORPG5L0031, CORPG5K0031, CMRPG5K0151, and CMRPG5K0152), Taiwan. The funding agencies played no role in this research.

Institutional Review Board Statement: This study was approved by the Institutional Review Board (IRB) of the Chang Gung Medical Foundation (IRB No. 202201282B0).

Informed Consent Statement: As participation was voluntary and survey responses were anonymous, the IRB waived the need for informed consent.

Data Availability Statement: All of the experimental data are included in the figures and manuscript. The data presented in this study are available upon request from the corresponding author.

Conflicts of Interest: The authors declare no conflict of interest.

References

1. Del Rio, C.; Malani, P.N. COVID-19-New Insights on a Rapidly Changing Epidemic. *JAMA* **2020**, *323*, 1339–1340. [CrossRef] [PubMed]
2. Woods, J.A.; Hutchinson, N.T.; Powers, S.K.; Roberts, W.O.; Gomez-Cabrera, M.C.; Radak, Z.; Berkes, I.; Boros, A.; Boldogh, I.; Leeuwenburgh, C.; et al. The COVID-19 pandemic and physical activity. *Sports Med. Health Sci.* **2020**, *2*, 55–64. [CrossRef] [PubMed]
3. Coronavirus Disease 2019 (COVID-19) Situation Report-41. Available online: https://www.who.int/docs/default-source/coronaviruse/situation-reports/20200301-sitrep-41-covid-19.pdf (accessed on 1 March 2020).
4. Wang, C.J.; Ng, C.Y.; Brook, R.H. Response to COVID-19 in Taiwan: Big Data Analytics, New Technology, and Proactive Testing. *JAMA* **2020**, *323*, 1341–1342. [CrossRef] [PubMed]
5. Cheng, H.Y.; Li, S.Y.; Yang, C.H. Initial rapid and proactive response for the COVID-19 outbreak—Taiwan's experience. *J. Formos. Med. Assoc.* **2020**, *119*, 771–773. [CrossRef]
6. Lee, T.L. Legal preparedness as part of COVID-19 response: The first 100 days in Taiwan. *BMJ Glob. Health* **2020**, *5*, e002608. [CrossRef]
7. Chiu, W.-T.; Laporte, R.P.; Wu, J. Determinants of Taiwan's Early Containment of COVID-19 Incidence. *Am. J. Public Health* **2020**, *110*, 943–944. [CrossRef]
8. Chen, P.; Mao, L.; Nassis, G.P.; Harmer, P.; Ainsworth, B.E.; Li, F. Coronavirus disease (COVID-19): The need to maintain regular physical activity while taking precautions. *J. Sport Health Sci.* **2020**, *9*, 103–104. [CrossRef]
9. Hossain, M.M.; Sultana, A.; Purohit, N. Mental health outcomes of quarantine and isolation for infection prevention: A systematic umbrella review of the global evidence. *Epidemiol. Health* **2020**, *42*, e2020038. [CrossRef]
10. Martinez-Ferran, M.; de la Guia-Galipienso, F.; Sanchis-Gomar, F.; Pareja-Galeano, H. Metabolic Impacts of Confinement during the COVID-19 Pandemic Due to Modified Diet and Physical Activity Habits. *Nutrients* **2020**, *12*, 1549. [CrossRef]
11. Simpson, R.J.; Campbell, J.P.; Gleeson, M.; Krüger, K.; Nieman, D.C.; Pyne, D.B.; Turner, J.E.; Walsh, N.P. Can exercise affect immune function to increase susceptibility to infection? *Exerc. Immunol. Rev.* **2020**, *26*, 8–22.
12. Piercy, K.L.; Troiano, R.P.; Ballard, R.M.; Carlson, S.A.; Fulton, J.E.; Galuska, D.A.; George, S.M.; Olson, R.D. The Physical Activity Guidelines for Americans. *JAMA* **2018**, *320*, 2020–2028. [CrossRef] [PubMed]
13. Be Active during COVID-19. Available online: https://www.who.int/emergencies/diseases/novel-coronavirus-2019/question-and-answers-hub/q-a-detail/coronavirus-disease-covid-19-staying-active (accessed on 27 March 2020).
14. Taiwanese Version of the International Physical Activity Questionnaire 91 Short Form (IPAQ-SF). Available online: https://www.hpa.gov.tw/Pages/Detail.aspx?nodeid=876&pid=4900 (accessed on 1 March 2018).
15. Diet Behavior Questionnaire from Health Promotion Administration, Ministry of Health and Welfare, Taiwan (HPA-MOHW). Available online: https://health99.hpa.gov.tw/onlineQuiz/eatingBehavior (accessed on 1 September 2022).
16. Tu, W.-L. Development and Verification of Validity and Reliability of the International Physical Activity Questionnaire: Taiwan Show-Card Version. Master's Thesis, National Yang-Ming University, Taipei, Taiwan, 2010. [CrossRef]
17. Craig, C.L.; Marshall, A.L.; Sjöström, M.; Bauman, A.E.; Booth, M.L.; Ainsworth, B.E.; Pratt, M.; Ekelund, U.; Yngve, A.; Sallis, J.F.; et al. International physical activity questionnaire: 12-country reliability and validity. *Med. Sci. Sports Exerc.* **2003**, *35*, 1381–1395. [CrossRef] [PubMed]

18. Lee, P.H.; Macfarlane, D.J.; Lam, T.H.; Stewart, S.M. Validity of the International Physical Activity Questionnaire Short Form (IPAQ-SF): A systematic review. *Int. J. Behav. Nutr. Phys. Act.* **2011**, *8*, 115. [CrossRef] [PubMed]
19. Ammar, A.; Brach, M.; Trabelsi, K.; Chtourou, H.; Boukhris, O.; Masmoudi, L.; Bouaziz, B.; Bentlage, E.; How, D.; Ahmed, M.; et al. Effects of COVID-19 Home Confinement on Eating Behaviour and Physical Activity: Results of the ECLB-COVID19 International Online Survey. *Nutrients* **2020**, *12*, 1583. [CrossRef] [PubMed]
20. Martinez-de-Quel, O.; Suarez-Iglesias, D.; Lopez-Flores, M.; Perez, C.A. Physical activity, dietary habits and sleep quality before and during COVID-19 lockdown: A longitudinal study. *Appetite* **2021**, *158*, 105019. [CrossRef]
21. Di Renzo, L.; Gualtieri, P.; Cinelli, G.; Bigioni, G.; Soldati, L.; Attina, A.; Bianco, F.F.; Caparello, G.; Camodeca, V.; Carrano, E.; et al. Psychological Aspects and Eating Habits during COVID-19 Home Confinement: Results of EHLC-COVID-19 Italian Online Survey. *Nutrients* **2020**, *12*, 2152. [CrossRef]
22. Di Renzo, L.; Gualtieri, P.; Pivari, F.; Soldati, L.; Attina, A.; Cinelli, G.; Leggeri, C.; Caparello, G.; Barrea, L.; Scerbo, F.; et al. Eating habits and lifestyle changes during COVID-19 lockdown: An Italian survey. *J. Transl. Med.* **2020**, *18*, 229. [CrossRef]
23. Qin, F.; Song, Y.; Nassis, G.; Zhao, L.; Cui, S.; Lili, L.; Wu, Z.; Xu, M.; Qu, C.; Dong, Y.; et al. Prevalence of Insufficient Physical Activity, Sedentary Screen Time and Emotional Well-Being During the Early Days of the 2019 Novel Coronavirus (COVID-19) Outbreak in China: A National Cross-Sectional Study. *SSRN Electron. J.* **2020**, *17*, 5170. [CrossRef]
24. Age Structure of Taiwan Population on 2020. Available online: https://www.ris.gov.tw/app/portal/346 (accessed on 14 April 2021).
25. Survey on Education Level of Taiwan Population. Available online: https://ws.moi.gov.tw/Download.ashx?u=LzAwMS9VcGxvYWQvNDAwL3JlbGZpbGUvMC8xNDAxMS8yMjE5YjU1NS0wM2QwLTQ0NjMtYTRmZi0xZmIwMGQyN2U1MmYucGRm&n=MTEw5bm056ysMTbpgLHlhafmlL%2fntbHoqIjpgJrloLFf5pWZ6IKy56iL5bqmLnBkZg%3d%3d (accessed on 14 April 2021).
26. Whitaker, C.; Stevelink, S.; Fear, N. The Use of Facebook in Recruiting Participants for Health Research Purposes: A Systematic Review. *J. Med. Internet Res.* **2017**, *19*, e290. [CrossRef]
27. Rahman, M.E.; Islam, M.S.; Bishwas, M.S.; Moonajilin, M.S.; Gozal, D. Physical inactivity and sedentary behaviors in the Bangladeshi population during the COVID-19 pandemic: An online cross-sectional survey. *Heliyon* **2020**, *6*, e05392. [CrossRef]
28. Chang, Y.K.; Hung, C.L.; Timme, S.; Nosrat, S.; Chu, C.H. Exercise Behavior and Mood during the COVID-19 Pandemic in Taiwan: Lessons for the Future. *Int. J. Environ. Res. Public Health* **2020**, *17*, 7092. [CrossRef] [PubMed]
29. Wilke, J.; Rahlf, A.L.; Füzéki, E.; Groneberg, D.A.; Hespanhol, L.; Mai, P.; de Oliveira, G.M.; Robbin, J.; Tan, B.; Willwacher, S.; et al. Physical Activity During Lockdowns Associated with the COVID-19 Pandemic: A Systematic Review and Multilevel Meta-analysis of 173 Studies with 320,636 Participants. *Sports Med. Open.* **2022**, *8*, 125. [CrossRef] [PubMed]
30. Bowden Davies, K.A.; Sprung, V.S.; Norman, J.A.; Thompson, A.; Mitchell, K.L.; Halford, J.C.G.; Harrold, J.A.; Wilding, J.P.H.; Kemp, G.J.; Cuthbertson, D.J. Short-term decreased physical activity with increased sedentary behaviour causes metabolic derangements and altered body composition: Effects in individuals with and without a first-degree relative with type 2 diabetes. *Diabetologia* **2018**, *61*, 1282–1294. [CrossRef] [PubMed]
31. Nosova, E.V.; Yen, P.; Chong, K.C.; Alley, H.F.; Stock, E.O.; Quinn, A.; Hellmann, J.; Conte, M.S.; Owens, C.D.; Spite, M.; et al. Short-term physical inactivity impairs vascular function. *J. Surg. Res.* **2014**, *190*, 672–682. [CrossRef]
32. Bowden Davies, K.A.; Pickles, S.; Sprung, V.S.; Kemp, G.J.; Alam, U.; Moore, D.R.; Tahrani, A.A.; Cuthbertson, D.J. Reduced physical activity in young and older adults: Metabolic and musculoskeletal implications. *Ther. Adv. Endocrinol. Metab.* **2019**, *10*, 2042018819888824. [CrossRef]
33. Guthold, R.; Stevens, G.A.; Riley, L.M.; Bull, F.C. Worldwide trends in insufficient physical activity from 2001 to 2016: A pooled analysis of 358 population-based surveys with 1·9 million participants. *Lancet Glob. Health* **2018**, *6*, e1077–e1086. [CrossRef]
34. Heffernan, K.S.; Jae, S.Y. Exercise as medicine for COVID-19: An ACE in the hole? *Med. Hypotheses* **2020**, *142*, 109835. [CrossRef]
35. de Luis Román, D.A.; Izaola, O.; Primo Martín, D.; Gómez Hoyos, E.; Torres Torres, B.; López Gómez, J.J. Effect of lockdown for COVID-19 on self-reported body weight gain in a sample of obese patients. *Nutr. Hosp.* **2020**, *37*, 1232–1237. [CrossRef]
36. Zachary, Z.; Brianna, F.; Brianna, L.; Garrett, P.; Jade, W.; Alyssa, D.; Mikayla, K. Self-quarantine and weight gain related risk factors during the COVID-19 pandemic. *Obes. Res. Clin. Pract.* **2020**, *14*, 210–216. [CrossRef]
37. Zeigler, Z. COVID-19 Self-quarantine and Weight Gain Risk Factors in Adults. *Curr. Obes. Rep.* **2021**, *10*, 423–433. [CrossRef]
38. Mirzay-Razaz, J.; Hassanghomi, M.; Ajami, M.; Koochakpoor, G.; Hosseini-Esfahani, F.; Mirmiran, P. Effective food hygiene principles and dietary intakes to reinforce the immune system for prevention of COVID-19: A systematic review. *BMC Nutr.* **2022**, *8*, 53. [CrossRef] [PubMed]
39. Taiwan Network Information Center-2020 Taiwan Internet Report. Available online: https://www.twnic.tw/doc/twrp/202012d.pdf (accessed on 30 September 2020).
40. Rosenberg, D.E.; Bull, F.C.; Marshall, A.L.; Sallis, J.F.; Bauman, A.E. Assessment of sedentary behavior with the International Physical Activity Questionnaire. *J. Phys. Act. Health* **2008**, *5* (Suppl. 1), S30–S44. [CrossRef] [PubMed]
41. Meh, K.; Jurak, G.; Sorić, M.; Rocha, P.; Sember, V. Validity and Reliability of IPAQ-SF and GPAQ for Assessing Sedentary Behaviour in Adults in the European Union: A Systematic Review and Meta-Analysis. *Int. J. Environ. Res. Public Health* **2021**, *18*, 4602. [CrossRef] [PubMed]

42. Hagströmer, M.; Oja, P.; Sjöström, M. The International Physical Activity Questionnaire (IPAQ): A study of concurrent and construct validity. *Public Health Nutr.* **2006**, *9*, 755–762. [CrossRef]
43. Staying Active during the Coronavirus Pandemic. Available online: https://www.exerciseismedicine.org/assets/page_documents/EIM_Rx%20for%20Health_%20Staying%20Active%20During%20Coronavirus%20Pandemic.pdf (accessed on 18 November 2020).

nutrients

Article

Acute Responses to Resistance Training on Body Composition, Muscular Fitness and Flexibility by Sex and Age in Healthy War Veterans Aged 50–80 Years

Mario Kasović [1,2], Lovro Štefan [1,2,3,*] and Zvonimir Kalčik [4]

1 Department of General and Applied Kinesiology, Faculty of Kinesiology, University of Zagreb, 10 000 Zagreb, Croatia
2 Division of Sport Motorics and Methodology in Kinanthropology, Faculty of Sports Studies, Masaryk University, 625 00 Brno, Czech Republic
3 Recruitment and Examination (RECETOX), Faculty of Science, Masaryk University, 625 00 Brno, Czech Republic
4 Home of Croatian Veterans, 10 000 Zagreb, Croatia
* Correspondence: lovro.stefan1510@gmail.com

Abstract: Background: Although evidence suggests that resistance training should be prescribed as a method to enhance or maintain physical fitness, these findings are mostly based on research on younger men. Studies investigating responses by sex and age to resistance training, especially in war veterans aged ≥50 years, are lacking. Therefore, the main purpose of this study was to examine whether a 4-week resistance training program would have similar effects on body composition, muscular fitness, and flexibility in men and women aged 50–80 years. Methods: Seven-hundred and sixty-four participants were recruited and categorized into two groups each of men and women aged 50–64 and 65–80 years. The training intervention lasted 4 weeks and consisted of three 60 min sessions per week. All participants were tested for each of the following physical fitness components: body composition, push-ups in 30 s, chair-stands in 30 s, sit-ups in 30 s, and a sit-and-reach test. Results: Over the intervention period of 4 weeks, body weight (p = 0.002) and the percent of fat mass ($p < 0.001$) decreased, while the percent of lean mass ($p < 0.001$) in push-ups in 30 s ($p < 0.001$), chair-stands in 30 s ($p < 0.001$), sit-ups in 30 s ($p < 0.001$), and sit-and-reach ($p < 0.001$) increased. Significant time*age interactions were shown for push-ups in 30 s ($F_{1,763}$ = 4.348, p = 0.038) and chair-stands in 30 s ($F_{1,763}$ = 9.552, p = 0.002), where men and women aged 50–64 years exhibited larger time-induced changes compared to their older (65–80 yr) counterparts. Effect sizes were similar between sex- and age-specific groups. Conclusions: The 4-week resistance training produced similar pronounced positive effects on body composition, muscular fitness, and flexibility, while men and women aged 50–64 years displayed significantly larger improvements in upper and lower muscular fitness compared with their 65–80-year-old counterparts.

Keywords: aging; performance; sex differences; age differences; strength; intervention-induced changes

Citation: Kasović, M.; Štefan, L.; Kalčik, Z. Acute Responses to Resistance Training on Body Composition, Muscular Fitness and Flexibility by Sex and Age in Healthy War Veterans Aged 50–80 Years. *Nutrients* **2022**, *14*, 3436. https://doi.org/10.3390/nu14163436

Academic Editors: Roberto Pippi, Carmine G. Fanelli and Matteo Vandoni

Received: 17 July 2022
Accepted: 18 August 2022
Published: 21 August 2022

1. Background

The prevalence of middle-aged and older adults is expanding worldwide [1]. The process of aging predominantly leads to physiological decline, often accompanied by reductions in lean mass [2,3], power [4], and strength [5]. These declines have been associated with negative health-related outcomes, such as an increased risk of falls [6], hip fractures [7], functional limitations [8], and all-cause mortality [9,10].

Due to structural and physiological losses during aging, previous studies examined efficient methods to increase or even postpone such changes [11]. Studies have documented that resistance training serves as a safe intervention that can increase the level of physical fitness from young to old in both sexes [12–18]. Furthermore, several studies have shown that resistance training has multiple health-related benefits for overall health [19,20]. However, whether there are sex- and age-specific adaptations to the same training is still unknown [13,18,21].

When considering sex, studies have found that men can increase absolute strength more than women [22,23], although increases in relative strength and hypertension have been similar between the sexes [24,25]. Others have found that women have a greater relative strength increase than men [26–28]. The most recent systematic review and meta-analysis showed that men and women adapt to resistance training with similar effect sizes for hypertrophy and lower-body strength, yet women have a larger effect for relative upper-body strength, due to differences in the skeletal muscle level between the sexes [18]. However, well-designed studies with a larger sample size are relatively scare, and sex-related responses to resistance training need to be interpreted with caution.

Age-specific responses to resistance training have been the topic of a few previous studies [12,13,26,29]. Ivey et al. [26] found that young women experience a significantly greater muscle-quality response to resistance training than young men, older men, and older women. In the same study, all groups, except older women, retained resistance-training-induced increases in muscle quality for 31 weeks after the cessation of training [26]. Furthermore, another study demonstrated that young subjects exhibited greater increases in one-repetition maximum compared with the older subjects [12], while Kittilsen et al. [13] found that older adults improved their one-repetition maximum to the same extent as younger groups.

Findings regarding sex and age responses to resistance training are still inconsistent. Men and women of different age groups have different rates of fatiguability and neuromuscular performance, partially because of differences in anatomy and physiology [30]. Moreover, older individuals may require shorter rest intervals to recover from resistance training, explained by the increase in type I fibers and atrophy of type II fibers occurring with aging [31]. Although resistance training has been recommended for all age groups, its positive effects on neuromuscular impairments and the maintenance of functional performance are especially observed in individuals aged over 50 years [32,33]. By examining sex- and age-specific responses to resistance training, health-related professionals and trainers would be able to plan and program protocols consisting of different training modes, frequencies, and durations to achieve maximum efficiency.

Therefore, the main purpose of the study was to examine whether a 4-week resistance training program would have similar effects on body composition, muscular fitness, and flexibility in middle-aged (50–64 yr) and older (65–80 yr) men and women. We hypothesized that all sex and age groups would have different acute responses to resistance training.

2. Methods

2.1. Study Participants

Seven hundred and sixty-four middle-aged (range 50–64 yr, mean age ± SD 56.4 ± 5.3 yr) and older (range 65–80 yr, 69.3 ± 4.0) men and women volunteered to participate in this study. All participants went through a rehabilitation center program established by the Ministry of Croatian Veterans (N = 2500). The main goal of the center is to improve and enhance the care system and quality of life. The second goal is to reintegrate them into everyday activities, such as social gatherings or sports. The accommodation program usually includes the use of services for up to 30 days. Before entering the study, participants needed to meet the following inclusion criteria: 1) being without chronic diseases, 2) having no psychiatric symptoms or diagnoses, and 3) being without locomotor disabilities (being able to perform exercises with a full range of motion and without pain and discomfort), in order to perform exercises in the4-week intervention program. Of the 2500 participants whose activity was measured, 764 met the inclusion criteria. Such a sample size (N = 764) with a two-tailed test, p-value set at 0.05, and statistical power of 0.95 would be able to detect a minimum effect size of 0.13. Not all the participants engaged in physical activity in the past 12 months, so the inactive ones were categorized as being sedentary. Prior to the intervention protocol, all participants gave written informed consent for participation, and they all agreed that the data generated from this study could be used for scientific purposes. During the study, the procedures were anonymous and each participant received a unique coded number. We followed the methods of the principles of the Declaration of Helsinki [34], and the Ethical Committee of The Home of War Veterans approved the study (Ethics code number: 2017/4).

2.2. Body Composition

Body composition was estimated using bioelectrical impedance analysis (Omron BF500 Body Composition Monitor, Omron Medizintechnik, Hamburg, Germany). The participants needed to stand on metal footpads barefoot and grasp a pair of electrodes fixed on a handle with arms extended in front of the chest [35]. The software used pre-programmed regression equations to predict lean mass and fat mass in percentages. Each participant was instructed not to consume food or water 2 h before the testing procedure. A Seca portable 202 scale (Seca, Hamburg, Germany) and a digital scale (Seca, model 769) were used to measure the standing height (cm) and weight (kg) with a precision of 0.1 cm and 0.1 kg. The body mass index was calculated using the following formula: weight (kg)/height (m^2).

2.3. Muscular Fitness

To assess muscular fitness, three tests were applied: (1) push-ups in 30 s, (2) chair-stands in 30 s, and (3) sit-ups in 30 s. The push-up test measures dynamic muscular endurance [36]. If the participant was not able to regularly perform the test, the test was carried out on the knees, as recommended by previous studies [36]. The final score was recorded as the number of push-ups in 30 s. The chair-stand test estimates lower body strength [37]. The measurer recorded the number of standing up and sitting down sets from a standard chair 40 cm in height, while the participant looked straight ahead with their back in an upright position, legs fully extended and arms folded across the chest. The final score involved counting the number of stand-ups in 30 s. The sit-up test was performed to assess repetitive upper body strength [38]. Before the testing, each participant laid on a soft mat in a supine position, holding the knees bent at an angle of 90° and placing the arms on the chest with the hands on opposite shoulders. The correct attempt included performing a full sit-up to the upright position with elbows touching the thighs and returning to the initial position when shoulders touched the mat surface [38]. The final score was the number of correct sit-ups completed in 30 s.

2.4. Flexibility

To assess flexibility, we used the sit-and-reach test [39]. The participant was instructed to reach forward with the arms overlapping along the centimeter tape taped on the floor, while sitting with legs straight under an angle of 90°. The test was measured three times and the best score was recorded in centimeters.

2.5. Resistance Training Program

All participants took part in a 4-week resistance training program performed 3 times per week with at least 1 day of rest between each session. All training sessions were supervised by 2 trained exercise specialists who had finished master studies in sports science and had experience in testing of >5 years. Both instructors were familiar with the training exercises and practical lessons given to the participants. The instructors' role was to supervise the exercises and track the maintenance of intensity. The resistance training was designed to increase lean mass, muscular fitness, and flexibility. Before starting the program, all participants attended two familiarization sessions, as in previous studies [40]. Following familiarization and prior to the intervention, the participants completed the initial one-day testing. Body composition was measured in the morning hours between 9:00 and 11:00 h. Muscular fitness and flexibility were assessed using four tests in the afternoon between 17:00 and 19:00 h. The rest interval between each test was set to 5 min to avoid fatigue. The testing was performed in groups of 15 participants. The same principles were applied to post-intervention testing with similar testing hours (± 1 h) as for the initial testing.

Each resistance training session consisted of a general warm-up period for 5–10 min at moderate intensity, including cycling or performing leg presses. After the warm-up, participants performed 5 different exercises. The exercises included leg presses, knee flexions and knee extensions, horizontal chest presses, seated rows, back pulls, arm curls, and arm extensions. An indirect measurement of the maximum load was calculated, based on the training load at 50% and 60% of the one-repetition maximum. During the first 2 weeks, the participants exercised with ≈50% of the one-repetition maximum in 3 sets (10 repetitions), while in the second 2 weeks, the volume-load increased to ≈60% of the one-repetition maximum in 4 sets (8 repetitions). The pause between the sets was 2 min. All sessions were performed at the same time between 15:00 and 18:00 h with an air-conditioned room temperature of 22 °C and 24 °C. The training sessions were conducted at the same time during the day inside the rehabilitation facility. Two gyms with standardized equipment (machines, free weights, elastic bands, small/big balls, sticks, and mattresses) were used for the testing protocols and training.

2.6. Statistical Analysis

Basic descriptive statistics of the study participants are presented as mean and standard deviation. Kolmogorov–Smirnov and Levene's tests were applied to examine the normality of the distribution and homogeneity of variance for all data before the testing. Within-group changes (initial to final) were tested with the repeated measures ANOVA, while univariate ANOVA was used to calculate between-group differences. If a significant p-value was noted, the Bonferroni post hoc test was used to determine the differences among groups. The intervention-induced changes, presented in percent, were analyzed as follows: ((final score-initial score)/initial score). To establish the magnitude of the group difference in body composition, muscular fitness and flexibility, Cohen's d effect sizes were calculated with the following classification: (i) <0.2 (trivial), (ii) 0.2–0.5 (moderate), (iii) 0.5–0.8 (large), and (iv) >0.8 (very large) [41]. Two-sided p-values were used, and the significance was set at $\alpha < 0.05$. All the analyses were calculated in Statistical Packages for Social Sciences v.23 (SPSS, Chicago, IL, USA).

3. Results

The number of participants within each sex and age group who undertook the initial and final measurements is given in Table 1.

Table 1. The number of the participants (N) with both initial and final measurement, according to sex (men/women) and age in years (yr).

Sex	**Men**				**Women**			
Age	**50–64 yr**		**65–80 yr**		**50–64 yr**		**65–80 yr**	
Study Variables	**Initial**	**Final**	**Initial**	**Final**	**Initial**	**Final**	**Initial**	**Final**
Body mass (kg)	271	271	112	112	148	148	52	52
Body mass index (kg·m^{-2})	265	265	111	111	148	148	52	52
Lean mass (%)	244	244	94	94	127	127	50	50
Fat mass (%)	243	243	93	93	127	127	50	50
Push-ups in 30 s (reps)	198	198	70	70	115	115	24	24
Chair-stands in 30 s (reps)	230	230	82	82	129	129	33	33
Sit-ups in 30 s (reps)	192	192	66	66	115	115	24	24
Sit-and-reach (cm)	229	229	79	79	131	131	32	32

The basic descriptive statistics of the study participants before and after the 4-week training intervention are presented in Table 2. Over the 4 weeks, significant decreases were observed for body weight ($F_{1,763}$ = 9.257, p = 0.002), and the percentage of fat mass ($F_{1,763}$ = 63.271, p < 0.001), while the increases in the percentage of lean mass ($F_{1,763}$ = 21.134, p < 0.001), push-ups in 30 s ($F_{1,763}$ = 122.417, p < 0.001), chair-stands in 30 s ($F_{1,763}$ = 200.653, p < 0.001), sit-ups in 30 s ($F_{1,763}$ = 54.627, p < 0.001), and sit-and-reach test ($F_{1,763}$ = 40.172, p < 0.001) were obtained. Significant time*age interactions were shown for push-ups in 30 s ($F_{1,763}$ = 4.348, p = 0.038) and chair-stands in 30 s ($F_{1,763}$ = 9.552, p = 0.002), where men and women aged 50–64 years exhibited larger time-induced changes compared with their older (65–80 yr) counterparts. No significant time*sex, time*age or time*sex*age interactions for other variables were noted.

Table 2. Body composition, muscular physical fitness, and flexibility for men and women of different ages before and after the 4-week training intervention.

Sex	Men				Women			
Age	**50–64 yr**		**65–80 yr**		**50–64 yr**		**65–80 yr**	
Study Variables	**Initial**	**Final**	**Initial**	**Final**	**Initial**	**Final**	**Initial**	**Final**
Body mass (kg)	95.2 ± 16.5	94.4 ± 17.1	92.9 ± 15.5	92.0 ± 16.8	78.4 ± 15.6	78.1 ± 15.7	80.6 ± 13.2	80.4 ± 13.2
Body mass index (kg·m^{-2})	29.9 ± 5.0	29.8 ± 5.0	29.8 ± 4.7	29.7 ± 4.8	29.3 ± 5.3	29.2 ± 5.4	30.4 ± 4.4	30.1 ± 4.5
Lean mass (%)	32.5 ± 4.2	33.5 ± 4.6	31.9 ± 3.3	33.2 ± 3.4	27.9 ± 5.4	28.7 ± 5.1	26.4 ± 4.1	27.8 ± 3.4
Fat mass (%)	27.2 ± 6.8	26.1 ± 6.6	26.1 ± 7.0	25.4 ± 6.2	38.7 ± 7.3	37.4 ± 7.6	40.0 ± 6.8	38.8 ± 6.4
Push-ups in 30 s (reps)	11.3 ± 7.0	14.0 ± 7.9	7.4 ± 5.9	8.9 ± 7.2	9.0 ± 5.0	11.3 ± 5.9	7.6 ± 5.3	9.6 ± 6.7
Chair-stands in 30 s (reps)	12.8 ± 4.8	15.2 ± 5.1	10.2 ± 5.4	11.6 ± 6.2	10.3 ± 3.9	12.8 ± 4.6	10.6 ± 3.8	12.3 ± 4.4
Sit-ups in 30 s (reps)	10.3 ± 5.7	12.6 ± 6.7	8.1 ± 7.1	9.2 ± 7.2	8.5 ± 5.1	10.4 ± 5.8	8.6 ± 6.2	10.2 ± 7.0
Sit-and-reach (cm)	40.8 ± 15.9	45.7 ± 16.7	35.5 ± 16.9	38.5 ± 18.5	48.1 ± 15.8	53.1 ± 17.4	45.6 ± 16.6	48.4 ± 16.4

Figures 1 and 2 show sex- and age-specific intervention-induced changes (%) and effect sizes. After the 4 weeks, women exhibited significantly larger changes for chair-stands in 30 s compared with men in both age groups (24.3% and 16.0% vs. 18.8% and 13.7%, respectively). Additionally, women aged 65–80 years performed better in sit-ups in 30 s (18.6%) than 65–80-year-old men (13.6%). Similarly induced changes in body composition and flexibility in both sex and age groups were observed (p > 0.05). The largest effect sizes for muscular fitness were obtained (ranging from 0.15 for sit-ups in 30 s in men aged 65–80 yr to 0.59 for chair-stands in 30 s in women aged 50–64 yr), followed by flexibility (ranging from 0.17 in men and women aged 65–80 yr to 0.30 in men and women aged 50–64 yr). For body composition, the largest effect sizes were observed for the percent of lean mass in men and women aged 65–80 years (0.39 and 0.37, respectively), while for fat mass, the effect sizes ranged from 0.11 in 65–80-year-old men to 0.18 in 65–80-year-old women.

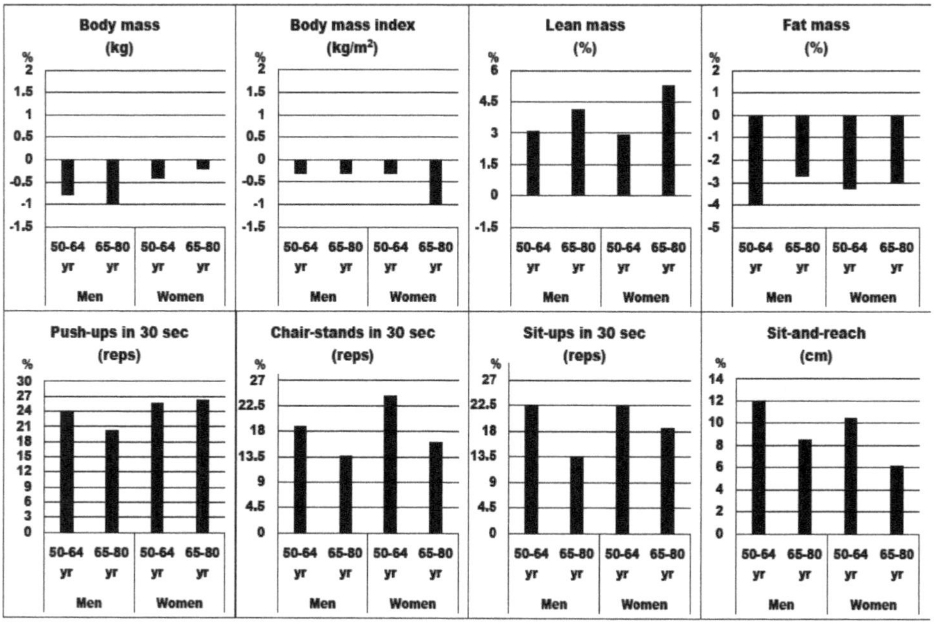

Figure 1. Intervention-induced changes (%) for body composition, muscular fitness, and flexibility before and after the 4-week resistance training across the age groups in years (yr).

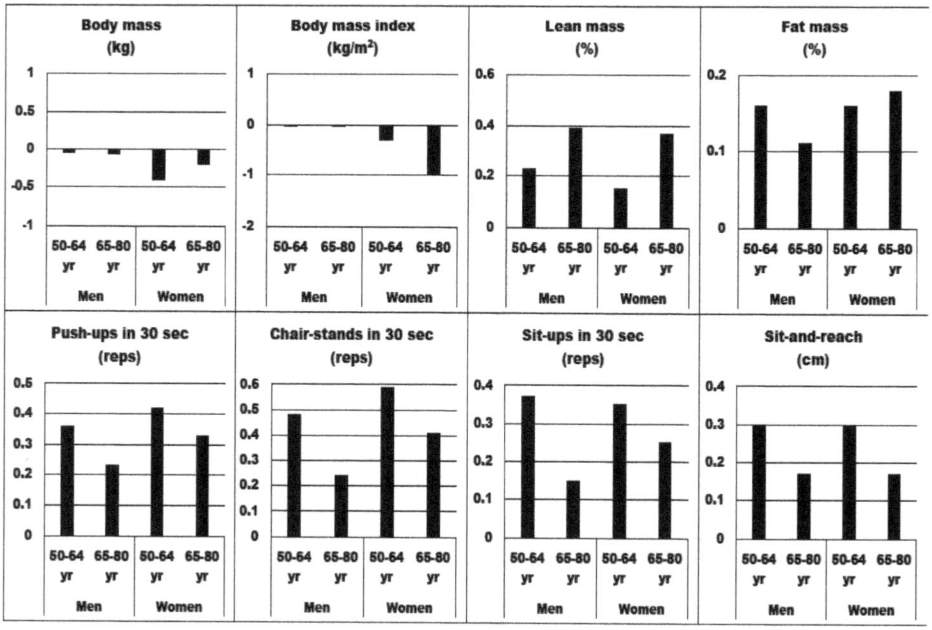

Figure 2. Effect sizes for body composition, muscular fitness and flexibility before and after the 4-week resistance training across the age groups in years (yr).

4. Discussion

The main purpose of this study was to examine the effects of a 4-week resistance training program on body composition, muscular fitness, and flexibility in middle-aged (50–64 yr) and older (65–80 yr) men and women. The main findings were: (1) significant time changes in all sex and age groups were observed, (2) 50–64 year-old men and women had somewhat larger changes in push-ups in 30 s and chair-stands in 30 s tests compared with their older counterparts, and (3) similar intervention-induced changes (%) and effect sizes between groups occurred.

Studies found that relative upper-body strength increased by 29% in women compared with 17% in men, whereas the increases in lower-body strength were similar [42], which are comparable to our findings in this study. The increases in muscular fitness may be explained by the increases in lean mass and decreases in fat mass, as in previous studies [12]. This statement can be confirmed, because we found significant correlations between lean mass, fat mass, and muscular fitness ($p < 0.05$). Studies showed that different neuromuscular adaptations are one factor contributing to the larger increases in upper-body strength for women, whereas acute recovery following resistance training may be slower in men [18]. Women generally have lower initial levels of physical fitness, causing a ceiling effect for motor skills and better training adaptations compared with men [18]. Although we did not find significant time*sex interactions for any of the study variables, women exhibited larger intervention-induced changes for chair-stands in 30 s. This may be explained by two potential mechanisms. First, women have a greater proportion of type I fibers in the vastus medialis and biceps brachii, indicating better muscular endurance [43,44]. Second, studies showed that men have longer-lasting muscle soreness than women [45]. Most recently, a study by Roberts et al. [18] showed no significant differences between men and women in hypertrophy (effect size = 0.07 ± 0.06, $p = 0.31$) or lower-body strength (effect size = -0.21 ± 0.16, $p = 0.20$); yet, there was a significant effect favoring women for upper-body strength (effect size = -0.60 ± 0.16, $p = 0.002$). Although the changes for push-ups in 30 s were larger for women in our study, unfortunately, we did not collect additional data regarding biological and physiological characteristics, although previous evidence suggests that women tend to have larger strength gains and more muscle growth during the follicular phase [46]. However, our sample size was based on women aged $\geq$50 yr, and it was reported that the menopausal age starts roughly at the age of 50, dismissing the effects of the menstrual cycle on resistance training [47].

We also found that younger men and women (50–64 yr) had larger effects in push-ups in 30 s and chair-stands in 30 s compared with their older (65–80 yr) counterparts, which is in line with the findings of previous studies [12,48]. Specifically, Lemmer et al. [12] found that younger participants increased their one-repetition maximum strength significantly more than older participants (34% $\pm$ 3% vs. 28% $\pm$ 3%). Another study showed that young participants had better performance in specific strength for knee extensions and experienced less fatigue across repetitions compared with old participants [48]. Older adults experience physiological changes in terms of age-associated loss of type II fiber number and size, which significantly contribute to the ability to increase strength in response to resistance training [12]. On the other hand, one study reported the same improvements in one-repetition maximum in all age groups from young adults in their twenties and thirties, middle-aged in their forties and fifties and up, to older adults in their sixties and seventies [13]. Along with mechanical and architectural factors associated with the same sex and age responses to resistance training, previous studies acknowledged that the mechanism for similar training-induced increases in muscle quality lies in the increases in motor unit recruitment and decreases in the coactivation of the antagonist muscle groups following training in older adults [26]. Moreover, the ratio between type I and type II fibers may help improve neuromuscular adaptations that enhance the contractile properties of the muscles [26].

Our findings support previous evidence of similar acute responses to resistance training, irrespective of sex and age. Researchers have well-documented that the differences are largely influenced by neural, muscular, and motor learning adaptations [18]. Nevertheless, it is important to understand how resistance training may affect body composition, muscular fitness, and flexibility in men and women of different ages in practice.

This study is not without limitations. First, although we found significant time changes, the 4-week resistance training intervention may have been relatively short compared with those in previous studies with longer study durations (between 6 and 24 weeks) [18]. Second, we did not collect data on the participants' biological, physiological, or sociodemographic characteristics, which can mediate the resistance training effects. Furthermore, we did not collect data on the level of physical activity prior to the intervention; thus, it is possible that physically active individuals might have had different basal activity compared with untrained individuals. Future research should collect more detailed information regarding the anthropological and health-related status of the participants. In addition to our finding significant changes in physical fitness after the 4-week resistance training, it would be clinically relevant to study the appropriate intervention duration and training mode for producing the largest effects on health-related physical fitness.

5. Conclusions

To the best of our knowledge, this is the first study to report marked improvements in body composition, muscular fitness, and flexibility in a large sample of middle-aged and older adults categorized as war veterans, according to sex and age. We found significant changes in all sex and age groups for all variables. Resistance training produced larger improvements in younger men and women in push-ups in 30 s and chair-stands n 30 s compared with older men and women. To conclude, resistance training for 4 weeks increased lean mass, muscular fitness, and flexibility and decreased body weight, body mass index, and fat mass across the groups. Therefore, even a relatively short resistance training intervention may lead to higher physical fitness levels in men and women aged 50–80 years.

Author Contributions: Conceptualization, L.Š. and Z.K.; methodology, L.Š.; software, L.Š.; validation, L.Š.; formal analysis, L.Š.; investigation, L.Š. and Z.K.; resources, L.Š. and Z.K.; data curation, L.Š.; writing—original draft preparation, M.K., L.Š. and Z.K.; writing—review and editing, L.Š.; visualization, L.Š.; supervision, L.Š. and Z.K.; project administration, Z.K.; funding acquisition, Z.K. All authors have read and agreed to the published version of the manuscript.

Funding: This research received no external funding.

Institutional Review Board Statement: The study was approved by the Ethical Committee of The Home of War Veterans (Ethics code number: 2017/4).

Informed Consent Statement: Informed consent was voluntarily signed by the participants.

Data Availability Statement: The datasets used and/or analyzed during the current study are available from the corresponding author on reasonable request.

Acknowledgments: The authors would like to thank all the participants and training supervisors for their enthusiastic participation in the study.

Conflicts of Interest: The authors declare no conflict of interest.

References

1. World Health Organization (WHO). *World Report on Aging and Health*; WHO: Geneva, Switzerland, 2015; Available online: https://apps.who.int/iris/bitstream/handle/10665/186463/9789240694811_eng.pdf?sequence=1&isAllowed=y (accessed on 12 July 2022).
2. Reid, K.F.; Fielding, R.A. Skeletal muscle power: A critical determinant of physical functioning in older adults. *Exerc. Sport Sci. Rev.* **2012**, *40*, 4–12. [CrossRef] [PubMed]
3. Boutari, C.; Mantzoros, C.S. Decreasing lean body mass with age: Challenges and opportunities for novel therapies. *Endocrinol. Metab.* **2017**, *32*, 422–425. [CrossRef] [PubMed]

4. Alcazar, J.; Alegre, L.M.; Van Roie, E.; Magalhães, J.P.; Nielsen, B.R.; González-Gross, M.; Júdice, P.B.; Casajús, J.A.; Delecluse, C.; Sardinha, L.B.; et al. Relative sit-to-stand power: Aging trajectories, functionally relevant cut-off points, and normative data in a large European cohort. *J. Cachexia Sarcopenia Muscle* **2021**, *12*, 921–932. [CrossRef] [PubMed]
5. Keller, K.; Engelhardt, M. Strength and muscle mass loss with aging process. Age and strength loss. *Muscles Ligaments Tendons J.* **2013**, *3*, 346–350. [CrossRef]
6. Yang, N.P.; Hsu, N.W.; Lin, C.H.; Chen, H.C.; Tsao, H.M.; Lo, S.S.; Chou, P. Relationship between muscle strength and fall episodes among the elderly: The Yilan study, Taiwan. *BMC Geriatr.* **2018**, *18*, 90. [CrossRef]
7. Testa, G.; Vescio, A.; Zuccalà, D.; Petrantoni, V.; Amico, M.; Russo, G.I.; Sessa, G.; Pavone, V. Diagnosis, treatment and prevention of sarcopenia in hip fractured patients: Where we are and where we are going: A systematic review. *J. Clin. Med.* **2020**, *9*, 2997. [CrossRef]
8. Jindai, K.; Nielson, C.M.; Vorderstrasse, B.A.; Quiñones, A.R. Multimorbidity and functional limitations among adults 65 or older, NHANES 2005–2012. *Prev. Chronic Dis.* **2016**, *13*, 151. [CrossRef]
9. Spahillari, A.; Mukamal, K.J.; DeFilippi, C.; Kizer, J.R.; Gottdiener, J.S.; Djoussé, L.; Lyles, M.F.; Bartz, T.M.; Murthy, V.L.; Shah, R.V. The association of lean and fat mass with all-cause mortality in older adults: The Cardiovascular Health Study. *Nutr. Metab. Cardiovasc. Dis.* **2016**, *26*, 1039–1047. [CrossRef]
10. Alcazar, J.; Navarrete-Villanueva, D.; Mañas, A.; Gómez-Cabello, A.; Pedrero-Chamizo, R.; Alegre, L.M.; Villa, G.; Gusi, N.; González-Gross, M.; Casajús, J.A.; et al. 'Fat but powerful' paradox: Association of muscle power and adiposity markers with all-cause mortality in older adults from the EXERNET multicentre study. *Br. J. Sports Med.* **2021**, *55*, 1204–1211. [CrossRef]
11. Taylor, J.; Walsh, S.; Kwok, W.; Pinheiro, M.B.; de Oliveira, J.S.; Hassett, L.; Bauman, A.; Bull, F.; Tiedemann, A.; Sherrington, C. A scoping review of physical activity interventions for older adults. *Int. J. Behav. Nutr. Phys. Act.* **2021**, *18*, 82. [CrossRef]
12. Lemmer, J.T.; Hurlbut, D.E.; Martel, G.F.; Tracy, B.L.; Ivey, F.M.; Metter, E.J.; Fozard, J.L.; Fleg, J.L.; Hurley, B.F. Age and gender responses to strength training and detraining. *Med. Sci. Sports Exerc.* **2000**, *32*, 1505–1512. [CrossRef] [PubMed]
13. Kittilsen, H.T.; Goleva-Fjellet, S.; Freberg, B.I.; Nicolaisen, I.; Støa, E.M.; Bratland-Sanda, S.; Helgerud, J.; Wang, E.; Sæbø, M.; Støren, Ø. Responses to maximal strength training in different age and gender groups. *Front. Physiol.* **2021**, *12*, 636972. [CrossRef] [PubMed]
14. Da Boit, M.; Sibson, R.; Meakin, J.R.; Aspden, R.M.; Thies, F.; Mangoni, A.A.; Gray, S.R. Sex differences in the response to resistance exercise training in older people. *Physiol. Rep.* **2016**, *4*, 12834. [CrossRef]
15. Kojić, F.; Mandić, D.; Ilić, V. Resistance training induces similar adaptations of upper and lower-body muscles between sexes. *Sci. Rep.* **2021**, *11*, 23449. [CrossRef] [PubMed]
16. Støren, Ø.; Helgerud, J.; Sæbø, M.; Støa, E.M.; Bratland-Sanda, S.; Unhjem, R.J.; Hoff, J.; Wang, E. The effect of age on the V˙O2max response to high-intensity interval training. *Med. Sci. Sports Exerc.* **2017**, *49*, 78–85. [CrossRef] [PubMed]
17. Wang, E.; Nyberg, S.K.; Hoff, J.; Zhao, J.; Leivseth, G.; Tørhaug, T.; Husby, O.S.; Helgerud, J.; Richardson, R.S. Impact of maximal strength training on work efficiency and muscle fiber type in the elderly: Implications for physical function and fall prevention. *Exp. Gerontol.* **2017**, *91*, 64–71. [CrossRef]
18. Roberts, B.M.; Nuckols, G.; Krieger, J.W. Sex Differences in resistance training: A systematic review and meta-analysis. *J. Strength Cond. Res.* **2020**, *34*, 1448–1460. [CrossRef]
19. Phillips, S.M.; Winett, R.A. Uncomplicated resistance training and health-related outcomes: Evidence for a public health mandate. *Curr. Sports Med. Rep.* **2010**, *9*, 208–213. [CrossRef]
20. El-Kotob, R.; Ponzano, M.; Chaput, J.P.; Janssen, I.; Kho, M.E.; Poitras, V.J.; Ross, R.; Ross-White, A.; Saunders, T.J.; Giangregorio, L.M. Resistance training and health in adults: An overview of systematic reviews. *Appl. Physiol. Nutr. Metab.* **2020**, *45*, 165–179. [CrossRef]
21. Grgić, J.; Shoenfeld, B. A case for considering age and sex when prescribing rest intervals in resistance training. *Kinesiology* **2019**, *51*, 78–82.
22. Dias, R.M.; Cyrino, E.S.; Salvador, E.S.; Nakamura, F.Y.; Cheche Pina, F.L.; de Oliveira, A.R. Impact of an eight-week weight training program on the muscular strength of men and women. *Rev. Bras. Med. Esporte* **2005**, *11*, 213–218.
23. Roth, S.M.; Ivey, F.M.; Martel, G.F.; Lemmer, J.T.; Hurlbut, D.E.; Siegel, E.L.; Metter, E.J.; Fleg, J.L.; Fozard, J.L.; Kostek, M.C.; et al. Muscle size responses to strength training in young and older men and women. *J. Am. Geriatr. Soc.* **2001**, *49*, 1428–1433. [CrossRef] [PubMed]
24. Kosek, D.J.; Kim, J.S.; Petrella, J.K.; Cross, J.M.; Bamman, M.M. Efficacy of 3 days/wk resistance training on myofiber hypertrophy and myogenic mechanisms in young vs. older adults. *J. Appl. Physiol.* **2006**, *101*, 531–544. [CrossRef] [PubMed]
25. Salvador, E.P.D.R.; Gurjao, A.L.; Avelar, A.; Pinto, L.G.; Cyrino, E.S. Effect of eight weeks of strength training on fatigue resistance in men and women. *Isokinet. Exerc. Sci.* **2009**, *17*, 101–106. [CrossRef]
26. Ivey, F.M.; Tracy, B.L.; Lemmer, J.T.; NessAiver, M.; Metter, E.J.; Fozard, J.L.; Hurley, B.F. Effects of strength training and detraining on muscle quality: Age and gender comparisons. *J. Gerontol. Ser. A Biol. Sci. Med. Sci.* **2000**, *55*, 152–157, discussion 158–159. [CrossRef]
27. Kell, R.T. The influence of periodized resistance training on strength changes in men and women. *J. Strength Cond. Res.* **2011**, *25*, 735–744. [CrossRef]
28. Ribeiro, A.S.; Avelar, A.; Schoenfeld, B.J.; Trindade, M.C.; Ritti-Dias, R.M.; Altimari, L.R.; Cyrino, E.S. Effect of 16 weeks of resistance training on fatigue resistance in men and women. *J. Hum. Kinet.* **2014**, *42*, 165–174. [CrossRef]

29. Häkkinen, K.; Pakarinen, A.; Kraemer, W.J.; Newton, R.U.; Alen, M. Basal concentrations and acute responses of serum hormones and strength development during heavy resistance training in middle-aged and elderly men and women. *J. Gerontol. Ser. A Biol. Sci. Med. Sci.* **2000**, *55*, 95–105.
30. Hunter, S.K. Sex differences in human fatigability: Mechanisms and insight to physiological responses. *Acta Physiol.* **2014**, *210*, 768–789. [CrossRef]
31. Charette, S.L.; McEvoy, L.; Pyka, G.; Snow-Harter, C.; Guido, D.; Wiswell, R.A.; Marcus, R. Muscle hypertrophy response to resistance training in older women. *J. Appl. Physiol.* **1991**, *70*, 1912–1916. [CrossRef]
32. Straight, C.R.; Lindheimer, J.B.; Brady, A.O.; Dishman, R.K.; Evans, E.M. Effects of resistance training on lower-extremity muscle power in middle-aged and older adults: A systematic review and meta-analysis of randomized controlled trials. *Sports Med.* **2016**, *46*, 353–364. [CrossRef] [PubMed]
33. Lavin, K.M.; Roberts, B.M.; Fry, C.S.; Moro, T.; Rasmussen, B.B.; Bamman, M.M. The importance of resistance exercise training to combat neuromuscular aging. *Physiology* **2019**, *34*, 112–122. [CrossRef] [PubMed]
34. World Medical Association. World Medical Association Declaration of Helsinki: Ethical principles for medical research involving human subjects. *JAMA* **2013**, *310*, 2191–2194. [CrossRef] [PubMed]
35. Pietiläinen, K.H.; Kaye, S.; Karmi, A.; Suojanen, L.; Rissanen, A.; Virtanen, K.A. Agreement of bioelectrical impedance with dual-energy X-ray absorptiometry and MRI to estimate changes in body fat, fat-free and visceral fat during a 12-month weight loss intervention. *Br. J. Nutr.* **2013**, *9*, 1910–1916. [CrossRef]
36. Suni, J.H.; Oja, P.; Miilunpalo, S.I.; Pasanen, M.E.; Vuori, I.M.; Bös, K. Health-related fitness test battery for adults: Associations with perceived health, mobility, and back function and symptoms. *Arch. Phys. Med. Rehabil.* **1998**, *79*, 559–569. [CrossRef]
37. Rikli, R.E.; Jones, C.J. Development and validation of criterion-referenced clinically relevant fitness standards for maintaining physical independence in later years. *Gerontologist* **2013**, *53*, 255–267. [CrossRef]
38. Abe, T.; Yaginuma, Y.; Fujita, E.; Thiebaud, R.S.; Kawanishi, M.; Akamine, T. Associations of sit-up ability with sarcopenia classification measures in Japanese older women. *Interv. Med. Appl. Sci.* **2016**, *8*, 152–157. [CrossRef]
39. President's Council on Physical Fitness and Sports (PCPFS). The President's Challenge Physical Fitness Test: V-Sit Reach. 2012. Available online: https://www.presidentschallenge.org/challenge/physical/activities/v-sit-reach.shtml (accessed on 12 July 2022).
40. Schaun, G.Z.; Bamman, M.M.; Andrade, L.S.; David, G.B.; Krüger, V.L.; Marins, E.F.; Nunes, G.N.; Häfele, M.S.; Mendes, G.F.; Gomes, M.L.B.; et al. High-velocity resistance training mitigates physiological and functional impairments in middle-aged and older adults with and without mobility-limitation. *Geroscience* **2022**, *44*, 1175–1197. [CrossRef]
41. Cohen, J. A power primer. *Psychol. Bull.* **1992**, *112*, 155–159. [CrossRef]
42. Wilmore, J.H. Alterations in strength, body composition and anthropometric measurements consequent to a 10-week weight training program. *Med. Sci. Sports* **1974**, *6*, 133–138. [CrossRef]
43. Roberts, B.M.; Lavin, K.M.; Many, G.M.; Thalacker-Mercer, A.; Merritt, E.K.; Bickel, C.S.; Mayhew, D.L.; Tuggle, S.C.; Cross, J.M.; Kosek, D.J.; et al. Human neuromuscular aging: Sex differences revealed at the myocellular level. *Exp. Gerontol.* **2018**, *106*, 116–124. [CrossRef]
44. Haizlip, K.M.; Harrison, B.C.; Leinwand, L.A. Sex-based differences in skeletal muscle kinetics and fiber-type composition. *Physiology* **2015**, *30*, 30–39. [CrossRef] [PubMed]
45. Dannecker, E.A.; Liu, Y.; Rector, R.S.; Thomas, T.R.; Fillingim, R.B.; Robinson, M.E. Sex differences in exercise-induced muscle pain and muscle damage. *J. Pain* **2012**, *13*, 1242–1249. [CrossRef]
46. Wikström-Frisén, L.; Boraxbekk, C.J.; Henriksson-Larsén, K. Effects on power, strength and lean body mass of menstrual/oral contraceptive cycle based resistance training. *J. Sports Med. Phys. Fitness* **2017**, *57*, 43–52. [CrossRef] [PubMed]
47. Rahman, S.; Salehin, F.; Iqbal, A. Menopausal symptoms assessment among middle age women in Kushtia, Bangladesh. *BMC Res. Notes* **2011**, *4*, 188. [CrossRef] [PubMed]
48. Petrella, J.K.; Kim, J.S.; Tuggle, S.C.; Hall, S.R.; Bamman, M.M. Age differences in knee extension power, contractile velocity, and fatigability. *J. Appl. Physiol.* **2005**, *98*, 211–220. [CrossRef]

nutrients

MDPI

Article

Prevalence of Orthorexia in Groups of Students with Varied Diets and Physical Activity (Silesia, Poland)

Mateusz Grajek [1,2], Karolina Krupa-Kotara [3,*], Krzysztof Sas-Nowosielski [2], Ewa Misterska [4] and Joanna Kobza [1]

1 Department of Public Health, Faculty of Health Sciences in Bytom, Medical University of Silesia in Katowice, 41902 Katowice, Poland; mgrajek@sum.edu.pl (M.G.); jkobza@sum.edu.pl (J.K.)
2 Department of Humanistic Foundations of Physical Culture, Faculty of Physical Education, Jerzy Kukuczka Academy of Physical Education in Katowice, 40065 Katowice, Poland; gmattgrayek@gmail.com
3 Department of Epidemiology, Faculty of Health Sciences in Bytom, Medical University of Silesia in Katowice, 41902 Bytom, Poland
4 Department of Pedagogy and Psychology, Faculty of Social Studies in Poznań, Poznań School of Security, 60778 Poznań, Poland; emisterska1@wp.pl
* Correspondence: kkrupa@sum.edu.pl

Abstract: (1) Background: The literature emphasizes the role of many factors influencing the onset of eating disorders (EDs) and their mutual influence on each other. Therefore, this study aimed to evaluate and compare the prevalence of orthorexic behaviors in groups of health-related and non-health-related students in terms of their differential health behaviors—diet and physical activity levels. (2) The study included 300 individuals representing two equal groups of fields of study, which for the study were called the health-related field (HRF) and the non-health-related field (NRF). (3) Results: Based on the results of the dietary assessment, it was found that the best dietary model was characterized by the HRF group; in this group, 97.2% of students were characterized by a very good and good dietary mode. The NRF group, on the other hand, was dominated by a sufficient dietary mode for 64.4% of all cases in this group (94 people), while the dietary model marked as "good" was less popular, at 24.6% of this group (36 people). (4) Conclusions: Based on the cited self-research and information from the literature, it can be concluded that the problem of orthorexia is still a new issue at the level of social sciences, medical sciences, and health sciences. The psychometric tools used in this study allowed us to demonstrate the prevalence of the aforementioned eating disorders in the sample groups of students.

Keywords: eating disorders; eating behaviors; students; nutrition; orthorexia; lifestyle; diet; physical activity; health-related; non-health-related

Citation: Grajek, M.; Krupa-Kotara, K.; Sas-Nowosielski, K.; Misterska, E.; Kobza, J. Prevalence of Orthorexia in Groups of Students with Varied Diets and Physical Activity (Silesia, Poland). *Nutrients* **2022**, *14*, 2816. https://doi.org/10.3390/nu14142816

Academic Editors: Roberto Pippi, Carmine G. Fanelli and Matteo Vandoni

Received: 20 June 2022
Accepted: 7 July 2022
Published: 8 July 2022

1. Introduction

Proper nutrition and adequate physical activity are the most important factors that promote health. However, sometimes, the interaction of certain factors leads to the manifestation of eating disorders (EDs). The literature emphasizes the role of many factors influencing the onset of eating disorders and their mutual influence on each other, the most frequently mentioned being physiological, psychological, and socio-cultural factors [1,2]. Eating disorders form a group of behavioral disorders that involve excessive weight control and focusing thoughts on food. According to the American Psychiatric Association's classification (DSM-V), there are two primary groups of eating disorders—specific and nonspecific [3]. Specific eating disorders include anorexia (mental anorexia), bulimia (mental gluttony), and sometimes a mixed disorder (bulimorexia) [4]. Nonspecific eating disorders form a group of behaviors not classified in the DSM-V, but this does not mean that these individuals do not cause serious health consequences for the person who suffers from them [5]. Nonspecific eating disorders include pathological eating behaviors such as emotional eating or food fanaticism. According to the International Statistical Classification of

Diseases and Health Disorders (ICD-10), eating disorders are classified as mental disorders from the group of behavioral disorders, associated with physiological disturbances and psychological factors. Eating disorders are classified as compulsive disorders due to the compulsion to restrict or overindulge in food. Among the most characteristic symptoms of these disorders are anxiety, depression, obsessive-compulsive disorder, self-aggression, or reduced quality of life [1,2]. Major risk factors for EDs include [6,7]:

- Physiological factors: female gender, abnormal functioning of neurotransmitters and neuromodulators (serotonin, dopamine, norepinephrine), genetic predisposition, abnormalities in hormonal axes (hypothalamic-pituitary).
- Collective psychological factors: disturbed family and peer relations, the occurrence of psychological problems in the family (depression, anxiety disorders, obsessive-compulsive disorders), abnormal family patterns (dysfunctional family, overprotection from the mother or father, sexual abuse).
- Individual psychological factors: distorted self-image, low self-esteem, perfectionism, intrapsychic and interpersonal communication difficulties, sense of responsibility, suppression of aggression, submissiveness.
- Socio-cultural factors: the cult of a slim figure created by the media, social expectations of the role.

Namysłowska [8], on the other hand, indicates that factors influencing the development of eating disorders should be considered in terms of a causal sequence or vicious circle. The first group of factors mentioned by the author are predisposing factors, among which are the individual characteristics of the person at risk of developing the disorder, but also family and social issues (excessive ambitions, aggression, violence, social expectations). The second category of factors are triggered, and here behavioral disturbances within the desire for self-monitoring of body weight and the drive for self-acceptance are indicated. In the third category are the maintenance factors, which are defined by the effect of drastic dieting and physical activity in the form of starvation, which drive to maintain such a state of affairs—the person with an eating disorder feels satisfaction through achieving a given effect, and this causes the problem to worsen. Eating disorders are a significant public health problem. Their prevalence in the general population is quite high, despite difficult epidemiological studies. EDs are estimated to affect 2–4% of the population, and the prevalence of eating disorders is significantly higher in some age and social groups than in others [7,9]. Diagnosing eating disorders is a complex process, primarily due to the presence of nonspecific somatic symptoms that mask the underlying illness, thus prolonging the diagnosis process and making it more costly. In addition, the treatment of eating disorders is a lengthy and multi-step process that requires collaboration between the patient's case manager, a psychologist or psychotherapist, and a nutritionist [2,4].

Nowadays, with the cult of slimness and care for a healthy lifestyle, there is a lot of talk about health risks associated with healthism, i.e., excessive attention to health. One can say that the eating disorder resulting from such behavior is orthorexia. Orthorexia nervosa is an informally diagnosed condition characterized by an obsessive preoccupation with eating healthy and "clean" food. In this condition, it is the quality, not the quantity, of food that is crucial [10,11]. Orthorexia nervosa, sometimes called radical eating, is a condition in which a pathological obsession with eating the "right" food is manifested. It is more commonly diagnosed in women and affluent individuals regardless of gender. Orthorexia affects 7% of the general population [1], and research by Dunn and Bartman [12] suggests that the problem may affect up to 90% of members of certain social groups, as the problem is more common in people with high levels of physical activity to maintain fitness and health, as well as in people who strive to achieve the "ideal" body shape that is promoted by mass media [13]. In this disorder, as in classic anorexia, there is an obsessive, systematic focus on counting the caloric value of the foods consumed and giving up all fatty and hard-to-digest foods [13,14]. Unlike anorexia, on the other hand, the focus of the sufferer is not only on the quantity consumed and weight reduction, but more importantly on the quality of the food consumed and on achieving and maintaining health [15,16]. Individuals with orthorexia think obsessively about food, planning meals, imposing dietary discipline on themselves, and enforcing punishments for breaking the rules they have established. Such behavior stems from the conviction that only eating healthy, easily digestible food and strict adherence to a diet will allow them to prevent the occurrence of diseases characteristic of modern societies-chronic non-communicable diseases [12]. Therefore, the desire to live a healthy and long life, to stay healthy and fit, and to focus on the quality of the food consumed rather than the quantity of the food consumed makes this disease not easy to diagnose [10,17]. There are also cases where patients who eliminate more products start consuming only water while believing that only drinking strictly selected water will ensure full health [5]. Health consequences of chronic orthorexia include, but are not limited to, broken social ties along with avoidance of going out to eat, malnutrition secondary to elimination and reduction diets (including deficiencies of protein, vitamin B12, iron, sodium), rhabdomyolysis (muscle breakdown), metabolic acidosis, and elevated laboratory indicators (mainly liver enzymes and bilirubin) [18]. Due to the lack of unambiguous diagnostic criteria, and thus the very great difficulty in making the diagnosis, the exact number of people with orthorexia is still unknown (apart from the aforementioned estimates, which are based on small group studies). People with orthorexia are often treated by their environment as caring too much about their health, and their relatives do not recognize the features of the disorder in such behavior. The lack of accurate information on the size of the condition is also due to the reluctance of sufferers to report to specialists and their failure to notice such problems [11,19]. Therapy for orthorexia, like therapy for anorexia, consists primarily of compensating for any nutritional deficiencies and psychotherapy. Its goal is to show patients that not all foods they reject carry health risks [12].

Therefore, the main objective of this study was to evaluate and compare the prevalence of orthorexic behaviors in groups of health-related and non-health-related students in terms of their differential health behaviors—diet and physical activity levels.

The following research hypotheses were posed in preparation for the study:

1. Orthorexic behaviors are more common among people who have a rational diet.
2. Orthorexic behaviors are more common among individuals who represent high levels of physical activity and motivation to engage in physical activity.
3. Orthorexic behaviors are more common among people who overestimate the size and calorie portions of foods and foods.

2. Materials and Methods

2.1. Study Organization and Eligibility Criteria

The study included 300 individuals representing two equal groups of fields of study, which for the study were called the health-related field (HRF) and the non-health-related field (NRF).

The HRF group consisted of 150 final-year sophomore students with majors in dietetics and physical education. The key to selecting this group was the fact of having in-depth and professional knowledge in the field of rational nutrition and physical activity. The NRF group consisted of 150 students in their final year of second-degree studies with majors in management and computer science. The key to selecting this group was the fact that they did not have in-depth and professional knowledge in the field of rational nutrition and physical activity, at least at the university level. The assumption for the selection of these majors was that the gender groups were more or less equal. Such majors as dietetics and management are more often chosen by females, and physical education or computer science by males.

Individuals in the NRF group showing concurrent education (or past education) in a health-related field were excluded from the study. Individuals who had applied knowledge and skills in rational nutrition and physical activity in their professional work were treated similarly. The physiological state of the respondent was also taken into account. Persons suffering from diseases that influence the diet and/or physical activity of the respondent (e.g., allergies, food intolerances, metabolic diseases, tumors, etc.) were excluded from the research. The same was done with subjects who represented a specific dietary model (elimination diet or pregnancy and puerperium).

The final analyses included 290 (144 subjects in the HRF group and 146 subjects in the NRF group) correctly completed questionnaires that addressed the inclusion criteria described above. All participants were informed about the purpose and scope of the study and gave informed consent to participate.

The study was approved by the Bioethics Committee of the Medical University of Silesia in Katowice, in light of the Act on Medical and Dental Professions of 5 December 1996, which includes a definition of medical experimentation. The study participants consciously agreed to participate in the study.

2.2. Study Procedure and Research Tool

A diagnostic survey method was used in this study. The survey was conducted using an online form, which is an acceptable method in psychological research. The research was conducted using a survey technique. The survey consisted of a survey questionnaire and a scrapbook of sample foods and dishes. To record information from the research, a research tool was used, which included the following:

I. The questionnaire of the survey consisted of a metric (data of the subject: gender, age, a field of study and occupation, anthropometric data—declared height and body weight); the author's questionnaire of dietary habits based on the guidelines and standards of the National Institute of Public Health and the NCEZ [18,20]; questions about the physical activity practiced and its level based on WHO guidelines [21]; standardized questionnaires such as the Exercise Motivation Inventory (EMI-2) (validated by Sas-Nowosielski and Nowicka [22]), the Orthorexia Questionnaire (ORTO-15) (validated by Stochel et al. [23]; Brytek-Matera [24]). The survey questionnaire was available online from May–June 2021.

II. An album of sample foods and dishes to verify the ability to estimate the size and calorie content of portions, consisting of 12 photographs consistent with the division of foods into 12 groups (one photograph per group) [25,26]. The study using the album was conducted with the sensory panel of the Department of Dietetics, Faculty of Health Sciences in Bytom, Silesian Medical University in Katowice, Poland, from July–August 2021. Before each study, visual perception (perception of images) was tested using a scrapbook. For this purpose, selected Ishihara boards and optical illusion boards were used. Both tools are commonly used to assess so-called visual daltonism and the perception of objects in pictures (e.g., size, shape, length). To link the results of the questionnaire with the album, each participant of the study was given an individual number while filling in the questionnaire, which was then also entered in the album. The study was conducted according to scientific ethics, anonymity rules, and the RODO clause (Polish Law on Respect for Classified Information).

2.3. Interpretation of the Tools Used

Body mass index was calculated using the formula: BMI [kg/m^2] = body weight [kg]/height [m]^2. The results were then interpreted using a scale [27]: >30 kg/m^2—obesity (alarming score); 25–29.9 kg/m^2—overweight (elevated body weight); 20–24.9 kg/m^2—normal body weight; 17–19.9 kg/m^2—underweight (underweight); <17 kg/m^2—malnutrition (alarming score).

In the assessment of dietary intake, the author's tool based on nutrition standards for the Polish population [18,27] was used, which included 20 dietary indices (e.g., frequency of consumption of individual product groups, number of meals during the day, regularity of meals during the day, snacking, fluids drunk). One point was awarded for each correct answer (in accordance with the applied standards), so the highest possible total score was 20. To prioritize the results, the following scale was adopted: 18–20 points—very good nutrition; 14–17 pts.—good; 10–13 pts.—moderate, $\leq$9 pts.—poor nutrition (bad).

Based on the physical activity score in the questionnaire, respondents were assigned a physical activity index (PAL), which takes the following values, based on current recommendations for physical activity, respectively [21,28]: 1.2—no physical activity; 1.4—low physical activity (approximately 140 min per week); 1.6—medium physical activity (approximately 280 min per week); 1.8—high physical activity (approximately 420 min per week); 2.0—very high physical activity (approximately 560 min per week).

The EMI-2 questionnaire consists of 56 variables grouped into 14 categories corresponding to motives for exercising. In each subscale, the respondent could receive 5 points, where 0 means the highest priority for the motivator and 5 the lowest; the lower the scores for a given motivator, the higher the motivation [29].

The ORTO-15 questionnaire consists of 15 questions, each to be answered on a 4-point scale (always, often, rarely, or never). Answers indicating a tendency toward orthorexic behavior receive 1 point, while those corresponding to normal eating receive 4 points. According to the creators, the cutoff point is a score of 40 points; scoring below this score indicates a tendency toward orthorexia [13].

2.4. Statistical Compilation

Tables and figures were prepared for all extracted data from the survey questionnaire and descriptive statistics (percentages (%), counts (N; n), mean (X) or median (M)values, standard deviations (SD), minimum and maximum values (MIN and MAX)) were included. Detailed statistical analyses were conducted, regarding the demonstration of differences between the represented behaviors (pro-health or anti-health) and the occurrence of orthorexia in the sample group. To analyze the above material, the χ^2 (chi-square) test for nonparametric variables and the V-Cramér coefficient of the strength of the relationship (with Yates and Fisher's correction) were used, as well as the nonparametric equivalent of the one-way analysis of variance, the Kruskal–Wallis test with the coefficient ε^2. A probability level of $p = 0.05$ was assumed for the study.

3. Results

In terms of gender distribution, the sample groups were as follows: women, 60.0%—174 persons (HRF: 47.1%, n = 82; NRF: 52.9%, n = 92); men, 40.0%—116 persons (HRF: 53.4%, n = 62; NRF: 46.6%, n = 54). All respondents were students in the final year of their master's degree (second year of their second degree). Based on the medical history, it was observed that 5.2% (15 persons) had been diagnosed with chronic diseases, although these were seasonal allergies (pollen, house dust mite, insect venom), i.e., diseases that do not significantly affect their lifestyle. The age of the respondents was 26 years (±2 years). Dietetics was studied by 48.6% of subjects (n = 70) and physical education by 51.4% of subjects (n = 72)—these subjects constituted the HRF group (144 subjects). Management was studied by 47.3% of individuals (n = 69) and computer science by 52.7% (n = 77)—these individuals constituted the NRF group (146 individuals). Among the respondents, 249 people (85.9%) lived in large cities (over 100,000 inhabitants), 23 people (7.9%) lived in smaller cities (under 100,000 inhabitants), and 18 people (6.2%) lived in villages. As far as their occupation was concerned, only 13.1% of the respondents (38 persons) had permanent employment, i.e., in telecommunication, service, and administration-office sectors. The main addiction in the surveyed groups was smoking tobacco, with 3.8% of students (11 persons) admitting to this habit. There were no subjects who compulsively consumed alcohol or took other psychoactive drugs.

None of the subjects in the study were characterized as malnourished. More than 15.2% of the subjects were characterized as underweight (44 subjects in the HRF group). Normal weight was a characteristic of 178 subjects (61.3%). Overweight and obesity were present only in the NRF group with a total of 68 subjects (23.4%). These differences were statistically significant (T = 11.281; V = 0.621, $p = 0.001$). The results of the calculations are presented in Table 1.

Table 1. Body mass indexes (BMI) of the students (N = 290).

Group	Malnutrition	Underweight	Normoweight	Overweight	Obesity
HRF (n = 144)	0 (0.0%)	44 (30.6%)	100 (69.4%)	0 (0.0%)	0 (0.0%)
NRF (n = 146)	0 (0.0%)	0 (0.0%)	78 (54.4%)	61 (41.7%)	7 (3.9%)
Total (N = 290)	0 (0.0%)	44 (15.2%)	178 (61.3%)	61 (21.0%)	7 (2.4%)
T	-		-	**11.281**	
p	>0.05		>0.05	**0.0001**	

HRF—health-related field students; NRF—non-health-related field. Bold values are statistically significant.

Based on the results of the dietary assessment, it was found that the best dietary model was characterized by the HRF group; in this group, 97.2% of students were characterized by a very good and good dietary mode (84.0%—121 persons, 13.4%—19 persons, respectively). The NRF group, on the other hand, was dominated by sufficient dietary mode, at 64.4% of all cases in this group (94 people). Less popular was the dietary model marked as "good", with only 24.6% of this group (36 people). It should be emphasized that an incorrect dietary pattern was represented only by people from the HRF group (3.9% of the total number of subjects—11 people). Detailed results of the students' dietary assessment are shown in Figure 1.

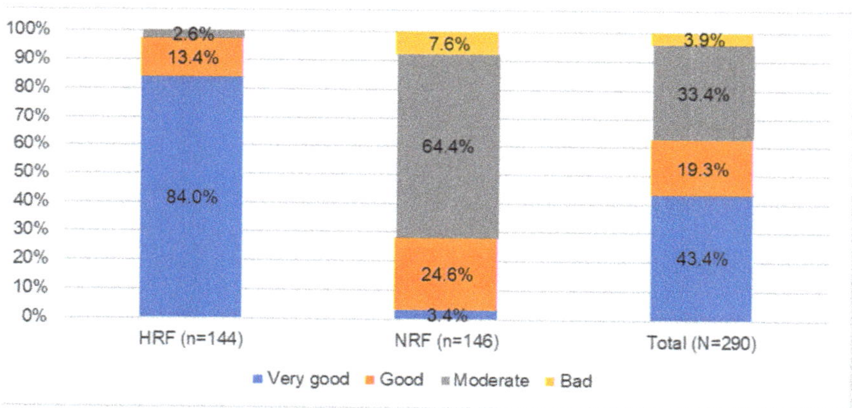

Figure 1. Students' dietary assessment (N = 290): HRF—health-related field students; NRF—non-health-related field.

The next stage of the study was to assess the physical activity and motivation of the respondents to undertake physical activity. The level of physical activity was assessed by answering four questions regarding the fact of exercise, type of exercise, frequency, and duration of physical activity. Based on the data obtained, it was observed that 98.6% (142 persons) of the HRF group and 83.6% (122 persons) of the NRF group were physically active. Correspondingly, 2 individuals from the HRF and 24 individuals from the NRF did not engage in any physical exercise daily (1.4% vs. 16.4%)—these individuals were not included in Figure 2 which categorizes physical activity levels by PAL index.

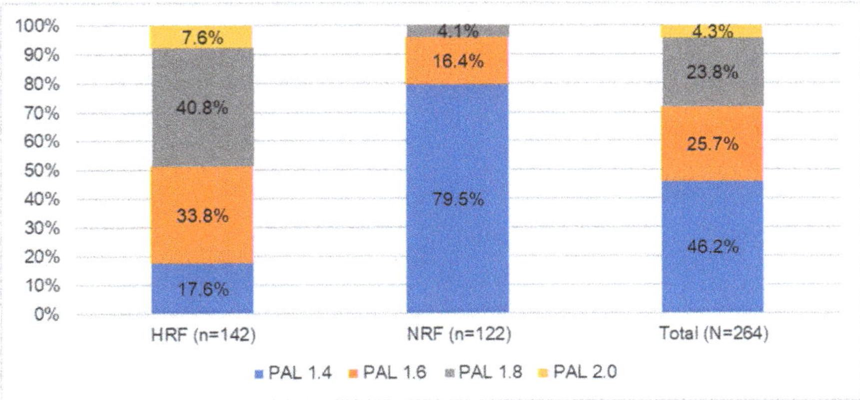

Figure 2. Students' physical activity level ratings (N = 264).

Low physical activity was characteristic for 46.2% of respondents (122 persons), and most often chosen by persons from the NRF group (79.5%—97 persons). Medium physical activity was observed in 25.7% of the respondents (68 persons); this activity concerned both the HRF group (33.8%—48 persons) and the NRF group (16.4%—20 persons). Physical activity at a high and very high level concerned 28.1% of the students (75 persons), these were mainly persons from the HRF group (48.4%—70 persons) (Figure 2).

The level of motivation to undertake physical exercise and its reasons in the sample group varied, and were assessed using the EMI-2 questionnaire. In the sample group, the pleasure derived from physical activity was the most important motivation to undertake it (1.79 ± 1.78). Psychological regeneration (1.81 ± 1.73), maintaining health (1.91 ± 1.82), building strength and endurance (1.93 ± 1.81), taking care of appearance (1.96 ± 1.86), and avoiding ill health (1.99 ± 1.71) were also strong motivators. The least important motivation for exercise was health pressure (2.77 ± 2.22), followed by social recognition (2.62 ± 1.93) and the desire to belong to a group (2.37 ± 2.02). There were no statistically significant differences between groups. The results were comparable in both groups of students (Table 2).

Table 2. EMI-2 subscales by group (N = 290).

Subscale	Mean (X ± SD) HRF (n = 144)	NRF (n = 146)	Total (N = 290)	T	*p*
Stress Management	2.20 (±1.32)	1.80 (±2.02)	2.00 (±1.72)	-	>0.05
Mental Regeneration	1.82 (±1.74)	1.79 (±1.72)	1.81 (±1.73)		
Pleasure	1.80 (±1.79)	1.78 (±1.77)	1.79 (±1.78)		
Challenges	2.04 (±1.81)	2.06 (±1.83)	2.05 (±1.82)		
Social Recognition	2.63 (±1.92)	2.61 (±1.94)	2.62 (±1.93)		
Group Membership	2.36 (±2.01)	2.38 (±2.03)	2.37 (±2.02)		
Competition	2.32 (±2.04)	2.35 (±2.06)	2.34 (±2.05)		
Health Pressure	2.78 (±2.23)	2.76 (±2.21)	2.77 (±2.22)		
Avoiding Ill Health	2.00 (±1.74)	1.98 (±1.68)	1.99 (±1.71)		
Staying Healthy	1.95 (±1.83)	1.86 (±1.81)	1.91 (±1.82)		
Weight Control	2.03 (±1.89)	2.09 (±1.95)	2.06 (±1.92)		
Appearance	1.90 (±1.80)	2.02 (±1.92)	1.96 (±1.86)		
Strength and Endurance	1.90 (±1.84)	1.96 (±1.78)	1.93 (±1.81)		
Agility and Flexibility	2.00 (±1.70)	2.18 (±1.72)	2.09 (±1.71)		

Before evaluating the size and caloric value of the portions using the albums of exemplary products and dishes, each participant had to pass a visual perception test consisting of the evaluation of six images divided into two groups: (1) Ishihara boards—assessing the perception of colors, and representing in turn: the number 12, the number 96 and the absence of a specific shape; and (2) optical illusion boards—assessing the perception of space (size, length, and shape). Each correct indication in the visual perception test was scored one point, and a total of six points could be gained. In the sample group, 89.6% (n = 282) scored from five to six points, and 10.4% (n = 30) scored three to four points. The greatest difficulty for the subjects turned out to be the Ishihara board, which does not represent a specific shape, and the optical illusion board, which assesses shape perception (assessing the straightness of the lines depicted). Due to the overall good performance on the test, it was not decided to exclude any participant in the remainder of the study.

The visual perception assessment was followed by the actual test of estimating portion sizes and calories. Each participant received individual albums of sample products and dishes, which contained 12 photographs of food products and ready meals. The evaluator's task was to estimate the size and caloric value of the given item using the variants listed under the photographs (four variants for size (g), and four for energy supply (kcal)). The variants were selected so that one indicated the correct value; one smaller or larger in the range of 8–12% from the correct value, but still treated as a correct answer; and two incorrect variants, underestimated and overestimated in the range of 28–32% relative to the correct value. Based on the data obtained, it was determined what percentage of respondents correctly and incorrectly (over- or underestimated) the size and calorie content of the servings.

Figure 3 shows the results of the portion size estimation test.

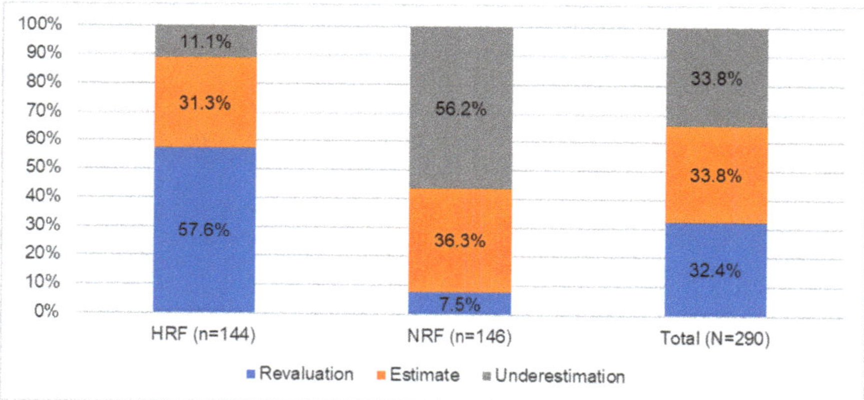

Figure 3. Level of portion size estimation across student groups (N = 290).

Based on the test on the ability to estimate the size of the portions based on photographs, it was found that 32.4% (94 people) overestimated the size of the portions of products and dishes indicated in the photographs. In this group, there were mostly people studying in health faculties—57.6% (83 people); less often, there are people from other faculties—7.5% (11 people). In the case of underestimation (33.8%, n = 98), the situation was reversed—people from the NRF group mainly underestimated the size of products and dishes—56.2% (n = 82); in the HRF group, much fewer people underestimated (11.1%, n = 16). The remaining persons correctly indicated the size of the portion—33.8% (98 people).

Figure 4 shows the results of the caloric estimation test for portions.

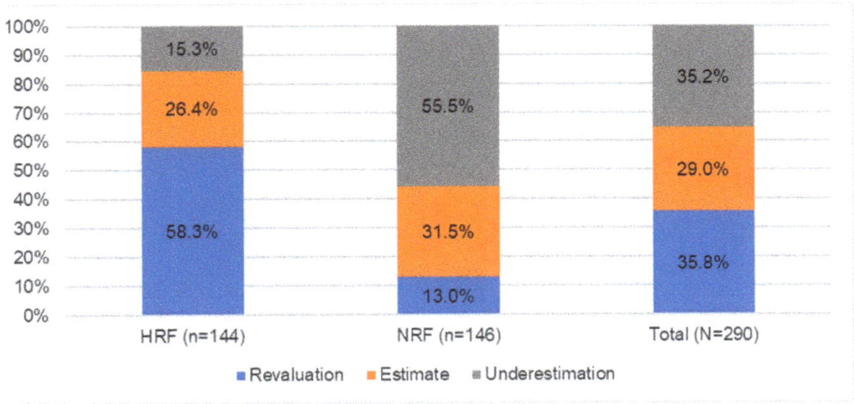

Figure 4. Level of calorie estimation of servings in student groups (N = 290).

Analyzing the results of the test on the ability to estimate the calorie content of portions based on photographs, it was observed that 35.8% (104 people) overestimated the calorie content of the products and dishes indicated in the photographs. This group included mainly health-related people (58.3%—84 people), and less frequently, non-health-related people (13.0%—19 people). On the other hand, in the case of underestimation of the energy of dishes (35.2%, n = 102), people from the NRF group mostly underestimated the caloric value of products and dishes presented in the album (55.5%, n = 81); in the HRF group, such cases were much less (15.3%, n = 22). The remaining persons correctly indicated the calorie content of the portion—29.0% (84).

Using the ORTO-15 questionnaire, it was found that, among the subjects, 44.5% (129 subjects) scored below 40, indicating an increased risk of orthorexia. This was more frequent in the HRF group than in the NRF group (63.5% vs. 25.8%), with 92 and 37 subjects, respectively, from the student groups. Based on statistical inference, it was found that low BMI values occur in individuals from the HRF group, which indicates the presence of a statistically significant relationship between the indicated characteristics (T = 13.238; V = 0.723; p = 0.0001). Similarly, also in the case of diet, individuals representing good (27.6%) and very good (16.2%) nutrition were more likely to belong to the group of people with an increased risk of orthorexia. In this case, as well, a statistically significant correlation with HRF group membership was shown (T = 10.984; V = 0.683; p = 0.0001) (Table 3).

Table 3. Relationship between BMI and diet and the group at increased risk for orthorexia (n = 129).

BMI vs. ORTO-15	Malnutrition	Underweight	Normoweight	Overweight	Obesity	T	p
	0	44 (15.2%)	85 (29.3%)	0	0		
HRF (n = 92)	0	44 (15.2%)	48 (16.6%)	0	0	**13.238**	**0.0001**
NRF (n = 37)	0	0	37 (12.8%)	0	0		
Diet vs. ORTO-15	Bad	Moderate	Good	Very Good		T	p
	0	2 (0.7%)	80 (27.6%)	47 (16.2%)			
HRF (n = 92)	0	0	45 (15.5%)	47 (16.2%)		**10.984**	**0.0001**
NRF (n = 37)	0	2 (0.7%)	35 (12.1%)	0			

Bold values are statistically significant.

Next, it was decided to verify the relationships between the occurrence of orthorexic behavior and the represented level of physical activity. Based on the statistical inference performed, it was found that high PAL values occur in the HRF group, which indicates the presence of a statistically significant relationship between the indicated characteristics (T = 8.117; V = 0.597; p = 0.002) (Table 4).

Table 4. Relationship between physical activity level and the group at increased risk for orthorexia (n = 129).

PAL vs. ORTO-15	PAL 1.4	PAL 1.6	PAL 1.8	PAL 2.0	T	*p*
	19 (6.6%)	27 (9.3%)	51 (17.6%)	32 (11.0%)		
HRF (n = 92)	10 (3.4%)	15 (5.2%)	35 (12.1%)	32 (11.0%)	**8.117**	**0.002**
NRF (n = 37)	9 (3.1%)	12 (4.1%)	16 (5.5%)	0		

Bold values are statistically significant.

The last verification concerned the relationship between the occurrence of orthorexic behaviors in the sample group and the ability of the respondents to estimate portion sizes and calories. Based on the results presented in Table 5 and the statistical analyses performed, it was concluded that there is a statistical relationship both in the case of estimation of portion size and caloricity of meals; individuals from the HRF group characterized by orthorexic behavior are more likely to overestimate the size and caloricity of the meal ($p < 0.05$).

Table 5. Relationship between demonstrated ability to estimate portion size and group at increased risk for orthorexia (n = 129).

Estimating Portion Size vs. ORTO-15/TFEQ-13	Underestimation	Estimate	Revaluation	T	*p*
Orthorexic Behavior (n = 129)	0	32 (11.0%)	95 (32.8%)		
HRF (n = 92)	0	12 (4.1%)	78 (26.9%)	**12.467**	**0.0001**
NRF (n = 37)	0	20 (6.9%)	17 (5.9%)		
Estimating Caloric Intake vs. ORTO-15	**Underestimation**	**Estimate**	**Revaluation**	**T**	***p***
Orthorexic Behavior (n = 129)	18 (6.2%)	22 (7.6%)	87 (30.0%)		
HRF (n = 92)	8 (2.8%)	12 (4.1%)	70 (24.1%)	**11.551**	**0.0001**
NRF (n = 37)	10 (3.4%)	10 (3.4%)	17 (5.9%)		

Bold values are statistically significant.

4. Discussion

Several studies indicate that an occupational group with an increased risk of orthorexic behaviors are people who practice sports (representing various sports disciplines, including those that require a very slim and limber body). Due to the extreme difficulty in making a definitive diagnosis, the exact number of people with orthorexia is still unknown. Dunn and Bartman [12] estimate that between 6 and 90% of people may be affected depending on their social group (this spectrum is dictated by the different prevalence of the condition in different populations). People with orthorexia are very often treated by their environment as caring too much about their health, and their loved ones do not find features of the disorder in such behavior. The lack of accurate information on the size of the condition is also due to the reluctance of affected individuals to report to specialists and their failure to notice such problems.

Although orthorexia is not commonly recognized as an eating disorder, there is ongoing research on the condition of overeating, limiting food intake, and leading a pathologically pro-healthy lifestyle. The following is a review of studies that look at the relationship between psychological state, occupation/field of study, practicing physical activity, or anthropometric indices, and the occurrence of orthorexic behavior. In recent years, there have been several papers regarding the condition of orthorexia. Current scientific evidence is presented below and compared with the results of our research.

In our own study, the occurrence of orthorexia depended on the field of study chosen by the participants of the study. Of course, the authors do not suggest that it is the field of study that influences the incidence of orthorexia, but rather the personality conditions that determine its choice, which also influence the development of orthorexic behavior. In the current study, it was observed that orthorexia occurs twice as often in people from the health-related group than in non-health-related people (63.5% vs. 25.8%). In addition, Kinzl et al. [30] in their study checked the prevalence of orthorexia among 283 Austrian female dietitians. They used the German version of the FEV questionnaire, which examines three dimensions of eating behavior, and the ORTO-15 questionnaire to verify the presence of orthorexia. In the sample group, more than one-third were individuals who had recently changed their eating habits. Among the respondents, some orthorexic behavior was presented in 34.9% of people, while orthorexia was found in 12.8% of people. Individuals in the last group were more likely than others to have experienced eating disorders recently. From the FEV questionnaire, it was found that 40% of individuals significantly controlled their eating behavior. A study by Haddad et al. [31] analyzed a group of 811 Lebanese people, from each province. The paper also used the ORTO-15 questionnaire and adopted the same cut-off point as in our study. The study found that 75.2% of the respondents exhibited tendencies and behaviors indicative of orthorexia. There was a significant association of orthorexia in the group of women, with people starving themselves to lose weight, urging others to "go on a diet", and claiming that eating out is unhealthy.

The current study confirmed that people with higher physical activity are more likely to engage in orthorexic behavior. The demonstrated dependence showed that the higher the PAL index, the higher the risk of orthorexic behaviors. Moreover, the PAL index at the level of 2.0 was present only in the group of people with a positive ORTO-15 result. Malmborg et al. [32] investigated health status, physical activity, and frequency of orthorexia among physical education and management students. Respondents completed the Short Form Quality of Life Assessment Questionnaire (SF-36), the International Physical Activity Questionnaire (IPAQ), and the ORTO-15 questionnaire. Of 188 students, 144 (76.6%) had an ORTO-15 score indicating orthorexia, of which 84.5% were physical education students. Orthorexia combined with high levels of physical activity was more commonly observed in male physical education students than in female physical education students (45.1% vs. 8.3%). This would support the hypothesis posed in our study—those who participate intensively in sports may have a significantly higher exposure to orthorexia than those with lower levels of physical activity. This hypothesis is also supported by other research conducted by the author of the present study; in the 2020 study, the risk of orthorexia estimated based on ORTO-15 was determined for three-quarters of the sample group (300 out of 400 ballet schoolgirls in Silesian province) [33].

In addition, in our own study, it was shown that there is a true relationship, which indicates that orthorexia may occur in the group of people with a low BMI index; however, it was first of all noticed that it is appropriate for the group of people with normal body weight, regardless of the field of study they represented (HRF vs. NRF–16.6% vs. 12.8%). Similarly, Agopyan et al. [34] conducted a study to determine the relationship between orthorexia and the body composition of female students at Marmara University. The participants of the study were female students whose scores on the ORTO-15 questionnaire and EAT-40 eating attitude test indicated the presence of orthorexia. Evaluation of the respondents' body composition indices (bioelectrical impedance on a Tanita SC-330 device) showed that there was no significant difference between the EAT-40 and ORTO-15 scores in terms of body composition. The vast majority of female respondents (70.6%) had high ORTO-15 scores, and there was a significant negative correlation ($p < 0.05$) between EAT-40 and ORTO-15 scores. The final results of the data analysis showed that although abnormal tendencies were common among the female students, they were able to maintain normal body composition. Similarly, a study by Grammatikopoulou et al. [35] showed that health sciences students, especially nutrition and dietetics students, have a higher prevalence of eating disorders. A total of 176 undergraduate students from the Faculty of Nutrition and Dietetics in Greece participated in the study. The study monitored food intake and examined the frequency of eating as a result of emotion and stress (EADES). Among the students participating in the study, 4.5% showed food addiction, and 68.2% showed orthorexia. No differences were observed between males and females in food addiction and orthorexia. Students with orthorexia showed increased BMI. Orthorexics consumed more low-energy foods, including vegetables, and less high-energy foods (meat and fat). Multiple linear regression analysis showed that orthorexic behavior was associated with increased BMI, waist circumference, and energy intake. Lower BMI was associated with the ability to cope with EADES.

Farchakh et al. [36] conducted a study to assess the association between orthorexic behaviors (ORTO-15), eating habits (EAT-40), and anxiety levels (HAM-A) among a representative sample of medical students in Lebanese universities. A total of 627 medical students participated in the study. Linear regression results showed that a higher EAT-40 questionnaire score was significantly associated with lower ORTO-15 scores (more orthorexic behaviors), while a higher HAM-A anxiety score was significantly associated with higher ORTO-15 scores (less orthorexic behaviors). The results obtained in this study suggest an association between eating habits indicative of an eating disorder and orthorexic behaviors. In addition, individuals with orthorexia were shown to be less likely to experience anxiety. The self-reported study also highlighted the fact that there is an association between eating patterns and the occurrence of specific disorders. Barnes and Caltabiano [37] examined the correlations between perfectionism, body image, attachment style, self-esteem, and the occurrence of orthorexia. In total, 220 subjects completed a questionnaire consisting of the ORTO-15 questionnaire, the Multidimensional Perfectionism Scale (MPS), the Multidimensional Body Image Questionnaire (MBSRQ-AS), the Relationship Scale Questionnaire (RSQ), and the Rosenberg Self-Esteem Scale (RSES). The study confirmed a significant association of orthorexia prevalence among individuals with scores indicating perfectionism, appearance orientation, preoccupation with overweight and self-esteem, and aversion to attachment. However, the association of orthorexia prevalence with self-esteem was not confirmed. In our study, the occurrence of orthorexia nervosa was not compared with the mental state of the respondents, but an important correlation was shown that people suffering from this disorder more often overestimate the energy and volume value of food portions, which may indicate that among these people, similarly to other EDs, there are cognitive disorders associated with the incorrect perception of not only your own body, but also food intended for consumption. This condition should be the subject of further research on this topic.

Strengths and Limitations

The research on the prevalence of orthorexic behaviors among students of different majors allowed us to understand the basic mechanisms, cause–effect relationships, and determinants of the occurrence of the indicated disorders. Conducting the research required a lot of work and preparation in the form of developing research tools and becoming familiar with existing psychometric tools measuring the risk of orthorexia. Of course, the paper does not suggest that it is the field of study that influences the development of the disorder, but rather that individuals who choose it are characterized by certain traits that predispose them to it. This should be understood in the way that, thanks to the results of the study, it is possible to detect groups of people who should be included in the observation in terms of the control and safety of their lifestyle.

An important limitation of the study is that causation cannot be described as it is a cross-sectional study. The main difficulties during the conduct of the study were access to the student group because the study was conducted in the period of May–June 2021, and it should be emphasized that this was the period immediately adjacent to the lifting of the COVID-19 pandemic restrictions, so it was necessary to use the method of online surveying using Google package forms. In addition, data such as height or weight, because the study was conducted using the CAWI method, were provided by the respondents themselves, which may result in a mistake caused by the self-assessment of these indicators by the participants. The use of an Internet survey still raises some doubts among researchers as to the reliability of filling out the questionnaires. It is worth emphasizing here that despite many reservations about online surveys, it is currently one of the main and most acceptable forms of conducting them. The second part of the research, which involved the use of food and dishes photo albums, was conducted face-to-face. This approach was chosen because of the extensive nature of the research tools and concerns about respondents' reluctance to fill out the extensive questionnaire. In addition, contemporary reports confirm that people are more willing to participate in research when the researcher provides a comfortable research experience (online methods, neutral environment, interesting setting) [38]. The research material presented in this study, in light of scientific reports, appears to be a rather novel approach to the topic of nonspecific eating disorders, as research rarely uses methods from psychology and dietetics simultaneously. This approach has allowed for a comprehensive analysis and elaboration of the collected research material.

5. Conclusions

Based on the cited self-research and information from the literature, it can be concluded that the problem of orthorexia is still a new issue at the level of social sciences, medical sciences, and health sciences. The mechanisms of development of these disorders are still poorly understood, and any data resulting from the study are only a signpost for further scientific investigation. The psychometric tools used in this study allowed us to demonstrate the prevalence of the aforementioned eating disorders in the studied groups of students, along with their determinants, and the photo album of selected foods and dishes allowed us to estimate the respondents' skills in estimating the weight and energy of food intake. Nevertheless, it is worth noting that the methods used were characterized by certain limitations; therefore, in the future, it would be worth extending the scope of the study to other social groups, a wider range of research tools, and deepening the existing ones.

The conducted research allowed us to verify the set research hypotheses and to formulate the following conclusions: orthorexic behaviors are characteristic of a group of people who are associated with health, and who take care of their lifestyle, diet, and participate in physical activity. Individuals who are at increased risk for orthorexia tend to overestimate the size and caloric content of their meals. The dietary condition discussed in the paper should be under constant control, and all health promotion activities should focus on the nutrition education and psychoeducation of young adults.

In conclusion, it should be noted that a necessary aspect of further research on the topic of nonspecific eating disorders should be the development of actions aimed at the prevention of eating disorder development in young adults. This can be achieved by including mental problems of nutritional nature in the National Health Program and the National Mental Health Program, or by planning and implementing nationwide health policy programs that include such tasks as comprehensive health education, with particular emphasis on nutritional education and psychoeducation from the early school years. It should be noted that eating disorders are an important multidisciplinary problem. Apart from the well-known disorders, the less-known ones, whose background may be found in the trend for a "fit life", are more frequently discussed. Therefore, the mentioned education should be provided not only by psychologists, but also by pedagogues, dieticians, personal trainers, and representatives of other professions connected with the problem.

Author Contributions: Conceptualization, M.G.; methodology, M.G., K.S.-N. and E.M.; validation, K.S-N.; formal analysis, M.G.; investigation, M.G.; resources, M.G. and K.K.-K.; data curation, M.G.; writing—original draft preparation, M.G.; writing—review and editing, M.G. and K.K.-K.; visualization, K.K.-K.; supervision, K.S.-N. and J.K.; project administration, E.M., M.G. and K.K.-K. All authors have read and agreed to the published version of the manuscript.

Funding: This research received no external funding.

Institutional Review Board Statement: Not applicable.

Informed Consent Statement: Informed consent was obtained from all subjects involved in the study.

Data Availability Statement: The original contributions presented in the study are included in the article; further inquiries can be directed to the corresponding author.

Acknowledgments: The authors would like to thank all the participants in the study.

Conflicts of Interest: The authors declare that the research was conducted in the absence of any commercial or financial relationships that could be construed as a potential conflict of interest.

References

1. Brytek-Matera, A. *Psychodietetyka*; PZWL: Warszawa, Poland, 2020; pp. 61–80.
2. Grajek, M.; Nowak, J. *Interwencje Psychodietetyczne We Wybranych Zaburzeniach Odżywiania*; Śląski Uniwersytet Medyczny w Katowicach: Katowice, Poland, 2021; pp. 57–61.
3. American Psychiatric Association. *Diagnostic and Statistical Manual of Mental Disorders (DSM-5)*; American Psychiatric Publishing: Philadelphia, PA, USA, 2013.
4. Żechowski, C. Zaburzenia odżywiania się—Problem współczesnej młodzieży. *Ośr. Rozw. Edukac.* **2016**, *5*, 1–14.
5. Ryman, F.V.M.; Cesuroglu, T.; Bood, Z.M.; Syurina, E.V. Orthorexia Nervosa: Disorder or Not? Opinions of Dutch Health Professionals. *Front Psychol.* **2019**, *10*, 555. [CrossRef] [PubMed]
6. Zipfel, S.; Giel, K.E.; Bulik, C.M. Anorexia nervosa: Aetiology, assessment, and treatment. *Lancet Psychiatry* **2015**, *2*, 1099–1111. [CrossRef]
7. Kotwas, A.; Krakiewicz-Krawczyk, K.; Zabielska, P. Występowanie zaburzeń odżywiania wśród uczennic szkół ponadgimnazjalnych. *Psychiatr. Pol.* **2019**, *127*, 253–263.
8. Namysłowska. Podstawowe Grupy Zaburzeń Odżywiania. 2014. Available online: https://podyplomie.pl/psychiatria/16026,podstawowe-grupy-zaburzen-odzywiania (accessed on 6 October 2021).
9. Grajek, M.; Rej, A.; Kryska, S.; Sobczyk, K. Problematyka zaburzeń odżywiania w ocenie adolescentów. *Nauczyciel I Szkoła* **2014**, *2*, 187–198.
10. Gkiouleka, M.; Stavraki, C.; Sergentanis, T.N.; Vassilakou, T. Orthorexia Nervosa in Adolescents and Young Adults: A Literature Review. *Children* **2022**, *9*, 365. [CrossRef] [PubMed]
11. Niedzielski, A.; Kaźmierczak-Wojtaś, N. Prevalence of Orthorexia Nervosa and Its Diagnostic Tools—A Literature Review. *Int. J. Environ. Res. Public Health* **2021**, *18*, 5488. [CrossRef]
12. Dunn, T.M.; Bratman, S. On orthorexia nervosa: A review of the literature and proposed diagnostic criteria. *Eat Behav.* **2016**, *21*, 11–17. [CrossRef]
13. Dittfeld, A. *Ortoreksja—Nowe Zaburzenie Odżywiania*; Annales Academiae Medicae Silesiensis: Katowice, Poland, 2013; p. 67.
14. Koven, N.S.; Abry, A.W. The clinical basis of orthorexia nervosa: Emerging perspectives. *Neuropsychiatr. Dis. Treat.* **2015**, *11*, 385–394. [CrossRef]
15. Strahler, J.; Hermann, A.; Walter, B.; Stark, R. Orthorexia nervosa: A behavioral complex or a psychological condition? *J. Behav. Addict.* **2018**, *7*, 1143–1156. [CrossRef]
16. Grajek, M.; Mitera, A. *Psychodietetyka We Współczesnym Poradnictwie Żywieniowym*; Śląski Uniwersytet Medyczny w Katowicach: Katowice, Poland, 2020; pp. 58–73.
17. Segura-Garcia, C.; Ramacciotti, C.; Rania, M. The prevalence of orthorexia nervosa among eating disorder patients after treatment. *Eat Weight Disord.* **2015**, *20*, 161–166. [CrossRef] [PubMed]
18. Jarosz, M.; Rychlik, E.; Stoś, K. *Normy Żywienia Dla Populacji Polskiej i ich Zastosowanie*; NIZP-PZH: Warszawa, Poland, 2020; pp. 103–110.
19. Dunn, T.M.; Gibbs, J.; Whitney, N.; Starosta, A. Prevalence of orthorexia nervosa is less than 1%: Data from a US sample. *Eat Weight Disord.* **2017**, *22*, 185–192. [CrossRef] [PubMed]
20. NCEZ: Talerz Zdrowego Żywienia. Narodowe Centrum Edukacji Żywieniowej. 2020. Available online: https://ncez.pzh.gov.pl/abc-zywienia/talerz-zdrowego-zywienia/ (accessed on 6 October 2021).
21. WHO. Physical Activity. 2020. Available online: https://www.who.int/news-room/fact-sheets/detail/physical-activity (accessed on 6 October 2021).
22. Sas-Nowosielski, K.; Nowicka, M. Motywy i bariery uczestnictwa kobiet w zajęciach fitnessu. *Rozpr. Nauk. Akadem. Wych. Fiz. We Wroc.* **2017**, *56*, 3–9.
23. Stochel, M.; Janas-Kozik, M.; Zejda, J. Walidacja kwestionariusza ORTO-15 w grupie młodzieży miejskiej w wieku 15–21 lat. *Psychiatr. Pol.* **2015**, *49*, 119–134. [CrossRef]
24. Brytek-Matera, A.; Krupa, M.; Poggiogalle, E.; Donini, L.M. Adaptation of the ORTHO-15 test to Polish women and men. *Eat Weight Disord.* **2014**, *19*, 69–76. [CrossRef] [PubMed]
25. Gawęcki, J. Żywienie człowieka. In *Podstawy Nauki o Żywieniu*; PWN: Warszawa, Poland, 2017; pp. 57–80.
26. Ciborowska, H.; Rudnicka, A. *Dietetyka Żywienie Zdrowego I Chorego Człowieka*; PZWL: Warszawa, Poland, 2019; p. 118.

27. WHO. Body Mass Index—BMI. 2021. Available online: https://www.euro.who.int/en/health-topics/disease-prevention/nutrition/a-healthy-lifestyle/body-mass-index-bmi (accessed on 6 October 2021).
28. FAO. Total Energy Expenditure (TEE) and Physical Activity Levels (PAL) in Adults: Doubly-Labelled Water Data. Energy and Protein Requirements, Proceedings of an IDECG Workshop. United Nations University. 1994. Available online: https://archive.unu.edu/unupress/food2/UID01E/UID01E08.HTM (accessed on 6 October 2021).
29. Markland, D.; Ingledew, D.K. The measurement of exercise motives: Factorial validity and invariance across gender of a revised Exercise Motivations Inventory. *Br. J. Health Psychol.* **1997**, *2*, 361–376. [CrossRef]
30. Kinzl, J.F.; Hauer, K.; Traweger, C.; Kiefer, I. Orthorexia nervosa in dieticians. *Psychother. Psychosom.* **2006**, *75*, 395–396. [CrossRef]
31. Haddad, C.; Obeid, S.; Akel, M. Correlates of orthorexia nervosa among a representative sample of the Lebanese population. *Eat Weight Disord.* **2019**, *24*, 481–493. [CrossRef]
32. Malmborg, J.; Bremander, A.; Olsson, M.C.; Bergman, S. Health status, physical activity, and orthorexia nervosa: A comparison between exercise science students and business students. *Appetite* **2017**, *109*, 137–143. [CrossRef]
33. Grajek, M. Dietary habits and orthorexic behaviours of dancing school female students. *J. Phys. Edu. Sport* **2020**, *20*, 3102–3107. [CrossRef]
34. Agopyan, A.; Kenger, E.B.; Kermen, S. The relationship between orthorexia nervosa and body composition in female students of the nutrition and dietetics department. *Eat Weight Disord.* **2019**, *24*, 257–266. [CrossRef] [PubMed]
35. Grammatikopoulou, M.G.; Gkiouras, K.; Markaki, A.; Theodoridis, X.; Tsakiri, V.; Mavridis, P.; Dardavessis, T.; Chourdakis, M. Food addiction, orthorexia, and food-related stress among dietetics students. *Eat Weight Disord.* **2018**, *23*, 459–467. [CrossRef] [PubMed]
36. Farchakh, Y.; Hallit, S.; Soufia, M. Association between orthorexia nervosa, eating attitudes and anxiety among medical students in Lebanese universities: Results of a cross-sectional study. *Eat Weight Disord.* **2019**, *24*, 683–691. [CrossRef] [PubMed]
37. Barnes, M.A.; Caltabiano, M.L. The interrelationship between orthorexia nervosa, perfectionism, body image, and attachment style. *Eat Weight Disord.* **2017**, *22*, 177–184. [CrossRef] [PubMed]
38. Kuś, J.; Stefańska, K.; Bukowska, A. Metodologia badań psychologicznych prowadzonych w przestrzeni Internetu. *Studia Metodol.* **2015**, *34*, 209–237.

nutrients

MDPI

Article

Weekend–Weekday Differences in Adherence to the Mediterranean Diet among Spanish University Students

Luis M. Béjar

Department of Preventive Medicine and Public Health, School of Medicine, University of Seville, 41004 Seville, Spain; lmbprado@us.es; Tel.: +34-954-551-771

Abstract: Daily routines may influence eating patterns; however, differences in intake on weekdays and at weekends have rarely been explored. Furthermore, these differences have not been analyzed among university students (a particularly interesting group among the younger generations). The aim of the study was to evaluate weekend–weekday variation in the Mediterranean diet among Spanish university students, while investigating the potential influence of age, gender, studies, body mass index, smoking status and physical activity status. A repeated-measurement 28-day cross-sectional observational study with self-reported dietary intake collected using the e12HR app was conducted. There were 361 participants: average age 20.6 years; 72.9% women; 58.2% students of Pharmacy; average BMI 21.9 kg/m^2; 91.4% nonsmokers; 77.6% performed ≥150 min/week of physical activity. Outcome measurements were adherence to the Mediterranean diet (AMD) index and percentage of participants meeting recommendations for each food group on weekdays and at weekends. In all subgroups, Spanish university students' global diet was associated with low AMD, with poorer diet quality (>12% reductions in mean scores of AMD index and >26% reductions in adequate adherence scores (≥9)) at weekends. In conclusion, weekend health behaviors of Spanish university students displayed less favorable eating behavior, making the weekend an important target for public health interventions aiming to improve dietary intake.

Keywords: Mediterranean diet; food; feeding behavior; nutrition assessment; university; smartphone; mobile applications; information technology

Citation: Béjar, L.M. Weekend–Weekday Differences in Adherence to the Mediterranean Diet among Spanish University Students. *Nutrients* **2022**, *14*, 2811. https://doi.org/10.3390/nu14142811

Academic Editors: Roberto Pippi, Carmine G. Fanelli and Matteo Vandoni

Received: 16 June 2022
Accepted: 6 July 2022
Published: 8 July 2022

1. Introduction

In 2004, the World Health Organization (WHO) adopted the Global Strategy on Diet, Physical Activity and Health, the overall goal of which was to promote and protect health through diet and physical activity [1]. Since then, improving diet quality has been essential for health promotion strategy.

Within the international debate on changing diets and food systems to more adequate ones, the Mediterranean diet (MD) is potentially the best diet based on evidence as it is at once healthy and sustainable. The MD combines: 1. Important health benefits: a growing body of evidence supports the protective role of the MD, in terms of primary and secondary prevention, against cardiovascular disease, arteriosclerosis, cancer, diabetes mellitus, metabolic syndrome, excess weight/obesity, respiratory disease (asthma and sleep apnea), mental disorders (cognitive decline and depression) and renal disease [2–6]. Non-nutritional aspects, linked in one way or another to food consumption, have been suggested to contribute to the beneficial effect of the MD; these include, among others, physical activity [7]; and 2. Sustainability [6,8–13]: an aspect which has been under debate in recent years regarding dietary patterns is that they should not only be beneficial for all people but also for the environment, for all countries and, as such, for the planet [6,8]. The MD does this as it has a low environmental impact and richness of biodiversity, a high sociocultural value is placed on the foods, and it provides positive local economic benefits [6].

The MD (with its health benefits and sustainability) is faced with great difficulties in its implementation in other geographic and cultural regions and, paradoxically, it is even struggling to stay alive in traditionally Mediterranean regions (influenced by unhealthy dietary habits as a result of global acculturation) [4] where it is being abandoned, mainly by younger generations [12].

People's day to day lives are punctuated by work, education, domestic chores, sleep and food. Alterations in daily patterns contribute significantly to changes in dietary patterns [14]. Characterization of food consumption across the days of the week can help target health promotion initiatives that are striving to improve dietary intake of the population [15]. However, while much research has focused on the identification of dietary patterns, less attention has been paid to temporal variation of dietary intake [15].

A limited number of studies have analyzed weekly variation dietary patterns in diverse populations (e.g., children/adolescents [15–31] and adults [15,29–37]) residing in different countries (e.g., United States [16–19,26,29,32–34,36,37], Denmark [15,20,21], Australia [25,28], Canada [31,35], Brazil [30], New Zealand [22], France [24], Korea [27], Belgium, Cyprus, Estonia, Germany, Hungary, Italy, Spain and Sweden (multicentric study) [23]).

In general, findings have previously reported less healthful dietary intakes at weekends in comparison to those at weekdays. Compared with weekdays, weekend days have shown higher energy intake [15,20,29,30,32–35], higher percentage of energy from fat [16,17,29,30,32,34], higher consumption of added sugar [15,23], alcohol [15,32,34,35], discretionary foods [15,25,32], sugar-sweetened beverages [15,20–22,30,32], sweets [20], chocolate [20], white bread [20], and hot chips [22,30], lower consumption of dietary fiber [15,32], vegetables [15,17,20,21,24,32,34], fruit [15–17,20,21,24,32,34], milk/yogurt [24,34] and wholegrain products [15,20,24,34], a consistent pattern of more frequent consumption and larger portions of unhealthy foods and beverages [19], and an increase in the prevalence of fast-food and full-service restaurant consumption [32]. Additionally, some studies have provided lower dietary quality scores on weekends than on weekdays, such as the Dietary Guidelines Index for Children and Adolescents score [25] and the Healthy Eating Index [34,35]. However, the nature of weekday–weekend variation in dietary intake among university students (a particularly interesting group among the younger generations) has remained unknown.

The university phase may be the first phase of life when most teenagers start making their own food choices. For this reason, universities may provide an ideal forum for reaching out to many young adults through nutrition education programs that may positively influence students' eating habits [38]. Research on the timing of dietary behaviors is essential for understanding the complexity of dietary patterns in this novel group and necessary to inform nutrition-related health policies and recommendations, which, regarding the MD, could help reverse the abandonment observed especially in the younger generations.

Therefore, to our knowledge, this paper serves as the first attempt to evaluate weekend–weekday differences in the MD among Spanish university students through 28 days of dietary recording, while investigating the potential influence of age, gender, studies, body mass index (BMI), smoking status and physical activity status as determinants for weekly variation. We hypothesized that individuals would display a less healthy diet during the weekends compared with that of the weekdays and furthermore that these differences were heterogeneous across population subgroups under examination.

2. Materials and Methods

2.1. Participant Recruitment

A repeated-measurement 28-day cross-sectional observational study was conducted. The recruitment of participants took place in April 2022.

The study took place with students at the Faculties of Medicine and Pharmacy at the University of Seville (Andalusia, Spain, South of Europe), selecting 4 random classrooms in each school.

A member of the research team presented the project to the students providing information on:

1. The objectives and participation in the study: to participate, interested students had to send an email to the address provided for the study;
2. Inclusion criteria: over the age of 18; no chronic pathologies, food intolerances or pregnancy (situations that could require specialized dietary recommendations); be a student at the Faculties of Medicine or Pharmacy (University of Seville); and possess a mobile telephone with Internet access and an iOS or Android operating system;
3. How the e-12HR app works.

After receiving an e-mail from the interested students, a member of the research team responded with another e-mail that contained the following documents and information:

1. Informed consent: the student had to sign and return it to the same e-mail address;
2. An initial document with personal information (date of birth, gender, center of study, height, weight, smoking status): the student must complete and return to the same e-mail address;
3. Their assigned personal alphanumeric code;
4. The method for downloading the e-12HR app: the app is free to download in the Apple Store (for iOS operating systems) or the Play Store (for devices with the Android operating system);
5. A user manual with detailed information for using the e-12HR app.

This procedure was implemented to promote participation in the study, avoiding unnecessary travel in order to sign or fill in documents, as well as to avoid the unnecessary use of paper and to promote conservation.

Participation in the study was incentivized with a raffle for school materials (valued at 500 euros) among the participants who completed the study.

2.2. e-12HR App

e-12HR is a previously validated application that allows for long-term collection of data on dietary intake of food groups [39–43].

After downloading, the first time that a participant used the e-12HR mobile application, they had to activate it by introducing a personally assigned alphanumeric code. After this step, the participants registered the number of standard portions consumed during the day for each of the 18 food groups included in the study: fruits, vegetables, breakfast cereals, pasta, rice, bread, olive oil, milk and dairy products, nuts, fermented beverages (wine and beer), potatoes, legumes, eggs, fish, white meat, red meat and sweets. The application also allowed users to register the number of minutes of moderate and intense physical activity performed throughout the day.

The participants were instructed to use the app after finishing their last meal of the day [44,45]. The app could only be completed between 8PM and 4AM, a time range that might seem strange at first glance but was chosen to provide users with sufficient time to complete the task. Taking into account that the university students, young adults, who made up the sample often go out in the evening and eat and drink until late at night, this time period allowed users to also register those foods/drinks in the application.

At the end of each day of monitoring, an alert appeared on the mobile phone of the participant to let them know it was time to use the app (each participant was allowed to establish the time for the alert according to their own preference). From that moment on, the participant could access the task and register the number of standard servings consumed throughout the day for each of the previously mentioned food groups, and the number of minutes of physical activity.

In order to assist in estimating the number of standard servings consumed, each food group was accompanied by an explanatory text with different homemade measurements (as the research team considered that it would be more appropriate and easier to follow for people without experience in dietetics). The standard servings used by e-12HR are based on a semiquantitative food frequency questionnaire (FFQ) previously validated for the Spanish population [46]. For example, when using the app, participants would see the following: How many servings of fruits (orange, apple, pear, peach, strawberry, watermelon, etc., including fresh juice) have you consumed today? One serving = 150–200 g. Homemade measures: 1 serving = A medium-sized piece of apple, pear or orange, a cup of cherries or strawberries, two slices of melon, a glass of natural juice. Participants would introduce the corresponding number in the "Answer" section and then they would tap the "Next" button to continue on to the following food group. The app also allowed participants to use decimals to better estimate the number of portions consumed. If an error occurred when registering information, participants could return to the previous page by tapping the "Previous" button, and they could begin the process again (Figure 1).

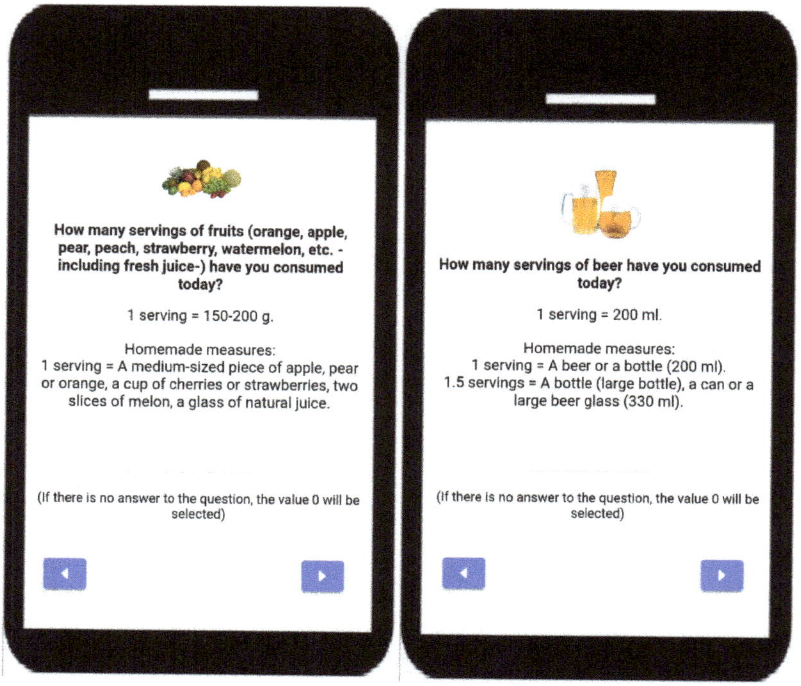

Figure 1. Screenshots from the e-12HR app.

To make the app easier to use, the list of food groups appeared in the same order every day (Appendix A, Table A1) and each food group was accompanied by a representative image.

After completing the daily questionnaire on the app, the collected information was automatically sent to the website of the study administrators, so the participants could not change their previous responses nor access the application until the following day when they would complete the next questionnaire.

Registration of dietary data using the e-12HR app was scheduled for twenty-eight consecutive days. Participants could know if they had completed the study period as the application presented a counter with the number of days the task was successfully completed.

2.3. Usability Rating Questionnaire for e-12HR

Finally, at the end of the 28-day study period, a member of the research team sent an e-mail to each participant that contained a usability rating questionnaire [43,47–49] for the e-12HR app, comprised of five questions about the completion the daily e-12HR task (Appendix A, Table A2).

Each participant was required to complete and return this usability rating questionnaire to the same e-mail address.

2.4. Adherence to Mediterranean Diet (AMD) Assessment

To calculate the adherence to Mediterranean diet (AMD) index, it took into account previously established rules [50] which consider:

1. Specific food groups (compatible with the MD);
2. Recommendations for consumption frequency for standard servings (per meal, daily or weekly);
3. A numerical score assigned to each item (Appendix A, Table A3).

However, it was necessary to make some modifications in order to adapt them to the characteristics of e-12HR (Table 1).

Table 1. Mediterranean diet Serving Score for e-12HR.

Scoring of Food Groups Calculated on a Daily Basis		
Food Group	**Servings Per Day**	**Score (e-12HR)**
Fruits	3–6 servings	3
Vegetables	≥6 servings	3
Cereals	3–6 servings	3
Olive oil	3–4 servings	3
Milk and dairy products	2–3 servings	2
Nuts	1–2 servings	2
Fermented beverages	1–2 servings	1
Scoring of food groups calculated on a weekly basis		
Food group	**Servings per week**	**Score (e-12HR)**
Potatoes	≤3 servings	1
Legumes	≥2 servings	1
Eggs	2–4 servings	1
Fish	≥2 servings	1
White meat	2–3 servings	1
Red meat	<2 servings	1
Sweets	≤2 servings	1
Total maximum score		24

Cereals: breakfast cereals, pasta, rice and bread. Olive oil: used on salads or bread or for frying. Milk and dairy products: milk, yogurt and cheese. Fermented beverages: wine and beer. White meat: poultry. Red meat: pork, beef and lamb. Sweets: sugar, candies, pastries, sweetened fruit juices and soft drinks.

For food groups that have scores greater than 1, the scoring rules are as follows [51]:

1. Fruits contribute 1 point for 1 to 2 servings, 2 points for 2 to 3 servings, and 3 points for 3–6 servings per day.
2. Vegetables contribute 1 point for 2 to 4 servings, 2 points for 4 to 6 servings, and 3 points for ≥6 servings per day.
3. Cereals contribute 1 point for 1 to 2 servings, 2 points for 2 to 3 servings, and 3 points for 3–6 servings per day.
4. Olive oil contributes 1 point for 1 to 2 serving, 2 points for 2 to 3 servings, and 3 points for 3–4 servings per day.
5. Milk and dairy products contribute 1 point for 1 to 2 servings and 2 points for 2–3 servings per day.
6. Nuts contribute 2 points for 1–2 servings per day.

For each food group, if the indicated recommendations were not followed, a value of zero was assigned for that group.

Scorings for the AMD index were calculated manually by the research team (using the data sent by the application to the study website and the rules shown in Table 1).

The information from each participant was analyzed considering three time periods: 1. Total monitoring period; 2. Weekdays (Monday–Thursday); and 3. Weekend days (Friday–Sunday and holidays).

For each period of time, for each individual food group, the average daily number of standard portions registered throughout the period in question was first added all together, and the result was then divided by the number of days for which the task was completed during that same period. For each period of time, for food groups which used the weekly averages for the number of standard servings, as opposed to daily, the result from the previous operation was multiplied by 7.

Obvious errors produced during data entry were modified (as it was considered that the data must have been introduced as grams or milliliters instead of standard servings). For example, on one occasion, a value of 150 was introduced for the question "How many servings of vegetables (tomato, carrot, bell pepper, lettuce, zucchini, etc.) have you consumed today?". The research team considered that this value indicated a consumption of 150 g, which is the equivalent of one serving. In any case, the data were modified by the research team on only 1080 occasions out of a total of 196,452 registered data points (0.55%).

To complete the process, all of the values were added up, and scoring of the AMD index was generated, which could vary between zero and twenty-four.

On top of this, the score on the AMD index was related with one of three levels of AMD [51]: low (0–8 points), moderate (9–15 points) or high (16–24 points).

2.5. Statistical Analysis

Discrete variables are presented as a number followed by percentages. Continuous variables are presented using means and standard deviations and median and interquartile range (IQR).

The data rwee tested for normality using the nonparametric Kolmogorov–Smirnov test.

For unpaired samples, Students *t*-test or the nonparametric Mann–Whitney U-test were used for the analysis of quantitative variables, and the chi-square test was used for the comparison of proportions.

For paired samples, Students *t*-test or the nonparametric Wilcoxon test were used for the analysis of quantitative variables, and McNemar's test was used for the comparison of proportions.

The results were considered significant if p-value < 0.05.

Statistical analyses were performed using the SPSS statistical software package version 26.0 (SPSS Inc., Chicago, IL, USA).

3. Results

3.1. Database

The informed consent forms were signed by 439 students who fulfilled the inclusion requirement for the study. Of them, 78 were considered as nonresponsive (as they completed the task on the app for less than 14 days); the data for these individuals was not included in the later statistical analysis. There were no significant statistical differences in the variables studied between the participants who completed the study and those who did not. The study response rate was 82.2% (361 of 439 students completed the task on the app for at least 14 days).

As has been mentioned previously, dietary data registration through the e-12HR app was scheduled for twenty-eight consecutive days. The majority of the responsive participants, 79.2%, completed the monitoring period and of note, more than a third of them, 39.6%, continued using the app for more than thirteen days on their own initiative. The vast majority of the participants completed the application at least seven days both on weekdays and weekend days. The information on the number of days for which the task was completed is shown in Table 2.

Table 2. Characteristics of study participants.

Characteristics	N (%)	Mean (SD)	Median (IQR)
Participants who completed the study	361 (82.2)	-*	-
Participants who did not complete the study	78 (17.8)	-	-
Number of days app task completed	-	-	-
>30 days	143 (39.6)	-	-
28–30 days	143 (39.6)	-	-
21–27 days	55 (15.2)	-	-
14–20 days	20 (5.5)	-	-
Number of days app task completed (weekdays: Monday–Thursday)	-	-	-
15–32 days	287 (79.5)	-	-
7–14 days	73 (20.2)	-	-
3–6 days	1 (0.3)	-	-
Number of days app task completed (weekend days: Friday–Sunday and holidays)	-	-	-
15–32 days	137 (37.9)	-	-
7–14 days	212 (58.7)	-	-
3–6 days	12 (3.3)	-	-
Age (years)	-	20.6 (2.8)	20.0 (2.0)
<20	185 (51.2)	-	-
≥20	176 (48.8)	-	-
Gender	-	-	-
Females	263 (72.9)	-	-
Males	98 (27.1)	-	-
Studies	-	-	-
Pharmacy	210 (58.2)	-	-
Medicine	151 (41.8)	-	-
BMI (kg/m^2)	-	21.9 (3.3)	21.1 (4.0)
<25	317 (87.8)	-	-
≥25	44 (12.2)	-	-
Smoking status	-	-	-
No	330 (91.4)	-	-
Yes	31 (8.6)	-	-
Physical activity status (minutes/week)	-	-	-
≥150	280 (77.6)	-	-
<150	81 (22.4)	-	-

* Not applicable.

The average age of the participants was 20.6 years old. The gender distribution of women/men was 72.9%/27.1%. More than half of them were students at the School of Pharmacy, 58.2%. The average BMI was 21.9 kg/m^2. The majority of the participants were nonsmokers, 91.4%, and performed 150 min or more of moderate/intense physical activity each week, 77.6% (Table 2).

The participants who completed the study registered their daily consumption for the 18 food groups included in the study for 10,914 days taken together (representing a collected total of 196,452 data points on daily consumption for the food groups).

3.2. Scores and Levels of the AMD Index

Table 3 shows the scores and levels of the AMD index in the total monitoring period in the whole study sample and in different subgroups thereof (by age, gender, studies, BMI, smoking status and physical activity status). The mean score of the AMD index was 8.7 (SD = 2.9), by subgroups varying between 7.6 (<150 min/week) and 9.2 (males). There were statistically significant differences in the subgroups by gender, BMI and physical activity status: adherence scores were higher in subgroups of males (9.2), <25 kg/m^2 (8.8) and ≥150 min/week (9.0), respectively. An adequate adherence score (≥9) was observed in 47.9% of the participants (although of them, only 1.9% (seven subjects) presented a high level (16–24 points)). By subgroups, the lowest percentage of an adequate AMD score was found among <150 min/week (30.9%), and the highest percentage among ≥150 min/week (52.9%). There was a statistically significant difference in the subgroups by physical activity status.

Table 3. Scores and levels of the AMD index (total monitoring period).

Total Monitoring Period	Index			Level		
	Mean (SD)	Median (IQR)	*p* *	Low: 0–8	Moderate–High ≥ 9	*p* **
All	8.7 (2.9)	8.0 (3.0)		188 (52.1)	173 (47.9)	
Age (years)						
<20	8.7 (2.8)	8.0 (4.0)	0.860	99 (53.5)	86 (46.5)	0.576
≥20	8.7 (2.9)	8.0 (3.0)		89 (50.6)	87 (49.4)	
Gender						
Females	8.5 (2.8)	8.0 (3.0)	0.049	141 (53.6)	122 (46.4)	0.339
Males	9.2 (3.1)	9.0 (4.0)		47 (48.0)	51 (52.0)	
Studies						
Pharmacy	8.6 (2.9)	8.0 (3.0)	0.496	113 (53.8)	97 (46.2)	0.437
Medicine	8.8 (2.8)	9.0 (4.0)		75 (49.7)	76 (50.3)	
BMI (kg/m^2)						
<25	8.8 (2.9)	8.0 (4.0)	0.026	159 (50.2)	158 (49.8)	0.050
≥25	7.8 (2.4)	7.0 (3.0)		29 (65.9)	15 (34.1)	
Smoking status						
No	8.8 (2.9)	8.0 (3.0)	0.078	169 (51.2)	161 (48.8)	0.283
Yes	7.7 (2.6)	7.0 (3.0)		19 (61.3)	12 (38.7)	
Physical activity status (minutes/week)						
≥150	9.0 (2.9)	9.0 (4.0)	0.000	132 (47.1)	148 (52.9)	0.000
<150	7.6 (2.5)	7.0 (3.0)		56 (69.1)	25 (30.9)	

SD: standard deviation. IQR: interquartile range. * Evaluated by the Mann–Whitney U-test. ** Evaluated by the chi-square test.

Tables 4 and 5 report the scores and levels of the AMD index on weekdays and weekend days. The differences were statistically significant, considering the scores and levels of the AMD index, in the whole study sample and in all subgroups thereof (except in smoking status yes for the level of the AMD index).

Compared with the weekday average, the Mediterranean diet Serving Score (MDSS) for the weekend average was 1.2 points lower (12.6% reduction). By subgroups, the reduction varied between 18.1% (smoking status yes) and 12.0% (smoking status no) (Table 4).

Compared with that of the weekdays, the adequate adherence score (≥9) for weekends was 17.8 percentage points lower (31.8% reduction). By subgroups, the reduction varied between 26.3% (≥20 years) and 41.2% (<150 min/week) (Table 5).

Table 4. Scores of the AMD index (weekdays–weekends).

	Weekdays		Weekends		
	Mean (SD)	**Median (IQR)**	**Mean (SD)**	**Median (IQR)**	*p*
All	9.3 (3.0)	9.0 (4.0)	8.1 (2.9)	8.0 (4.0)	0.000 **
Age (years)					
<20	9.3 (3.0)	9.0 (4.0)	8.1 (3.0)	8.0 (4.0)	0.000 **
≥20	9.2 (3.0)	9.0 (4.0)	8.1 (2.8)	8.0 (4.0)	0.000 **
Gender					
Females	9.0 (2.9)	9.0 (4.0)	7.9 (2.8)	8.0 (4.0)	0.000 **
Males	9.9 (3.2)	10.0 (4.0)	8.6 (3.2)	8.0 (4.0)	0.000 **
Studies					
Pharmacy	9.1 (2.9)	9.0 (4.0)	8.0 (3.0)	8.0 (4.0)	0.000 **
Medicine	9.4 (3.0)	9.0 (4.0)	8.2 (2.8)	8.0 (3.0)	0.000 **
BMI (kg/m^2)					
<25	9.4 (3.0)	9.0 (4.0)	8.2 (2.9)	8.0 (4.0)	0.000 **
≥25	8.5 (2.5)	8.0 (4.0)	7.4 (2.7)	7.0 (5.0)	0.001 *
Smoking status					
No	9.3 (3.0)	9.0 (4.0)	8.2 (3.0)	8.0 (4.0)	0.000 **
Yes	8.5 (2.7)	8.0 (4.0)	7.0 (2.4)	7.0 (4.0)	0.000 **
Physical activity status (minutes/week)					
≥150	9.6 (3.0)	9.0 (4.0)	8.4 (2.9)	8.0 (4.0)	0.000 **
<150	8.1 (2.4)	8.0 (4.0)	7.0 (2.7)	7.0 (4.0)	0.000 **

SD: standard deviation. IQR: interquartile range. * Evaluated by t-test. ** Evaluated by the Wilcoxon test.

Table 5. Levels of the AMD index (weekdays–weekends).

	Weekdays		Weekends		*p* *
	Low: 0–8	**Moderate–High ≥ 9**	**Low: 0–8**	**Moderate–high ≥ 9**	
	N (%)	**N (%)**	**N (%)**	**N (%)**	
All	159 (44.0)	202 (56.0)	223 (61.8)	138 (38.2)	0.000
Age (years)					
<20	78 (42.2)	107 (57.8)	117 (63.2)	68 (36.8)	0.000
≥20	81 (46.0)	95 (54.0)	106 (60.2)	70 (39.8)	0.000
Gender					
Females	124 (47.1)	139 (52.9)	170 (64.6)	93 (35.4)	0.000
Males	35 (35.7)	63 (64.3)	53 (54.1)	45 (45.9)	0.002
Studies					
Pharmacy	94 (44.8)	116 (55.2)	135 (64.3)	75 (35.7)	0.000
Medicine	65 (43.0)	86 (57.0)	88 (58.3)	63 (41.7)	0.001
BMI (kg/m^2)					
<25	136 (42.9)	181 (57.1)	192 (60.6)	125 (39.4)	0.000
≥25	23 (52.3)	21 (47.7)	31 (70.5)	13 (29.5)	0.021
Smoking status					
No	141 (42.7)	189 (57.3)	200 (60.6)	130 (39.4)	0.000
Yes	18 (58.1)	13 (41.9)	23 (74.2)	8 (25.8)	0.125
Physical activity status (minutes/week)					
≥150	112 (40.0)	168 (60.0)	162 (57.9)	118 (42.1)	0.000
<150	47 (58.0)	34 (42.0)	61 (75.3)	20 (24.7)	0.007

* Evaluated by McNemar's test.

3.3. Stratification of AMD Items (Food Groups)

Table 6 shows the stratification of AMD items (food groups) in the total monitoring period. Fruits, vegetables, cereals, olive oil, milk and dairy products and nuts (food groups which contribute the highest scores to the MDSS index, Table 1) were consumed according to recommendations by less than 25% of the participants, in the whole study sample and in all subgroups thereof (except for cereals in males, milk and dairy products in smoking status yes and physical activity status ≥150 min/week). Other food groups that were also consumed according to the recommendations by less than 25% of the participants were red meat (in the whole study sample and in all subgroups thereof), sweets (in subgroups <20 years, females, BMI ≥25 kg/m^2, smoking status yes and physical activity status <150 min/week) and legumes (in smoking status yes). There were statistically significant differences in the subgroups by gender (eight food groups), physical activity status (five food groups), age and smoking status (two food groups), studies and BMI (one food group).

Table 6. Stratification of adherence to MD items (food groups) (total monitoring period).

Total Monitoring Period	All	Age (Years)		Gender	
-	-	<20	≥20	Female	Male
Food group	**N (%)**	**N (%)**	**N (%)**	**N (%)**	**N (%)**
Fruits	22 (6.1)	17 (9.2)	5 (2.8) *	16 (6.1)	6 (6.1)
Vegetables	0 (0.0)	0 (0.0)	0 (0.0)	0 (0.0)	0 (0.0)
Cereals	52 (14.4)	28 (15.1)	24 (13.6)	22 (8.4)	30 (30.6) *
Olive oil	15 (4.2)	6 (3.2)	9 (5.1)	10 (3.8)	5 (5.1)
Milk and dairy products	85 (23.5)	44 (23.8)	41(23.3)	61 (23.2)	24 (24.5)
Nuts	28 (7.8)	16 (8.6)	12 (6.8)	15 (5.7)	13 (13.3) *
Fermented beverages	351 (97.2)	181 (97.8)	170 (96.6)	261 (99.2)	90 (91.8) *
Potatoes	147 (40.7)	77 (41.6)	70 (39.8)	117 (44.5)	30 (30.6) *
Legumes	116 (32.1)	54 (29.2)	62 (35.2)	75 (28.5)	41 (41.8) *
Eggs	171 (47.4)	76 (41.1)	95 (54.0) *	141 (53.6)	30 (30.6) *
Fish	230 (63.7)	124 (67.0)	106 (60.2)	161 (61.2)	69 (70.4)
White meat	306 (84.8)	156 (84.3)	150 (85.2)	218 (82.9)	88 (89.8)
Red meat	59 (16.3)	31 (16.8)	28 (15.9)	51 (19.4)	8 (8.2) *
Sweets	95 (26.3)	43 (23.2)	52 (29.5)	61 (23.2)	34 (34.7) *
Total monitoring period	**All**	**Studies**		**BMI (kg/m^2)**	
-	-	**Pharmacy**	**Medicine**	**<25**	**≥25**
Food group	**N (%)**	**N (%)**	**N (%)**	**N (%)**	**N (%)**
Fruits	22 (6.1)	10 (4.8)	12 (7.9)	21 (6.6)	1 (2.3)
Vegetables	0 (0.0)	0 (0.0)	0 (0.0)	0 (0.0)	0 (0.0)
Cereals	52 (14.4)	26 (12.4)	26 (17.2)	45 (14.2)	7 (15.9)
Olive oil	15 (4.2)	10 (4.8)	5 (3.3)	14 (4.4)	1 (2.3)
Milk and dairy products	85 (23.5)	51 (24.3)	34 (22.5)	77 (24.3)	8 (18.2)
Nuts	28 (7.8)	15 (7.1)	13 (8.6)	26 (8.2)	2 (4.5)
Fermented beverages	351 (97.2)	202 (96.2)	149 (98.7)	309 (97.5)	42 (95.5)
Potatoes	147 (40.7)	88 (41.9)	59 (39.1)	136 (42.9)	11 (25.0) *
Legumes	116 (32.1)	66 (31.4)	50 (33.1)	105 (33.1)	11 (25.0)
Eggs	171 (47.4)	111 (52.9)	60 (39.7) *	151 (47.6)	20 (45.5)
Fish	230 (63.7)	139 (66.2)	91 (60.3)	199 (62.8)	31 (70.5)
White meat	306 (84.8)	175 (83.3)	131 (86.8)	269 (84.9)	37 (84.1)
Red meat	59 (16.3)	33 (15.7)	26 (17.2)	54 (17.0)	5 (11.4)
Sweets	95 (26.3)	54 (25.7)	41 (27.2)	86 (27.1)	9 (20.5)

Table 6. *Cont.*

Total Monitoring Period	All	Smoking Status		Physical Activity Status (Minutes/Week)	
-	-	No	Yes	≥150	<150
Food group	**N (%)**	**N (%)**	**N (%)**	**N (%)**	**N (%)**
Fruits	22 (6.1)	22 (6.7)	0 (0.0)	21 (7.5)	1 (1.2) *
Vegetables	0 (0.0)	0 (0.0)	0 (0.0)	0 (0.0)	0 (0.0)
Cereals	52 (14.4)	48 (14.5)	4 (12.9)	44 (15.7)	8 (9.9)
Olive oil	15 (4.2)	13 (3.9)	2 (6.5)	12 (4.3)	3 (3.7)
Milk and dairy products	85 (23.5)	77 (23.3)	8 (25.8)	74 (26.4)	11 (13.6) *
Nuts	28 (7.8)	27 (8.2)	1 (3.2)	24 (8.6)	4 (4.9)
Fermented beverages	351 (97.2)	325 (98.5)	26 (83.9) *	272 (97.1)	79 (97.5)
Potatoes	147 (40.7)	141 (42.7)	6 (19.4) *	111 (39.6)	36 (44.4)
Legumes	116 (32.1)	110 (33.3)	6 (19.4)	92 (32.9)	24 (29.6)
Eggs	171 (47.4)	153 (46.4)	18 (58.1)	122 (43.6)	49 (60.5) *
Fish	230 (63.7)	212 (64.2)	18 (58.1)	184 (65.7)	46 (56.8)
White meat	306 (84.8)	278 (84.2)	28 (90.3)	244 (87.1)	62 (76.5) *
Red meat	59 (16.3)	57 (17.3)	2 (6.5)	46 (16.4)	13 (16.0)
Sweets	95 (26.3)	89 (27.0)	6 (19.4)	81 (28.9)	14 (17.3) *

* Statistically significant differences. Evaluated by the chi-square test.

Table 7 reports the stratification of AMD items (food groups) on the weekdays and weekend days. The consumption on weekends was similar to that on the weekdays in the whole study sample and in all subgroups thereof for the food groups which contribute the highest scores to the MDSS index (fruits, vegetables, cereals, olive oil and nuts (except for olive oil and nuts among student of Medicine)) and fish. A lower percentage of participants complied with the recommendations in consumption at weekends than on weekdays in sweets (in the whole study sample and in all subgroups), fermented beverages (in the whole study sample and 11 subgroups), potatoes and legumes (in the whole study sample and 10 subgroups), milk and dairy products (in the whole study sample and eight subgroups), red meat (in the whole study sample and six subgroups), eggs (in the whole study sample and five subgroups) and white meat (in the whole study sample and three subgroups).

Table 7. Stratification of adherence to MD items (food groups) (weekdays–weekends).

	All		Age (Years)			
	-		<20		≥20	
	N (%)		N (%)		N (%)	
Food Group	**Weekdays**	**Weekends**	**Weekdays**	**Weekends**	**Weekdays**	**Weekends**
Fruits	22 (6.1)	20 (5.5)	16 (8.6)	16 (8.6)	6 (3.4)	4 (2.3)
Vegetables	1 (0.3)	0 (0.0)	1 (0.5)	0 (0.0)	0 (0.0)	0 (0.0)
Cereals	58 (16.1)	54 (15.0)	34 (18.4)	29 (15.7)	24 (13.6)	25 (14.2)
Olive oil	18 (5.0)	17 (4.7)	8 (4.3)	8 (4.3)	10 (5.7)	9 (5.1)
Milk and dairy products	98 (27.1)	76 (21.1) *	53 (28.6)	40 (21.6) *	45 (25.6)	36 (20.5) *
Nuts	31 (8.6)	28 (7.8)	18 (9.7)	16 (8.6)	13 (7.4)	12 (6.8)
Fermented beverages	355 (98.3)	335 (92.8) *	182 (98.4)	170 (91.9) *	173 (98.3)	165 (93.8) *
Potatoes	187 (51.8)	127 (35.2) *	96 (51.9)	64 (34.6) *	91 (51.7)	63 (35.8) *
Legumes	151 (41.8)	89 (24.7) *	76 (41.1)	41 (22.2) *	75 (42.6)	48 (27.3) *
Eggs	152 (42.1)	126 (34.9) *	75 (40.5)	54 (29.2) *	77 (43.8)	72 (40.9)
Fish	216 (59.8)	205 (56.8)	111 (60.0)	111 (60.0)	105 (59.7)	94 (53.4)
White meat	299 (82.8)	278 (77.0) *	156 (84.3)	146 (78.9)	143 (81.3)	132 (75.0)
Red meat	85 (23.5)	59 (16.3) *	42 (22.7)	32 (17.3)	43 (24.4)	27 (15.3) *
Sweets	145 (40.2)	70 (19.4) *	73 (39.5)	32 (17.3) *	72 (40.9)	38 (21.6) *

Table 7. *Cont.*

	All		Gender			
	-		Female		Male	
	N (%)		N (%)		N (%)	
Food Group	**Weekdays**	**Weekends**	**Weekdays**	**Weekends**	**Weekdays**	**Weekends**
Fruits	22 (6.1)	20 (5.5)	16 (6.1)	15 (5.7)	6 (6.1)	5 (5.1)
Vegetables	1 (0.3)	0 (0.0)	1 (0.4)	0 (0.0)	0 (0.0)	0 (0.0)
Cereals	58 (16.1)	54 (15.0)	30 (11.4)	26 (9.9)	28 (28.6)	28 (28.6)
Olive oil	18 (5.0)	17 (4.7)	10 (3.8)	12 (4.6)	8 (8.2)	5 (5.1)
Milk and dairy products	98 (27.1)	76 (21.1) *	68 (25.9)	56 (21.3) *	30 (30.6)	20 (20.4) *
Nuts	31 (8.6)	28 (7.8)	19 (7.2)	14 (5.3)	12 (12.2)	14 (14.3)
Fermented beverages	355 (98.3)	335 (92.8) *	263 (100.0)	251 (95.4) *	92 (93.9)	84 (85.7)*
Potatoes	187 (51.8)	127 (35.2) *	141 (53.6)	98 (37.3) *	46 (46.9)	29 (29.6) *
Legumes	151 (41.8)	89 (24.7) *	102 (38.8)	59 (22.4) *	49 (50.0)	30 (30.6) *
Eggs	152 (42.1)	126 (34.9) *	126 (47.9)	103 (39.2) *	26 (26.5)	23 (23.5)
Fish	216 (59.8)	205 (56.8)	150 (57.0)	143 (54.4)	66 (67.3)	62 (63.3)
White meat	299 (82.8)	278 (77.0) *	212 (80.6)	198 (75.3)	87 (88.8)	80 (81.6)
Red meat	85 (23.5)	59 (16.3) *	73 (27.8)	50 (19.0) *	12 (12.2)	9 (9.2)
Sweets	145 (40.2)	70 (19.4) *	95 (36.1)	41 (15.6) *	50 (51.0)	29 (29.6) *
	All		**Studies**			
	-		**Pharmacy**		**Medicine**	
	N (%)		N (%)		N (%)	
Food group	**Weekdays**	**Weekends**	**Weekdays**	**Weekends**	**Weekdays**	**Weekends**
Fruits	22 (6.1)	20 (5.5)	9 (4.3)	9 (4.3)	13 (8.6)	11 (7.3)
Vegetables	1 (0.3)	0 (0.0)	0 (0.0)	0 (0.0)	1 (0.7)	0 (0.0)
Cereals	58 (16.1)	54 (15.0)	34 (16.2)	25 (11.9)	24 (15.9)	29 (19.2)
Olive oil	18 (5.0)	17 (4.7)	8 (3.8)	13 (6.2)	10 (6.6)	4 (2.6) *
Milk and dairy products	98 (27.1)	76 (21.1) *	57 (27.1)	43 (20.5) *	41 (27.2)	33 (21.9)
Nuts	31 (8.6)	28 (7.8)	14 (6.7)	18 (8.6)	17 (11.3)	10 (6.6) *
Fermented beverages	355 (98.3)	335 (92.8) *	205 (97.6)	193 (91.9) *	150 (99.3)	142 (94.0) *
Potatoes	187 (51.8)	127 (35.2) *	112 (53.3)	71 (33.8) *	75 (49.7)	56 (37.1) *
Legumes	151 (41.8)	89 (24.7)*	87 (41.4)	49 (23.3) *	64 (42.4)	40 (26.5) *
Eggs	152 (42.1)	126 (34.9)*	101 (48.1)	73 (34.8) *	51 (33.8)	53 (35.1)
Fish	216 (59.8)	205 (56.8)	132 (62.9)	124 (59.0)	84 (55.6)	81 (53.6)
White meat	299 (82.8)	278 (77.0)*	173 (82.4)	162 (77.1)	126 (83.4)	116 (76.8)
Red meat	85 (23.5)	59 (16.3)*	50 (23.8)	34 (16.2) *	35 (23.2)	25 (16.6)
Sweets	145 (40.2)	70 (19.4)*	84 (40.0)	39 (18.6) *	61 (40.4)	31 (20.5) *
	All		**BMI (kg/m^2)**			
	-		**<25**		**≥25**	
	N (%)		N (%)		N (%)	
Food group	**Weekdays**	**Weekends**	**Weekdays**	**Weekends**	**Weekdays**	**Weekends**
Fruits	22 (6.1)	20 (5.5)	20 (6.3)	19 (6.0)	2 (4.5)	1 (2.3)
Vegetables	1 (0.3)	0 (0.0)	1 (0.3)	0 (0.0)	0 (0.0)	0 (0.0)
Cereals	58 (16.1)	54 (15.0)	49 (15.5)	46 (14.5)	9 (20.5)	8 (18.2)
Olive oil	18 (5.0)	17 (4.7)	17 (5.4)	15 (4.7)	1 (2.3)	2 (4.5)
Milk and dairy products	98 (27.1)	76 (21.1) *	89 (28.1)	69 (21.8) *	9 (20.5)	7 (15.9)
Nuts	31 (8.6)	28 (7.8)	29 (9.1)	27 (8.5)	2 (4.5)	1 (2.3)
Fermented beverages	355 (98.3)	335 (92.8) *	311 (98.1)	298 (94.0) *	44 (100.0)	37 (84.1) *
Potatoes	187 (51.8)	127 (35.2) *	170 (53.6)	115 (36.3) *	17 (38.6)	12 (27.3)
Legumes	151 (41.8)	89 (24.7) *	139 (43.8)	78 (24.6) *	12 (27.3)	11 (25.0)
Eggs	152 (42.1)	126 (34.9)*	133 (42.0)	107 (33.8) *	19 (43.2)	19 (43.2)
Fish	216 (59.8)	205 (56.8)	188 (59.3)	181 (57.1)	28 (63.6)	24 (54.5)
White meat	299 (82.8)	278 (77.0) *	263 (83.0)	242 (76.3) *	36 (81.8)	36 (81.8)
Red meat	85 (23.5)	59 (16.3) *	77 (24.3)	54 (17.0) *	8 (18.2)	5 (11.4)
Sweets	145 (40.2)	70 (19.4) *	127 (40.1)	60 (18.9) *	18 (40.9)	10 (22.7) *

Table 7. *Cont.*

	All		Smoking Status			
	-		No		Yes	
	N (%)		N (%)		N (%)	
Food Group	**Weekdays**	**Weekends**	**Weekdays**	**Weekends**	**Weekdays**	**Weekends**
Fruits	22 (6.1)	20 (5.5)	22 (6.7)	20 (6.1)	0 (0.0)	0 (0.0)
Vegetables	1 (0.3)	0 (0.0)	1 (0.3)	0 (0.0)	0 (0.0)	0 (0.0)
Cereals	58 (16.1)	54 (15.0)	54 (16.4)	52 (15.8)	4 (12.9)	2 (6.5)
Olive oil	18 (5.0)	17 (4.7)	16 (4.8)	15 (4.5)	2 (6.5)	2 (6.5)
Milk and dairy products	98 (27.1)	76 (21.1) *	88 (26.7)	71 (21.5) *	10 (32.3)	5 (16.1)
Nuts	31 (8.6)	28 (7.8)	29 (8.8)	27 (8.2)	2 (6.5)	1 (3.2)
Fermented beverages	355 (98.3)	335 (92.8) *	326 (98.8)	313 (94.8) *	29 (93.5)	22 (71.0) *
Potatoes	187 (51.8)	127 (35.2) *	176 (53.3)	121 (36.7) *	11 (35.5)	6 (19.4)
Legumes	151 (41.8)	89 (24.7) *	142 (43.0)	83 (25.2) *	9 (29.0)	6 (19.4)
Eggs	152 (42.1)	126 (34.9) *	136 (41.2)	114 (34.5)	16 (51.6)	12 (38.7)
Fish	216 (59.8)	205 (56.8)	199 (60.3)	187 (56.7)	17 (54.8)	18 (58.1)
White meat	299 (82.8)	278 (77.0) *	270 (81.8)	252 (76.4) *	29 (93.5)	26 (83.9)
Red meat	85 (23.5)	59 (16.3) *	80 (24.2)	57 (17.3) *	5 (16.1)	2 (6.5)
Sweets	145 (40.2)	70 (19.4) *	134 (40.6)	67 (20.3) *	11 (35.5)	3 (9.7) *

	All		Physical activity status (minutes/week)			
	-		≥150		<150	
	N (%)		N (%)		N (%)	
Food group	**Weekdays**	**Weekends**	**Weekdays**	**Weekends**	**Weekdays**	**Weekends**
Fruits	22 (6.1)	20 (5.5)	22 (7.9)	19 (6.8)	0 (0.0)	1 (1.2)
Vegetables	1 (0.3)	0 (0.0)	1 (0.4)	0 (0.0)	0 (0.0)	0 (0.0)
Cereals	58 (16.1)	54 (15.0)	52 (18.6)	47 (16.8)	6 (7.4)	7 (8.6)
Olive oil	18 (5.0)	17 (4.7)	16 (5.7)	12 (4.3)	2 (2.5)	5 (6.2)
Milk and dairy products	98 (27.1)	76 (21.1) *	84 (30.0)	66 (23.6) *	14 (17.3)	10 (12.3)
Nuts	31 (8.6)	28 (7.8)	27 (9.6)	25 (8.9)	4 (4.9)	3 (3.7)
Fermented beverages	355 (98.3)	335 (92.8) *	275 (98.2)	259 (92.5) *	80 (98.8)	76 (93.8)
Potatoes	187 (51.8)	127 (35.2) *	144 (51.4)	103 (36.8) *	43 (53.1)	24 (29.6) *
Legumes	151 (41.8)	89 (24.7) *	119 (42.5)	72 (25.7) *	32 (39.5)	17 (21.0) *
Eggs	152 (42.1)	126 (34.9) *	101 (36.1)	94 (33.6)	51 (63.0)	32 (39.5) *
Fish	216 (59.8)	205 (56.8)	171 (61.1)	161 (57.5)	45 (55.6)	44 (54.3)
White meat	299 (82.8)	278 (77.0) *	238 (85.0)	220 (78.6) *	61 (75.3)	58 (71.6)
Red meat	85 (23.5)	59 (16.3) *	69 (24.6)	47 (16.8) *	16 (19.8)	12 (14.8)
Sweets	145 (40.2)	70 (19.4) *	121 (43.2)	57 (20.4) *	24 (29.6)	13 (16.0) *

* Statistically significant differences. Evaluated by McNemar's test.

3.4. Usability Rating Questionnaire for e-12HR

The usability rating questionnaire was answered by 174 participants. The responses of the users are shown in Table 8.

Table 8. Responses of the study participants to the usability rating questionnaire for the e-12HR app.

	Questions, n (%)			
Options	**Easy to Complete**	**Interesting to Complete**	**Understandable Questions**	**I Would Be Willing to Complete Again**
Strongly agree	117 (67.2)	110 (63.2)	120 (69.0)	54 (31.0)
Agree	54 (31.0)	57 (32.7)	52 (29.9)	88 (50.6)
Neither agree nor disagree	3 (1.7)	6 (3.4)	2 (1.1)	28 (16.1)
Disagree	0 (0.0)	1 (0.6)	0 (0.0)	4 (2.3)
Strongly disagree	0 (0.0)	0 (0.0)	0 (0.0)	0 (0.0)

Table 8. *Cont.*

Options	Questions, n (%)
	Time to Complete the App
<1 min/day	16 (9.2)
Approximately 1 min/day	37 (21.3)
Approximately 2 min/day	63 (36.2)
Approximately 3 min/day	43 (24.7)
Approximately 4 min/day	11 (6.3)
5 min/day or more	4 (2.3)

4. Discussion

To our knowledge, this study is the first to evaluate weekend–weekday differences in diet among university students (specifically, MD and Spanish university students at the Faculties of Medicine and Pharmacy). As we hypothesized, dietary intake in this sample was found to fluctuate during the week, with weekend days displaying lower dietary quality compared with that of weekdays; however, the differences were very similar across the population subgroups under examination.

A rationale for the existence of distinct, temporally conditioned behavioral patterns, as observed in this study, could be provided by the fact that human behavior during the weekdays is highly structured and generally dictated by time spent at work/in school [14], and many health promotion initiatives target the weekdays. A change in daily structures during the weekend is likely to have consequences for habitual behaviors such as eating [15].

Spanish university students are a particularly interesting group among the younger generations for various reasons. University students are one of the populations with a high risk of having unhealthy habits [52]; generally, young adults, especially university students, present an important challenge due to the coincidence of a series of emotional, physiological and environmental changes. They select their food, are very receptive to fashionable trends such as following slimming diets, skipping meals or consuming snacks, soft drinks and other new products [53], and leading an unhealthy lifestyle, and the risk that these habits are preserved during adulthood represents a great inconvenience for these individuals, especially for students in fields related to Health Sciences [54]. The promotion of healthy habits in the population at large, such as maintaining a good diet, is one of the primary tasks of these future professionals. Therefore, they must not only know the basics of these habits, but also practice them [55].

Spanish university students at the Faculties of Medicine and Pharmacy (this study sample) have compulsory and optional subjects related to nutrition and dietetics: for students of Medicine, the subjects Preventive Medicine and Public Health (compulsory) and Health Promotion (optional); for Pharmacy students, the subjects Public Health (compulsory), Nutrition and Bromatology (compulsory) and Nutrition, Dietetics and Dietotherapy (optional). This training in nutrition/dietetics may have had an influence on the dietary habits of the participants. For this reason, future research will focus on determining weekend–weekday differences in diet among other non-Health Science students (without training in health or nutrition) (see future research related to the current study section).

In general, in the present study, in the whole study sample and in all subgroups thereof (by age, gender, studies, BMI, smoking status and physical activity status): A. In the total monitoring period: Adherence to the MD (by mean scores of the AMD index and adequate adherence score (≥9)) was low (Table 3). This is similar to previous recent literature among Spanish university students (although using other AMD indexes) [56–59]. Among the categories, gender, BMI and physical activity status provided statistically significant differences (although physical activity status was the only one to show any statistically significant differences, in both the AMD index and adequate adherence score (≥9); gender and BMI only in the AMD index) (Table 3). The AMD index was higher in males compared to that in females, which was a finding that follows the trend shown in these recent studies [58,59]. Also in line with one of these previous studies was that maintaining low levels of physical activity was associated with a diet of worse quality [56]. In contrast, in these recent papers among Spanish university students, the relationship of a low score of the AMD index with overweight/obesity could not be observed [56,58,59]. The food groups which were consumed according to recommendations by less than 25% of the participants were fruits, vegetables, cereals, olive oil, milk and dairy products, nuts, red meat and sweets (Table 6). B. During weekend days, compared with the weekdays: Poorer diet quality was observed. This study confirmed findings from previous research in children/adolescents [15–31] and adults (not specifically university students) [15,29–37]: substantial reductions in following dietary guidelines were observed, with >12% reductions in mean scores of the AMD index and >26% reductions in adequate adherence scores (≥9) (Tables 4 and 5). There was no percentage variation in consumption of fruits, vegetables, cereals, olive oil, nuts and fish (Table 7). There was a lower percentage of participants who complied with the recommendations in consumption of sweets, fermented beverages, potatoes, legumes, milk and dairy products, red meat, eggs and white meat (Table 7).

The Spanish university students' diet was associated with poor diet quality in general and, especially at weekends, in the whole study sample and in all subgroups thereof. Among Spanish university students, policy interventions and public health campaigns are warranted to promote healthy eating focused on all time periods, on food groups that were consumed according to recommendations by less than 25% of the participants (fruits, vegetables, cereals, olive oil, milk and dairy products, nuts, red meat and sweets). In these food groups, the percentage of university students that meets the recommendations was below 25% and, additionally, no differences were observed between the weekends and the weekdays. These food groups (except red meat and sweets) contribute the highest scores to the MDSS index (Table 1), so an improvement in their consumption would be associated with notable increases in the AMD index. At the same time, focus should be placed on the weekends and food groups with a lower percentage of participants which complied with the consumption recommendations (sweets, fermented beverages, potatoes, legumes, milk and dairy products, red meat, eggs and white meat). An improvement in their consumption at the weekends could be associated with increases in the global AMD index. In this sense, future interventions should be applied to all subgroups by age, gender, studies, BMI, smoking status and physical activity status (with very similar results across subgroups under examination).

Only 174 of 361 (48.2%) participants answered the usability rating questionnaire. Regarding this point, on the one hand, the recruitment of the participants took place in April 2022. On the other, the monitoring period was 28 days, and only at the end of these 28 days of study was the email sent to the participants (with the usability rating questionnaire). Taking into account the participant recruitment period (April 2022) and the duration of the study (28 days), the email was received by the participants from the beginning of May onwards, close to the second semester exams. This fact could have influenced the low response rate to the usability rating questionnaire, since the students were already focused on preparing for exams at that time.

The strengths of this study include, among others, the 28-day dietary intake data collection period for each participant. While those participants who completed the app task for at least 14 days were considered responders, the majority of the participants repeated the task for at least 28 days, (Table 2). The decision to use the 14-day limit was due to other studies that included repeated dietary intake data collections for 14 days or less (2 days [25,26,29,30,32,37], 3 days [17,24,28], 5 days [33], 7 days [15,16,20,21], 14 days [18]), except for a single study that included a larger number of repetitions, specifically 52 repetitions in total [34]. In order to determine habitual dietary intake (or average long-term consumption) using short-term tools, it is necessary to repeat these measures multiple times, and more repetitions provide a clearer picture of habitual dietary intake. This has been possible thanks to the use of e-12HR. This app is, basically, a modified 24 h recall (24HR) which is completed once a day during the study period and does not require making photographs of the food groups consumed [39–43]. These characteristics result in a low workload for users of e-12HR and, at the same time, has allowed the research team to schedule a longer monitoring period. The majority of the participants in this study reported that the e-12HR app was easy and interesting to complete and contained understandable questions; that they would be willing to complete e-12HR app again; and that the task took 3 min or less per day to complete (Table 8); Another important strength of the study was the various subgroups that were analyzed (age, gender, studies, BMI, smoking status and physical activity status).

Nevertheless, a few limitations should be noted. e-12HR is a self-reporting method and, as a consequence, it presents the limitations inherent in this type of tool (amply described in [47,60–65]); among others, the dependence on the memory of each participant and, mainly, the difficulty of estimating the size of servings consumed. As far as the participant's memory is concerned, e-12HR reduces this disadvantage, as it only requires short-term memory, being completed at the end of each day. Indeed, the name e-12HR (electronic 12-Hour Dietary Recall) is a reference to how it differs from a 24HR. While 24HR registers consumption of food groups from the day before, e-12HR allows users to register their consumption during the same day (normally with a maximum period of time between consumption of the food and it being registered of 12 h). Regarding the difficulty of estimating the size of the servings consumed, we must take into account that AMD assessment does not require a precise estimation of the size of the foods consumed, but rather a precise recognition of the food groups consumed together with an approximate estimation of the servings [51]. In this sense, e-12HR allows for collecting data on consumption for all the food groups needed to calculate AMD. Newer alternative methods for determining dietary intake include audio signal processing, inertial sensing, image processing, non-intrusive near-infrared scanning and gesture recognition interfacing [66–69]. Some authors maintain that more research is needed to develop these and other tools, which are more objective and precise, and that resources should be invested to this end [65]. Until these alternatives are available and in spite of their limitations, digital technologies for self-reporting methods can, and must, be developed and utilized [39] as an improvement on traditional self-reporting methods, the progress of which constitutes one of the most important challenges to the field of nutritional epidemiology [48,70] in this day and age. The small number of individuals in some of the subgroups analyzed (e.g., smoking status yes (n = 31)) is another of the limitations of the study.

Future Research Related to the Current Study

Future research will focus on determining weekend–weekday differences in diet among Health Science students during nonschool periods as well as among other students (non-Health Science students). This will allow the research team to establish if the results observed in the present study are specific to Health Science students and to the school period or if, on the contrary, they are maintained in other periods (e.g., the summer holidays) and among other students (without training in health or nutrition).

5. Conclusions

This study has been carried out using the e-12HR application. This app is characterized by a low workload for users (allowing the research team to schedule a long monitoring period) as it only requires short-term memory use and allows for collecting data on consumption for all the food groups needed to calculate AMD. Preliminary evidence suggests that Spanish university students' diet was associated with poor diet quality in general and especially at the weekends in the whole study sample and in all subgroups thereof. These results could be used to improve public health campaigns to promote healthy eating among Spanish university students. In a practical way, the interventions could be focused, on the one hand, on all times periods, on food groups that were consumed according to recommendations by less than 25% of the participants (fruits, vegetables, cereals, olive oil, milk and dairy products, nuts, red meat and sweets), and on the other, on weekends, on food groups with a lower percentage of participants who complied with the consumption recommendations (sweets, fermented beverages, potatoes, legumes, milk and dairy products, red meat, eggs and white meat). Finally, future interventions should be applied to all subgroups by age, gender, studies, BMI, smoking status and physical activity status (with very similar results).

Funding: This research received no external funding.

Institutional Review Board Statement: The study was conducted according to the guidelines of the Declaration of Helsinki and approved by the Ethics Committee of the University of Seville, internal code 2813-N-21 (on 30 March 2022).

UNIVERSIDAD D SEVILLA 1505

VICERRECTORADO DE INVESTIGACIÓN

Comité de Ética de la Investigación

ACUERDO DEL COMITÉ DE ÉTICA DE LA INVESTIGACIÓN DE LA UNIVERSIDAD DE SEVILLA

Dª. Rosario Antequera Jurado, Secretaria Técnica del

Comité de Ética de la Investigación de la Universidad de Sevilla

CERTIFICA

Que el *Comité de Ética en la Investigación de la Unviersidad de Sevilla*, en su reunión del día 23 de Febrero de 2022 (Acta 06/22), tras la evaluación del estudio titulado: *"Efectividad de un programa de intervención personalizado para el fomento de la dieta mediterránea, basado en una aplicación de teléfono móvil (e12HR), en estudiantes de la Universidad de Sevilla "*, con código Interno PEIBA: 2813-N-21

ACUERDA: **Solicitar Aclaraciones Mayores**

*En el **protocolo** presentado no queda claro el procedimiento de captación de los participantes ¿Cómo se accede a sujetos de los grupos seleccionados aleatoriamente?. Es necesario incluir en la **hoja de información y consentimiento informado** el sorteo de material escolar. La **protección de datos** tiene que realizarse teniendo en cuenta que los datos no son anónimos (como se indica) sino que son seudoanonimizados con posibilidad de reidentificación. No se hace referencia sobre el alojamiento de la información y el encriptado de la misma, ni lo referido a la cesión, acceso y destrucción de los datos.*

Debe presentar (si existe) un informe anterior de un Comité de Ética por la reailzación o parcial previa del proyecto que ha presentado. Igualmente deberá enviar el cronograma actualizado.

Se le indica que, en el supuesto de no responder a todas las aclaraciones solicitadas en un **plazo máximo de tres meses,** se procederá a la cancelación del estudio en el Portal de Ética de la Investigación Biomédica de Andalucía (PEIBA).

Código Seguro De Verificación	1jkvQz4rzwsxxiNJvBfJ+Q==	Fecha	25/02/2022
Firmado Por	ROSARIO ANTEQUERA JURADO		
Url De Verificación	https://pfirma.us.es/verifirma/code/1jkvQz4rzwsxxiNJvBfJ+Q==	Página	1/1

Informed Consent Statement: Written informed consent has been obtained from the patient(s) to publish this paper.

Data Availability Statement: The data presented in this study are available on request from the corresponding author.

Acknowledgments: The author would like to thank the participants in this study.

Conflicts of Interest: The author declares no conflict of interests.

Appendix A

Table A1. Questionnaire used in e-12HR.

Questions About Food Groups:
1. How many servings of fruits (orange, apple, pear, peach, strawberry, watermelon, etc., including fresh juice) have you consumed today? 1 serving = 150–200 g. Homemade measures: 1 serving = A medium-sized piece of apple, pear or orange, a cup of cherries or strawberries, two slices of melon, a glass of natural juice.
2. How many servings of vegetables (tomato, carrot, bell pepper, lettuce, zucchini, etc.) have you consumed today? 1 serving = 150–250 g. Homemade measures: 1 serving = One normal single plate of salad, one normal single plate of cooked vegetables, one large tomato, two carrots.
3. How many servings of breakfast cereals have you consumed today? 1 serving = 20–30 g. Homemade measures: 1 serving = One individual normal bowl.
4. How many servings of pasta have you consumed today? 1 serving = 50–70 g. Homemade measures: 1 serving = One normal individual plate.
5. How many servings of rice have you consumed today? 1 serving = 50–70 g. Homemade measures: 1 serving = One normal individual plate.
6. How many servings of bread have you consumed today? 1 serving = 30–60 g. Homemade measures: 1 serving = Three or four slices of bread or a muffin.
7. How many servings of olive oil have you consumed today (used for salad, to add to bread or for cooking)? 1 serving = 15 mL. Homemade measures: 1 serving = One tablespoon.
8. How many servings of milk and dairy products (yogurt, fresh cheese, aged cheese) have you consumed today? 1 serving of milk = 200–250 mL. 1 serving of yogurt = 125 g. 1 serving of fresh cheese = 60–80 g. 1 serving of aged cheese = 30–40 g. Homemade measures: 1 serving = A glass of milk, a yogurt, a tub or individual portion of fresh cheese, two or three slices of aged cheese.
9. How many servings of nuts (almonds, walnuts, hazelnuts, etc.) and/or olives have you consumed today? 1 serving = 20–30 g. Homemade measures: 1 serving = A handful of olives (8–10 units), a handful of hazelnuts (18-20 units), three or four walnuts.
10. How many servings of beer have you consumed today? 1 serving = 200 mL. Homemade measures: 1 serving = A beer or a bottle (200 mL). 1.5 servings = A bottle (large bottle), a can or a large beer glass (330 mL).
11. How many servings of wine have you consumed today? 1 serving = 100 mL. Homemade measures: 1 serving = A glass of wine (100 mL).
12. How many servings of potatoes have you consumed today (cooked, roasted or fried)? 1 serving = 100–150 g. Homemade measures: 1 serving = One large potato or two small potatoes.
13. How many servings of legumes (lentils, beans, chickpeas, peas, etc.) have you consumed today? 1 serving = 50–70 g. Homemade measures: 1 serving = One normal individual plate.

Table A1. *Cont.*

Questions About Food Groups:
14. How many servings of eggs have you consumed today? 1 serving = One medium egg (50–70 g).
15. How many servings of fish (and / or shellfish) have you consumed today? 1 serving = 100–150 g. Homemade measures: 1 serving = One single regular steak. 0.5 servings = One can of tuna, etc.
16. How many servings of white meat (poultry) have you consumed today? 1 serving = 100–125 g. Homemade measures: 1 serving = One regular single filet or a chicken leg quarter. 0.5 servings = Two or three slices of chicken or turkey.
17. How many servings of red meat (beef, pork or lamb) have you consumed today? 1 serving = 100–125 g. Homemade measures: 1 serving = One single regular steak.
18. How many servings of processed meats (hamburgers, sausages) and/or cold cuts (salami, chorizo, cooked ham) have you consumed today? 1 serving = 90–100 g. Homemade measures: 1 serving = a hamburger, a large sausage or two small sausages, eight or ten thin slices of cold cuts (salami, chorizo), four or five thin slices of cooked ham.
19. How many sweets (sugar, candies, pastries, sweetened fruit juices and soft drinks) have you consumed today? Consider the number of units consumed regardless of the serving size.
Additional questions about physical activities:
20. For how many minutes have you practiced moderate physical activity today? Consider only those moderate physical activities that you practiced for at least 10 min at a time. According to the WHO, these activities require moderate effort, which perceptibly accelerates the heart rate. Examples: fast walking, cycling, dancing, housework, active participation in games and sports with children, etc.
21. For how many minutes have you practiced intense physical activity today? Consider only those intense physical activities that you practiced for at least 10 min at a time. According to the WHO, these activities require a great deal of effort and cause rapid breathing and a substantial increase in heart rate. Examples: running, cycling fast, competitive sports and games, etc.

Table A2. Usability rating questionnaire for e-12HR.

1. SI found e-12HR easy to complete:
Strongly agree. Agree. Neither agree nor disagree. Disagree. Strongly disagree.
2. I found e-12HR interesting to complete:
Strongly agree. Agree. Neither agree nor disagree. Disagree. Strongly disagree.
3. I found the questions of e-12HR understandable:
Strongly agree. Agree. Neither agree nor disagree. Disagree. Strongly disagree.

Table A2. *Cont.*

4. In the future, I would be willing to complete e-12HR again:
Strongly agree. Agree. Neither agree nor disagree. Disagree. Strongly disagree.
5. How much time was needed to complete the daily questionnaire on the app:
Less than 1 min per day. Approximately 1 min per day. Approximately 2 min per day. Approximately 3 min per day. Approximately 4 min per day. 5 min per day or more.

Table A3. Mediterranean diet Serving Scores (MDSS).

Food Group	Recommendation	Score
Fruits	1–2 servings/main meal	3
Vegetables	≥2 servings/main meal	3
Cereals	1–2 servings/main meal	3
Olive oil	1 serving/main meal	3
Milk and dairy products	2 servings/day	2
Nuts	1–2 servings/day	2
Fermented beverages	1–2 glass/day	1
Potatoes	≤3 servings/week	1
Legumes	≥2 servings/week	1
Eggs	2–4 servings/week	1
Fish	≥2 servings/week	1
White meat	2 servings/week	1
Red meat	<2 servings/week	1
Sweets	≤2 servings/week	1
Total maximum score		24

Main meal: breakfast, lunch and dinner. Cereals: breakfast cereals, pasta, rice and bread. Olive oil: used on salads or bread or for frying. Milk and dairy products: milk, yogurt and cheese. Fermented beverages: wine and beer (one glass for females and two glasses for males). White meat: poultry. Red meat: pork, beef and lamb. Sweets: sugar, candies, pastries, sweetened fruit juices and soft drinks.

References

1. WHO. Global Strategy on Diet, Physical Activity and Health. 2004. Available online: https://www.who.int/publications/i/item/9241592222 (accessed on 14 June 2022).
2. Gotsis, E.; Anagnostis, P.; Mariolis, A.; Vlachou, A.; Katsiki, N.; Karagiannis, A. Health benefits of the Mediterranean Diet: An update of research over the last 5 years. *Angiology* **2015**, *66*, 304–318. [CrossRef] [PubMed]
3. Ventriglio, A.; Sancassiani, F.; Contu, M.P.; Latorre, M.; Di Slavatore, M.; Fornaro, M.; Bhugra, D. Mediterranean Diet and its Benefits on Health and Mental Health: A Literature Review. *Clin. Pract. Epidemiol. Ment. Health* **2020**, *16*, 156–164. [CrossRef] [PubMed]
4. Lăcătușu, C.M.; Grigorescu, E.D.; Floria, M.; Onofriescu, A.; Mihai, B.M. The Mediterranean Diet: From an Environment-Driven Food Culture to an Emerging Medical Prescription. *Int. J. Environ. Res. Public Health* **2019**, *16*, 942. [CrossRef] [PubMed]
5. Katz, D.L.; Meller, S. Can we say what diet is best for health? *Annu. Rev. Public Health* **2014**, *35*, 83–103. [CrossRef] [PubMed]
6. Dernini, S.; Berry, E.M.; Serra-Majem, L.; La Vecchia, C.; Capone, R.; Medina, F.X.; Aranceta-Bartrina, J.; Belahsen, R.; Burlingame, B.; Calabrese, G.; et al. Med Diet 4.0: The Mediterranean diet with four sustainable benefits. *Public Health Nutr.* **2017**, *20*, 1322–1330. [CrossRef]
7. Karam, J.; Bibiloni, M.D.M.; Serhan, M.; Tur, J.A. Adherence to Mediterranean Diet among Lebanese University Students. *Nutrients* **2021**, *13*, 1264. [CrossRef]
8. Berry, E.M. Sustainable Food Systems and the Mediterranean Diet. *Nutrients* **2019**, *11*, 2229. [CrossRef]
9. Dernini, S.; Berry, E.M. Mediterranean Diet: From a Healthy Diet to a Sustainable Dietary Pattern. *Front. Nutr.* **2015**, *7*, 15. [CrossRef]

10. Berry, E.M.; Dernini, S.; Burlingame, B.; Meybeck, A.; Conforti, P. Food security and sustainability: Can one exist without the other? *Public Health Nutr.* **2015**, *18*, 2293–2302. [CrossRef]
11. Burlingame, B.; Dernini, S. *Sustainable Diets and Biodiversity*; Food and Agriculture Organization of the United Nations (FAO): Rome, Italy, 2012; p. 309.
12. Lacirignola, C.; Capone, R. *Mediterranean Food Consumption Patterns Diet, Environment, Society, Economy and Health*; Food and Agriculture Organization of the United Nations (FAO): Rome, Italy, 2015; p. 77.
13. Burlingame, B.; Dernini, S. Sustainable diets: The Mediterranean diet as an example. *Public Health Nutr.* **2011**, *14*, 2285–2287. [CrossRef]
14. McCarthy, S. Weekly patterns, diet quality and energy balance. *Physiol. Behav.* **2014**, *134*, 55–59. [CrossRef] [PubMed]
15. Nordman, M.; Matthiessen, J.; Biltoft-Jensen, A.; Ritz, C.; Hjorth, M.F. Weekly variation in diet and physical activity among 4–75-year-old Danes. *Public Health Nutr.* **2020**, *23*, 1350–1361. [CrossRef] [PubMed]
16. Cullen, K.W.; Lara, K.M.; de Moor, C. Children's dietary fat intake and fat practices vary by meal and day. *J. Am. Diet Assoc.* **2002**, *102*, 1773–1778. [CrossRef]
17. Hart, C.N.; Raynor, H.A.; Osterholt, K.M.; Jelalian, E.; Wing, R.R. Eating and activity habits of overweight children on weekdays and weekends. *Int. J. Pediatr. Obes.* **2011**, *6*, 467–742. [CrossRef] [PubMed]
18. Brazendale, K.; Rayan, S.; Eisenstein, D.; Blankenship, M.; Rey, A.; Garcia, J.; Odahowski, C.L.; Leon, A. Obesogenic Behaviors of Rural Children on School and Nonschool Days. *Child Obes.* **2021**, *17*, 483–492. [CrossRef]
19. Hoffmann, D.A.; Marx, J.M.; Burmeister, J.M.; Musher-Eizenman, D.R. Friday Night Is Pizza Night: A Comparison of Children's Dietary Intake and Maternal Perceptions and Feeding Goals on Weekdays and Weekends. *Int. J. Environ. Res. Public Health* **2018**, *11*, 720. [CrossRef]
20. Rothausen, B.W.; Matthiessen, J.; Hoppe, C.; Brockhoff, P.B.; Andersen, L.F.; Tetens, I. Differences in Danish children's diet quality on weekdays v. weekend days. *Public Health Nutr.* **2012**, *15*, 1653–1660. [CrossRef]
21. Rothausen, B.W.; Matthiessen, J.; Andersen, L.F.; Brockhoff, P.B.; Tetens, I. Dietary patterns on weekdays and weekend days in 4-14-year-old Danish children. *Br. J. Nutr.* **2013**, *109*, 1704–1713. [CrossRef]
22. Rockell, J.E.; Parnell, W.R.; Wilson, N.C.; Skidmore, P.M.; Regan, A. Nutrients and foods consumed by New Zealand children on schooldays and non-schooldays. *Public Health Nutr.* **2011**, *14*, 203–208. [CrossRef]
23. Svensson, A.; Larsson, C.; Eiben, G.; Lanfer, A.; Pala, V.; Hebestreit, A.; Huybrechts, I.; Fernández-Alvira, J.M.; Russo, P.; Koni, A.C.; et al. European children's sugar intake on weekdays versus weekends: The IDEFICS study. *Eur. J. Clin. Nutr.* **2014**, *68*, 822–828. [CrossRef]
24. Lachapelle, D.; Gamache, C.; Brodeur, J.M.; Sévigny, J. Frequency of food consumption in children: Weekdays versus weekends. *J. Can. Dent. Assoc.* **1989**, *55*, 61e5.
25. Dutch, D.C.; Golley, R.K.; Johnson, B.J. Diet Quality of Australian Children and Adolescents on Weekdays versus Weekend Days: A Secondary Analysis of the National Nutrition and Physical Activity Survey 2011–2012. *Nutrients* **2021**, *13*, 4128. [CrossRef] [PubMed]
26. Hanson, K.L.; Olson, C.M. School meals participation and weekday dietary quality were associated after controlling for weekend eating among U.S. school children aged 6 to 17 years. *J. Nutr.* **2013**, *143*, 714–721. [CrossRef] [PubMed]
27. Kim, M.J. Comparison of food and nutrient intake between weekday and weekend for elementary and middle school students by gender in Busan and some parts of Kyungsangnamdo. *J. Nutr. Health* **2013**, *46*, 332–345. [CrossRef]
28. Smith, K.L.; Straker, L.M.; Kerr, D.A.; Smith, A.J. Overweight adolescents eat what? And when? Analysis of consumption patterns to guide dietary message development for intervention. *J. Hum. Nutr. Diet.* **2015**, *28*, 80–93. [CrossRef]
29. Haines, P.S.; Hama, M.Y.; Guilkey, D.K.; Popkin, B.M. Weekend eating in the United States is linked with greater energy, fat, and alcohol intake. *Obes. Res.* **2003**, *11*, 945–949. [CrossRef]
30. Monteiro, L.S.; Hassan, B.K.; Estima, C.C.P.; Souza, A.M.; Verly, E.; Sichieri, R.; Pereira, R.A. Food Consumption According to the Days of the Week-National Food Survey, 2008–2009. *Rev. Saude Publica* **2017**, *51*, 93. [CrossRef]
31. Yang, P.H.W.; Black, J.L.; Barr, S.I.; Vatanparast, H. A temporal analysis of Canadian dietary choices using the Canadian Community Health Survey Cycle 2.2: Does nutrient intake and diet quality vary on weekends versus weekdays. *FASEB J.* **2013**, *27*, 354. [CrossRef]
32. An, R. Weekend-weekday differences in diet among U.S. adults, 2003–2012. *Ann. Epidemiol.* **2016**, *26*, 57–65. [CrossRef]
33. Racette, S.B.; Weiss, E.P.; Schechtman, K.B.; Steger-May, K.; Villareal, D.T.; Obert, K.A.; Holloszy, J.O. Influence of weekend lifestyle patterns on body weight. *Obesity* **2008**, *16*, 1826–1830. [CrossRef]
34. Jahns, L.; Conrad, Z.; Johnson, L.K.; Scheett, A.J.; Stote, K.S.; Raatz, S.K. Diet Quality Is Lower and Energy Intake Is Higher on Weekends Compared with Weekdays in Midlife Women: A 1-Year Cohort Study. *J. Acad. Nutr. Diet.* **2017**, *117*, 1080–1086. [CrossRef] [PubMed]
35. Yang, P.H.; Black, J.L.; Barr, S.I.; Vatanparast, H. Examining differences in nutrient intake and dietary quality on weekdays versus weekend days in Canada. *Appl. Physiol. Nutr. Metab.* **2014**, *39*, 1413–1417. [CrossRef] [PubMed]
36. Rhodes, D.G.; Cleveland, L.E.; Murayi, T.; Moshfegh, A.J. The effect of weekend eating on nutrient intakes and dietary patterns. *FASEB J.* **2007**, *21*, 835. [CrossRef]
37. Hartline-Grafton, H.L.; Rose, D.; Johnson, C.C.; Rice, J.C.; Webber, L.S. The influence of weekday eating patterns on energy intake and BMI among female elementary school personnel. *Obesity* **2010**, *18*, 736–742. [CrossRef]

38. Yahia, N.; Achkar, A.; Abdallah, A.; Rizk, S. Eating habits and obesity among Lebanese university students. *Nutr. J.* **2008**, *7*, 32. [CrossRef]
39. Béjar, L.M.; Sharp, B.N.; García-Perea, M.D. The e-EPIDEMIOLOGY Mobile Phone App for Dietary Intake Assessment: Comparison with a Food Frequency Questionnaire. *JMIR Res. Protoc.* **2016**, *5*, e208. [CrossRef]
40. Béjar, L.M.; Vázquez-Limón, E. Is there any alternative to traditional food frequency questionnaire for evaluating habitual dietary intake? *Nutr. Hosp.* **2017**, *34*, 880–888. [CrossRef]
41. Béjar, L.M. First evaluation steps of a new method for dietary intake estimation regarding a list of key food groups in adults and in different sociodemographic and health-related behaviour strata. *Public Health Nutr.* **2017**, *20*, 2660–2669. [CrossRef]
42. Béjar, L.M.; Reyes, Ó.A.; García-Perea, M.D. Electronic 12-Hour Dietary Recall (e-12HR): Comparison of a Mobile Phone App for Dietary Intake Assessment with a Food Frequency Questionnaire and Four Dietary Records. *JMIR Mhealth Uhealth* **2018**, *6*, e10409. [CrossRef]
43. Béjar, L.M.; García-Perea, M.D.; Reyes, Ó.A.; Vázquez-Limón, E. Relative Validity of a Method Based on a Smartphone App (Electronic 12-Hour Dietary Recall) to Estimate Habitual Dietary Intake in Adults. *JMIR Mhealth Uhealth* **2019**, *7*, e11531. [CrossRef]
44. Knudsen, V.K.; Hatch, E.E.; Cueto, H.; Tucker, K.L.; Wise, L.; Christensen, T.; Mikkelsen, E.M. Relative validity of a semi-quantitative, web-based FFQ used in the 'Snart Forældre' cohort—A Danish study of diet and fertility. *Public Health Nutr.* **2016**, *19*, 1027–1034. [CrossRef] [PubMed]
45. Medin, A.C.; Astrup, H.; Kåsin, B.M.; Andersen, L.F. Evaluation of a web-based food record for children using direct unobtrusive lunch observations: A validation study. *J. Med. Internet Res.* **2015**, *17*, e273. [CrossRef] [PubMed]
46. Rodríguez, I.T.; Ballart, J.F.; Pastor, G.C.; Jordà, E.B.; Val, V.A. Validation of a short questionnaire on frequency of dietary intake: Reproducibility and validity. *Nutr. Hosp.* **2008**, *23*, 242–252. [PubMed]
47. Forster, H.; Fallaize, R.; Gallagher, C.; O'Donovan, C.B.; Woolhead, C.; Walsh, M.C.; Macready, A.L.; Lovegrove, J.A.; Mathers, J.C.; Gibney, M.J.; et al. Online dietary intake estimation: The Food4Me food frequency questionnaire. *J. Med. Internet Res.* **2014**, *16*, e150. [CrossRef]
48. Svensson, A.; Larsson, C. A mobile phone app for dietary intake assessment in adolescents: An evaluation study. *JMIR Mhealth Uhealth* **2015**, *3*, e93. [CrossRef]
49. Hongu, N.; Pope, B.T.; Bilgiç, P.; Orr, B.J.; Suzuki, A.; Kim, A.S.; Merchant, N.C.; Roe, D.J. Usability of a smartphone food picture app for assisting 24-hour dietary recall: A pilot study. *Nutr. Res. Pract.* **2015**, *9*, 207–212. [CrossRef]
50. Monteagudo, C.; Mariscal-Arcas, M.; Rivas, A.; Lorenzo-Tovar, M.L.; Tur, J.A.; Olea-Serrano, F. Proposal of a Mediterranean Diet Serving Score. *PLoS ONE* **2015**, *10*, e0128594. [CrossRef]
51. Vasiloglou, M.F.; Lu, Y.; Stathopoulou, T.; Papathanail, I.; Fäh, D.; Ghosh, A.; Baumann, M.; Mougiakakou, S. Assessing Mediterranean Diet Adherence with the Smartphone: The Medipiatto Project. *Nutrients* **2020**, *12*, 3763. [CrossRef]
52. Duan, Y.P.; Wienert, J.; Hu, C.; Si, G.Y.; Lippke, S. Web-Based Intervention for Physical Activity and Fruit and Vegetable Intake Among Chinese University Students: A Randomized Controlled Trial. *J. Med. Internet Res.* **2017**, *19*, e106. [CrossRef]
53. García-Meseguer, M.J.; Burriel, F.C.; García, C.V.; Serrano-Urrea, R. Adherence to Mediterranean diet in a Spanish university population. *Appetite* **2014**, *78*, 156–164. [CrossRef]
54. Solera, A.; Gamero, A. Healthy habits in university students of health sciences and other branches of knowledge: A comparative study. *Rev. Esp. Nutr. Hum. Diet.* **2019**, *23*, 271–282.
55. Cancela-Carral, J.M.; Ayán-Pérez, C. Prevalence and relationship between physical activity and abnormal eating attitudes in Spanish women university students in Health and Education Sciences. *Rev. Esp. Salud Publica* **2011**, *85*, 499–505. [CrossRef] [PubMed]
56. Ramón-Arbués, E.; Granada-López, J.M.; Martínez-Abadía, B.; Echániz-Serrano, E.; Antón-Solanas, I.; Jerue, B.A. Factors Related to Diet Quality: A Cross-Sectional Study of 1055 University Students. *Nutrients* **2021**, *13*, 3512. [CrossRef] [PubMed]
57. Telleria-Aramburu, N.; Bermúdez-Marín, N.; Rocandio, A.M.; Telletxea, S.; Basabe, N.; Rebato, E.; Arroyo-Izaga, M. Nutritional quality and carbon footprint of university students' diets: Results from the EHU12/24 study. *Public Health Nutr.* **2022**, *25*, 183–195. [CrossRef]
58. López-Moreno, M.; Garcés-Rimón, M.; Miguel, M.; Iglesias-López, M.T. Adherence to Mediterranean Diet, Alcohol Consumption and Emotional Eating in Spanish University Students. *Nutrients* **2021**, *13*, 3174. [CrossRef]
59. Cobo-Cuenca, A.I.; Garrido-Miguel, M.; Soriano-Cano, A.; Ferri-Morales, A.; Martínez-Vizcaíno, V.; Martín-Espinosa, N.M. Adherence to the Mediterranean Diet and Its Association with Body Composition and Physical Fitness in Spanish University Students. *Nutrients* **2019**, *11*, 2830. [CrossRef]
60. Willett, W. *Nutritional Epidemiology*, 3rd ed.; Oxford University Press: New York, NY, USA, 2013; p. 552.
61. Rutishauser, I.H. Dietary intake measurements. *Public Health Nutr.* **2005**, *8*, 1100–1107. [CrossRef]
62. Tucker, K.L.; Smith, C.E.; Lai, C.Q.; Ordovas, J.M. Quantifying diet for nutrigenomic studies. *Annu. Rev. Nutr.* **2013**, *33*, 349–371. [CrossRef]
63. Gibson, R. *Principles of Nutritional Assessment*, 2nd ed.; Oxford University Press: New York, NY, USA, 2005; p. 908.
64. Martín-Moreno, J.M.; Gorgojo, L. Assessment of dietary intake at the population level through individual questionnaires: Meth-odological shadows and lights. *Rev. Esp. Salud Publica* **2007**, *81*, 507–518. [CrossRef]

65. Dhurandhar, N.V.; Schoeller, D.; Brown, A.W.; Heymsfield, S.B.; Thomas, D.; Sørensen, T.I.; Speakman, J.R.; Jeansonne, M.; Allison, D.B.; Energy Balance Measurement Working Group. Energy balance measurement: When something is not better than nothing. *Int. J. Obes.* **2015**, *39*, 1109–1113. [CrossRef]
66. Illner, A.K.; Freisling, H.; Boeing, H.; Huybrechts, I.; Crispim, S.P.; Slimani, N. Review and evaluation of innovative technologies for measuring diet in nutritional epidemiology. *Int. J. Epidemiol.* **2012**, *41*, 1187–1203. [CrossRef] [PubMed]
67. Steele, R. An overview of the state of the art of automated capture of dietary intake information. *Crit. Rev. Food Sci. Nutr.* **2015**, *55*, 1929–1938. [CrossRef] [PubMed]
68. Hassannejad, H.; Matrella, G.; Ciampolini, P.; De Munari, I.; Mordonini, M.; Cagnoni, S. Automatic diet monitoring: A review of computer vision and wearable sensor-based methods. *Int. J. Food Sci. Nutr.* **2017**, *68*, 656–670. [CrossRef] [PubMed]
69. Thong, Y.J.; Nguyen, T.; Zhang, Q.; Karunanithi, M.; Yu, L. Predicting food nutrition facts using pocket-size near-infrared sensor. *Annu. Int. Conf. IEEE Eng. Med. Biol. Soc.* **2017**, *2017*, 742–745. [CrossRef]
70. Carroll, R.J.; Midthune, D.; Subar, A.F.; Shumakovich, M.; Freedman, L.S.; Thompson, F.E.; Kipnis, V. Taking advantage of the strengths of 2 different dietary assessment instruments to improve intake estimates for nutritional epidemiology. *Am. J. Epidemiol.* **2012**, *175*, 340–347. [CrossRef]

nutrients

MDPI

Review

The Effectiveness of Wearable Devices in Non-Communicable Diseases to Manage Physical Activity and Nutrition: Where We Are?

Valentina Natalucci [1,*], Federica Marmondi [2], Michele Biraghi [3] and Matteo Bonato [3,4]

1 Department of Biomolecular Sciences, Division of Exercise and Health Sciences, University of Urbino Carlo Bo, 61029 Urbino, Italy
2 Department of Infection Diseases, IRCCS San Raffaele Scientific Institute, 20132 Milan, Italy
3 Department of Biomedical Sciences for Health, Università degli Studi di Milano, 20122 Milan, Italy
4 IRCCS Istituto Ortopedico Galeazzi, 20161 Milan, Italy
* Correspondence: valentina.natalucci@uniurb.it

Abstract: Wearable devices are increasingly popular in clinical and non-clinical populations as a tool for exercise prescription, monitoring of daily physical activity and nutrition, and health-related parameters management. In this regard, smart devices not only assist people in pursuing a healthier lifestyle, but also provide a constant stream of physiological and metabolic data for management of non-communicable diseases (NCDs). Although the benefits of lifestyle-based interventions (exercise and nutrition) for NCDs are well known, the potential of wearable devices to promote healthy behaviors in clinical populations is still controversial. In this narrative review, we aimed to discuss the current application of wearable devices in NCDs, highlighting their role in prescribing and monitoring daily physical activity and dietary habits in the population living with chronic diseases. None of the studies considered specifically addressed the efficacy of the use of wearable devices, and limited are those that incorporate monitoring of both physical activity and nutrition for NCDs. However, there is evidence that such devices have helped improve physical activity levels, physical fitness, body composition, and metabolic and psychological parameters. Therefore, the authors believe that the benefits obtained from the use of wearable devices are likely to translate to public health and represent one of the important tools for the development of prevention plans in everyday life and clinical practice for optimal patient management.

Keywords: physical activity; exercise; nutrition; wearable devices; lifestyle assessment; health; non-communicable diseases

Citation: Natalucci, V.; Marmondi, F.; Biraghi, M.; Bonato, M. The Effectiveness of Wearable Devices in Non-Communicable Diseases to Manage Physical Activity and Nutrition: Where We Are? *Nutrients* **2023**, *15*, 913. https://doi.org/10.3390/nu15040913

Academic Editor: Joerg Koenigstorfer

Received: 9 January 2023
Revised: 28 January 2023
Accepted: 7 February 2023
Published: 11 February 2023

1. Introduction

The major non-communicable diseases (NCDs), also known as chronic diseases, continue to become exceedingly ingrained in everyday life and represent the main killers in the modern era. Although chronic disease is not contagious, its long duration and progress slowly has a negative impact on the population's health, accounting for 74% of all deaths globally [1] and representing a high cost to healthcare systems worldwide [2]. The risk factors underlying NCDs include unhealthy behaviors, such as smoking, overeating, alcohol consumption, and sedentary lifestyle, all behaviors that are considered modifiable risk factors. The reversal of these bad health habits can be achieved through leading a healthier lifestyle, with the aim to extend the period of being free from NCDs (primary prevention), to improve managing the disease (secondary prevention), and increasing the quality of life in people with NCDs (tertiary prevention) [3]. To achieve increased adoption of healthy behaviors in the three levels of prevention, integrated action by all clinical and non-clinical stakeholders that looks beyond the traditional model of healthcare and is increasingly in step with the social context is needed.

In the last 10 years, wearable technology has gained in popularity, both in the general population and in people with NCDs, for physical activity and health monitoring, representing nowadays one of the most popular trends in health and fitness [4]. It is well known that physical activity is associated with numerous health benefits, preventing the onset of non-communicable diseases, and resulting in a lower risk of mortality [5]. Recently, Strain et al. [6] showed that higher volumes of device-based physical activity energy expenditure was associated with reduced mortality rates. The public health relevance of such devices is increasing and may impact areas such as physical activity, wellbeing, cardiovascular health, mortality risk, and dietary habits [4]. In fact, commercial wearable devices have the potential to allow for population-level measurement of physical activity and large-scale behavior change. A common example is represented by the self-monitoring of physical activity in terms of step numbers and minutes of daily activity, as well as physiological parameters (e.g., heart rate) or dietary intake (e.g., energy expenditure), depending on the characteristics of the device. Some products also remind one to stop sedentary activities or introduce meals through notification messages [7]. All this data can be used by users to plan, organize, and monitor their daily physical activity or dietary habits, but can also provide immediate feedback that can eliminate the barriers between the patient and healthcare professional. Moreover, wearable technology can also aid researchers in planning study designs with the aim to use physical activity monitor devices, especially in people with NCDs [8].

In this regard, the actual wide use of wearable devices connected to the internet, social media, and databases, increases the use of real-world data in the medical and healthcare field to monitor patient health status [9]. In fact, new advances in technology for objective assessment of physical activity using wearable devices in research enable testing the efficacy of interventions and give the opportunity to prescribe and monitor patients' home-based physical activity and its effect on health. As technology advances, these devices took the top spot in the American College of Sports Medicine (ACSM) list in 2017, 2019, 2020, and 2022, with nutrition devices also growing in popularity over the past 3 years [10–12].

Although the use of wearable devices has consistently entered society, currently there is a lack of sufficient evidence and data on how wearable devices can be implemented in the NCDs population in both the clinical and non-clinical setting. Therefore, the aim of this narrative review is to discuss the current application of wearable devices in NCDs, highlighting their role in prescribing and monitoring daily physical activity and dietary habits in the population living with chronic diseases. In the following sections, we will first provide an overview of the relationships between NCDs and major, modifiable, behavioral risk factors, such as exercise and nutrition. We will examine the utility of wearable devices for prescribing and monitoring modifiable lifestyle behaviors (exercise and nutrition) and provide an overview of randomized-controlled studies that have included the use of wearable devices for prescribing and monitoring exercise and nutrition habits in the population living with NCDs. We will end with a discussion of the effectiveness and potential role of emerging technologies for prescribing and monitoring daily physical activity and dietary habits, in addition to discussion of the barriers to the integration of the technology into the population and into research and clinical settings.

2. Relationships between Non-Communicable Diseases and Modifiable Behavioral Risk Factors

2.1. Sedentary Risks or Unhealthy Physical Activity Levels

In clinical and non-clinical populations, insufficient physical activity levels in all stages of life are a well-documented public health issue [13]. Between 2001 and 2016, the levels of insufficient physical activity decreased marginally globally in high-income countries, which reported a 5% increase in the prevalence of physical inactivity [14]. Moreover, during the COVID-19 pandemic, due to contagion reduction policies based on home confinement and social distancing, a reduction of 33% from 108 to 72 min per week and an increment of 28% of time spent sitting from 5 to 8 h per day was observed in different chronic diseases [15–18].

High levels of sedentary behavior have a negative impact on the human body at the level of the muscular, cardiovascular, metabolic, endocrine, and nervous systems [19], resulting in an increased risk of developing a variety of chronic diseases, including cardiovascular diseases, type 2 diabetes, cancers, and mental illness [20]. To date, people with low levels of physical activity use significantly more healthcare services than active people [21]. The novel aspect to counteract the extraordinary burden of insufficient physical activity and improve understanding of its negative effects lies in the application and monitoring of physical activity components in a new human evolutionary context different from that of our ancestors (hunter-gatherers), who were forced to be physically active to survive.

Physical activity is defined as "any bodily movement produced by the contraction of skeletal muscles that results in energy expenditure" [22]. In this regard, growing evidence suggests a clear dose–response relationship between the volume of physical activity and the difference in mortality rates for chronic disease [23]. The updated current adults physical activity guidelines of the World Health Organization (WHO) recommend undertaking 150–300 min of moderate intensity or 75–150 min of vigorous intensity aerobic physical activity, or some equivalent combination of moderate-intensity and vigorous-intensity aerobic physical activity per week [24]. The same guidelines suggest that adults should also perform moderate- or higher-intensity muscle-strengthening activities involving all major muscle groups 2 or more days a week. In addition, an increase in attention is also directed to daily steps as an important part of preventing chronic disease [25–28]. Even if the guidelines refer to the general healthy population for primary prevention, different thresholds have been recommended for secondary and tertiary prevention for different chronic conditions considering the several components (i.e., the FITT principle [frequency, intensity, time, and type]) of physical activity. There is currently a lack of knowledge regarding the minimum amount of exercise needed to prevent and mitigate different chronic diseases, but promising evidence exists on how individual components of FITT affect the development and progression of chronic diseases. Today, we can talk about 'exercise medicine', in which the response to exercise is specific and predictable for optimal adjuvant treatment of over 30 chronic diseases [29]. The expanded understanding of exercise physiology and molecular biology has provided strong evidence on how different components and combinations of exercise (i.e., frequency, intensity, time, and type of exercise) may play a critical role in the persistent, low-grade inflammation that characterizes chronic diseases [30–34]. Evidence from epidemiological studies and clinical research demonstrates that the exercise component also exerts its effects on mental diseases. As with other chronic diseases with an impact on physical function, mental diseases include symptoms that, while they are different for everyone, can benefit from exercise [35–37].

Although the link between exercise and signaling pathways at the cellular and molecular levels can induce beneficial effects on physical and mental health, more than 80% of people do not meet physical activity guidelines [38].

2.2. Dietary Risks or Unhealthy Foods Consumption

When macronutrients are consumed in appropriate proportions to support energetic and physiologic needs without excess intake, while also providing sufficient micronutrients and hydration to meet the physiologic needs of the body, it is called a 'healthy diet' [39]. However, over the past 40 years, population diets have shifted toward a greater consumption of processed and ultra-processed foods that are low in nutrients and high in energy [40], with major public health consequences [41].

Unhealthy diet patterns, including the intake of foods high in saturated fat, refined carbohydrates, and excess sodium, coupled with lower physical activity levels, have resulted in higher prevalence rates of obesity, cardiovascular disease, type 2 diabetes, site-specific cancers, and respiratory diseases [42–47]. According to data from the NCD Risk Factor Collaboration and the Global Burden of Disease Study, NCDs, including those listed above, are responsible for almost 70% of all deaths worldwide, while changes in eating habits play a crucial role in preventing up to 80% of major NCDs [48].

In the modern era, unhealthy nutritional behaviors continue to be recorded in people with and without NCDs. These behaviors are not only limited to extreme social conditions, such as the latest COVID-19 pandemic [49]. Indeed, there is compelling evidence that diet can be influenced by many social and economic factors that evolve over time and interact in a complex manner (e.g., income, food prices, individual preferences and beliefs, cultural traditional, geographical, and environmental aspects). While there is no clear model that can pinpoint the people who adopt an unhealthy diet, on the other hand, the effects that the high consumption of trans-fatty acids has on the deterioration of health conditions are well document. The first consequence is low-grade systemic inflammation, which is positively correlated with type 2 diabetes, cardiovascular disease, cancer, and premature death [50,51]. In addition, particular attention is also paid to the consequences of intra-abdominal fat accumulation as an important risk factor for the promotion of insulin resistance, which can lead to glucose intolerance, elevated triglycerides, and low high-density lipoprotein, as well as hypertension [52–54].

With the aim to counter global unhealthy diets and to prevent a range of NCDs, WHO has developed evidence-based guidelines [55]. As with the exercise guidelines, the exact composition of a healthy diet also depends on individual characteristics (e.g., age, gender, lifestyle, and level of physical activity), cultural context, locally available foods, and dietary customs. Following a healthy diet could be easier in those countries where certain nutritional models, such as the Mediterranean diet (i.e., Euro-Mediterranean countries), are rooted. Paradoxically, that is not the case, and there is compelling evidence that most people from industrialized countries do not meet the current dietary recommendations [56].

3. The Utility of Wearable Devices on Lifestyle Behaviors

The use of smart technology has a dual role in the clinical and non-clinical context (healthcare and social). Particularly, it represents an important prevention tool, characterized by the possibility of the individual to measure and monitor health parameters because of his lifestyle-related behaviors. Furthermore, it also represents an important continuous monitoring tool, through which clinicians and non-clinician professionals can personalize the exercise prescription and nutritional intake of the individual living with or without NCDs.

3.1. Wearable Devices for Prescription and Monitoring Physical Activity

To counteract sedentary behavior, defined as an insufficient physical activity level, according to WHO recommendations, is physical activity. Humans' evolutionary history suggests that today, people must be active, but paradoxically find themselves in an increasingly industrialized context, forced to be sedentary [57]. In fact, the effects of the competing demands of activity and inactivity on the body represent an evolutionary paradox that could be countered by the evolutionary thrust of technology.

Advances in 21st century technology have introduced the use of commercial off-the-shelf activity trackers that allow users to self-monitor their daily physical activity [58]. These devices allow objectively monitoring physical activity using several consumer-based activity trackers equipped with different sensors, including accelerometers, heart rate (HR), Global Positioning System (GPS) technology, gyroscope, barometer and altimeters, and algorithms built into smartphones or wearable technology (e.g., bracelets, bands, rings, etc.), which determine a device output, such as step-count, distance traveled, energy expenditure, activity intensity, and HR [59]. This need arises from the consequences that self-reported questionnaires and diaries suffer from participants' biases as self-report measures, such as social desirability or imprecise recall [60]. According to Chan et al. [61], wearable devices represent a promising intervention tool for population-wide physical activity promotion, providing real remote monitoring of users' physical fitness. In particular, activity trackers offer a significant source of personalized physical activity data from users that would provide insights into healthcare analytics and user feedback on health status, assisting clinicians and experts in the field (e.g., sport scientists) in providing a more holistic care [62].

3.2. Wearable Devices for Prescription and Monitoring Dietary Intake

As with exercise, wearable technology, websites, and smartphone applications could estimate the nutritional intake of individuals. In the modern era, the self-reported method using smartphones has discouraged the use of conventional paper-based self-assessment methods both for more practical reasons and for reasons of data accuracy [63–65]. The network capacity of a smartphone also allows this modern approach to have more features, such as a response from clinicians and real-time self-monitoring [66]. The new systems allow participants to record entire days of meals and to monitor their intake of kilocalories and macronutrients. In addition, depending on the applications, there are also other features that allow the consumer to set goals, plans meals, or even track micronutrients.

Over time, research has also demonstrated that the timing and frequency of self-monitoring dietary intake are significantly related to weight outcomes [67]. These findings related to the importance of the frequency of self-monitoring within each day, as well as the consistency throughout a month, amplify the importance of increasingly accessible and practical tools that enable the development of very specific self-monitoring dietary goals.

3.3. Wearable Devices in Non-Communicable Diseases: Where We Are

In the last decade, researchers have begun to take advantage of this wearable technology by incorporating these devices in their research studies.

In this regard, here we have reviewed all the longitudinal RCTs from 2016 to 2022 that used wearable devices, focusing on the outcomes that could be relevant for improving physical activity and health-related outcomes in people with NCDs (Table 1). To date, 23 RCTs have been published [68–90]. The NCDs studied were cancer (31%), obesity (26%), cardiovascular diseases (22%), metabolic syndrome (13%), diabetes, and COPD (4%) (Figure 1A). Study protocols had a mean duration of 22 weeks, ranging from 2 to 96 weeks. Participants were a mean of 59 years old, ranging from 31 to 72 years old. The physical activity protocols performed during the RCTs were mainly aerobic (87%), followed by the combination of aerobic and resistance training (13%). None of the RCTs analyzed used a resistance training protocol alone (Figure 1B). The wearable devices used during the studies were Fitbit (44%), Garmin (13%), Polar (9%), and others (30%) (Figure 1C). Drop-out rates during the studies were a mean of 11%, ranging from 0% to 60%. Analyzing the RCTs, all the physical activity protocols showed an increase of physical activity levels with an increase of self-reported physical activity, daily steps, moderate to vigorous physical activity, and motivation to perform physical exercise, with a general reduction of sedentary time. This increase in physical activity levels improved cardiorespiratory fitness, with a reduction of the parameters associated with body composition (body weight, body mass index, fat mass, and waist circumference) and metabolic parameters (glycated hemoglobin and systolic and diastolic blood pressure), and an improvement in psychological parameters (anxiety and depression scores). Regarding nutrition, only eight studies considered this aspect. Particularly, 3 studies monitored diet during the experimental protocol using a 3-day [77] or 7-day food diary [71,79]. Three studies provided nutritional counselling for self-monitoring food intake, planning specific educational sessions with weekly and monthly phone recall [69,82,87]. One study assessed with a specific questionnaire the adherence to the Mediterranean diet [88]. Finally, only one study prescribed a calorie-restricted diet. To date, this was linked with an improvement of body composition and metabolic parameters in obese postmenopausal women [86].

Table 1. Summary of the exercise- and nutrition-based intervention and wearable devices for health-related outcomes of the included studies.

Author, Year [Reference]	Study Design (Duration)	Sample Size (Non-Communicable Disease)	Age (Years)	Exercise-Based Interventions	Nutrition Counselling/ Monitoring	Exercise Prescription/ Monitoring (Wearable Device)	Results
Alley et al., 2022 [68]	RCT (12 weeks)	243 (obese people)	69 ± 4	Tailored advice only (n = 96): web-based program with 6 modules of tailored advice delivered biweekly for reaching 30 min of moderate-intensity physical activity on at least 5 days each week, including 2 to 3 sessions of resistance and flexibility activity. Tailoring + Fitbit (n = 78): same protocol but with use of the wearable devices. Control group (n = 69): usual care.	Not considered	Fitbit	(i) Drop out: 60%. (ii) Tailored advice only: ↔ moderate to vigorous physical activity. (iii) Tailoring + Fitbit: ↑ moderate to vigorous physical activity. (iv)All groups: ↑ self-reported physical activity.
Ferrante et al., 2022 [69]	RCT (12 months)	44 (African American/Black women breast cancer survivors)	21–75 *	5% wight loss goal, 1200–1500 kcal daily, and 10 to 30 min per day of moderate physical activity and 10,000 steps per day (n = 44). Fitbit only (n = 17). Fitbit + SparkPeople (n = 17). Fitbit + SparkPeople Premium (n = 10).	Participants with SparkPeople device were educated for self-monitoring nutrition and weigh tracking.	(a) Fitbit (b) SparkPeople	(i) Drop out: 0%. (ii) Devices helped to improve activity levels.
Agarwal et al., 2021 [70]	RCT (12 weeks)	180 (obese people)	56 ± 13	12-week game with points and levels designed using behavioral economic principles to reach step goals (n = 180). Gamification with social support group (n = 60). Gamification + financial incentives group (n = 60). Control group (n = 60).	Not considered.	(a) Fitbit (b) Inspire (c) Way to Health platform	(i) Drop out: 1%. (ii)Gamification with social support group: ↔ daily steps. (iii) Gamification + financial incentives group: ↑ daily steps. (iv)Control group: ↔ daily steps.
Haufe et al., 2021 [71]	RCT (6 months)	314 (people with metabolic syndrome)	47 ± 8	Exercise group (n = 160): personal counselling with recommendations aiming to perform 150 min of moderate–intense physical activity per week. Control group (n = 154): usual care.	Exercise group completed a 7-day food diary which was analyzed and reviewed by dietitians for macronutrient and micronutrient content using professional nutrition analysis software.	Garmin Forerunner 35	(i) Drop out: 13%. (ii) Exercise group: ↑ Questionnaire-estimated exercise activities; ↑ maximum power output. (iii) Control group: not applicable.

Table 1. *Cont.*

Author, Year [Reference]	Study Design (Duration)	Sample Size (Non-Communicable Disease)	Age (Years)	Exercise-Based Interventions	Nutrition Counselling/ Monitoring	Exercise Prescription/ Monitoring (Wearable Device)	Results
Patel et al., 2021 [72]	RCT (12 months)	361 (people with type-2 diabetes)	53 ± 10	Conducted goal setting and entered a 1-year game designed using insights from behavioral economics with points and levels to reach step goals and weight loss targets (n = 361). Gamification with support (n = 92). Gamification with collaboration (n = 95). Gamification with competition (n = 87). Control group (n = 87).	Not considered.	Withings Activite Steel	(i) Drop out: 7%. (ii) Gamification with support, Gamification with collaboration, Gamification with competition and Control group: ↑ mean daily steps; ↓ weight; ↓ glycated hemoglobin.
Hardcastle et al., 2021 [73]	RCT (12 weeks)	68 (cancer survivors)	64 ± 8	Intervention group (n = 34): reducing bouts of sedentary behavior and responding to the automatic Fitbit prompts to take steps, in addition to encouraging planned bouts of moderate to vigorous physical activity. Control group (n = 34): only received printed materials containing the physical activity guidelines.	Not considered.	Fitbit Alta	(i) Drop out: 6%. (ii) Intervention group: ↑ moderate-to-vigorous physical activity. (iii) Control group: ↓ moderate-to-vigorous physical activity.
Pinto et al., 2021 [74]	RCT (12 weeks)	20 (older (65+ years) cancer survivors)	72 ± 4	Adjust step goals every week (n = 20). Audiobook group (n = 12). Comparison group (n = 8).	Not considered.	(a) Fitbit Charge 2 (b) Hoopla	(i) Drop out: 5%. (ii) Audiobook group: ↑ steps per day. (iii) Comparison group: ↔ steps per day.

Table 1. *Cont.*

Author, Year [Reference]	Study Design (Duration)	Sample Size (Non-Communicable Disease)	Age (Years)	Exercise-Based Interventions	Nutrition Counselling/ Monitoring	Exercise Prescription/ Monitoring (Wearable Device)	Results
Chen et al., 2021 [75]	RCT (24 weeks)	602 (obese people)	39 ± 10	Strive for their daily step goal in which participants compete against each other or work together depending on group (n = 602). Class 1 (n = 328): more extroverted and more motivated; had previously used a wearable device. - Control group (n = 71). - Gamification with support (n = 81). - Gamification with collaboration (n = 86). - Gamification with competition (n = 90). Class 2 (n = 121): less active and less social; never used a wearable device. - Control group (n = 33). - Gamification with support (n = 30). - Gamification with collaboration (n = 29). - Gamification with competition (n = 29). Class 3 (n = 153): less motivated and at risk. - Control group (n = 47). - Gamification with support (n = 40). - Gamification with collaboration (n = 35). - Gamification with competition (n = 31).	Not considered.	Withings Activite Steel	(i) Drop out: 2%. (ii) Class 1: ↑ mean daily step counts in the gamification + competition arm. (iii) Class 2: ↑ mean daily steps relative to control during the intervention period. (iv) Class 3: ↔ mean daily steps relative to control for any of the gamification arms.
Peacock et al., 2020 [76]	RCT (12 months)	204 (people with cardiovascular disease and/or type II diabetes)	64 ± 6	Intervention group (n = 134): Personal multidimensional aerobic physical activity feedback using a customized digital system and app for 3 months, plus 5 health trainer-led sessions. Control group (n = 70): usual care.	Not considered.	(a) BodyMedia Core (b) SenseWear® Pro 8.0	(i) Drop out: 10%. (ii) Intervention group and Control group: ↔ mean physical activity levels.

Table 1. *Cont.*

Author, Year [Reference]	Study Design (Duration)	Sample Size (Non-Communicable Disease)	Age (Years)	Exercise-Based Interventions	Nutrition Counselling/ Monitoring	Exercise Prescription/ Monitoring (Wearable Device)	Results
Roberts et al., 2019 [77]	RCT (8 weeks)	40 (adults with coronary artery disease events)	70 ± 7	Exercise group (n = 20): aerobic and resistance exercises, twice weekly. Counselling on reducing sedentary behavior and increasing non-exercise physical activity. Exercise + non-exercise physical activity (n = 20): also tracking non-exercise physical activity with Fitbit.	All participants performed a 3-day diet recall.	(a) Polar Ft2 (b) Fitbit Zip	(i) Drop out: 10%. (ii) Exercise group: ↑ daily steps; ↓ sedentary time; ↓ systolic and diastolic blood pressure. (iii) Exercise + non exercise physical activity: ↔ in all outcomes.
Singh et al., 2020 [78]	RCT (12 weeks)	52 (women with stage II-IV breast cancer)	51 ± 9	Physical activity counselling (n = 26): physical activity levels, moderate to vigorous physical activity, were assessed using physical activity counselling and surveys; 150 min physical activity per week. Physical activity counselling + Fitbit (n = 26): also received an activity tracker.	Not considered.	(a) Fitbit Charge HR (b) Actigraph® GT3X+	(i) Drop out: 4%. (ii) Physical activity counselling: ↔ steps/day. (iii) Physical activity counselling + Fitbit: ↑ steps/day during moderate to vigorous physical activity.
Haufe et al., 2019 [79]	RCT (6 months)	314 (people with metabolic syndrome)	48 ± 8	Exercise group (n = 160): personal counselling with recommendations aiming to do 150 min of moderately intense physical activity per week. Control group (n = 154): usual care.	All participants completed a 7-day food diary, which was analyzed and reviewed by dietitians for macronutrient and micronutrient content. All participants in the exercise group received nutritional counselling, which provided background information on healthy food choices.	(a) Garmin Forerunner 35	(i) Drop out: 13%. (ii)Exercise group: ↓ metabolic syndrome severity. (iii) Control group: ↔ metabolic syndrome severity.
Lynch et al., 2019 [80]	RCT (12 weeks)	83 (women with stage I–III breast cancer)	62 ± 6	Intervention group (n = 43): face-to-face session. Acoustic and visual alerts for inactivity were set. Telephone-delivered behavioral counselling. Control group (n = 40): usual care.	Not considered.	(a) Garmin Vivofit 2 (b) Actigraph (c) ActivPAL	(i) Drop out: 4%. (ii) Intervention group: ↑ levels of moderate to vigorous physical activity. (iii) Control group: ↔ levels of moderate to vigorous physical activity.

Table 1. *Cont.*

Author, Year [Reference]	Study Design (Duration)	Sample Size (Non-Communicable Disease)	Age (Years)	Exercise-Based Interventions	Nutrition Counselling/ Monitoring	Exercise Prescription/ Monitoring (Wearable Device)	Results
Van Blarigan et al., 2019 [81]	RCT (2 weeks)	42 (people with colorectal cancer)	54 ± 11	Intervention group (n = 21): 150 min/week of moderate activities or 75 min/week of vigorous activities; 2–3 times per week. Control group (n = 21): received print educational materials about physical activity after cancer.	Not considered.	(a) Fitbit Flex™ (b) ActiGraph GT3X+	(i) Drop out: 7%. (ii) Intervention group: ↑ activity levels; ↑ motivation to exercise. (iii) Control group: ↑ activity levels.
Lee et al., 2019 [82]	RCT (12 weeks)	96 (prostate cancer patients)	69 ± 7	Intervention smartphone group (n = 50): home-based aerobic and resistance exercises, provided with Smart After-Care app and a wearable InbodyBand digital pedometer. Pedometer control group (n = 50): conventional pedometer to record the number of steps and minutes of physical activity performed, and to record the number of resistance exercise sessions performed weekly.	Nutrition information was provided by the application, and participants received weekly feedback consultations about the intervention by telephone.	(a) Android smartphone (b) Smart After-Care app (c) InbodyBand digital pedometer	(i) Drop out: 18%. (ii) Intervention smartphone group: ↑ physical function. (iii) Pedometer control group: ↑ physical function.
Varas et al., 2018 [83]	RCT (8 weeks)	40 (patients with COPD)	68 ± 8	Experimental group (n = 17): walking 5 days a week for 30–60 min. Control group (n = 16): general recommendations to walk more every day.	Not considered.	(a) OMRON Walking Style X (b) Pocket HJ-320e digital (c) Pedometer	(i) Drop out: 18%. (ii) Experimental group: ↑ endurance shuttle test; ↑ steps/day; ↑ Baecke scores; ↓ total St. George's Respiratory; ↔ dyspnea; ↔ exacerbation. (iii) Control group: ↔ in all outcomes.
Chokshi et al., 2018 [84]	RCT (24 weeks)	105 (ischemic heart disease patients)	60 ± 11	Incentive arm (n = 50): received personalized step goals and daily feedback with remote monitoring for all 24 weeks. Control arm (n = 55): usual care with step monitoring.	Not considered.	Misfit Shine	(i) Drop out: 2%. (ii) Incentive arm: ↑ daily steps. (iii) Control arm: ↔ daily steps.

Table 1. *Cont.*

Author, Year [Reference]	Study Design (Duration)	Sample Size (Non-Communicable Disease)	Age (Years)	Exercise-Based Interventions	Nutrition Counselling/ Monitoring	Exercise Prescription/ Monitoring (Wearable Device)	Results
McDermott et al., 2018 [85]	RCT (9 months)	200 (patients with peripheral artery disease)	70 ± 10	Intervention group (n = 99): home-based exercise with advice to walk 5 days per week (indoors or outdoors), 10–15 min, up to 50 min per session. Control group (n = 101): usual care.	Not considered.	Fitbit Zip	(i) Drop out: 11%. (ii) Intervention group: ↔ 6 min walk distance; ↔ mean steps per day; ↔ mean score for walking impairment questionnaire distance. (iii) Control group: ↔ in all outcomes.
Grossman et al., 2018 [86]	RCT (16 weeks)	11 (obese postmenopausal women)	59 ± 5	Daily energy intake goal between 1200/1500 calories (n = 11). High intensity interval training group (n = 6): five different 10 min workouts (total body, cardio, lower body, abs, and yoga flex) per 4–5 workouts per week. Endurance group (n = 5): walking, jogging, cycling, swimming, or other cardiovascular exercise 60 to 250 min per week.	Both groups followed a calorie-restricted diet.	Fitbit Charge HR	(i) Drop out: 9%. (ii) High intensity interval training group: ↓ fat mass, ↓ BMI; ↓fat free mass. (iii) Endurance group: ↓ Body mass; ↓ BMI; ↓ waist circumference; ↓ average calories consumed.
Tran et al., 2017 [87]	RCT (6 months)	422 (adults with metabolic syndrome)	57 ± 5	Intervention group (n = 214): four 2 h education sessions followed by walking aerobic training protocol. Control group (n = 203): one session of standard advice.	The intervention group received nutrition program during the four 2 h education sessions.	Yamax SW-200	(i) Drop out: 10%. (ii) Intervention group: ↑ moderate activity participation, walking time and total physical activity; ↑ steps on average on 7 consecutive days; ↓ sitting time. (iii) Control group: ↔ in all outcomes.

Table 1. *Cont.*

Author, Year [Reference]	Study Design (Duration)	Sample Size (Non-Communicable Disease)	Age (Years)	Exercise-Based Interventions	Nutrition Counselling/ Monitoring	Exercise Prescription/ Monitoring (Wearable Device)	Results
Heron et al., 2017 [88]	RCT (6 weeks)	15 (stroke patients)	69 ± 7	Manual group (n = 5): standard care and intervention program based on moderate intensity activity. Manual + pedometer (n = 5): also received activity tracker, and were encouraged to keep a daily step-count diary. Control group (n = 5): received standard post-transient ischemic attack or minor stroke care.	Assessment of adherence to Mediterranean Diet.	Fitbit Charge or pedometer	(i) Drop out: 0%. (ii) Manual group: ↑ physical activity, ↑ 2 min walk distance, ↑ hospital anxiety and depression scores, ↓ hours sitting per day. (iii) Manual + pedometer: ↑ daily steps, ↑ 2 min walk distance, ↑ hospital anxiety and depression scores. (iv) Control group: ↑ 2 min walk distance.
Swartz et al., 2017 [89]	RCT (12 weeks)	40 (obese patients)	62 ± 6	Intervention group (n = 20): provided an activity tracker and set a step goal of 7000 steps per day by the end of the intervention. Control group (n = 20): usual care.	Not considered.	Jawbone™ Up24	(i) Drop out: 13%. (ii) Intervention group: ↑ steps per week. (iii) Control group: ↔ steps per week.
Jakicic et al., 2016 [90]	RCT (24 months)	470 (obese adults)	18–35 *	Received a behavioral weight loss intervention (n = 470). Standard behavioral weight loss intervention (n = 233). Technology-enhanced intervention (n = 237).	Not considered.	BodyMedia Fit	(i) Drop out: 25%. (ii) Standard behavioral weight loss intervention: ↓ Body mass; ↓ sedentary time, sedentary time, and light-intensity physical activity across time, ↔ fat mass, ↔ lean mass, ↔body fat, ↔bone mineral content, ↔bone mineral density; ↔cardiorespiratory fitness. ↔ total moderate-to-vigorous physical activity. (iii) Technology-enhanced intervention group: ↓ Body mass.

Age values are presented as mean ± standard deviation, unless otherwise noted. * Range reported, rather than standard deviation. Abbreviation: RCT = randomized controlled trial; HR = heart rate; BMI = body mass index; COPD = chronic obstructive pulmonary disease; ↔ = no changes; ↓ = decrease; ↑ = increase.

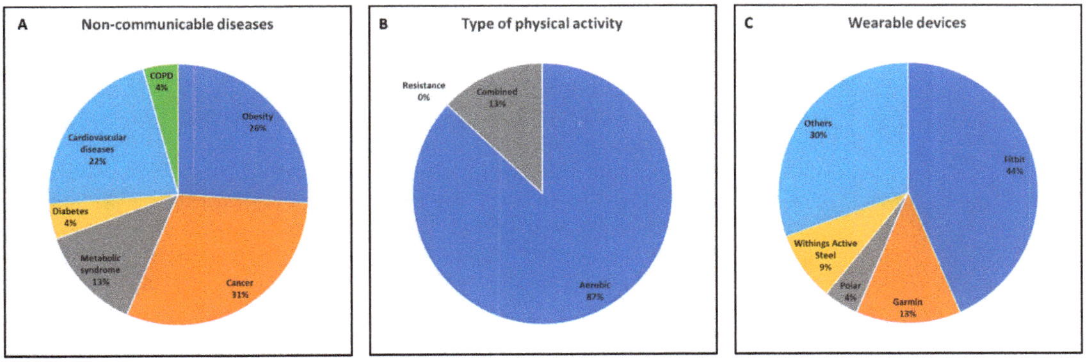

Figure 1. Pie charts of non-communicable diseases (**A**), type of physical activity (**B**), and wearable devices (**C**) used in the RCTs from 2016 to 2022.

4. Discussion

This review analyzed 23 RCTs in a narrative manner to highlight the role of wearable devices in prescribing and monitoring daily physical activity and dietary habits in people with NCDs. In particular, it emerged that the prevalent use of wearable devices is aimed at the prescription and monitoring of the physical activity protocol to increase physical activity levels. Wearable devices have been used to prescribe and monitor different types of exercise. As reported in Figure 1B, aerobic exercise was prescribed the most (87%) [69–76,78–81,83–85,87–90], followed by combined exercise (13%) (i.e., aerobic and resistance) [68,77,82,86]. However, it is well documented in the literature that resistance exercise alone can bring about significant health changes in numerous chronic conditions [91]. This lack, which we find in the studies analyzed, could depend on the current low propensity of wearable devices to monitor functional parameters, such as the muscle strength of the lower and upper limbs. In fact, although by apps it is possible to prescribe resistance exercises to the subject, monitoring is poor due to the lack of accurate wearable devices. To date, the main specific metrics that can be derived from exercise monitoring wearables are shifted towards physiological parameters, such as the number of steps, distance traveled, and cardiometabolic parameters (e.g., HR, energy expenditure, maximum oxygen consumption, oxygen saturation, and blood pressure).

In pursuing physical activity with health implications, tracking daily step count is an invaluable component. The Fitbit was the most used wearable technology in the studies analyzed (Figure 1C). However, as reported in a 2020 systemic review [8], wearable devices are accurate for measuring step count in the laboratory, but exhibit a wider range of inaccuracy in free-living environments. In addition, another major problem is the estimation of the number of steps: some devices overestimate, while others underestimate, and such variability in terms of reliability exists intra-device (i.e., the step count may differ not only within the same company, but also within the same device).

These issues were also found in standard measurements of maximum oxygen consumption (VO_{2max}). Though VO_2 estimation has become more common in wearable devices, the validity and reliability among wearable devices measuring this parameter is still controversial, and none of the popular smartwatches has been well validated [4,92]. If we consider that VO_{2max} has proven to be a powerful indicator of health and has recently been proposed as a clinical vital sign by the American Heart Association [93], it is disheartening to note that among the studies analyzed, this parameter was only considered in one study [90]. In fact, the major outcomes of the studies analyzed were: (i) number of daily or weekly steps [70,72,74,75,77,78,83–85,87,89]; (ii) physical activity levels in terms of intensity increments (e.g., from moderate to vigorous), total minutes of daily activity, reduction in sedentary time, and daily walking time [68,69,71,73,76,77,80,81,87,88]. In two studies, the outcomes were also measured subjectively through questionnaires for daily physical activity levels: the Freiburger Physical Activity Questionnaire and work ability index [71] and the Walking Impairment Questionnaire [86].

Less commonly, clinical outcomes, such as blood pressure [77], metabolic syndrome [79], and physical function [82,83], or psychological parameters, such as anxiety and depression [88] and exercise motivation [81], were explored.

The selection of suitable activity trackers in populations living with NCDs should be able to offer patients and healthcare professionals the reading of the main outcomes of interest that should be monitored for health purposes, without excluding anyone. Therefore, collaboration with activity tracker companies to overcome existing discrepancies remains crucial and should focus on the accuracy and validity of the device. In fact, the accuracy in the monitoring of the different parameters needs to be more precise to collect the physiological and activity outcomes. While wearable activity trackers offer considerable promise for helping people's lifestyle behaviors, there are numerous barriers researchers and users find when using them. First, prolonged use of activity trackers may cause study participants to experience behavioral problems, such as health status monitoring-induced anxiety. Secondly, breakage or loss of the device and technical difficulties with the accompanying device/software were noted as other barriers [94]. Consequently, these barriers may negatively impact study participants' adherence to wearing trackers [95]. Another important barrier is also represented by the reading of the results themselves. In fact, understanding the results could be an incentive for wearable device users, while, as highlighted in a survey, understanding the data is often unknown. Device users find themselves asking for the help of a physician or health coach to guide them in understanding the data of their wearable technology to make lifestyle changes. Moreover, they are often willing to pay for this service, as well [4]. In the field of exercise, an expert in sport sciences with a master's degree in Preventive and Adapted Physical Activity is essential for the correct prescription and correct monitoring of physical activity in population living with NCDs. His role lies in being able to accompany the subject with chronic disease step by step in achieving his health goals by managing the continuous comparison and readjustment of the exercise proposals. Furthermore, it can represent valid support both for healthcare professionals (medical specialists) and for the patient in reading the objective data derived from wearable devices.

Regarding nutrition, only eight studies [69,71,77,79,82,86–88] considered and analyzed nutritional aspects in their trials. Unlike exercise prescription and monitoring, nutritional aspects were predominantly delivered through face-to-face or remote (e.g., by telephone) educational counselling and monitored through a food diary analyzed and reviewed by dietitians. The lack of precision control for eating habits certainly represents a bias in reading the results. In fact, poor monitoring of nutritional aspects can influence the observation of possible improvements in physical fitness, body composition, and metabolic parameters. In this regard, articles that have considered nutritional aspects, in addition to physical activity, have stated that this combination can lead to greater health outcomes than those of exercise alone or nutrition alone. Therefore, accurate and objective monitoring of both lifestyle aspects is desirable for the development of appropriate health promotion interventions.

To date, evidence indicates that wearable devices have not yet reached such a level of development to effectively help researchers or clinicians in monitoring nutrition and, consequently, caloric intake. For both exercise and nutritional aspects, collaboration and regular feedback from exercise specialists and dietitians with other health professionals and device users is still critical to accurately monitoring lifestyle behaviors. For this reason, an integration between health and non-health professionals should be encouraged to limit this shortage and promote a healthy lifestyle in people living with chronic diseases.

5. Current Lifestyle Models and Future Directions

Despite the benefits of a healthy lifestyle based on correct physical activity levels and healthy foods being well documented, an unhealthy lifestyle is rapidly becoming a major global concern, with health, economic, environmental, and social consequences [96]. Nowadays, any lifestyle intervention should consider physical activity and nutrition as two parallel lines of intervention. The first intervention on physical activity has a twofold objective: the first one aims to reduce sedentary behavior, with daily strategies for carrying out physical activity (e.g., using the stairs instead of the lift, parking away from the workplace, etc.); and the second aims to introduce a structured exercise program into daily life with specific goals [28]. Similarly, the intervention on nutrition also has a twofold objective: the first aims to introduce healthy foods into everyday life; and the second aims to introduce a nutritional program with specific objectives in the presence of NCDs.

The emerging literature contains many examples of interventions, in which physical activity and nutrition are part of the same model, some of which are applied to populations living with NCDs, and the results demonstrate that this can be a model to scale up [97–99]. The success and feasibility of introducing this new model of care, which complements standard care, requires the implementation of specific action plans that may differ from country to country. This may depend on who is authorized to prescribe the exercise or diet, but also on the health system of the country where the model is to be implemented. In this regard, to be effective, this model needs to overcome the barriers of each country and become integrated into a delivery system; this is often guaranteed by the involvement of different health professionals (general practitioners, specialist doctors, dietitians, exercise specialists, and psychologists), who create the so-called multidisciplinary team, in which technology also plays an important role. However, in many countries, benefits stop outside research programs.

To bypass this problem, healthcare institutions and policy makers should make it easier to use wearable devices, which are often very expensive, and make the reality of a multidisciplinary team at the service of the patient more robust. The results of this narrative review may be useful for the development of new remote healthcare services via mobile devices that researchers or clinicians could consider for population health.

6. Strengths and Limitations

This is an emerging field of investigation, and our RCT analysis work provides the best evidence, to our knowledge, to shed light on the benefits of wearable devices in NCDs to date. Compared to other studies, our approach takes a holistic view of wearable device usage. Indeed, we reviewed the two most important lifestyle aspects (exercise and nutrition) to enable: (i) a better understanding of the use of wearable devices, in NCDs, in lifestyle change; and (ii) the development of new questions for future research. In this regard, a strength of this work is that it can help advance the field by clarifying the use of different devices in prescribing and monitoring healthy lifestyles and by offering, albeit preliminarily, sufficient data to understand the applicability to the different NCDs, on which wearable devices for monitoring and prescribing healthy behaviors have already been applied. The overview provided a solid foundation, upon which to direct future studies to achieve health improvements in clinical populations and age groups. The magnitude of the strength of this literature review is of clinical significance, and based on early results, the gains appear to be promising. We also have some limitations of our work. First, this is a narrative and not a systematic review; therefore, it did not allow drawing firm conclusions on the efficacy of wearable devices to prescribe and monitor physical activity protocols and nutritional aspects to reach beneficial health effects. Second, studies utilizing smartphone apps are not incorporated in this review. Although smartphone apps are gaining much attention in research, many are still not validated for usage in scientific research [100].

7. Conclusions

With the growing interest in the use of wearable devices and the global need to reduce the health burden of people living with chronic diseases, this study highlighted that more efforts are needed for wearable technologies to integrate them reliably into the field of prevention.

This study has shown that wearable devices have the promise to be an effective method for physical activity monitoring for the prevention, treatment, and improvement of the health and quality of life in people with NCDs. However, the devices are predominantly used to monitor and intervene in physical activity, rather than other daily activities (e.g., diet and sleep) or physiological parameters. Taken together, findings support wearable devices as a valuable tool to reduce the workload of medical personnel and hospitals, allowing, where possible, autonomous management of daily habits in terms of physical activity and nutrition. In the near future, there is a need for innovative measurement tools that are accurate, reliable, and effective for both exercise-related and nutritional aspects, as well as better training for their use. To date, these devices cannot do that without a continuous dialogue between the patient and healthcare professionals.

Author Contributions: Conceptualization, V.N. and M.B. (Matteo Bonato); methodology, V.N. and M.B. (Matteo Bonato); investigation, M.B. (Matteo Bonato), V.N. and M.B. (Michele Biraghi); data curation, M.B. (Matteo Bonato), V.N. and M.B. (Michele Biraghi); writing—original draft preparation, V.N. and M.B. (Matteo Bonato); writing—review and editing, V.N., M.B. (Matteo Bonato), F.M. and M.B. (Michele Biraghi); visualization, M.B. (Matteo Bonato); supervision, M.B. (Matteo Bonato). All authors have read and agreed to the published version of the manuscript.

Funding: This work was supported by the Italian Ministry of Health (Ricerca Corrente).

Institutional Review Board Statement: Non applicable.

Informed Consent Statement: Non applicable.

Data Availability Statement: Non applicable.

Conflicts of Interest: The authors declare no conflict of interest.

References

1. World Health Organization. Noncommunicable Diseases. Available online: https://www.who.int/en/news-room/fact-sheets/detail/noncommunicable-diseases (accessed on 16 December 2022).
2. Ding, D.; Lawson, K.D.; Kolbe-Alexander, T.L.; Finkelstein, E.A.; Katzmarzyk, P.T.; van Mechelen, W.; Pratt, M.; Lancet Physical Activity Series 2 Executive Committee. The economic burden of physical inactivity: A global analysis of major non-communicable diseases. *Lancet* **2016**, *388*, 1311–1324. [CrossRef] [PubMed]
3. Kontis, V.; Mathers, C.D.; Rehm, J.; Stevens, G.A.; Shield, K.D.; Bonita, R.; Riley, L.M.; Poznyak, V.; Beaglehole, R.; Ezzati, M. Contribution of six risk factors to achieving the 25 × 25 non-communicable disease mortality reduction target: A modelling study. *Lancet* **2014**, *384*, 427–437. [CrossRef]
4. Shei, R.J.; Holder, I.G.; Oumsang, A.S.; Paris, B.A.; Paris, H.L. Wearable activity trackers-advanced technology or advanced marketing? *Eur. J. Appl. Physiol.* **2022**, *122*, 1975–1990. [CrossRef]
5. Isath, A.; Virani, S.S.; Wang, Z.; Lavie, C.J.; Naidu, S.S.; Messerli, F.H.; Krittanawong, C. Meta-analysis of Per-Day Step Count and All-Cause Mortality. *Am. J. Cardiol.* **2022**, *180*, 166–168. [CrossRef] [PubMed]
6. Strain, T.; Wijndaele, K.; Dempsey, P.C.; Sharp, S.J.; Pearce, M.; Jeon, J.; Lindsay, T.; Wareham, N.; Brage, S. Wearable-device-measured physical activity and future health risk. *Nat. Med.* **2020**, *26*, 1385–1391. [CrossRef]
7. Carpenter, C.A.; Ugwoaba, U.A.; Cardel, M.I.; Ross, K.M. Using self-monitoring technology for nutritional counseling and weight management. *Digit. Health* **2022**, *8*, 20552076221102774. [CrossRef]
8. Fuller, D.; Colwell, E.; Low, J.; Orychock, K.; Tobin, M.A.; Simango, B.; Buote, R.; Van Heerden, D.; Luan, H.; Cullen, K.; et al. Reliability and Validity of Commercially Available Wearable Devices for Measuring Steps, Energy Expenditure, and Heart Rate: Systematic Review. *JMIR Mhealth Uhealth* **2020**, *8*, e18694. [CrossRef]
9. Liu, F.; Demosthenes, P. Real-world data: A brief review of the methods, applications, challenges and opportunities. *BMC Med. Res. Methodol.* **2022**, *22*, 287. [CrossRef] [PubMed]
10. Shi, Z.; Li, X.; Shuai, Y.; Lu, Y.; Liu, Q. The development of weareable technologies and their potential for measuring nutrient intake: Towards precision nutrient. *Nutr. Bull.* **2022**, *47*, 388–406. [CrossRef]
11. Riffenburg, K.M.; Spartano, N.L. Physical activity and weight maintenance: The utility of wearable devices and mobile health technology in research and clinical settings. *Curr. Opin. Endocrinol. Diabetes Obes.* **2018**, *25*, 310–314. [CrossRef]
12. Thompson, W.R. Worldwide Survey of Fitness Trends for 2022. *ACSM's Health Fit. J.* **2022**, *26*, 11–20. [CrossRef]
13. Jake-Schoffman, D.E.; Baskin, M.L. Promoting Physical Activity Across the Life Span: Progress and Promise. *J. Public Health Manag. Pract.* **2019**, *25*, 30–31. [CrossRef]
14. Guthold, R.; Stevens, G.A.; Riley, L.M.; Bull, F.C. Worldwide trends in insufficient physical activity from 2001 to 2016: A pooled analysis of 358 population-based surveys with 1·9 million participants. *Lancet Glob. Health* **2018**, *6*, e1077–e1086. [CrossRef]

15. Wedig, I.J.; Duelge, T.A.; Elmer, S.J. Infographic. Stay physically active during COVID-19 with exercise as medicine. *Br. J. Sports Med.* **2021**, *55*, 346–347. [CrossRef] [PubMed]
16. Pérez-Gisbert, L.; Torres-Sánchez, I.; Ortiz-Rubio, A.; Calvache-Mateo, A.; López-López, L.; Cabrera-Martos, I.; Valenza, M.C. Effects of the COVID-19 Pandemic on Physical Activity in Chronic Diseases: A Systematic Review and Meta-Analysis. *Int. J. Environ. Res. Public Health* **2021**, *18*, 12278. [CrossRef] [PubMed]
17. Park, A.H.; Zhong, S.; Yang, H.; Jeong, J.; Lee, C. Impact of COVID-19 on physical activity: A rapid review. *J. Glob. Health* **2022**, *12*, 05003. [CrossRef]
18. Natalucci, V.; Villarini, M.; Emili, R.; Acito, M.; Vallorani, L.; Barbieri, E.; Villarini, A. Special Attention to Physical Activity in Breast Cancer Patients during the First Wave of COVID-19 Pandemic in Italy: The DianaWeb Cohort. *J. Pers. Med.* **2021**, *11*, 381. [CrossRef]
19. Narici, M.; Vito, G.; Franchi, M.; Paoli, A.; Moro, T.; Marcolin, G.; Grassi, B.; Baldassarre, G.; Zuccarelli, L.; Biolo, G.; et al. Impact of sedentarism due to the COVID-19 home confinement on neuromuscular, cardiovascular and metabolic health: Physiological and pathophysiological implications and recommendations for physical and nutritional countermeasures. *Eur. J. Sport Sci.* **2021**, *21*, 614–635. [CrossRef]
20. Garber, C.E.; Blissmer, B.; Deschenes, M.R.; Franklin, B.A.; Lamonte, M.J.; Lee, I.M.; Nieman, D.C.; Swain, D.P. Quantity and quality of exercise for developing and maintaining cardiorespiratory, musculoskeletal, and neuromotor fitness in apparently healthy adults: Guidance for prescribing exercise. *Med. Sci. Sports Exerc.* **2011**, *43*, 1334–1359. [CrossRef]
21. Sari, N. Physical inactivity and its impact on healthcare utilization. *Health Econ.* **2009**, *18*, 885–901. [CrossRef] [PubMed]
22. Centers for Disease Control and Prevention Prevention. Physical Activity and Health: A Report of the Surgeon General. Available online: https://www.cdc.gov/nccdphp/sgr/index.htm (accessed on 16 December 2022).
23. Geidl, W.; Schlesinger, S.; Mino, E.; Miranda, L.; Pfeifer, K. Dose-response relationship between physical activity and mortality in adults with noncommunicable diseases: A systematic review and meta-analysis of prospective observational studies. *Int. J. Behav. Nutr. Phys. Act.* **2020**, *17*, 109. [CrossRef]
24. World Health Organisation. WHO Guidelines on Physical Activity and Sedentary Behaviour. Available online: https://apps.who.int/iris/bitstream/handle/10665/336656/9789240015128-eng.pdf?sequence=1&isAllowed=y (accessed on 16 December 2022).
25. Lee, I.M.; Buchner, D.M. The importance of walking to public health. *Med. Sci. Sports Exerc.* **2008**, *40*, S512–S518. [CrossRef] [PubMed]
26. King, A.C.; Whitt-Glover, M.C.; Marquez, D.X.; Buman, M.P.; Napolitano, M.A.; Jakicic, J.; Fulton, J.E.; Tennant, B.L. Physical Activity Promotion: Highlights from the 2018 Physical Activity Guidelines Advisory Committee Systematic Review. *Med. Sci. Sports Exerc.* **2019**, *51*, 1340–1353. [CrossRef] [PubMed]
27. Kraus, W.E.; Janz, K.F.; Powell, K.E.; Campbell, W.W.; Jakicic, J.M.; Troiano, R.P.; Sprow, K.; Torres, A.; Piercy, K.L. Daily Step Counts for Measuring Physical Activity Exposure and Its Relation to Health. *Med. Sci. Sports Exerc.* **2019**, *51*, 1206–1212. [CrossRef]
28. Bull, F.C.; Al-Ansari, S.S.; Biddle, S.; Borodulin, K.; Buman, M.P.; Cardon, G.; Carty, C.; Chaput, J.P.; Chastin, S.; Chou, R.; et al. World Health Organization 2020 guidelines on physical activity and sedentary behaviour. *Br. J. Sports Med.* **2020**, *54*, 1451–1462. [CrossRef]
29. Pedersen, B.K. The Physiology of Optimizing Health with a Focus on Exercise as Medicine. *Annu. Rev. Physiol.* **2019**, *81*, 607–627. [CrossRef] [PubMed]
30. Pedersen, B.K.; Febbraio, M.A. Muscle as an endocrine organ: Focus on muscle-derived interleukin-6. *Physiol. Rev.* **2008**, *88*, 1379–1406. [CrossRef] [PubMed]
31. Pedersen, B.K. Exercise-induced myokines and their role in chronic diseases. *Brain Behav. Immun.* **2011**, *25*, 811–816. [CrossRef]
32. Handschin, C.; Spiegelman, B.M. The role of exercise and PGC1alpha in inflammation and chronic disease. *Nature* **2008**, *454*, 463–469. [CrossRef]
33. Winding, K.M.; Munch, G.W.; Iepsen, U.W.; Van Hall, G.; Pedersen, B.K.; Mortensen, S.P. The effect on glycaemic control of low-volume high-intensity interval training versus endurance training in individuals with type 2 diabetes. *Diabetes Obes. Metab.* **2018**, *20*, 1131–1139. [CrossRef]
34. Gibala, M.J. High-intensity interval training: A time-efficient strategy for health promotion? *Curr. Sports Med. Rep.* **2007**, *6*, 211–213. [CrossRef]
35. Mikkelsen, K.; Stojanovska, L.; Polenakovic, M.; Bosevski, M.; Apostolopoulos, V. Exercise and mental health. *Maturitas* **2017**, *106*, 48–56. [CrossRef] [PubMed]
36. Cooney, G.M.; Dwan, K.; Greig, C.A.; Lawlor, D.A.; Rimer, J.; Waugh, F.R.; McMurdo, M.; Mead, G.E. Exercise for depression. *Cochrane Database Syst. Rev. vol.* **2013**, *9*, CD004366. [CrossRef]
37. Chekroud, S.R.; Gueorguieva, R.; Zheutlin, A.B.; Paulus, M.; Krumholz, H.M.; Krystal, J.H.; Chekroud, A.M. Association between physical exercise and mental health in 1·2 million individuals in the USA between 2011 and 2015: A cross-sectional study. *Lancet Psychiatry* **2018**, *5*, 739–746. [CrossRef]
38. Piercy, K.L.; Troiano, R.P.; Ballard, R.M.; Carlson, S.A.; Fulton, J.E.; Galuska, D.A.; George, S.M.; Olson, R.D. The Physical Activity Guidelines for Americans. *JAMA* **2018**, *320*, 2020–2028. [CrossRef]
39. Stark, C. Guidelines for Food and Nutrient Intake. In *Biochemistry, Physiology and Molecular Aspects of Human Nutrition*, 3rd ed.; Stipanuk, M.H., Caudill, M.A., Eds.; Elsevier Saunders: St. Louis, MO, USA, 2013; pp. 34–47.

40. Ng, M.; Fleming, T.; Robinson, M.; Thomson, B.; Graetz, N.; Margono, C.; Mullany, E.C.; Biryukov, S.; Abbafati, C.; Abera, S.F.; et al. Global, regional, and national prevalence of overweight and obesity in children and adults during 1980–2013: A systematic analysis for the Global Burden of Disease Study 2013. *Lancet* **2014**, *384*, 766–781. [CrossRef]
41. GBD 2017 Diet Collaborators. Health effects of dietary risks in 195 countries, 1990–2017: A systematic analysis for the Global Burden of Disease Study 2017. *Lancet* **2019**, *393*, 1958–1972. [CrossRef]
42. Jayedi, A.; Soltani, S.; Abdolshahi, A.; Shab-Bidar, S. Healthy and unhealthy dietary patterns and the risk of chronic disease: An umbrella review of meta-analyses of prospective cohort studies. *Br. J. Nutr.* **2020**, *124*, 1133–1144. [CrossRef]
43. Bechthold, A.; Boeing, H.; Schwedhelm, C.; Hoffmann, G.; Knüppel, S.; Iqbal, K.; De Henauw, S.; Michels, N.; Devleesschauwer, B.; Schlesinger, S.; et al. Food groups and risk of coronary heart disease, stroke and heart failure: A systematic review and dose-response meta-analysis of prospective studies. *Crit. Rev. Food Sci. Nutr.* **2019**, *59*, 1071–1090. [CrossRef] [PubMed]
44. Schwingshackl, L.; Schwedhelm, C.; Hoffmann, G.; Knüppel, S.; Iqbal, K.; Andriolo, V.; Bechthold, A.; Schlesinger, S.; Boeing, H. Food Groups and Risk of Hypertension: A Systematic Review and Dose-Response Meta-Analysis of Prospective Studies. *Adv. Nutr.* **2017**, *8*, 793–803. [CrossRef]
45. Schwingshackl, L.; Hoffmann, G.; Lampousi, A.M.; Knüppel, S.; Iqbal, K.; Schwedhelm, C.; Bechthold, A.; Schlesinger, S.; Boeing, H. Food groups and risk of type 2 diabetes mellitus: A systematic review and meta-analysis of prospective studies. *Eur. J. Epidemiol.* **2017**, *32*, 363–375. [CrossRef]
46. World Cancer Research Fund; American Institute for Cancer Research. Diet, Nutrition, Physical Activity and Cancer: A Global Perspective. Continuous Update Project Expert Report. 2018. Available online: https://www.wcrf.org/dietandcancer (accessed on 20 December 2022).
47. Zheng, P.F.; Shu, L.; Si, C.J.; Zhang, X.Y.; Yu, X.L.; Gao, W. Dietary Patterns and Chronic Obstructive Pulmonary Disease: A Meta-analysis. *COPD* **2016**, *13*, 515–522. [CrossRef]
48. World Health Organization—Regional Office for Europe. European Food and Nutrition Action Plan 2015–2020. Available online: https://www.euro.who.int/__data/assets/pdf_file/0003/294474/European-Food-Nutrition-Action-Plan-20152020-en.pdf (accessed on 20 December 2022).
49. Azzouzi, S.; Stratton, C.; Muñoz-Velasco, L.P.; Wang, K.; Fourtassi, M.; Hong, B.Y.; Cooper, R.; Balikuddembe, J.K.; Palomba, A.; Peterson, M.; et al. The Impact of the COVID-19 Pandemic on Healthy Lifestyle Behaviors and Perceived Mental and Physical Health of People Living with Non-Communicable Diseases: An International Cross-Sectional Survey. *Int. J. Environ. Res. Public Health* **2022**, *19*, 8023. [CrossRef]
50. Phillips, C.M.; Chen, L.W.; Heude, B.; Bernard, J.Y.; Harvey, N.C.; Duijts, L.; Mensink-Bout, S.M.; Polanska, K.; Mancano, G.; Suderman, M.; et al. Dietary Inflammatory Index and Non-Communicable Disease Risk: A Narrative Review. *Nutrients* **2019**, *11*, 1873. [CrossRef] [PubMed]
51. Restrepo, B.J.; Rieger, M. Denmark's Policy on Artificial Trans Fat and Cardiovascular Disease. *Am. J. Prev. Med.* **2016**, *50*, 69–76. [CrossRef] [PubMed]
52. Hocking, S.; Samocha-Bonet, D.; Milner, K.L.; Greenfield, J.R.; Chisholm, D.J. Adiposity and insulin resistance in humans: The role of the different tissue and cellular lipid depots. *Endocr. Rev.* **2013**, *34*, 463–500. [CrossRef] [PubMed]
53. De Mutsert, R.; Gast, K.; Widya, R.; de Koning, E.; Jazet, I.; Lamb, H.; le Cessie, S.; de Roos, A.; Smit, J.; Rosendaal, F.; et al. Associations of Abdominal Subcutaneous and Visceral Fat with Insulin Resistance and Secretion Differ Between Men and Women: The Netherlands Epidemiology of Obesity Study. *Metab. Syndr. Relat. Disord.* **2018**, *16*, 54–63. [CrossRef]
54. Després, J.P. Abdominal obesity as important component of insulin-resistance syndrome. *Nutrition* **1993**, *9*, 452–459.
55. World Health Organization. Healthy Diet. Available online: https://www.who.int/news-room/fact-sheets/detail/healthy-diet (accessed on 20 December 2022).
56. Harika, R.K.; Eilander, A.; Alssema, M.; Osendarp, S.J.; Zock, P.L. Intake of fatty acids in general populations worldwide does not meet dietary recommendations to prevent coronary heart disease: A systematic review of data from 40 countries. *Ann. Nutr. Metab.* **2013**, *63*, 229–238. [CrossRef]
57. Raichlen, D.A.; Pontzer, H.; Zderic, T.W.; Harris, J.A.; Mabulla, A.Z.P.; Hamilton, M.T.; Wood, B.M. Sitting, squatting, and the evolutionary biology of human inactivity. *Proc. Natl. Acad. Sci. USA* **2020**, *117*, 7115–7121. [CrossRef]
58. St Fleur, R.G.; St George, S.M.; Leite, R.; Kobayashi, M.; Agosto, Y.; Jake-Schoffman, D.E. Use of Fitbit Devices in Physical Activity Intervention Studies Across the Life Course: Narrative Review. *JMIR Mhealth Uhealth* **2021**, *9*, e23411. [CrossRef]
59. Tedesco, S.; Sica, M.; Ancillao, A.; Timmons, S.; Barton, J.; O'Flynn, B. Accuracy of consumer-level and research-grade activity trackers in ambulatory settings in older adults. *PLoS ONE* **2019**, *14*, e0216891. [CrossRef] [PubMed]
60. Sallis, J.F.; Saelens, B.E. Assessment of physical activity by self-report: Status, limitations, and future directions. *Res. Q Exerc. Sport* **2000**, *71*, S1–S14. [CrossRef]
61. Chan, A.; Chan, D.; Lee, H.; Ng, C.C.; Yeo, A.H.L. Reporting adherence, validity and physical activity measures of wearable activity trackers in medical research: A systematic review. *Int. J. Med. Inform.* **2022**, *160*, 104696. [CrossRef] [PubMed]
62. Hoy, M.B. Personal Activity Trackers and the Quantified Self. *Med. Ref. Serv. Q* **2016**, *35*, 94–100. [CrossRef]
63. Pendergast, F.J.; Ridgers, N.D.; Worsley, A.; McNaughton, S.A. Evaluation of a smartphone food diary application using objectively measured energy expenditure. *Int. J. Behav. Nutr. Phys. Act.* **2017**, *14*, 30. [CrossRef] [PubMed]

64. Rangan, A.M.; O'Connor, S.; Giannelli, V.; Yap, M.L.; Tang, L.M.; Roy, R.; Louie, J.C.; Hebden, L.; Kay, J.; Allman-Farinelli, M. Electronic Dietary Intake Assessment (e-DIA): Comparison of a Mobile Phone Digital Entry App for Dietary Data Collection With 24-Hour Dietary Recalls. *JMIR Mhealth Uhealth* **2015**, *3*, e98. [CrossRef]
65. Hutchesson, M.J.; Rollo, M.E.; Callister, R.; Collins, C.E. Self-monitoring of dietary intake by young women: Online food records completed on computer or smartphone are as accurate as paper-based food records but more acceptable. *J. Acad. Nutr. Diet.* **2015**, *115*, 87–94. [CrossRef]
66. Wohlers, E.M.; Sirard, J.R.; Barden, C.M.; Moon, J.K. Smart phones are useful for food intake and physical activity surveys. In Proceedings of the 2009 Annual International Conference of the IEEE Engineering in Medicine and Biology Society, Minneapolis, MN, USA, 3–6 September 2009; pp. 5183–5186. [CrossRef]
67. Harvey, J.; Krukowski, R.; Priest, J.; West, D. Log Often, Lose More: Electronic Dietary Self-Monitoring for Weight Loss. *Obesity* **2019**, *27*, 380–384. [CrossRef]
68. Alley, S.J.; van Uffelen, J.; Schoeppe, S.; Parkinson, L.; Hunt, S.; Power, D.; Waterman, N.; Waterman, C.; To, Q.G.; Duncan, M.J.; et al. The Effectiveness of a Computer-Tailored Web-Based Physical Activity Intervention Using Fitbit Activity Trackers in Older Adults (Active for Life): Randomized Controlled Trial. *J. Med. Internet Res.* **2022**, *24*, e31352. [CrossRef]
69. Ferrante, J.M.; Lulla, A.; Williamson, J.D.; Devine, K.A.; Ohman-Strickland, P.; Bandera, E.V. Patterns of Fitbit Use and Activity Levels Among African American Breast Cancer Survivors During an eHealth Weight Loss Randomized Controlled Trial. *Am. J. Health Promot.* **2022**, *36*, 94–105. [CrossRef] [PubMed]
70. Agarwal, A.K.; Waddell, K.J.; Small, D.S.; Evans, C.; Harrington, T.O.; Djaraher, R.; Oon, A.L.; Patel, M.S. Effect of Gamification with and Without Financial Incentives to Increase Physical Activity Among Veterans Classified as Having Obesity or Overweight: A Randomized Clinical Trial. *JAMA Netw. Open* **2021**, *4*, e2116256. [CrossRef] [PubMed]
71. Haufe, S.; Hupa-Breier, K.L.; Bayerle, P.; Boeck, H.T.; Rolff, S.; Sundermeier, T.; Kerling, A.; Eigendorf, J.; Kück, M.; Hanke, A.A.; et al. Telemonitoring-Supported Exercise Training in Employees with Metabolic Syndrome Improves Liver Inflammation and Fibrosis. *Clin. Transl. Gastroenterol.* **2021**, *12*, e00371. [CrossRef]
72. Patel, M.S.; Small, D.S.; Harrison, J.D.; Hilbert, V.; Fortunato, M.P.; Oon, A.L.; Rareshide, C.A.L.; Volpp, K.G. Effect of Behaviorally Designed Gamification with Social Incentives on Lifestyle Modification Among Adults with Uncontrolled Diabetes: A Randomized Clinical Trial. *JAMA Netw. Open* **2021**, *4*, e2110255. [CrossRef] [PubMed]
73. Hardcastle, S.J.; Maxwell-Smith, C.; Hince, D.; Bulsara, M.K.; Boyle, T.; Tan, P.; Levitt, M.; Salama, P.; Mohan, G.R.K.A.; Salfinger, S.; et al. The wearable activity technology and action-planning trial in cancer survivors: Physical activity maintenance post-intervention. *J. Sci. Med. Sport* **2021**, *24*, 902–907. [CrossRef]
74. Pinto, B.M.; Kindred, M.; Franco, R.; Simmons, V.; Hardin, J. A 'novel' multi-component approach to promote physical activity among older cancer survivors: A pilot randomized controlled trial. *Acta Oncol.* **2021**, *60*, 968–975. [CrossRef]
75. Chen, X.S.; Changolkar, S.; Navathe, A.S.; Linn, K.A.; Reh, G.; Szwartz, G.; Steier, D.; Godby, S.; Balachandran, M.; Harrison, J.D.; et al. Association between behavioral phenotypes and response to a physical activity intervention using gamification and social incentives: Secondary analysis of the STEP UP randomized clinical trial. *PLoS ONE* **2020**, *15*, e0239288. [CrossRef]
76. Peacock, O.J.; Western, M.J.; Batterham, A.M.; Chowdhury, E.A.; Stathi, A.; Standage, M.; Tapp, A.; Bennett, P.; Thompson, D. Effect of novel technology-enabled multidimensional physical activity feedback in primary care patients at risk of chronic disease—The MIPACT study: A randomised controlled trial. *Int. J. Behav. Nutr. Phys. Act.* **2020**, *17*, 99. [CrossRef]
77. Roberts, L.M.; Jaeger, B.C.; Baptista, L.C.; Harper, S.A.; Gardner, A.K.; Jackson, E.A.; Pekmezi, D.; Sandesara, B.; Manini, T.M.; Anton, S.D.; et al. Wearable Technology to Reduce Sedentary Behavior And CVD Risk In Older Adults: A Pilot Randomized Clinical Trial. *Clin. Interv. Aging* **2019**, *14*, 1817–1828. [CrossRef]
78. Singh, B.; Spence, R.R.; Sandler, C.X.; Tanner, J.; Hayes, S.C. Feasibility and effect of a physical activity counselling session with or without provision of an activity tracker on maintenance of physical activity in women with breast cancer—A randomised controlled trial. *J. Sci. Med. Sport* **2020**, *23*, 283–290. [CrossRef]
79. Haufe, S.; Kerling, A.; Protte, G.; Bayerle, P.; Stenner, H.T.; Rolff, S.; Sundermeier, T.; Kück, M.; Ensslen, R.; Nachbar, L.; et al. Telemonitoring-supported exercise training, metabolic syndrome severity, and work ability in company employees: A randomised controlled trial. *Lancet Public Health* **2019**, *4*, e343–e352. [CrossRef]
80. Lynch, B.M.; Nguyen, N.H.; Moore, M.M.; Reeves, M.M.; Rosenberg, D.E.; Boyle, T.; Vallance, J.K.; Milton, S.; Friedenreich, C.M.; English, D.R. A randomized controlled trial of a wearable technology-based intervention for increasing moderate to vigorous physical activity and reducing sedentary behavior in breast cancer survivors: The ACTIVATE Trial. *Cancer* **2019**, *125*, 2846–2855. [CrossRef]
81. Van Blarigan, E.L.; Chan, H.; Van Loon, K.; Kenfield, S.A.; Chan, J.M.; Mitchell, E.; Zhang, L.; Paciorek, A.; Joseph, G.; Laffan, A.; et al. Self-monitoring and reminder text messages to increase physical activity in colorectal cancer survivors (Smart Pace): A pilot randomized controlled trial. *BMC Cancer* **2019**, *19*, 218. [CrossRef] [PubMed]
82. Lee, B.J.; Park, Y.H.; Lee, J.Y.; Kim, S.J.; Jang, Y.; Lee, J.I. Smartphone Application Versus Pedometer to Promote Physical Activity in Prostate Cancer Patients. *Telemed. J. E Health* **2019**, *25*, 1231–1236. [CrossRef] [PubMed]
83. Varas, A.B.; Córdoba, S.; Rodríguez-Andonaegui, I.; Rueda, M.R.; García-Juez, S.; Vilaró, J. Effectiveness of a community-based exercise training programme to increase physical activity level in patients with chronic obstructive pulmonary disease: A randomized controlled trial. *Physiother. Res. Int.* **2018**, *23*, e1740. [CrossRef] [PubMed]

84. Chokshi, N.P.; Adusumalli, S.; Small, D.S.; Morris, A.; Feingold, J.; Ha, Y.P.; Lynch, M.D.; Rareshide, C.A.L.; Hilbert, V.; Patel, M.S. Loss-Framed Financial Incentives and Personalized Goal-Setting to Increase Physical Activity Among Ischemic Heart Disease Patients Using Wearable Devices: The ACTIVE REWARD Randomized Trial. *J. Am. Heart Assoc.* **2018**, *7*, e009173. [CrossRef]
85. McDermott, M.M.; Spring, B.; Berger, J.S.; Treat-Jacobson, D.; Conte, M.S.; Creager, M.A.; Criqui, M.H.; Ferrucci, L.; Gornik, H.L.; Guralnik, J.M.; et al. Effect of a Home-Based Exercise Intervention of Wearable Technology and Telephone Coaching on Walking Performance in Peripheral Artery Disease: The HONOR Randomized Clinical Trial. *JAMA* **2018**, *319*, 1665–1676. [CrossRef]
86. Grossman, J.A.; Arigo, D.; Bachman, J.L. Meaningful weight loss in obese postmenopausal women: A pilot study of high-intensity interval training and wearable technology. *Menopause* **2018**, *25*, 465–470. [CrossRef]
87. Tran, V.D.; Lee, A.H.; Jancey, J.; James, A.P.; Howat, P.; Mai, L.T. Physical activity and nutrition behaviour outcomes of a cluster-randomized controlled trial for adults with metabolic syndrome in Vietnam. *Trials* **2017**, *18*, 18. [CrossRef]
88. Heron, N.; Kee, F.; Mant, J.; Reilly, P.M.; Cupples, M.; Tully, M.; Donnelly, M. Stroke Prevention Rehabilitation Intervention Trial of Exercise (SPRITE)—A randomised feasibility study. *BMC Cardiovasc. Disord.* **2017**, *17*, 290. [CrossRef]
89. Swartz, M.C.; Lewis, Z.H.; Swartz, M.D.; Martinez, E.; Lyons, E.J. Brief Report: Active Ingredients for Adherence to a Tracker-Based Physical Activity Intervention in Older Adults. *J. Appl. Gerontol.* **2019**, *38*, 1023–1034. [CrossRef]
90. Jakicic, J.M.; Davis, K.K.; Rogers, R.J.; King, W.C.; Marcus, M.D.; Helsel, D.; Rickman, A.D.; Wahed, A.S.; Belle, S.H. Effect of Wearable Technology Combined with a Lifestyle Intervention on Long-term Weight Loss: The IDEA Randomized Clinical Trial. *JAMA* **2016**, *316*, 1161–1171. [CrossRef] [PubMed]
91. Momma, H.; Kawakami, R.; Honda, T.; Sawada, S.S. Muscle-strengthening activities are associated with lower risk and mortality in major non-communicable diseases: A systematic review and meta-analysis of cohort studies. *Br. J. Sport. Med.* **2022**, *56*, 755–763. [CrossRef] [PubMed]
92. Molina-Garcia, P.; Notbohm, H.L.; Schumann, M.; Argent, R.; Hetherington-Rauth, M.; Stang, J.; Bloch, W.; Cheng, S.; Ekelund, U.; Sardinha, L.B.; et al. Validity of Estimating the Maximal Oxygen Consumption by Consumer Wearables: A Systematic Review with Meta-analysis and Expert Statement of the INTERLIVE Network. *Sport. Med.* **2022**, *52*, 1577–1597. [CrossRef]
93. Ross, R.; Blair, S.N.; Arena, R.; Church, T.S.; Després, J.P.; Franklin, B.A.; Haskell, W.L.; Kaminsky, L.A.; Levine, B.D.; Lavie, C.J.; et al. Importance of Assessing Cardiorespiratory Fitness in Clinical Practice: A Case for Fitness as a Clinical Vital Sign: A Scientific Statement from the American Heart Association. *Circulation* **2016**, *134*, e653–e699. [CrossRef]
94. Maher, C.; Ryan, J.; Ambrosi, C.; Edney, S. Users' experiences of wearable activity trackers: A cross-sectional study. *BMC Public Health* **2017**, *17*, 880. [CrossRef]
95. Albergoni, A.; Hettinga, F.J.; La Torre, A.; Bonato, M.; Sartor, F. The Role of Technology in Adherence to Physical Activity Programs in Patients with Chronic Diseases Experiencing Fatigue: A Systematic Review. *Sports Med. Open* **2019**, *12*, 41. [CrossRef] [PubMed]
96. Bonato, M.; Vitale, J.A.; López Sánchez, G.F.; Codella, R. Editorial: Exercise Prescription and Psychological Determinants for Healthy Living. *Front. Psychol.* **2022**, *13*, 851852. [CrossRef]
97. Pistelli, M.; Natalucci, V.; Scortichini, L.; Agostinelli, V.; Lenci, E.; Crocetti, S.; Merloni, F.; Bastianelli, L.; Taus, M.; Fumelli, D.; et al. The Impact of Lifestyle Interventions in High-Risk Early Breast Cancer Patients: A Modeling Approach from a Single Institution Experience. *Cancers* **2021**, *13*, 5539. [CrossRef]
98. Grazioli, E.; Tranchita, E.; Marrone, G.; Urciuoli, S.; Di Lauro, M.; Cerulli, C.; Piacentini, N.; Murri, A.; Celotto, R.; Romani, A.; et al. The Impact of Functional Bars and Adapted Physical Activity on Quality of Life in Chronic Kidney Disease: A Pilot Study. *Int. J. Environ. Res. Public Health* **2022**, *19*, 3281. [CrossRef]
99. Natalucci, V.; Ferri Marini, C.; De Santi, M.; Annibalini, G.; Lucertini, F.; Vallorani, L.; Rocco Panico, A.; Sisti, D.; Saltarelli, R.; Donati Zeppa, S.; et al. Movement and health beyond care, MoviS: Study protocol for a randomized clinical trial on nutrition and exercise educational programs for breast cancer survivors. *Trials* **2023**, *23*. *in press*.
100. Bonato, M.; Turrini, F.; de Zan, V.; Meloni, A.; Plebani, M.; Brambilla, E.; Giordani, A.; Vitobello, C.; Caccia, R.; Piacentini, M.F.; et al. A Mobile Application for Exercise Intervention in People Living with HIV. *Med. Sci. Sports Exerc.* **2020**, *52*, 425–433. [CrossRef] [PubMed]

nutrients

MDPI

Systematic Review

Unraveling Barriers to a Healthy Lifestyle: Understanding Barriers to Diet and Physical Activity in Patients with Chronic Non-Communicable Diseases

Massimiliano Cavallo [1,†], Giovanni Morgana [2,†], Ivan Dozzani [3], Alessandro Gatti [4], Matteo Vandoni [4], Roberto Pippi [5,*], Giacomo Pucci [1], Gaetano Vaudo [1,‡] and Carmine Giuseppe Fanelli [5,‡]

1 Department of Medicine and Surgery, University of Perugia, Unit of Internal Medicine, Terni University Hospital, Piazzale Tristano Di Joannuccio, 1, T05100 Terni, Italy; massimilianocavallotr@gmail.com (M.C.); giacomo.pucci@unipg.it (G.P.); gaetano.vaudo@unipg.it (G.V.)
2 Post-Graduate School of Sports Medicine, Department of Medicine and Surgery, University of Perugia, 06123 Perugia, Italy; giovamorga94@gmail.com
3 Post-Graduate School of Clinical Nutrition and Dietetics, Department of Medicine and Surgery, University of Perugia, Piazzale Gambuli 1, 06132 Perugia, Italy; dozzaniivan@gmail.com
4 Laboratory of Adapted Motor Activity (LAMA), Department of Public Health, Experimental Medicine and Forensic Science, University of Pavia, 27100 Pavia, Italy; alessandro.gatti08@universitadipavia.it (A.G.); matteo.vandoni@unipv.it (M.V.)
5 Healthy Lifestyle Institute, C.U.R.I.A.Mo. (Centro Universitario Ricerca Interdipartimentale Attività Motoria), Department of Medicine and Surgery, University of Perugia, 06126 Perugia, Italy; carmine.fanelli@unipg.it
* Correspondence: roberto.pippi@unipg.it
† These authors equally contributed to this manuscript.
‡ These authors equally contributed to this manuscript.

Abstract: Although the important contribution of nutrition and physical activity to people's health is known, it is equally well known that there are many barriers to adherence to healthy habits (i.e., of an organizational, economic, and/or psychological nature) experienced by the general population, as well as by people with non-communicable diseases. Knowledge of these barriers seems essential to the implementation of the activities and strategies needed to overcome them. Here, we aim to highlight the most frequent barriers to nutrition and exercise improvement that patients with chronic-degenerative diseases experience. Drawing from the Pubmed database, our analysis includes quantitative or mixed descriptive studies published within the last 10 years, involving adult participants with non-communicable diseases. Barriers of an organizational nature, as well as those of an environmental, economic, or psychological nature, are reported. The study of patients' barriers enables healthcare and non-health professionals, stakeholders, and policymakers to propose truly effective solutions that can help both the general population and those with chronic pathologies to adhere to a healthy lifestyle.

Keywords: barriers; physical activity; healthy nutrition

Citation: Cavallo, M.; Morgana, G.; Dozzani, I.; Gatti, A.; Vandoni, M.; Pippi, R.; Pucci, G.; Vaudo, G.; Fanelli, C.G. Unraveling Barriers to a Healthy Lifestyle: Understanding Barriers to Diet and Physical Activity in Patients with Chronic Non-Communicable Diseases. *Nutrients* **2023**, *15*, 3473. https://doi.org/10.3390/nu15153473

Academic Editor: Hayato Tada

Received: 14 July 2023
Revised: 2 August 2023
Accepted: 3 August 2023
Published: 5 August 2023

1. Introduction

It is widely recognized that nutrition and physical activity (PA) are two of the main determinants of maintaining optimal health for the individual [1,2]. Many studies show that following an unbalanced diet [3,4] and being inactive (defined as an accumulation of fewer than 150 min a week of moderate or vigorous PA [5]) are two risk factors for many cardiovascular and chronic degenerative pathologies. However, it is equally well known that many barriers prevent the general population from achieving constant adherence to healthy nutritional and PA habits [6] and that the main barriers encountered are those of an organizational, economic, and/or psychological nature [7]. Indeed, a recent analysis found that more than 27% of the world global population did not reach the suggested guidelines for PA [8], and as reported by Liu et al. [9], more than 85% of American adults consume junk food daily. Several nutrition and PA strategies have been adopted internationally to encourage the achievement of a healthier lifestyle [10,11]. While these issues may initially appear to be primarily related only to healthy adults, they are equally significant in patients with chronic non-communicable diseases (NCDs). In fact, for individuals with NCDs, proper dietary habits together with regular engagement in PA represent key non-pharmacologic therapeutic strategies [10,12]. A well-balanced diet and regular PA support optimal bodily functions, strengthen the immune system, and promote overall well-being [13–15]. Additionally, they help control blood sugar levels, manage weight, reduce inflammation, and improve cardiovascular health [15–17]. Among well-balanced diet patterns, the Mediterranean diet (MED) has been proposed as an ideal nutritional model against cardiovascular problems [17,18]. MED is considered the gold standard for treatment for preventing and treating NCDs such as diabetes [19], some types of cancer [20], obesity [21–23], and neurodegenerative pathologies in old people [24,25]. Moreover, a positive association between adherence to the Mediterranean diet (MED) and muscle strength was observed in the elderly [16]. MED, as shown by Martínez-González et al. [17], has been also strongly associated with a reduced risk of developing coronary heart disease and ischemic stroke, while also promoting improved cardiovascular health.

More in detail, MED is a nutritional model characterized by a balanced combination of seasonal fruit and vegetables, fish, whole grains, legumes, and extra virgin olive oil, with moderate consumption of white meat, dairy products, and red wine [26].

Concurrently promoting the MED and PA is likely to provide an opportunity for metabolic risk reduction [27] and is a strategic key to both prevent and control the development of NCDs [28]. Therefore, understanding and identifying the barriers to a healthy diet and regular PA becomes imperative in order to develop effective interventions to overcome them.

For these reasons, our study aims to highlight the barriers that patients with chronic-degenerative diseases experience in implementing a healthier diet and an exercise-based therapeutic program, by using a quantitative approach to develop a point-by-point list of the most frequent barriers to both nutritional improvement and exercise. By recognizing and addressing these barriers, it is possible to empower patients with NCDs to adopt healthier lifestyles, enhance their quality of life (QoL), and reduce the burden of NCD management. In the last ten years, there has been a significant advancement in the treatment of patients with NCDs. To ensure that we have the latest and most relevant information, we analyzed only studies published between 2013 and 2023. We decided to consider this period with the aim of providing a recent cross-section of the barriers experienced by the world population, to provide ideas for solving current problems. Moreover, we choose to consider adult people because they conduct very similar lifestyles with the aim of making the population homogeneous.

2. Materials and Methods

This study used the PRISMA guideline and methodology for systematic review [19]. This review was not registered.

Search Strategy

The search for studies was conducted by drawing from the Pubmed database using the following search string "(physical activity OR exercise OR diet) (prescription OR participation) AND barriers NOT rehabilitation". To be eligible, studies must have the following characteristics:

Quantitative or mixed descriptive studies.

Adult population with chronic pathologies of a non-neurological or psychiatric nature.

Interventions of a non-rehabilitative nature.

Period of publication not exceeding 10 years.

The search produced 432 results (Figure 1). The selection of the studies was performed firstly by reading the titles, then by reading the abstracts and excluding duplicates, and finally, the selection of the remaining studies (Table 1) took place with the aid of the Mixed Methods Appraisal Tool (MMAT) version 2018.

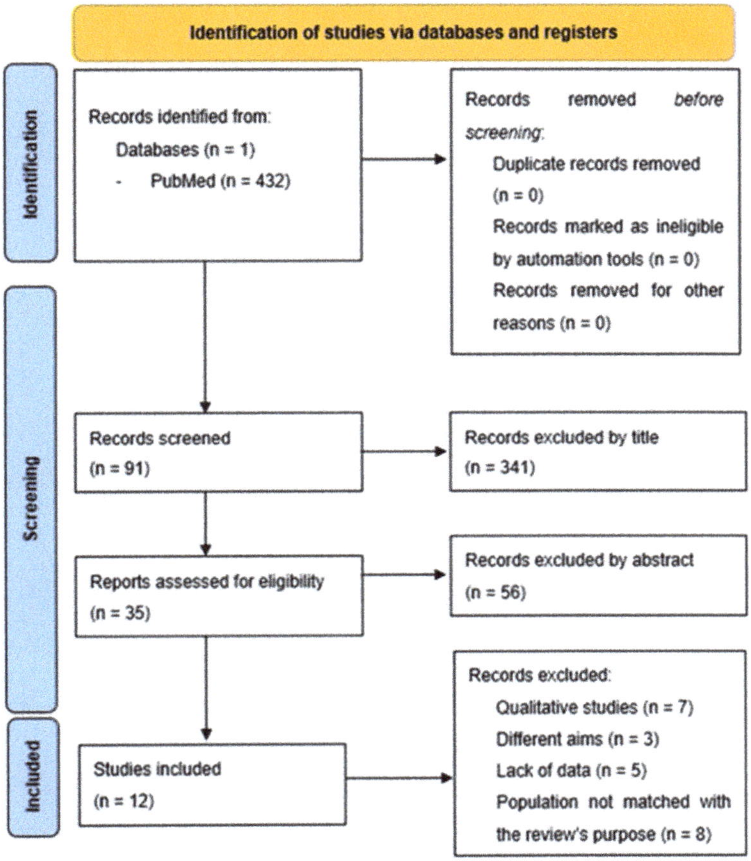

Figure 1. PRISMA [29] 2020 flow diagram for new systematic reviews.

Table 1. Summary of the population characteristics of each study and relative common barriers.

	Population	Gender	Mean Age (% of Population)	Nationality	Ethnicity	Comorbidity	BMI (% of Population)	Common Barriers
Sheshadri 2020 [30]	25	93% M 7% F	60 ± 7	USA	13% white 47% black 20% asian 20% others	93% hypertension 33% and diabetes 37% chronic ischemic heart disease 30% heart failure 7% stroke 13% peripheral arterial disease 20% arrhytmias 100% hemodyalisis	29.1 ± 3.8	Health status
Rogers 2014 [31]	183	53.3% M 46.7% M	62 ± 2 (32.2) 67 ± 2 (32.2) 73 ± 2 (35.5)	Great Britain	100% white	58.5% with 1 or more NCDs 16.8% with musculoskeletal diseases	>25 (59.6)	Environment Health status
Venditti 2014 [32]	1076	31.8% M 68.2% F	34 ± 9 (33.08) 52 ± 7 (45.26) >60 (21.65)	Multicentric International study	53.71% white 18.86% afro-american 16.54% hispanic 5.57% asian	-	33.9	Lack of time Environment Insigths
Thomson 2016 [33]	43	100% F	30.3 ± 6.2	Australia	-	100% PCOS	36.4 ± 5.6	Insights
Rosa 2015 [34]	98	57% M 43% F	51.6 ± 15.7	Brazil	59% white or others 39% black	55% hypertension/diabetes 36% metabolic syndrome 92% cardiovascular diseases 16% musculoskeletal diseases	-	Lack of time Insights
Kang 2022 [35]	52	100% M	63.4 ± 7.1	Canada	89% white 11% others	60% artrhitis 31% hypertension 100% prostate cancer survivors	29 ± 4.7	Environment Health status
Koutoukidis 2017 [36]	83	100% F	62.6 ± 9	Great Britain	-	100% uterine cancer survivors	-	Health status
Miller 2020 [37]	54	100% F	61.2	USA	77% non-hispanic white 8% non-hispanic black 4% hispanic 6% others	100% breast cancer survivors	<18.5 (4) 18.5–24.9 (32) 25–29.9 (25) >30 (40)	Environment Insights Health status
Clark-Cutaia 2018 [38]	30	63% M 37% F	<65 (47) >65 (53)	USA	53% white 47% afro-american	100% haemodyalisis 60% cardiovascular diseases	-	Economic and financial Environment Health status Insights

Table 1. *Cont.*

	Population	Gender	Mean Age (% of Population)	Nationality	Ethnicity	Comorbidity	BMI (% of Population)	Common Barriers
Bernard-Davilla 2015 [39]	102	100% F	56.4 ± 9.6	South America	25.7% black 40% white 2.9% native americans 15.7% others	100% breast cancer survivors	-	Lack of time Environment Economic and financial Health status Insights
Mendonça 2019 [40]	1483	12.94% M 87.05% F	30 ± 9 (9.8) 50 ± 9 (47.13) >60 (43.08)	Brazil	-	53.67% hypertension 43.42% dyslipidemia 8.5% diabetes	-	Lack of time Environment Economic and financial Health status Insights
Mofleh 2021 [41]	216	2.3% M 97.7% F	41.1 ± 11.9	USA	78.2% white 21.8% others	100% and metabolic syndrome or obesity	30.1 ± 8	Economic and financial Health status

3. Results

3.1. Barriers to a Healthy Diet

The five selected studies enrolled a total of 1855 subjects. These studies are nearly unanimous in indicating as barriers to maintaining adequate compliance with a healthy diet: lack of time, organizational and family problems, the high (or presumed high) cost of a healthy balanced diet, concerns about one's body/figure/physical health, and motivational difficulty in changing one's lifestyle.

Gender-related differences. Excepting from the work of Clark-Cutaia et al. [38] in which women represent 37% of the studied population with a limited cohort not letting a deep comparison between male and female, in all the other examined studies the majority of the involved population is composed by women (100% in Bernard-Davila et al. [39] consisting in breast cancer Hispanic survivors; in Mofleh et al. [41], 97.7% of a population of educators from USA; 87% in Mendonça et al. [40] from the Health Academy Program in Brazil; 58% in Miller et al. [37] consisting in breast cancer survivors). Among women, as a synthetic result of all the analyzed studies, differences in the encountered barriers are especially linked to own's body perception, grade of education, being employed, need to take care of families, and economic concerns. Being younger and with lower income, for example, represents a risk factor for food insecurity in Mofleh et at. [41].

Ethnicity-related differences. In Clark-Cutaia et al. [38] the studied population is quite equally divided between Caucasian and African-American but the sample is too little to understand differences in terms of ethnicity. Bernard-Davila et al. [39] choose Hispanic people according to their being the main minority in the US but, at the same time, one of the less involved communities in clinical studies. In her work, Spanish monolingualism is one of the main determinants of lack of enrollment in the protocol together with being unemployed and considering the study cost-consuming. Ethnicity seems to not represent a statistically significant element in terms of adherence to a nutritional intervention with or without in-person counseling in Miller et al. [37]. In Mofleh et al. [41], being white or not does not represent a statistically significant condition for food insecurity in a population of educators from Pennsylvania.

Lack of time. Clark-Cutaia et al. [38] enrolled 30 patients (mean age 63.3 $\pm$ 13.3 years) with end-stage renal failure on hemodialysis replacement therapy who underwent semi-structured telephone interviews to understand the barriers to following the recommended diet recognized as assisting substitution therapy in the treatment of the underlying disease. Among the main barriers indicated were those related to the time required. The long dialysis sessions, which included the transfer time between home and the dialysis center, led patients to skip a main meal with consequent difficulty in preparing healthy meals and a reduced desire to consume them.

In the work of Bernard-Davila et al. [39], albeit indirectly, it emerges that having a job represents a barrier to adherence to a dietary improvement intervention by a group of Hispanic breast cancer survivors (about 38.2% agreement). Similar factors can also be deduced from the work of Mendonça et al. [40] who also adds the time necessary to look after the family as another time constraint. Moreover, in the study by Mendonça et al. [40], although adherence to the intervention implemented at the Brazilian Primary Health Care service was high (possibly due to subject-related factors, the research scenario [health care service: Health Academy Program], the intervention methodology, and/or the bond-building among participants, professionals and the research team), adherence did seem to have been reduced due to 15 issues related to the incompatibility of situations that included work, self-care, care for the other(s), and service working hours (morning).

In contrast, Farmer Miller et al. [37] showed that for cancer survivors an eight-week course of nutrition education, with guaranteed face-to-face psychological support, was more effective, even though more time-consuming than the same intervention carried out electronically with printed material.

Environmental barriers. In the work of Clark-Cutaia et al. [38], the distance from the hemodialysis site combined with the need to utilize various means of transportation represented a further barrier to maintaining adequate adherence to the recommended diet.

Mendonça et al. [40] emphasize in their paper that an adequate setting for nutritional visits is a factor that promotes adherence.

Reading Miller's [37] work from another point of view, we can see how face-to-face interaction represents a fundamental motivational factor in increasing adherence to a healthy diet in a group of cancer survivors.

Bernard-Davila et al. [39] recognized the monolingualism of Hispanic cancer survivors in an English-speaking setting as a barrier to participation in the dietary intervention envisaged by the study.

Economic and financial barriers. Clark-Cutaia et al. [38] point out that approximately 50% of their enrolled patients said they did not have adequate finances to ensure the maintenance of a suitable diet for end-stage renal failure. Patients reported that dietary recommendations were expensive both in terms of the quantity and quality of the foods recommended. Another common patient concern was the greater ease of obtaining groceries at large stores with the possibility of finding discounted or less expensive items more easily. Some said that they sometimes had to give up drugs due to economic constraints, consequently making food choices immediately subject to direct economic sustainability.

In the work of Mofleh et al. [41], it emerged that in a population of educators of school-age children, the greatest degree of food insecurity manifested itself in younger subjects (31.5% of the population examined), with BMIs compatible with grade I obesity, with fewer years of teaching, and with lower salary levels.

Bernard Davila et al. [39], acknowledge unemployment and concern about the possible costs of the protocol as barriers to enrollment in the nutritional program provided for Hispanic women who survived breast cancer (about 64.3% strongly agreed that it would cost too much).

In contrast, Mendonça et al. [40] in their study aimed to improve fruit and vegetable consumption, found that instead of economic factors, work, having to care for others, and self-care were greater barriers to fruit and vegetable consumption.

Health status. Clark-Cutaia et al. [38] showed that many patients with end-stage renal failure considered their disease status and its consequences (hemodialysis with its timing and related distress) as a barrier to adherence to the best diet regimen.

A reported higher BMI (32.4 mean) in statistically significant terms characterized educators with greater food insecurity in the study by Mofleh et al. [41].

A lower degree of satisfaction with one's body image was a factor significantly related to lower adherence to the nutritional intervention proposed in the work of Mendonça et al. [40]. This was regardless of the general state of health (presence of metabolic and cardiovascular comorbidities).

Among the factors that affected participation in the nutritional intervention planned by the group of Bernard-Davila et al. [39], was concerned about one's own health status and degree of disease (Hispanic breast cancer survivor patients). A total of 37% of the participants thought that a dietary intervention could lead to side effects that doctors cannot predict. On the other hand, perceived health status was not a factor significantly correlated with the greater success of an in-person versus remote nutritional education protocol in the cancer survivor population in the work of Miller et al. [37].

Psychological barriers/insights. In the work of Clark-Cutaia et al. [38], hemodialysis patients reported that poor personalization of dietary intervention as a set of general rules to follow represents a barrier to adherence to the intended diet.

An adherence of more than one year to the nutritional intervention outlined in the work of Mendonça et al. [40] was correlated with better outcomes indirectly, how the proactive attitude towards lifestyle change is fundamental.

Bernard-Davila et al. [39] found that improved confidence in the positive outcome of the research appears to be an inducing factor in participation in the nutritional intervention.

3.2. Barriers to Exercise

Out of a total population of 1560 subjects tested through a questionnaire regarding the barriers encountered in undertaking physical exercise, 339 declared that they did not have enough time to dedicate to it (22.3%). Another very frequent problem cited was the distance from the gym or unfavorable weather conditions (8.63%, n = 131). A total of 242 attributed their state of health as an obstacle to embarking on a healthier life (15.95%). Of these 242, 123 belong to a very fragile category of patients who were undergoing dialysis therapy; a therapy that very often leads to symptoms related to hypotension, fever, joint pain, and fatigue. Furthermore, 33% of the patients involved in the studies had to interrupt the activity due to problems that required hospitalization. A total of 107 complained of mood disorders and showed little motivation to undertake a course in PA (7.05%). Finally, 71 (5.15%) refused to participate in the study as they did not consider it advantageous for their state of health.

Gender-related differences. Several studies suggested that women with NCDs tend to experience greater barriers to PA than men. For example, Pereira et al. [37] found that women with NCDs were less likely to participate in PA than their male counterparts. Pereira et al. [42] proposed several reasons for this gender disparity, including greater involvement in household tasks such as childcare, meal preparation, and cleaning [43]. In addition, women face other barriers, such as a lack of support from their partners, who may not encourage them to engage in PA, safety concerns, and fear of violence in some places used for PA [44]. In addition, Venditti et al. [32] showed that women with NCDs perceive more barriers to PA and weight loss than men. These barriers include internal cues (such as thoughts and moods), social cues and time management, physical events (such as injury or illness), and challenges related to access and weather conditions.

Ethnicity-related differences. The study conducted by Venditti et al. [32], while exploring the primary barriers to PA, showed a strong association between barriers to PA and ethnicity. For example, American Indians viewed "self-control" as a greater challenge to participating in PA, while white adults saw "social cues" as a more crucial barrier. Moreover, Pereira et al. [42] revealed differences in PA levels between non-white and white Brazilian adults with NCDs. Non-white adults were found to be less active than their white counterparts. However, Rosa et al. [34] did not find any differences in PA levels based on skin color among adults undergoing hemodialysis.

Lack of time. The questionnaire results allow us to make a series of important conclusions regarding the perception of PA as a therapeutic tool and the barriers that prevent patients from utilizing it. First, it is immediately evident that one of the main motivations preventing patients from undertaking a more active lifestyle is worries about not having enough time available daily [31,32,34,36]. Exercise therapy requires an important weekly commitment with training sessions varying from three to five sessions of approximately 45–60 min each. Finding time to dedicate to PA during the day, especially for people busy with work [31,32,34,36], can, therefore, be extraordinarily complex. It is one of the main problems to consider when prescribing exercise.

In Rosa et al. [34] it emerged that 39.8% of patients did not have enough time for dedicated PA. This seems to be correlated with a sedentary lifestyle, since only 33% of those who already performed recreational PAreferred to lack of time as an effective barrier.

Environmental barriers. The difficulty in reaching the site for PA is another frequent type of barrier, which overlaps with the inconveniences of daily life. This also includes physical distance and adverse weather conditions which can discourage less motivated individuals [30,34,35].

Health status. Another interesting fact that we found is the low rate of recruitment to some protocols (30% in the case of Rogers et al. [31]; 20.3% in Koutoukidis et al. [36]). This rate was influenced by some characteristics of the population including youthful age, having one or more chronic conditions, and awareness of having a low level of PA [43,44]. Those who declined participation in the protocols mostly claimed to have a sufficient level of weekly activity [34]. This suggests that the suffering or sedentary patient perceives the possibility that movement can benefit health. In the study conducted by Sheshadri et al. [30], 73% of participants expressed willingness to participate in the protocol, believing that they could obtain a benefit of some kind that was related to QoL (30%) or be able to achieve a condition such that they could meet the criteria for renal transplantation (27%).

In cancer patients, the perception of pain and fatigue, also related to therapies, affected more than half of the cases undertaking an exercise-based protocol [30].

The results also show that deterrents to undertaking a therapeutic path based on exercise strongly depend on the type of disease involved, since, in the context of chronic pathologies such as diabetes or hypertension, lack of time or access to facilities limits those subjects [45], while in the contexts of more complex pathologies, the most prevalent deterrents are concerns for one's health and low motivation [30,44,45].

Sheshadri et al. [30] found that older age and a higher BMI were associated with increased motivational barriers related particularly to the presence of symptoms.

Psychological barriers/insights. From the data analyzed by Venditti et al. [32], another issue emerges in the maintenance of optimal levels of PA after the end of the experimental protocols. The six-month protocol completion rate by participants was an impressive 96%. In subsequent re-evaluations, however, participants had difficulty maintaining sufficient levels of PA; they reported this was related to poor time management, daily life commitments, and self-monitoring problems that prevented them from recording progress. This helps us understand that searching for and removing barriers is on a continuum that must also include the search for a way to ensure adequate maintenance of fitness levels. Additionally, the problem of a person's approach to physical exercise seems to be directly proportional to a person's degree of fitness and familiarity with the type of activity. In fact, in a study conducted by Thomson et al. [33], it emerged that the perceived barriers are greater in those who have had only dietary intervention and have not performed any type of PA. The study demonstrated that the extent of these barriers decreased over time only in the group that performed PA, while the group with only nutritional intervention did not show significant variation.

An interesting fact in Rosa et al. [34] is the degree of satisfaction derived from the exercises performed. Approximately 25.5% of the population involved in the study reported as a barrier the lack of propensity to perform certain exercises which could demotivate specific populations (such as people undergoing hemodialytic treatment) from following a therapeutic PA program.

Communication errors between Clinicians and Patients. Doctor–patient communication is perhaps the most important component of a treatment regimen [46]. A patient must trust the doctor and be well-informed by the doctor; a trusting, well-informed relationship often leads the person needing treatment to follow the doctor's advice to the letter. It is not surprising that if patients with a chronic-degenerative disease such as diabetes, are not educated to have a healthy awareness and acceptance of the condition through a broad and exhaustive informative interview, some may find themselves hesitant about what to do to deal with it. The need to develop a healthier lifestyle is often a topic dealt with superficially by the treating doctor, with little specific direction given as to methods for doing so.

4. Discussion

It should be noted that in literature it is easier to find qualitative rather than quantitative studies that evaluate the barriers to acquiring a healthier lifestyle through an adequate diet and regular physical activities. This is one of the peculiarities that makes this literary review innovative. In this discussion, we compare the result of our review of quantitative mixed studies and qualitative ones.

Patients suffering from chronic NCDs experience a condition of quoad vitam persistence of their morbid condition. The indefiniteness of the duration of the disease makes them particularly exposed to the risk of not adhering to recommended treatment, even in the context of a therapeutic alliance between doctor and patient. Although it is widely known that a healthy diet and maintenance of an adequate level of PA represent a fundamental component of the management and improvement of cardiovascular health [17] and most chronic NCDs in both clinical terms and QoL, it is equally commonly known that patients with NCDs experience numerous barriers to maintaining these prescriptions. Regarding adherence to recommendations, some elements must be considered. There could be an impact depending on the region of origin of the authors' study and the patients involved [17]. For example, many of the investigators who supported MED have born or lived in Mediterranean countries and this could have contributed to the adoption of their opinions on the benefits of MED [47]. This potential bias is not supported by the results of solid studies conducted in non-Mediterranean populations that have found similar benefits in adhering to MED [17]. Similarly, it was observed that adherence to WHO PA guidelines was lower among adults from Southern and Central European countries (Romania, Poland, Croatia, Cyprus, and Malta) and the USA than among Northern European countries (Iceland, Sweden, The Netherlands, and Denmark). Moreover, PA adherence was higher in men than in women [48]. Furthermore, our findings highlighted the presence of ethnicity and gender differences that frequently limit the participation of adults with NCDs in PA.

In our literature review, various similar barriers to healthy diet and exercise emerged. Among these, first, the time needed to be devoted to these two determinants of health is often considered unsustainable, especially for those who are engaged in work activities, who are caring for the family, or for those for whom the chronic disease itself involves considerable consumption of time (i.e., hemodialysis for chronic renal failure, time for therapy, and visits in cancer).

These results appear in agreement with that from qualitative research about these barriers. In Suderman et al. [49], for example, the lack of time is a barrier that remains both at the beginning of the intervention and at the end of it. In particular, workers, that tend to be younger than patients with NCDs seem to encounter this barrier more often. Considering that the number of younger people affected by NCDs is constantly growing in the last decades, especially due to the more effective screening campaign, the more effective diagnostic tools, and the greater sensitivity to their own health, it is particularly important to know this barrier in order to offer useful solutions to overcome them mitigating the severity of disease, especially in a pre-clinical phase or in an early stage in people employed in working activities. Taking care of their own family represents, also in qualitative studies, such as that of Attwood et al. [50] and Sebire et al. [51], an important barrier.

The importance of personalized counselling aimed at maintaining high motivation to achieve appropriate levels of PA and a balanced diet is consistently recognized as a crucial requirement for a broad range of individuals with chronic diseases. Even the accessibility of the exercise or dietary counselling site appears to be a vital element in increasing adherence to behavioral prescriptions. Economic barriers seem to detract more from maintaining adequate dietary levels. Moreover, the perception of a higher cost and a greater effort in procuring food hinders adherence to dietary recommendations. One's own perception of one's health and disease are a common barrier to diet and exercise. Patients with a negative subjective sense of well-being have more difficulty maintaining optimal levels of behavioral prescriptions. A close relationship between therapists and patients affected by NCDs, in terms of engagement and therapeutic alliance, appears to be a factor that can promote adherence to dietary recommendations and implementation of PA. In particular, an in-person individualized approach with repeated adherence assessments seems to represent the most effective strategy for supporting and strengthening the motivation to change [52,53]. Knowledge of the specific and common barriers to two key behavioral prescriptions (diet and PA) offers a fundamental opportunity to develop concrete approaches, individual and group, aimed at overcoming these barriers to improvement of the QoL and long-term control of NCDs.

All of these data seem to be similar to that from qualitative studies. In fact, among barriers frequently encountered in qualitative studies, consistent with the results of the review, there are those of an environmental nature and in particular, as noted by Suderman et al. [49], the fear of not finding competent personnel who are able to manage training programs for patients with chronic diseases. In this case, the issue concerns not only the problem of training competent personnel in the matter but also the scarce dissemination of information on the matter and the little trust that patients place both in the type of intervention and in who should be responsible for accompanying and supporting the patient along the course of care. Finally, the note reported by Suderman et al. [49] is noteworthy, in relation to the judgment of training programs, often considered punitive by the patients themselves. In Attwood et al. [50], instead, a good part of patients perceive such programs as constraints to change their lifestyle.

Comparing results from our literary review and data from qualitative studies, more similarities than differences could be appreciated. Due to the seminal importance of keeping an adequate diet and physical activity to counteract the ominous effects of NCDs, it is important to keep in mind that a lifestyle intervention of this type has a considerable impact on the patient's quality of life and for this reason, the prescription must necessarily take into consideration the needs and expectations of the patient himself. Compliance, in this type of patient, is a fundamental element for the success of the intervention, so in our opinion, the moment in which these therapeutic options are proposed is of fundamental importance. The patient must be aware of both the advantages and disadvantages and limitations that such an intervention can represent. The engagement of patients in their therapeutical plan is a decisive moment in the management of people suffering from NCDs and this could not take place without a complete and deep knowledge of the main behavioral barriers.

In relation to gender differences, women tend to report greater barriers, especially towards increasing levels of physical activity and these barriers are more frequently attributable to psychological problems, environmental barriers, and low motivation than men [28]. In dietary intervention, there are no differences in gender. Ethnic differences affect specifically diet-based interventions, and this is due to sociocultural and economic differences. Hispanic and African-American ethnicity, in the US context, do not enjoy high economic possibilities and often find themselves living in communities where mutual support is essential [50]. Clark-Cutaia [38] highlights how the assumption, by these patients, of a different lifestyle, would tend these subjects to exclude themselves from the community in which they live and to lose the social support of friends and relatives.

An increase in the number of barriers to diet has also been reported by Mofleh et al. [41], whose results show that there are differences regarding insecurities in one's own eating habits precisely in relation to ethnic and cultural differences. In physical activity intervention, there are differences in race too. If we consider the study taken by Venditti et al. [32] regarding non-Caucasian people, there are about 10–20% barriers more than among Caucasian people and this appears to be related to the socio-economic differences and to the difficulty to access the dedicated structure. In Sheshadri et al. [30], instead, there are no differences in gender in a pedometer intervention, this is probably attributed to the specific population (dialysis patients) and the type of intervention that does not require any gym or specific tools to be practiced.

Finally, as reported by Mendonça [40] and Clark-Cutaia [38], in Brazil and Iran, the level of education seems to be a determining factor for the adherence by these subjects to a healthier lifestyle, probably in relation to a degree of higher literacy.

It must be remembered that the time frame examined in this study (last ten years) also includes one of the greatest global health crisis periods in recent history. In fact, in February 2020 the World Health Organization (WHO) declared a public health emergency due to the SARS-CoV-2 virus, which is particularly dangerous for people with NCDs. To avoid the spread of the virus, containment measures were adopted with the ban to get away from their home. A "lockdown" and social isolation were imposed on some world countries, and it led to a drastic alteration of lifestyle habits (i.e., going to the grocery store was much more difficult and it was forbidden to go to eat meals in restaurants, with a consequent increase in meals cooked and eaten at home [54]. Moreover, PA outdoors are stopped, and exercising at home remained the only possibility to stay active during the COVID-19 pandemic [55]. These changes in habits lead to a reduction of PA levels [56] affecting psychological well-being, and worse nutritional habits [57] (i.e., an increase in the number of snacks consumed, an increase in comfort foods, and alcohol consumption). Anyway, during the COVID-19 pandemic were referred some specific barriers to healthy nutrition, such as, i.e., not having sufficient money to buy groceries and worrying about getting COVID-19 at the store [58]. While regarding PA barriers [59], laziness and fatigue, lack of motivation", and lack of time were the most prevalent, together with a lack of appropriate facilities, equipment, or space.

Strengths and Limitations. A considerable strength is that the large group of authors allowed us to carefully evaluate and double-check the entirety of all the articles. In fact, in the first phase, one group dealt with diet and another with physical activity, based on the authors' degrees and areas of expertise. Subsequently, the articles selected were evaluated by all the authors. This allowed us to better identify some categories of barriers common to both nutritional and PA recommendations.

The most important limitation, in our opinion, is that only one relevant database was searched (PubMed). Secondarily, only articles available in full-text versions were evaluated for inclusion in our review, which could restrict search opportunities.

Finally, the keywords used to study research were very detailed and could have conditioned the open-field search strategies.

5. Conclusions

Although it has been a consistent subject of research in recent years, the study of the barriers that prevent patients from adopting a healthy nutritional and PA lifestyle remains a crucial research focus. Greater knowledge of the various types of barriers patients face would allow clinical team professionals who care for patients with NDCs to more accurately understand the obstacles that hinder patients' adherence to a healthy lifestyle. Early identification of which barriers patients experience would improve awareness of their difficulties and enable healthcare and non-health professionals to propose truly effective solutions. Given the complex nature of some barriers, early identification would allow the various stakeholders to collaborate in the creation of environments, policies, and intervention programs that can help the general population as well as those with chronic pathologies to adhere to a healthy lifestyle, an effective tool for the prevention and treatment of NCDs. Tailoring lifestyle plans is a seminal element to improve NCD patients' compliance. Every patient, in fact, presents his/her own needs and motivations that turn away from spending time and resources to obtain a healthier lifestyle. All the members of the community could be engaged in social and political interventions having the aim of stimulating awareness of the real efficacy of a healthier lifestyle in improving global quality of life. An imperative role of health professionals has to educate, ameliorating people's awareness about NCDs and the most effective actions to counteract the ominous effects of them in terms of health and quality of life. Only a real paradigm shift from a simple taking care of health problems to a global approach to the person in terms of motivation, engagement, and deep knowledge of both physical and psychological barriers to a healthy lifestyle could reduce the burden of NCDs and consequent morbidity, mortality, and disability.

Author Contributions: Conceptualization, M.C. and G.M.; methodology, M.C. and G.M.; software, M.C. and G.M.; data curation, M.C. and G.M.; writing—original draft preparation, M.C., G.M., I.D., A.G. and R.P.; writing—review and editing, M.C., G.M., I.D., A.G., R.P., M.V., G.P., G.V. and C.G.F.; supervision, G.V. and C.G.F.; project administration, G.V. and C.G.F. All authors have read and agreed to the published version of the manuscript.

Funding: This research received no external funding.

Institutional Review Board Statement: Not applicable.

Informed Consent Statement: Not applicable.

Data Availability Statement: Not applicable.

Conflicts of Interest: The authors declare no conflict of interest.

References

1. Ministero della Salute. I Determinanti della Salute. Available online: https://www.salute.gov.it/imgs/C_17_pubblicazioni_1144_ulterioriallegati_ulterioreallegato_1_alleg.pdf (accessed on 30 June 2023).
2. Marmot, M.; Allen, J.; Bell, R.; Bloomer, E.; Goldblatt, P. Consortium for the European Review of Social Determinants of Health and the Health Divide. WHO European review of social determinants of health and the health divide. *Lancet* **2012**, *380*, 1011–1029. [CrossRef] [PubMed]
3. Pan, A.; Lin, X.; Hemler, E.; Hu, F.B. Diet and cardiovascular disease: Advances and challenges in population-based studies. *Cell Metab.* **2018**, *27*, 489–496. [PubMed]
4. GBD 2017 Diet Collaborators. Health effects of dietary risks in 195 countries, 1990–2017: A systematic analysis for the Global Burden of Disease Study 2017. *Lancet* **2019**, *393*, 1958–1972, Erratum in *Lancet* **2021**, *397*, 2466. [CrossRef]
5. Thivel, D.; Tremblay, A.; Genin, P.M.; Panahi, S.; Rivière, D.; Duclos, M. Physical Activity, Inactivity, and Sedentary Behaviors: Definitions and Implications in Occupational Health. *Front. Public Health* **2018**, *6*, 288. [CrossRef]
6. Deslippe, A.L.; Soanes, A.; Bouchaud, C.C.; Beckenstein, H.; Slim, M.; Plourde, H.; Cohen, T.R. Barriers and facilitators to diet, physical activity and lifestyle behavior intervention adherence: A qualitative systematic review of the literature. *Int. J. Behav. Nutr. Phys. Act.* **2023**, *20*, 14. [CrossRef]
7. Subramaniam, M.; Devi, F.; AshaRani, P.V.; Zhang, Y.; Wang, P.; Jeyagurunathan, A.; Roystonn, K.; Vaingankar, J.A.; Chong, S.A. Barriers and facilitators for adopting a healthy lifestyle in a multi-ethnic population: A qualitative study. *PLoS ONE* **2022**, *17*, e0277106. [CrossRef]
8. Guthold, R.; Stevens, G.A.; Riley, L.M.; Bull, F.C. Worldwide trends in insufficient physical activity from 2001 to 2016: A pooled analysis of 358 population-based surveys with 1·9 million participants. *Lancet Glob. Health* **2018**, *6*, e1077–e1086. [CrossRef]
9. Liu, J.; Lee, Y.; Micha, R.; Li, Y.; Mozaffarian, D. Trends in junk food consumption among US children and adults, 2001–2018. *Am. J. Clin. Nutr.* **2021**, *114*, 1039–1048. [CrossRef]
10. World Health Organization. Global Action Plan on Physical Activity 2018–2030: More Active People for a Healthier World. Available online: https://apps.who.int/iris/handle/10665/272722 (accessed on 30 June 2023).
11. Cooper, J.; Murphy, J.; Woods, C.; Van Nassau, F.; McGrath, A.; Callaghan, D.; Carroll, P.; Kelly, P.; Murphy, N.; Murphy, M.; et al. Barriers and facilitators to implementing community-based physical activity interventions: A qualitative systematic review. *Int. J. Behav. Nutr. Phys. Act.* **2021**, *18*, 118.
12. Anderson, E.; Durstine, J.L. Physical activity, exercise, and chronic diseases: A brief review. *Sports Med. Health Sci.* **2019**, *1*, 3–10. [CrossRef]
13. Calder, P.C.; Carr, A.C.; Gombart, A.F.; Eggersdorfer, M. Optimal Nutritional Status for a Well-Functioning Immune System Is an Important Factor to Protect against Viral Infections. *Nutrients* **2020**, *12*, 1181. [CrossRef] [PubMed]
14. Da Silveira, M.P.; da Silva Fagundes, K.K.; Bizuti, M.R.; Starck, É.; Rossi, R.C.; de Resende, E.; Silva, D.T. Physical exercise as a tool to help the immune system against COVID-19: An integrative review of the current literature. *Clin. Exp. Med.* **2021**, *21*, 15–28. [CrossRef]
15. Gilbert, L.; Gross, J.; Lanzi, S.; Quansah, D.Y.; Puder, J.; Horsch, A. How diet, physical activity and psychosocial well-being interact in women with gestational diabetes mellitus: An integrative review. *BMC Pregnancy Childbirth* **2019**, *19*, 60. [CrossRef]
16. Barrea, L.; Muscogiuri, G.; Di Somma, C.; Tramontano, G.; De Luca, V.; Illario, M.; Colao, A.; Savastano, S. Association between Mediterranean diet and hand grip strength in older adult women. *Clin. Nutr.* **2019**, *38*, 721–729. [CrossRef] [PubMed]
17. Martínez-González, M.A.; Gea, A.; Ruiz-Canela, M. The Mediterranean Diet and Cardiovascular Health. *Circ. Res.* **2019**, *124*, 779–798. [CrossRef] [PubMed]
18. Estruch, R.; Ros, E.; Salas-Salvadó, J.; Covas, M.I.; Corella, D.; Arós, F.; Gómez-Gracia, E.; Ruiz-Gutiérrez, V.; Fiol, M.; Lapetra, J.; et al. Primary prevention of cardiovascular disease with a Mediterranean diet supplemented with extra-virgin olive oil or nuts. *N. Engl. J. Med.* **2018**, *378*, e34. [CrossRef]
19. Martín-Peláez, S.; Fito, M.; Castaner, O. Mediterranean Diet Effects on Type 2 Diabetes Prevention, Disease Progression, and Related Mechanisms. A Review. *Nutrients* **2020**, *12*, 2236. [CrossRef]
20. Morze, J.; Danielewicz, A.; Przybyłowicz, K.; Zeng, H.; Hoffmann, G.; Schwingshackl, L. An updated systematic review and meta-analysis on adherence to mediterranean diet and risk of cancer. *Eur. J. Nutr.* **2021**, *60*, 1561–1586. [CrossRef]
21. Muscogiuri, G.; Verde, L.; Sulu, C.; Katsiki, N.; Hassapidou, M.; Frias-Toral, E.; Cucalón, G.; Pazderska, A.; Yumuk, V.D.; Colao, A.; et al. Mediterranean Diet and Obesity-related Disorders: What is the Evidence? *Curr. Obes. Rep.* **2022**, *11*, 287–304. [CrossRef]
22. Bray, G.A.; Frühbeck, G.; Ryan, D.H.; Wilding, J.P. Management of obesity. *Lancet* **2016**, *387*, 1947–1956. [CrossRef]
23. Mannarino, S.; Santacesaria, S.; Raso, I.; Garbin, M.; Pipolo, A.; Ghiglia, S.; Tarallo, G.; De Silvestri, A.; Vandoni, M.; Lucini, D.; et al. Benefits in Cardiac Function from a Remote Exercise Program in Children with Obesity. *Int. J. Environ. Res. Public Health* **2023**, *20*, 1544. [CrossRef]
24. Pippi, R.; Prete, D.; Ranucci, C.; Ministrini, S.; Pasqualini, L.; Fanelli, C. Physical activity level and mediterranean diet adherence evaluation in older people—observational, uncontrolled, pilot study. *Phys. Act. Rev.* **2022**, *10*, 119–129. [CrossRef]
25. Cybulska, B.; Kłosiewicz-Latoszek, L. Landmark studies in coronary heart disease epidemiology. The Framingham Heart Study after 70 years and the Seven Countries Study after 60 years. *Kardiol. Pol.* **2019**, *77*, 173–180. [CrossRef] [PubMed]

26. Urquiaga, I.; Echeverría, G.; Dussaillant, C.; Rigotti, A. Origin, components and mechanisms of action of the Mediterranean diet. *Rev. Medica De Chile* **2017**, *145*, 85–95.
27. Malakou, E.; Linardakis, M.; Armstrong, M.E.G.; Zannidi, D.; Foster, C.; Johnson, L.; Papadaki, A. The Combined Effect of Promoting the Mediterranean Diet and Physical Activity on Metabolic Risk Factors in Adults: A Systematic Review and Meta-Analysis of Randomised Controlled Trials. *Nutrients* **2018**, *10*, 1577. [CrossRef] [PubMed]
28. Caprara, G. Mediterranean-Type Dietary Pattern and Physical Activity: The Winning Combination to Counteract the Rising Burden of Non-Communicable Diseases (NCDs). *Nutrients* **2021**, *13*, 429. [CrossRef]
29. Page, M.J.; McKenzie, J.E.; Bossuyt, P.M.; Boutron, I.; Hoffmann, T.C.; Mulrow, C.D.; Shamseer, L.; Tetzlaff, J.M.; Akl, E.A.; Brennan, S.E.; et al. The PRISMA 2020 statement: An updated guideline for reporting systematic reviews. *BMJ* **2021**, *372*, n71. [CrossRef]
30. Sheshadri, A.; Kittiskulnam, P.; Delgado, C.; Sudore, R.; Lai, J.C.; Johansen, K.L. Association of motivations and barriers with participation and performance in a pedometer-based intervention. *Nephrol. Dial. Transplant.* **2020**, *35*, 1405–1411. [CrossRef]
31. Rogers, A.; Harris, T.; Victor, C.; Woodcock, A.; Limb, E.; Kerry, S.; Iliffe, S.; Whincup, P.; Ekelund, U.; Beighton, C.; et al. Which older people decline participation in a primary care trial of physical activity and why: Insights from a mixed methods approach. *BMC Geriatr.* **2014**, *14*, 46. [CrossRef]
32. Venditti, E.M.; Wylie-Rosett, J.; Delahanty, L.M.; Mele, L.; Hoskin, M.A.; Edelstein, S.L.; Diabetes Prevention Program Research Group. Short and long-term lifestyle coaching approaches used to address diverse participant barriers to weight loss and physical activity adherence. *Int. J. Behav. Nutr. Phys. Act.* **2014**, *11*, 16. [CrossRef]
33. Thomson, R.L.; Buckley, J.D.; Brinkworth, G.D. Perceived exercise barriers are reduced and benefits are improved with lifestyle modification in overweight and obese women with polycystic ovary syndrome: A randomised controlled trial. *BMC Womens Health* **2016**, *16*, 14. [CrossRef] [PubMed]
34. Rosa, C.S.; Bueno, D.R.; Souza, G.D.; Gobbo, L.A.; Freitas, I.F., Jr.; Sakkas, G.K.; Monteiro, H.L. Factors associated with leisure-time physical activity among patients undergoing hemodialysis. *BMC Nephrol.* **2015**, *16*, 192. [CrossRef]
35. Kang, D.W.; Boulé, N.G.; Field, C.J.; Fairey, A.S.; Courneya, K.S. Effects of supervised high-intensity interval training on motivational outcomes in men with prostate cancer undergoing active surveillance: Results from a randomized controlled trial. *Int. J. Behav. Nutr. Phys. Act.* **2022**, *19*, 126. [CrossRef] [PubMed]
36. Koutoukidis, D.A.; Beeken, R.J.; Manchanda, R.; Michalopoulou, M.; Burnell, M.; Knobf, M.T.; Lanceley, A. Recruitment, adherence, and retention of endometrial cancer survivors in a behavioural lifestyle programme: The diet and exercise in uterine cancer survivors (DEUS) parallel randomized pilot trial. *BMJ Open* **2017**, *7*, e018015. [CrossRef] [PubMed]
37. Miller, M.F.; Li, Z.; Habedank, M. A Randomized Controlled Trial Testing the Effectiveness of Coping with Cancer in the Kitchen, a Nutrition Education Program for Cancer Survivors. *Nutrients* **2020**, *12*, 3144. [CrossRef]
38. Clark-Cutaia, M.N.; Sevick, M.A.; Thurheimer-Cacciotti, J.; Hoffman, L.A.; Snetselaar, L.; Burke, L.E.; Zickmund, S.L. Perceived Barriers to Adherence to Hemodialysis Dietary Recommendations. *Clin. Nurs. Res.* **2019**, *28*, 1009–1029. [CrossRef]
39. Bernard-Davila, B.; Aycinena, A.C.; Richardson, J.; Gaffney, A.O.; Koch, P.; Contento, I.; Molmenti, C.S.; Alvarez, M.; Hershman, D.; Greenlee, H. Barriers and facilitators to recruitment to a culturally-based dietary intervention among urban Hispanic breast cancer survivors. *J. Racial Ethn. Health Disparities* **2015**, *2*, 244–255. [CrossRef]
40. Mendonça, R.D.; Guimarães, L.M.F.; Mingoti, S.A.; Magalhães, K.A.; Lopes, A.C.S. Barriers to and facilitators for adherence to nutritional intervention: Consumption of fruits and vegetables. *Nutrition* **2019**, *67*, 110568. [CrossRef] [PubMed]
41. Mofleh, D.; Ranjit, N.; Chuang, R.J.; Cox, J.N.; Anthony, C.; Sharma, S.V. Association Between Food Insecurity and Diet Quality Among Early Care and Education Providers in the Pennsylvania Head Start Program. *Prev. Chronic Dis.* **2021**, *18*, 200602. [CrossRef]
42. Pereira, Z.S.; da Silva, A.S.; Melo, J.C.; Dos Santos, J.C.; Sewo Sampaio, P.Y.; Silva, R.J.; Araújo, R.H.; Sampaio, R.A. Differential Factors Are Associated with Physical Activity in Older Adults in Brazil with and without Non-Communicable Chronic Diseases: A Cross-Sectional Analysis of the 2019 National Health Survey. *Int. J. Environ. Res. Public Health* **2023**, *20*, 6329. [CrossRef]
43. IBGE—Instituto Brasileiro de Geografia e Estatística. *Outras Formas de Trabalho: 2018*; Instituto Brasileiro de Geografia e Estatística—IBGE: Rio de Janeiro, Brazil. Available online: https://biblioteca.ibge.gov.br/index.php/biblioteca-catalogo?view=detalhes&id=2101650 (accessed on 14 February 2023).
44. Joseph, R.P.; Ainsworth, B.E.; Keller, C.; Dodgson, J.E. Barriers to Physical Activity Among African American Women: An Integrative Review of the Literature. *Women Health* **2015**, *55*, 679–699. [CrossRef]
45. Nocon, M.; Hiemann, T.; Müller-Riemenschneider, F.; Thalau, F.; Roll, S.; Willich, S.N. Association of physical activity with all-cause and cardiovascular mortality: A systematic review and meta-analysis. *Eur. J. Prev. Cardiol.* **2008**, *15*, 239–246. [CrossRef] [PubMed]
46. Bittner-Fagan, H.; Davis, J.; Savoy, M. Improving Patient Safety: Improving Communication. *FP Essent.* **2017**, *463*, 27–33.
47. Trichopoulou, A.; Lagiou, P. Healthy traditional Mediterranean diet: An expression of culture, history, and lifestyle. *Nutr. Rev.* **1997**, *55*, 383–389. [CrossRef] [PubMed]
48. Garcia-Hermoso, A.; López-Gil, J.F.; Ramírez-Vélez, R.; Alonso-Martínez, A.M.; Izquierdo, M.; Ezzatvar, Y. Adherence to aerobic and muscle-strengthening activities guidelines: A systematic review and meta-analysis of 3.3 million participants across 32 countries. *Br. J. Sports Med.* **2023**, *57*, 225–229. [CrossRef]

49. Suderman, K.; Dolgoy, N.; Yurick, J.; Sellar, C.; Nishimura, K.; Culos-Reed, S.N.; Joy, A.A.; McNeely, M.L. A Practical Approach to Using Integrated Knowledge Translation to Inform a Community-Based Exercise Study. *Int. J. Environ. Res. Public Health* **2020**, *17*, 3911. [CrossRef] [PubMed]
50. Attwood, S.; Morton, K.L.; Mitchell, J.; Van Emmenis, M.; Sutton, S.; VBI Programme Team. Reasons for non-participation in a primary care-based physical activity trial: A qualitative study. *BMJ Open* **2016**, *6*, e011577. [CrossRef]
51. Sebire, S.J.; Toumpakari, Z.; Turner, K.M.; Cooper, A.R.; Page, A.S.; Malpass, A.; Andrews, R.C. "I've made this my lifestyle now": A prospective qualitative study of motivation for lifestyle change among people with newly diagnosed type two diabetes mellitus. *BMC Public Health* **2018**, *18*, 204. [CrossRef]
52. Buratta, L.; Reginato, E.; Ranucci, C.; Pippi, R.; Aiello, C.; Tomaro, E.S.; Pazzagli, C.; Tirimagni, A.; Russo, A.; De Feo, P.; et al. Stage of Change and Motivation to a Healthier Lifestyle before and after an Intensive Lifestyle Intervention. *J. Obes.* **2016**, *2016*, 6421265. [CrossRef]
53. Centis, E.; Trento, M.; Cas, A.D.; Pontiroli, A.E.; De Feo, P.; Bruno, A.; Sasdelli, A.S.; Arturi, F.; Strollo, F.; Kreutzenberg, S.V.D.; et al. Stage change and motivation to healthy diet and habitual physical activity in type 2 diabetes. *Acta Diabetol.* **2014**, *51*, 559–566. [CrossRef]
54. Sarda, B.; Delamaire, C.; Serry, A.J.; Ducrot, P. Changes in home cooking and culinary practices among the French population during the COVID-19 lockdown. *Appetite* **2022**, *168*, 105743. [CrossRef] [PubMed]
55. ACSM. Staying Physically Active during the COVID-19 Pandemic. 2020. Available online: http://www.acsm.org/read-research/newsroom/news-releases/news-detail/2020/03/16/stayingphysically-active-during-COVID-19-pandemic (accessed on 25 July 2023).
56. Maugeri, G.; Castrogiovanni, P.; Battaglia, G.; Pippi, R.; D'Agata, V.; Palma, A.; Di Rosa, M.; Musumeci, G. The impact of physical activity on psychological health during COVID-19 pandemic in Italy. *Heliyon* **2020**, *6*, e04315. [CrossRef]
57. Bennett, G.; Young, E.; Butler, I.; Coe, S. The Impact of Lockdown During the COVID-19 Outbreak on Dietary Habits in Various Population Groups: A Scoping Review. *Front. Nutr.* **2021**, *8*, 626432. [CrossRef]
58. Reimold, A.E.; Grummon, A.H.; Taillie, L.S.; Brewer, N.T.; Rimm, E.B.; Hall, M.G. Barriers and facilitators to achieving food security during the COVID-19 pandemic. *Prev. Med. Rep.* **2021**, *23*, 101500. [CrossRef] [PubMed]
59. Farah, B.Q.; do Prado, W.L.; Malik, N.; Lofrano-Prado, M.C.; de Melo, P.H.; Botero, J.P.; Cucato, G.G.; de Almeida Correia, M.; Ritti-Dias, R.M. Barriers to physical activity during the COVID-19 pandemic in adults: A cross-sectional study. *Sport Sci. Health* **2021**, *17*, 441–447. [CrossRef] [PubMed]

nutrients

Systematic Review

Assessment Strategies to Evaluate the Mediterranean Lifestyle: A Systematic Review

Elisabet Montero-Sandiego, Rosario Ferrer-Cascales *, Nicolás Ruiz-Robledillo *, Borja Costa-López, Cristian Alcocer-Bruno and Natalia Albaladejo-Blázquez

Department of Health Psychology, Faculty of Health Science, University of Alicante, 03690 Alicante, Spain
* Correspondence: rosario.ferrer@ua.es (R.F.-C.); nicolas.ruiz@ua.es (N.R.-R.); Tel.: +34-965903400(N.R.-R.)

Abstract: The Mediterranean Lifestyle (MLS) has been related to better health and quality of life. However, there is no consensus on how to assess this lifestyle. The main objective of this work was to systematically review the methodology used in different studies on the evaluation of the MLS. The specific objectives were (1) to analyze the MLS components evaluated in previous studies, (2) to explore the assessment instruments available for the analysis of the MLS, and (3) to identify the psychometric properties of these instruments. The search was carried out using the PubMed, Scopus, Web of Science, and ScienceDirect databases with the purpose of identifying those published articles in which the MLS was assessed. The review included 26 studies linked to the assessment of the MLS. Of these studies, only four exclusively used a tool to analyze MLS components globally. These studies included two questionnaires and three different indexes. None of them, however, evaluated all of the recognized MLS components, and food preparation was the least frequently evaluated component. Given the clear importance of analyzing MLS adherence and the lack of consensus in previous research, an evaluation tool needs to be created to comprehensively assess all of the MLS dimensions by means of appropriate psychometric properties.

Keywords: Mediterranean Lifestyle; evaluation; questionnaire; index

Citation: Montero-Sandiego, E.; Ferrer-Cascales, R.; Ruiz-Robledillo, N.; Costa-López, B.; Alcocer-Bruno, C.; Albaladejo-Blázquez, N. Assessment Strategies to Evaluate the Mediterranean Lifestyle: A Systematic Review. *Nutrients* **2022**, *14*, 4179. https://doi.org/10.3390/nu14194179

Academic Editors: Roberto Pippi, Carmine G. Fanelli and Matteo Vandoni

Received: 4 September 2022
Accepted: 3 October 2022
Published: 8 October 2022

1. Introduction

Lifestyle (LS) is considered to be a set of repeated behavioral patterns maintained over time that characterize an individual's way of life [1]. The term has gained considerable relevance over recent years due to its close relationship with distinct pathologies and the higher levels of morbidity and mortality [2,3]. Lifestyle factors, such as physical activity, alcohol consumption, smoking, sleep, and diet have been found to be predictors of health status in both the general and the clinical population [4]. However, few studies have performed comprehensive analyses of the different so-called healthy lifestyles, such as the Mediterranean Lifestyle (MLS) [5]. This lifestyle, denominated after the countries situated near the Mediterranean Sea [2], displays the following factors: a high adherence to the Mediterranean Diet (MD); regular physical activity; good hydration and adequate rest (including regular naps); the consumption of seasonal and locally grown products; participation in food preparation and culinary activities; and frequent social interactions [2]. This lifestyle is the result of the interactions between these factors. Not only does the Mediterranean Diet pyramid incorporate recommendations regarding the frequency people should consume certain foods, and the amount of those foods, but it also refers to other dimensions that comprise the traditional Mediterranean life [6]. The MLS extends beyond a simple dietary pattern and is based on the interactions of different aspects of a healthy lifestyle. Different parameters, such as socialization, physical activity, leisure activities, appropriate rest, and, of course, diet, interact to create a healthy lifestyle, as in the case of an MLS [4]. In this way, different studies, although in isolation, have shown how the various components of the MLS are associated with better health and quality of life. For example, recent research has shown how meals shared with family members are associated with healthy weight and better eating habits [7]. Likewise, culinary activities constitute a behavior of great importance for health promotion, especially among children, as there are studies that show that it favors increased vegetable consumption [2]. In turn, the use of seasonal and locally grown products, another component of the MLS, allows avoiding the consumption of foods that have been processed for their maintenance during transportation and storage. Such processing negatively affects the nutrient content of the food, unlike local products that, after harvesting, are sold in a short time, preserving the freshness, taste, and quality of the product [2].

In relation to the practice of physical activity, there are very many studies that have shown how it is one of the most important protective factors against the development of numerous pathologies, reducing the risk of mortality and increasing life expectancy [8,9]. On the other hand, adequate night rest and characteristic naps are also protective factors against mortality from cardiovascular diseases, considering that both excess as well as lack of rest hours can become detrimental to health [5]. Likewise, socialization and participation in collective activities also provide the same benefits among the population, producing an increase in quality of life [2]. It can therefore be said that the MLS is a complex lifestyle formed by the interaction of different factors that provide great health benefits. Such benefits generally have been attributed only to dietary aspects, in which their protective role against diseases, such as diabetes, cancer, cardiovascular pathologies, obesity, and depression, is confirmed, without taking into account the other factors that configure the MLS [1,7]. Therefore, the MLS can be conceptualized as a complex lifestyle that is based on the interaction of different factors, which provide major combined health benefits. In fact, the MLS is considered a protective factor that reduces the risk of mortality and increases life expectancy [8,9].

According to numerous studies, the benefits of adhering to the MLS include a significant improvement in quality of life [10]. In this regard, many studies have shown that adherence to the MLS acts as a protective factor against chronic non-communicable diseases, including cardiovascular diseases, type 2 diabetes, hypertension [11–15], and metabolic syndrome [16], showing a lower prevalence of these diseases among people with strong adherence to the MLS [16]. In fact, the study by Hershey et al. showed that greater adherence to the MLS can be associated with 41% less mortality from cardiovascular disease [11]. Hence, MLS adherence acts as a protective factor against chronic diseases, especially in the elderly [10], given that adherence to this lifestyle is significantly associated with a lower risk of cardiovascular disease mortality [11–15]. Moreover, as previously indicated, adherence to the MLS is also closely related to a lower prevalence of metabolic syndrome [17] and has been linked to a lower development of glucose disorders in pregnant patients, subsequently reducing the rate of gestational diabetes [18]. In this sense, MLS adherence reduces the development of postpartum glucose disorders by 25%, and specifically by 35% in the rate of development of type 2 diabetes mellitus among women who have had gestational diabetes [18].

As for clinical populations, adherence to the MLS has been associated with an improved health status in renal disease groups that are not dialysis-dependent [16]. Adherence to the MLS among non-dialysis-dependent renal patients prevents progression of the disease [16]. Moreover, in a series of studies, Georgoulis et al. stated that adherence to the MLS is related to an improved cardiometabolic profile in patients with severe obstructive sleep apnea [19–21]. In this sense, a higher adherence to this lifestyle has been related to a reduction in the apnea and hypopnea index in daytime symptomatology, and it has been associated with an improvement in quality of life [19–21].

It should be added that adherence to the MLS not only has physical benefits, but also mental benefits, as it has been shown that adherence to the MLS reduces the risk of depression by 50% [22].

Despite the recognized importance of evaluating adherence to the MLS in different populations given its health benefits, to the best of our knowledge, there is no consensus as to the best strategy to reliably assess it. While some prior studies have used different questionnaires to evaluate the components of the MLS [10,19–21,23–28], others have used a specific index or questionnaire to assess global adherence to the MLS. However, little information exists with regard to the psychometric properties of the questionnaires created to examine the MLS [5]. Moreover, not all dimensions of the MLS have been included in the previously used evaluation strategies.

Given that past studies have relied on numerous heterogeneous assessment strategies and consensus has not yet been reached regarding the most valid and reliable strategy for the analysis of this type of lifestyle, this study attempted to systematically review and analyze the methodologies that were used in different studies to evaluate the MLS for both non-clinical and clinical populations. Moreover, the study was aimed to determine which components of the MLS were most frequently evaluated in past studies and which assessment instruments are currently being used to analyze these MLS components. Finally, the study also attempted to identify the psychometric properties of the available instruments that globally assess the MLS.

2. Materials and Methods

This study used a systematic review methodology that was based on the PRISMA statement [29].

2.1. Search Strategy

The main objective of the search strategy was to detect the published studies available in full text. The first step consisted of electronic searches carried out between December 2021 and May 2022 in the following databases: PubMed, Web of Science, Scopus, and Science Direct. This search strategy was designed to obtain original studies published on the assessment methods for MLS. A bulk search strategy was used by applying both descriptors and keywords in the titles and abstracts. Additionally, no date restrictions were applied to the articles' year of publication. Table 1 shows the search strategies used in the different databases.

Table 1. Search strategy.

Search Strategy
1. Mediterranean AND lifestyle (Title/Abstract/keyword)
2. "Mediterranean lifestyle" (Title/Abstract/keyword)
3."Mediterranean lifestyle" (Title/Abstract/keyword) AND Questionnaire (Title/Abstract/keyword)
4."Mediterranean lifestyle" (Title/Abstract/keyword) AND Review (Title/Abstract/keyword)
5."Mediterranean lifestyle" (Title/Abstract/keyword) AND Index (Title/Abstract/keyword)
6."Mediterranean lifestyle" (Title/Abstract/keyword) AND Evaluation (Title/Abstract/keyword)
7."Mediterranean lifestyle" (Title/Abstract/keyword) AND Assessment (Title/Abstract/keyword)

2.2. Inclusion and Exclusion Criteria

Inclusion criteria were (I) original articles in which at least two of the following MLS components were evaluated following the criteria proposed by Diolintzi et al. [2]: adherence to the Mediterranean Diet (MD), consumption of seasonal and locally grown products, participation in food preparation and culinary activities, regular physical activity, good hydration and adequate rest, including regular naps, and socialization; (II) articles that were available in full text and written in English or Spanish.

Exclusion criteria were (I) articles that were not related to the subject of the study; (II) articles having unreported results; (III) articles that did not refer to MLS assessment; (IV) articles that only referred to the Mediterranean Diet (MD); (V) articles that were reviews and meta-analyses; (VI) documents that were doctoral theses, reports, or conference summaries; and (VII) books and book chapters.

2.3. Selection of Studies

Once the search was performed in the databases, duplicates were discarded, as well as all works presented at congresses, reports, doctoral theses, and book chapters, among others.

The abstracts that were identified through the bibliographic search were independently evaluated by two authors to confirm whether or not the articles were valid according to the review's inclusion and exclusion criteria. Two authors of this paper evaluated each article independently and discrepancies were resolved by consulting with a third author.

2.4. Assessing the Methodological Quality of the Studies Included in the Review

The quality of each study was analyzed by applying a commonly used battery of instruments for the evaluation of methodological quality, CADIMA, which was developed at the Joanna Briggs Institute of the University of Adelaide, Australia [30]. This battery provides different evaluation instruments for each type of study design. Specifically, the instrument used for cross-sectional studies includes eight items, the instrument used for cohort studies has eleven items, and the instrument used for randomized trials contains thirteen items. All instruments include a response scale with four response options: "yes", "no", "unclear", or "not applicable". Two authors of this paper independently assessed the quality of each study included in the review and discrepancies were resolved by consulting with a third author. The results reflected an inter-subject reliability of between 0.60 and 0.85, according to Cohen's Kappa statistical parameter.

Tables S1–S3 in the Supplementary Material reveal the methodological quality of the assessment for the cross-sectional studies: randomized and cohort trials that were included in this review.

2.5. Data Extraction

The sample information extracted from each article consisted of the following elements: sample size, gender, origin, and age of the population under study. Regarding the information on the assessment methods, we extracted the Mediterranean Lifestyle components, the evaluation strategies used to analyze the MLS, the MLS evaluation instruments applied, and their psychometric properties. We also considered the study type and objective.

3. Results

3.1. Search Results

Table 2 shows the search strategies used in the different databases and details the corresponding number of total articles extracted per database.

Table 2. Bibliographic search strategies.

	PubMed	Scopus	Web of Science	Science Direct	Total
Mediterranean AND lifestyle (Title/Abstract/keyword)	1654	3536	2240	517	
"Mediterranean lifestyle" (Title/Abstract/keyword)	71	89	82	25	
"Mediterranean lifestyle" (Title/Abstract/keyword) AND Questionnaire (Title/Abstract/keyword)	10	18	10	0	
"Mediterranean lifestyle" (Title/Abstract/keyword) AND Review (Title/Abstract/keyword)	10	17	11	1	
"Mediterranean lifestyle" (Title/Abstract/keyword) AND Index (Title/Abstract/keyword)	24	27	22	8	
"Mediterranean lifestyle" (Title/Abstract/keyword) AND Evaluation (Title/Abstract/keyword)	5	8	4	5	
"Mediterranean lifestyle" (Title/Abstract/keyword) AND Assessment (Title/Abstract/keyword)	5	22	4	1	
Total	1772	3717	2373	557	8419
Total without duplicates					4707

As can be seen in Figure 1, a total of 8419 articles were obtained. After discarding duplicates, the total number was reduced to 4707 articles. A total of 3680 articles remained after discarding doctoral theses, reports, book chapters, etc. Following a review of the titles and abstracts, an additional 3484 articles were excluded. These articles were discarded mainly because they did not mention the MLS. Instead, they referred generally to lifestyles and included MD as a dietary pattern but did not name nor evaluate a minimum of two MLS components. In many other articles, the main objective was to evaluate the Mediterranean population's lifestyle, but without referencing the MLS as an LS. In these studies, the MD was the only characteristic relating directly to the Mediterranean population's LS, without considering any other characteristic component of the MLS.

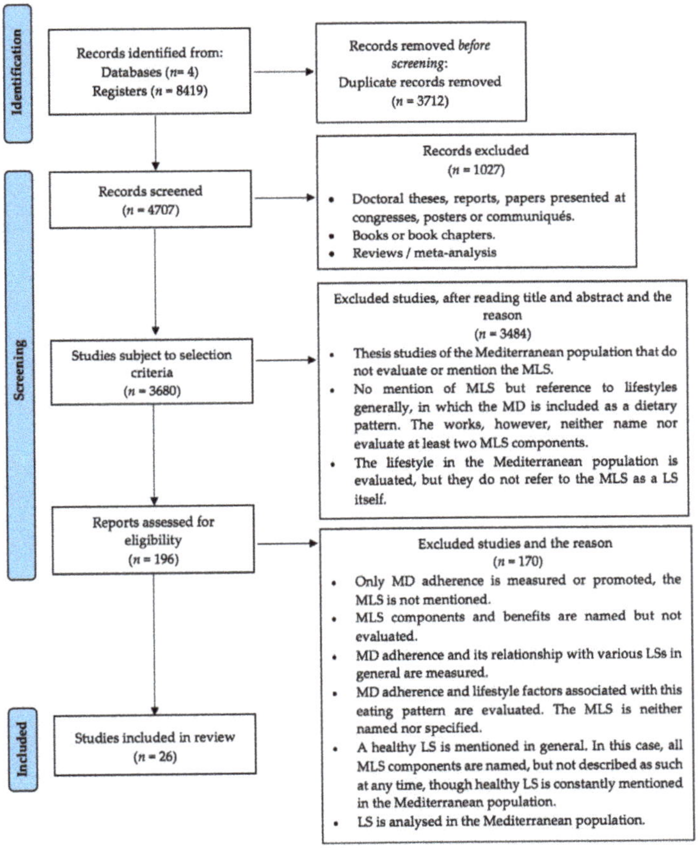

Figure 1. PRISMA flow diagram of studies evaluated in the systematic review.

After reading the full texts of the articles, an additional 170 were excluded. The reasons for their exclusion were as follows:

- MD adherence and its relationship with various LSs, in general, were measured. However, the MLS was not mentioned.
- MLS components and benefits were named but not evaluated.
- The Mediterranean population's LS was measured, and the MD was included, but no reference was made to the MLS nor its components.
- A healthy LS was mentioned in general. In this case, all MLS components were named but were not described as such at any time. Instead, a healthy LS in the Mediterranean population was constantly referred to.

Finally, after a rigorous search, a total of 26 articles were included in the review.

3.2. Characteristics of the Studies Included in the Review

Table 3 lists all of the studies that were used in the final review. The following information is listed per study: authors, study design, year of publication, country, population type, sample size, gender, age, and study objective.

Most of the articles considered a general population living in the Mediterranean Basin. However, some studies included participants having a specific pathology, such as: dementia [23], Chronic Renal Insufficiency [16], obesity and metabolic syndrome or sleep apnea [10,19–21], gestational diabetes [18], type 2 diabetes mellitus [31,32], and fatty liver disease [27].

The article having the largest number of participants had a sample size of 174,209 individuals [28]. In contrast, the study with the smallest sample size had a total of 63 participants [27]. With the exception of two articles, all of the articles specified the gender of the participants.

Most of the articles focused on a middle-aged population, except for one article, which focused on students aged 6 to 18 years old [28]. The study with the largest age range covered <30 to >70 years [33]. Finally, one article did not specify the age of its participants [26].

The main objective of all the articles was to evaluate the MLS in order to analyze the relationship between adherence to this lifestyle and other variables, either with other lifestyles [23,24,33], with the symptomatology of certain pathologies [10–17,22,25,28], or with the effectiveness of an intervention program in which the MLS was implemented in the daily lives of participants, comparing certain variables before and after the implementation of this LS [18–21,27,31,32]. Another study focused on the assessment of changes in adherence to the MLS after the COVID-19 pandemic [34]. Two other studies considered the designing of a questionnaire to measure MLS adherence and the verification of its reliability [5,35].

Of the studies included in this review, Table 3 reveals that nine were cross-sectional [12,16,17,23–25,28], ten were randomized controlled trials [10,15,18–21,27,31,32,35], and the remaining seven were cohort studies [5,11,13,14,22,26,33].

3.3. Conceptual Suitability

As illustrated in Table 3, the majority of the countries considered in the studies were part of the Mediterranean Basin—e.g., Spain, Italy, Greece, and Croatia—with the exception of the US and Australia, where a total of four studies were conducted [12,16,31,32]. In two other articles, collaboration took place between Mediterranean and non-Mediterranean countries, specifically Spain and Greece and the US [17,28].

The purpose of all of the studies was to evaluate the population's MLS adherence in order to promote this LS, and thereby use the results to demonstrate that high MLS adherence benefits the population's health, acting as a protective factor against various diseases, especially at a cardiovascular level. Therefore, the aim of the articles was both to promote MLS adherence among the population and to demonstrate its protective effect against different pathologies.

3.4. Applicability

In the study by Katsagoni et al. [28], the population sample was composed of students aged 16 to 18 years. Online questionnaires were used in the students' classrooms and there were trained teachers and/or Information Technology instructors who had been previously trained on the specific guidelines in order to help students correctly complete the questionnaires.

The remainder of the study questionnaires were administered by a trained dietitian, trained personnel, or through online questionnaires, in which the participants responded without the need for any external assistance.

Table 3. General characteristics of the studies included in the review.

Author(s)	Year	Country	Type of Population	Sample Size	Gender	Age				Objective of the Study	Study Design
						Average	SD	Range	Median		
Anastasiou et al. [23]	2018	Greece	Elderly population with dementia	n = 1716	Men: n = 693 Women: n = 1023	72.9	6.1	-	-	To investigate the relationship between cognitive function and LS, based on the MLS.	Cross-sectional study
Baldini et al. [24]	2009	Italy	University students from two Mediterranean regions (Italy/Spain)	n = 210	Men: n = 85 Women: n = 125	-	-	22–32	-	To compare the MLS between young Spaniards and Italians in order to check which group has the best LS.	Cross-sectional study
Bonaccio et al. [34]	2022	Italy	Elderly population	n =4400	Men: n = 1863 Women: n = 2537	-	-	65–99	-	To evaluate dietary changes during the COVID-19 pandemic.	Cross-sectional study
Bouzas et al. [10]	2020	Spain	Patients with obesity and metabolic syndrome	n = 6355	Men: n = 3268 Women: n = 3087	-	-	55–75	-	To analyze the association between adherence to the MLS and weight loss.	Randomized controlled trial
Bowden et al. [16]	2021	Australia	Patients with Chronic Renal Insufficiency	n = 99	Men: n = 64 Women: n = 35	73.2	10.5	-	-	To assess adherence to the MLS and its association with cardiometabolic markers and renal function in individuals with chronic renal failure who are not dependent on dialysis.	Cross-sectional study
Georgousopoulou et al. [25]	2017	Greece	Elderly population in the Mediterranean Basin	n = 2749	Men: n = 1369 Women: n = 1380	-	-	65–100	-	To assess the cardiovascular effects of adherence to the MLS.	Cross-sectional study
Georgoulis et al. [19]	2020	Greece	Overweight/ obese population + obstructive sleep apnea	n = 187 Standard LS n = 65 MD n = 62 MLS n = 60	Men: n = 141 Women: n = 46	49	10	-	-	To compare patients with severe obstructive sleep apnea by performing one or more of these three programs for six months: follow-up of a standard LS, MD adherence, or MLS adherence (MIMOSA Study).	Randomized controlled trial

Table 3. *Cont.*

Author(s)	Year	Country	Type of Population	Sample Size	Gender	Age				Objective of the Study	Study Design
						Average	SD	Range	Median		
Georgoulis et al. [20]	2020	Greece	Overweight/ obese population + obstructive sleep apnea	$n = 187$ Standard LS $n = 65$ MD $n = 62$ MLS $n = 60$	Men: $n = 141$ Women: $n = 46$	49	10	-	-	To measure the efficacy of interventions in patients with severe obstructive sleep apnea by implementing an MD or MLS adherence program (MIMOSA Study).	Randomized controlled trial
Georgoulis et al. [21]	2021	Greece	Overweight/ obese population + obstructive sleep apnea	$n = 187$ Standard LS $n = 65$ MD $n = 62$ MLS $n = 60$	Men: $n = 141$ Women: $n = 46$	49	10	-	-	To assess the efficacy of the MIMOSA program through MD or MLS adherence, and the prescription of continuous positive airway pressure (CPAP).	Randomized controlled trial
Grosso et al. [26]	2017	Italy	General population	Proposal of 1500 participants	-	-	-	-	-	To provide data to increase knowledge about the prevalence, incidence, and risk factors of age-related disorders in the Mediterranean region.	Cohort study
Hershey et al. [11]	2020	Spain	Graduate students	$n = 20{,}494$ Divided into four groups, according to the degree of MLS adherence, from lowest to highest adhesion: Q1: $n = 6390$ Q2: $n = 5783$ Q3: $n = 4820$ Q4: $n = 3501$	Men: $n = 8008$ Women: $n = 12{,}486$ Q1: Men: $n = 2681$ Women: $n = 3709$ Q2: Men: $n = 2348$ Women: $n = 3435$ Q3: Men: $n = 1857$ Women: $n = 2963$ Q4: Men: $n = 1122$ Women $n = 2379$	Q1: 37.25 Q2: 37.79 Q3: 37.94 Q4: 37.76	Q1: 12.46 Q2: 12.34 Q3: 12.34 Q4: 12.39	-	-	To associate the relationship between MLS and the causes of mortality.	Cohort study
Hershey et al. [17]	2021	US	US firefighters	$n = 249$ Divided into three groups according to MLS adherence, from lowest to highest adherence: T1: $n = 90$ T2: $n = 99$ T3: $n = 60$	Men: $n = 236$ Women: $n = 13$ T1: Men: $n = 88$ Women: $n = 2$ T2: Men: $n = 92$ Women: $n = 7$ T3: Men: $n = 56$ Women: $n = 4$	T1: 46.92 T2: 46.66 T3: 46.56	T1: 6.98 T2: 7.57 T3: 8.08	-	-	To associate the relationship between adherence to the MLS and metabolic syndrome in a non-Mediterranean population (US firefighters).	Cross-sectional study

Table 3. *Cont.*

Author(s)	Year	Country	Type of Population	Sample Size	Gender	Age				Objective of the Study	Study Design
						Average	SD	Range	Median		
Hershey et al. [36]	2021	Spain/US	General population	n = 15,279 Q1: n = 4865 Q2: n = 4387 Q3: n = 3520 Q4: n = 2507	Men: n = 6100 Women: n = 9179 Q1: Men: n = 1946 Women: n = 2919 Q2: Men: n = 1750 Women: n = 2637 Q3: Men: n = 1404 Women: n = 2116 Q4: Men: n = 1000 Women: n = 1507	Q1: 37.0 Q2: 37.0 Q3: 37.0 Q4: 37.0	Q1: 11.8 Q2: 11.5 Q3: 11.5 Q4: 11.7	-	-	To associate the relationship between the Mediterranean Lifestyle and the risk of depression.	Cohort study
Katsagoni et al. [28]	2020	Greece	Students aged 6 to 18 years	n = 174,209 Divided into three groups according to MLS adherence, from lowest to highest adherence: Low: n = 26,488 Average: n = 108,229 High: n = 39,492	Men: n = 89,174 Women: n = 85,035 Low: Men: n = 13,668 Women: n = 12,820 Average: Men: n = 55,089 Women: n = 53,140 High: Men: n = 20,417 Women: n = 19,075	-	-	-	Low: 11.8 Average: 11.2 High: 10.9	To analyze the relationship between adherence to the MLS and obesity in children and adolescents.	Cross-sectional study
Katsagoni et al. [27]	2018	Greece	Patients with fatty liver	n = 63 GC: n = 21 MDG MD: n = 21 MLG: n = 21	Men: n = 43 Women: n = 20 GC: Men: n = 13 Women: n = 8 MDG: Men: n = 13 Women: n = 8 MLG: Men: n = 17 Women: n = 4	-	-	-	GC: 47 MDG: 44 MLG: 48	Intervention to improve the weight of patients with fatty liver.	Randomized controlled trial
Lan et al. [12]	2020	USA	Active firefighters	n = 92 Divided into three groups according to MLS adherence, from lowest to highest adherence: Low: n = 10 Medium: n = 55 High: n = 27	Men: n = 89 Women: n = 3 Low: Men: n = 10 Women: n = 0 Medium: Men: n = 53 Women: n = 2 High: Men: n = 26 Women: n = 1	Low: 31.9 Medium: 27.6 High: 29.4	Low: 8.2 Medium: 3.9 High: 5.5	-	-	To analyze the relationship between adherence to the MLS and cardiovascular disease risk factors.	Cross-sectional study

Table 3. *Cont.*

Author(s)	Year	Country	Type of Population	Sample Size	Gender	Age				Objective of the Study	Study Design
						Average	SD	Range	Median		
Marventano et al. [33]	2017	Italy	Patients randomly selected from the lists of a group of doctors	n = 1952 Divided into four groups according to MD adherence, from lowest to highest adherence: Q1: n = 471 Q2: n = 600 Q3: n = 606 Q4: n = 285	Men: n = 813 Women: n = 1139 Q1: Men: n = 203 Women: n = 208 Q2: Men: n = 248 Women: n = 352 Q3: Men: n = 250 Women: n = 365 Q4: Men: n = 112 Women: n = 163	Range <30: 11.5 Range 30–39: 11.6 Range 40–49: 12.1 Range 50–59: 12.1 Range 60–69: 12.6 Range >70: 12.1	Range <30: 2.4 Range 30–39: 2.5 Range 40–49: 2.4 Range 50–59: 2.4 Range 60–69: 1.9 Range >70: 2.4	<30 30–39 4–49 50–59 60–69 >70	-	To evaluate the level of MD adherence and PA and its determinants in the Mediterranean healthy Eating, Aging, and Lifestyle (MEAL) study.	Cohort study
Mata-Fernández et al. [13]	2021	Spain	University graduates	n = 18,419 Divided into three groups according to MEDLIFE score: Low: n = 2928 Average: n = 9548 High: n = 5943	Men: n = 7267 Women: n = 11,152 Low: Men: n = 1232 Women: n = 1696 Medium: Men: n = 3976 Women: n = 5572 High: Men: n = 2059 Women: n = 3884	Low: 36.9 Medium: 38.3 High: 38.3	Low: 11.7 Medium: 12.2 High: 12.2	-	-	To assess the relationship between adherence to the MLS and the incidence of cardiovascular disease.	Cohort study
Pavicic-Žeželj et al. [15]	2018	Croatia	Workers in oil and gas companies	n = 366	Men: n = 177 Women: n = 189	37.2 Range <30: 26.8 Range 30–39: 35.1 Range 40–49: 44.0 Range ≥50: 52.3	8.6 Range <30: 1.4 Range 30–39: 2.5 Range 40–49: 2.7 Range ≥50: 1.9	<30 30–39 40–49 ≥50	-	To use the MEDLIFE questionnaire to analyze adherence to the MLS and compare the results with risk factors for cardiovascular pathologies.	Randomized controlled trial
Pérez-Ferre et al. [18]	2015	Spain	Pregnant women with gestational diabetes	n = 230 GC: n = 111 GI: n = 126	Women: n = 260	-	-	GC: 32–38 GI: 31–38	-	To perform an intervention in the LS implementing the MLS, in order to prevent glucose alterations in pregnant women with gestational diabetes.	Randomized controlled trial
Sánchez-Villegas et al. [22]	2016	Spain	University graduates	n = 11,800	Percentages: MD: T1 Men: 40.1 Women: 59.1 MD: T3 Men: 43.1 Women: 56.9 PA: T1 Men: 33.6 Women: 66.4 PA: T3 Men: 48.1 Women: 51.9 S: T1 Men: 51.9 Women: 48.1 S: T3 Men: 29.2 Women: 70.8	MD: T1: 34.3 MD: T3: 41.3 PA: T1: 36.8 PA: T3: 37.9 S: T1: 42.0 S: T3: 32.4	MD: T1: 10.0 MD: T3: 10.9 PA: T1: 10.9 PA: T3: 12.0 S: T1: 10.8 S: T3: 10.6	-	-	To analyze the relationship between depression and MLS, based on diet (MD), physical activity (PA), and socialization (S).	Cohort study

Table 3. *Cont.*

Author(s)	Year	Country	Type of Population	Sample Size	Gender	Age				Objective of the Study	Study Design
						Average	SD	Range	Median		
Sotos-Prieto et al. [14]	2021	Spain	General population	n = 11,090 Divided into four groups according to MEDLIFE score, from lowest to highest: Q1: n = 3. 042 Q2: n = 3. 435 Q3: n = 2. 917 Q4: n = 1. 696	Men: n = 5910 Women: n = 5181 Q1: Men: n = 1372 Women: n = 1670 Q2: Men: n = 1614 Women: n = 1821 Q3: Men: n = 1386 Women: n = 1531 Q4: Men: n = 807 Women: n = 889	Q1: 47.8 Q2: 45.8 Q3: 45.9 Q4: 46.3	Q1: 17.0 Q2: 16.1 Q3: 16.0 Q4: 15.0	-	-	To evaluate the MLS and its relationship with the risk of suffering from cardiovascular diseases.	Cohort study
Sotos-Prieto et al. [5]	2014	Spain	Workers at an automobile assembly plant	n = 988	-	-	-	40–55	-	To design a questionnaire that measures MLS adherence.	Cohort study
Sotos-Prieto et al. [35]	2015	Spain	Public school workers and family members involved in the school environment	n = 196	Men: n = 30 Women: n = 166	41.4	9.2	-	-	To study the reliability of the MEDLIFE questionnaire as a research tool.	Randomized controlled trial
Toobert et al. [31]	2005	USA	Post-menopausal women with type 2 diabetes mellitus	n = 279 GC: n = 116 GI: n = 163	Women: n = 279	61	-	39–74	-	To intervene in a population sample in which LS changes are implemented based on the MLS.	Randomized controlled trial
Toobert et al. [32]	2010	USA	Post-menopausal women with type 2 diabetes mellitus	n = 279 GC: n = 116 GI: n = 163	Women: n = 279	61	-	39–74	-	To examine the long-term effects of healthy behavioral changes following the implementation of the MLS program.	Randomized controlled trial

Lifestyle; MD: Mediterranean Diet; MLS: Mediterranean Lifestyle; Q: quartile; T: Tercile; GC: control group; MDG: group receiving a Mediterranean Diet intervention; MLG: group receiving a Mediterranean Lifestyle intervention; GI: intervention group; MD: T1: variable analysis group Mediterranean Diet: Tercile 1; MD: T3: variable analysis group Mediterranean Diet: Tercile 3; MLS: T1: variable analysis group Mediterranean Lifestyle: Tercile 1; MLS: T3: variable analysis group Mediterranean Lifestyle: Tercile 3; S: T1: variable analysis group socialization: Tercile 1; S: T3: variable analysis group socialization: Tercile 3.

3.5. Components of the Mediterranean Lifestyle Evaluated in Each Study

Table 4 includes the MLS components evaluated in each study. To analyze these components, the guidelines published in the study by Diolintzi et al. [2] were followed. The table shows that no article fully evaluated the MLS since none of them included participation in food preparation. MD adherence and the practice of physical activity (PA) were evaluated in all of them. Four studies focused on these two components [10,18,24,33], five also included night-time sleep [19–21,23,28], and three included MD, PA, and socialization [18,31,32]. Another study included MD, PA, and the use of locally grown, seasonal products [34]. Only six articles evaluated all of the MLS components, with the exception of the participation in food preparation and the consumption of locally grown and seasonal products [5,11,14,15,35,36]. Moreover, only two articles assessed all but one of the components, food preparation [16,17].

Table 4. Mediterranean Lifestyle components evaluated in each study.

Author(s)	Mediterranean Lifestyle Components							
	Mediterranean Diet	Hydration	Use of Seasonal/Locally Grown Products	Participation in Food Preparation	Physical Activity	Socialization	Rest (Napping)	Sleep (h/Night)
Anastasiou et al. [23]	+	-	-	-	+	-	-	+
Baldini et al. [24]	+	-	-	-	+	-	-	-
Bonaccio et al. [34]	+	-	+	-	+	-	-	-
Bouzas et al. [10]	+	-	-	-	+	-	-	-
Bowden et al. [16]	+	+	+	-	+	+	+	+
Georgousopoulou et al. [25]	+	-	-	-	+	+	+	-
Georgoulis et al. [19]	+	-	-	-	+	-	-	+
Georgoulis et al. [20]	+	-	-	-	+	-	-	+
Georgoulis et al. [21]	+	-	-	-	+	-	-	+
Grosso et al. [26]	+	-	-	-	+	+	-	+
Hershey et al. [11]	+	+	-	-	+	+	+	+
Hershey et al. [17]	+	+	+	-	+	+	+	+
Hershey et al. [36]	+	+	+	-	+	+	+	+
Katsagoni et al. [28]	+	-	-	-	+	-	+	+
Katsagoni et al. [27]	+	-	-	-	+	-	-	+
Lan et al. [12]	+	-	-	-	+	-	+	+
Marventano et al. [33]	+	-	-	-	+	-	-	-
Mata-Fernández et al. [13]	+	+	-	-	+	+	+	+
Pavicic-Žeželj et al. [15]	+	+	-	-	+	+	+	+
Pérez-Ferre et al. [18]	+	-	-	-	+	-	-	-

Table 4. *Cont.*

Author(s)	Mediterranean Lifestyle Components							
	Mediterranean Diet	Hydration	Use of Seasonal/Locally Grown Products	Participation in Food Preparation	Physical Activity	Socialization	Rest (Napping)	Sleep (h/Night)
Sánchez-Villegas et al. [22]	+	-	-	-	+	+	-	-
Sotos-Prieto et al. [14]	+	+	-	-	+	+	+	+
Sotos-Prieto et al. [5]	+	+	-	-	+	+	+	+
Sotos-Prieto et al. [35]	+	+	-	-	+	+	+	+
Toobert et al. [31]	+	-	-	-	+	+	-	-
Toobert et al. [32]	+	-	-	-	+	+	-	-

3.6. Evaluation Strategies Used to Analyze MLS Components

Table 5 was created with the purpose of organizing all of the extracted information and summarizing the different evaluation strategies used by the authors to analyze each MLS component.

It shows all of the MLS components together with the questionnaires or self-reported ad hoc questions that were used to evaluate each dimension, with the exception of six studies, which exclusively used a tool to analyze the MLS components globally. The MEDLIFE questionnaire, the MedCOVID-19 score, the Total Lifestyle Index (TLI), MEDiLIFE-index, and MEDI-Lifestyle index were used [12,16,23,28,34,36]. It should be noted that, in one of the studies, instead of applying the previously validated 28-item MEDLIFE questionnaire, Bowden et al. [16] used an initial pilot 32-item questionnaire that was created by the original authors, which included 4 questions that could not be validated in a second study [35]. In addition to all the ad hoc questions used for the assessment of each MLS component, both the MEDiLIFE-index and MEDI-Lifestyle indices do not include the assessment of MD adherence, but require a specific questionnaire for their evaluation, and therefore include the KIDMED and PREDIMED questionnaires, respectively. In this sense, the TLI index is made up of different questionnaires that assess each MLS dimension separately, such as the MedDiet Score questionnaire for MD adherence, the Athens Physical Activity Questionnaire (APAQ), the sleep scale of the Medical Outcomes Study (MOS), and the Sleep Index II.

In addition, seven articles used the MEDLIFE tool in combination with other questionnaires to evaluate certain dimensions of the MLS separately [5,11,13–15,17,35]. Hershey et al. [17] modified the original MEDLIFE questionnaire, making variations in a total of nine items.

Regarding the other studies, each MLS component was evaluated using different, previously validated, and specific questionnaires [10,18–22,24–27,31,32].

Table 5. Assessment tools used to analyze MLS components.

Author(s)	Mediterranean Lifestyle Components							
	Mediterranean Diet	**Hydration**	**Use of Seasonal/Locally Grown Products**	**Participation in Food Preparation**	**Physical Activity**	**Socialization**	**Rest (Naps)**	**Sleep (h/Night)**
Anastasiou et al. [23]	MedDiet Score [37]	-	-	-	Athens Physical Activity Questionnaire (APAQ) [38]	-	-	Medical Outcomes Study (MOS) Sleep Scale [39] Sleep Index II [40]
Baldini et al. [24]	Food Frequency Questionnaire (FFQ/FFQ-143/FFQ-136/FFQ-76) [41] MedDiet Score [37]	-	-	-	International Physical Activity Questionnaire (IPAQ) [42]	-	-	-
Bonaccio et al. [34]	MedCOVID-19 [34]	-	MedCOVID-19 [34]	-	MedCOVID-19 [34]	-	-	-
Bouzas et al. [10]	Food Frequency Questionnaire (FFQ/FFQ-143/FFQ-136/FFQ-76) [41] MedDiet Score [37]	-	-	-	Nurses' Health Study [43] Minnesota-REGICOR [44,45]	-	-	-
Bowden et al. [16]	MEDLIFE [35]	MEDLIFE [35]	MEDLIFE [35]	-	MEDLIFE [35]	MEDLIFE [35]	MEDLIFE [35]	MEDLIFE [35]
Georgousopoulou et al. [25]	Food Frequency Questionnaire (FFQ/FFQ-143/FFQ-136/FFQ-76) [41] MedDiet Score [37]	-	-	-	International Physical Activity Questionnaire (IPAQ) [42]	Short ad hoc self-reported questions	Ad hoc dichotomous questions	-
Georgoulis et al. [19]	Food Frequency Questionnaire (FFQ/FFQ-143/FFQ-136/FFQ-76) [41] MedDiet Score [37]	-	-	-	International Physical Activity Questionnaire (IPAQ) [42]	-	-	Short ad hoc self-reported questions
Georgoulis et al. [20]	Food Frequency Questionnaire (FFQ/FFQ-143/FFQ-136/FFQ-76) [41] MedDiet Score [37]	-	-	-	International Physical Activity Questionnaire (IPAQ) [42]	-	-	Short ad hoc self-reported questions

Table 5. *Cont.*

Author(s)	Mediterranean Lifestyle Components							
	Mediterranean Diet	**Hydration**	**Use of Seasonal/Locally Grown Products**	**Participation in Food Preparation**	**Physical Activity**	**Socialization**	**Rest (Naps)**	**Sleep (h/Night)**
Georgoulis et al. [21]	Food Frequency Questionnaire (FFQ/FFQ-143/FFQ-136/FFQ-76) [41] MedDiet Score	-	-	-	International Physical Activity Questionnaire (IPAQ) [42]	-	-	Short ad hoc self-reported questions
Grosso et al. [26]	Food Frequency Questionnaire (FFQ/FFQ-143/FFQ-136/FFQ-76) [41]	-	-	-	International Physical Activity Questionnaire (IPAQ) [42]	Short ad hoc self-reported question	-	Pittsburgh Sleep Quality Index (PAQI) [46]
Hershey et al. [11]	Food Frequency Questionnaire (FFQ/FFQ-143/FFQ-136/FFQ-76) [41] MEDLIFE [35]	MEDLIFE [35]	-	-	MEDLIFE [35]	MEDLIFE [35]	MEDLIFE [35]	MEDLIFE [35]
Hershey et al. [17]	Food Frequency Questionnaire (FFQ/FFQ-143/FFQ-136/FFQ-76) [41] MEDLIFE [35]	MEDLIFE [35]	MEDLIFE [35]	-	MEDLIFE [35]	MEDLIFE [35]	MEDLIFE [35]	MEDLIFE [35]
Hershey et al. [36]	FFQ-136 [41] MEDLIFE [35]	MEDLIFE [35]	MEDLIFE [35]		MEDLIFE [35] Nurses' Health Study [43]	MEDLIFE [35]	MEDLIFE [35]	MEDLIFE [35]
Katsagoni et al. [28]	Food Frequency Questionnaire (FFQ/FFQ-143/FFQ-136/FFQ-76) [41] MedDiet Score [37]	-	-	-	Athens Physical Activity Questionnaire (APAQ) [38]	-	Ad hoc dichotomous question	Short ad hoc self-reported question Athens Insomnia Scale [47]
Katsagoni et al. [27]	KIDMED (included in the MEDiLIFE-index questionnaire) [48]	-	-	-	Short ad hoc self-reported question	-	-	Short ad hoc self-reported question

Table 5. *Cont.*

Author(s)	Mediterranean Lifestyle Components							
	Mediterranean Diet	Hydration	Use of Seasonal/Locally Grown Products	Participation in Food Preparation	Physical Activity	Socialization	Rest (Naps)	Sleep (h/Night)
Lan et al. [12]	PREDIMED [49]	-	-	-	Short self-reported questions (h/week), based on the Metabolic Equivalent Activity Index (MET)	-	Ad hoc dichotomous question	Ad hoc dichotomous question
Marventano et al. [33]	Food Frequency Questionnaire (FFQ/FFQ-143/FFQ-136/FFQ-76) [41]	-	-	-	International Physical Activity Questionnaire (IPAQ) [42]	-	-	-
Mata-Fernández et al. [13]	Food Frequency Questionnaire (FFQ/FFQ-143/FFQ-136/FFQ-76) [41] MEDLIFE [35]	MEDLIFE [35]	-	-	MEDLIFE [35]	MEDLIFE [35]	MEDLIFE [35]	MEDLIFE [35]
Pavicic-Žeželj et al. [15]	Food Frequency Questionnaire (FFQ/FFQ-143/FFQ-136/FFQ-76) [41] MEDLIFE [35]	MEDLIFE [35]	-	-	International Physical Activity Questionnaire (IPAQ) [42] MEDLIFE [35]	Short ad hoc self-reported question MEDLIFE [35]	Short ad hoc self-reported question MEDLIFE [35]	Short ad hoc self-reported question MEDLIFE [35]
Pérez-Ferre et al. [18]	Food Frequency Questionnaire (FFQ/FFQ-143/FFQ-136/FFQ-76) [41]	-	-	-	Three questions taken from the "Lifestyle questionnaire" [50]	-	-	-
Sánchez-Villegas et al. [22]	Food Frequency Questionnaire (FFQ/FFQ-143/FFQ-136/FFQ-76) [41]	-	-	-	Short self-reported questionnaire of a total of 17 activities (h/week), based on the Metabolic Equivalent Activity Index (MET)	Short ad hoc self-reported question	-	-

Table 5. *Cont.*

Author(s)	Mediterranean Lifestyle Components							
	Mediterranean Diet	Hydration	Use of Seasonal/Locally Grown Products	Participation in Food Preparation	Physical Activity	Socialization	Rest (Naps)	Sleep (h/Night)
Sotos-Prieto et al. [14]	Food Frequency Questionnaire (FFQ/FFQ-143/FFQ-136/FFQ-76) [41] MEDLIFE [35]	MEDLIFE [35]	-	-	Nurses' Health Study [43] Health Professionals Follow-up Study (HPFS) physical activity questionnaires [51,52] MEDLIFE [35]	Short ad hoc self-reported question MEDLIFE [35]	Short ad hoc self-reported question MEDLIFE [35]	Short ad hoc self-reported question MEDLIFE [35]
Sotos-Prieto et al. [5]	Food Frequency Questionnaire (FFQ/FFQ-143/FFQ-136/FFQ-76) [41] MEDLIFE [35]	MEDLIFE [35]	MEDLIFE [35]	-	Nurses' Health Study [43] Health Professionals Follow-up Study (HPFS) physical activity questionnaires [51,52] MEDLIFE [35]	Short ad hoc self-reported question MEDLIFE [35]	MEDLIFE [35]	Short ad hoc self-reported question MEDLIFE [35]
Sotos-Prieto et al. [35]	MEDLIFE [35]	MEDLIFE [35]	-	-	Validated European Prospective EPIC Cohort Questionnaire [53] MEDLIFE [35]	MEDLIFE [35]	MEDLIFE [35]	MEDLIFE [35]
Toobert et al. [31]	Food Frequency Questionnaire (FFQ/FFQ-143/FFQ-136/FFQ-76) [41]	-	-	-	CHAMBS [54]	UCLA Social Support Inventory [55]	-	-
Toobert et al. [32]	Food Frequency Questionnaire (FFQ/FFQ-143/FFQ-136/FFQ-76) [41]	-	-	-	CHAMBS [54]	Short ad hoc self-reported question UCLA Social Support Inventory [55]	-	-

3.7. Indices for the Assessment of MLS

MEDiLIFE-index [28]

This index relies on a 3-point scoring system (0-1-2) and has a maximum final score of 8 points (the sum of all questionnaire components). The higher the score, the better the adherence to the MLS.

To evaluate MD adherence, the KIDMED questionnaire was applied. KIDMED ≥ 8 (high adherence) received 2 points; KIDMED 4 to 7 received 1 point; and KIDMED ≤ 3 received 0 points (weak adhesion). PA was measured as follows: 2 points for PA ≥ 60 min/day; 1 point for PA ≥ 30 and < 60 min/day; and 0 points for PA <30 min/day. For a sedentary lifestyle, 2 points were given for <1 h/d watching TV, videos, screens, etc.; 1 point for ≥ 1 and ≤ 2 h/d of sedentary activities; and 0 points for >2 h/d. For sleep, the American Academy of Sleep Medicine Guidelines were followed, taking into account the different age ranges (6–12 years 9/12 h; 13–18years 8/10 h): 2 points were given if the optimal duration was achieved; 1 point if the duration was longer; and 0 points if the duration was shorter. As observed, this questionnaire used short questions, and another questionnaire was used to measure MD adherence (the KIDMED questionnaire).

MEDI-Lifestyle [12]

This index consists of seven short ad hoc dichotomous questions. Scores range from 0 to 7, with a score of 7 representing the best degree of adherence, and 0 the poorest. The individual's weight was evaluated via BMI, receiving 1 point for a BMI <30 kg/m^2 and 0 points for a BMI ≥ 30 kg/m^2. Tobacco consumption was also included: 1 point if the person had not smoked in the last 6 months, 0 points if they smoked. The PREDIMED questionnaire evaluated the MD, receiving 1 point for high MD adherence (≥ 9) and 0 points for poor adherence (≤ 9). PA was also evaluated, with physically active individuals (≥ 16 h/week) receiving 1 point and physically inactive individuals (<16 h/week) receiving 0 points. Time watching TV received 1 point for <2 h/d and 0 points for ≥ 2 h/d. For sleep, 1 point was given for 7–8 h/d and 0 points for sleep <7 h or >8 h/d. Regarding naps, 1 point was given if a nap was taken, and 0 points were given if no nap was taken. In this case, two factors were included in the index that are not included in the MLS: weight and smoking.

Total Lifestyle Index (TLI) [23]

This index evaluates four dimensions of LS and includes a specific questionnaire for each: diet (MedDiet Score), physical activity (APAQ), sleep quality (MOS and Sleep Index II), and Instrumental Activities of Daily Living (IADL). The results obtained in each questionnaire were divided into quartiles. Values were assigned from 0, for the first quartile (worst score), to 1, 2, and 3 for the other quartiles (higher scores). The total TLI score ranged from 0 to 12. Higher values indicated a more beneficial LS. As in the MEDI-Lifestyle index, a factor that was not part of the MLS was also included: the Instrumental Activities of Daily Living.

MedCOVID-19 Score [34]

This questionnaire assesses the current intake of nine foods from the Mediterranean Diet and five MLS-related behaviors, in terms of decreased, maintained, or increased intake, making comparisons between 2019 and autumn 2020.

To estimate the dietary rating, the following scores were assigned:

- Score +1 point for the increased intake of foods that should be consumed more frequently (i.e., fruits, vegetables, legumes, cereals, fish, and olive oil), −1 point if their intake decreased, and 0 points if it remained the same.
- Score +1 point for the lowest self-reported intake of foods that should be consumed less frequently (i.e., meats, dairy products), −1 point for the highest intake, and 0 points if it remained the same.
- Score -1 point if the consumption of alcoholic beverages increased, +1 point if it decreased, and 0 points if it remained the same.
- Score +1 point for all dietary changes in behaviors related to the Mediterranean Lifestyle, i.e., (a) increased consumption of local and (b) ecological food; (c) increased physical activity; (d) decreased intake of home delivery food; and (e) decreased

consumption of pre-cooked foods: −1 point for changes in undesired behaviors, and 0 points if they remained the same.

Diet and behavior scores were equaled to obtain a total mark ranging from −14 to 14. Once the score had been calculated, the population was classified as follows: stable population (score = 0), population with an improved MLS (>1), and population with a worsened MLS (score < 0).

MEDLIFE questionnaire [5,35]

This questionnaire was designed specifically to evaluate the MLS, without using other supplementary questionnaires to analyze each dimension separately.

It is divided into three blocks. The first block consists of 15 items and measures the consumption of Mediterranean foods. The second block is composed of seven items and measures the habits of the Mediterranean Diet, including hydration. The third block includes six items and measures PA, rest, social habits, and conviviality. The range varies from 0 (low MLS adherence) to 28 (high MLS adherence).

To analyze the reliability of the questionnaire, Cohen's Kappa coefficient, the intraclass correlation coefficient (ICC), and the limit of agreement (LOA) were used. A comparison was performed using a 142-item questionnaire (full-Q) from which the 28 items constituting the MEDLIFE questionnaire were derived [5,35].

According to the authors, the MEDLIFE questionnaire is a valid instrument to measure MLS adherence in middle-aged adults and can be used for clinical and epidemiological studies in this population. Its generalizability and predictive validity have yet to be examined [35].

In a study by Sotos-Prieto et al. [35], 4 additional questions were included to evaluate food seasonality and moderation, resulting in a 32-item instrument. Despite this, they were not included in the final questionnaire since a comparison with other tools was not possible. Thus, their validity could not be evaluated, and they were excluded from this questionnaire. However, this 32-item questionnaire was used in a recent study by Bowden et al. [16].

The original MEDLIFE questionnaire was also modified in another study. The following specific changes were made [17].

- Block 1 (Mediterranean food consumption):

1. The item relating to the consumption of processed meats was eliminated.
2. The item relating to the consumption of nuts and olives was changed to the consumption of nuts.
3. The item relating to the consumption of herbs, spices, and garnishes was eliminated.

- Block 2 (Mediterranean dietary habits):

1. The item relating to the consumption of wine was changed to the consumption of wine or other common alcoholic beverages.
2. The item "limit nibbling between meals" was removed.
3. The item "consumption of local, seasonal, or organic products" was added.

- Block 3 (PA, rest, social habits, and conviviality):

1. The items "going out with friends" and "practice team sports" were eliminated.
2. The item "time spent eating" was added.

For the modified MEDLIFE questionnaire [17], scores varied from 0 to 26, following the same criteria as the original questionnaire. Although it is indicated that the modified MEDLIFE questionnaire presents a total of 26 items, it only includes 25.

3.8. Statistical Analysis Conducted to Create a Mediterranean Lifestyle Score in the Studies Included in the Review

Table 6 shows the different methods that researchers have suggested so far to create a questionnaire or index for assessing the MLS as a global dimension. Thus, most of the studies have employed different statistical analyses to integrate punctuations from diet adherence or dietary intake, sleep quality, or physical activity in a global MLS score. Moreover, the methodologies used to examine the structure of these questionnaires or indices are related to PCA, KMO, and also reliability and validity analyses [5,28,34,35].

Table 6. Statistical analysis to create a Mediterranean Lifestyle score in the studies included in the review that have created an index or questionnaire.

Authors	MLS Index/Questionnaire	Psychometric Analysis	Global MLS Component
Anastasiou et al. [23]	TLI: Total Lifestyle Index	-	The total score is calculated by adding up the scores of the index's dimensions distributed into different quartiles. The global MLS score ranges from 0 to 12.
Katsagoni et al. [28]	MEDiLIFE-index.	Principal Component Analysis (PCA) > 0.3 Kaiser–Meyer–Olkin (KMO) = 0.5	The total score is calculated by adding up the scores of the index's dimensions. Each dimension is evaluated by a 3-point rating scale (0-1-2) The global MLS score ranges from 0 to 8.
Lan et al. [12]	MEDI-Lifestyle	-	The total score is calculated by adding up the scores of the index's dimensions. Each dimension is categorized dichotomously (0-1). The global MLS score ranges from 0 to 7.
Bonaccio et al. [34]	MedCOVID-19 Score	Reliability: Internal consistency Cronbach's alpha coefficient = 0.83	The global score is obtained by adding up all the dimensions' scores. The dimensions are scored from −1 to +1. This total MLS score ranges from −14 to 14.
Sotos-Prieto et al. [5,35]	MEDLIFE	Convergent validity: – Degree of correlation between the two instruments: 0.626 Reliability: – Internal consistency Cronbach's alpha coefficient = 0.75 – Inter-rater correlation coefficient: 0.544 – Limits of agreement: from 4.66 to 7.45 (Mean = 1.40) – Kappa coefficient: Very good concordance (k = 0.81–1) was observed for 'limit salt in meals', 'nibbling', and 'nap' (10.7% of the items). Good (k = 0.61-0.80) to moderate (k = 0.41–0.60) agreement was found for most of the items evaluated (21.4%) such as wine, moderate consumption of red meat, legumes, fruit, and olive oil consumption) and fair (0.21–0.40) for 32.1% of the items.	The total score is calculated by adding up the scores of all the items. Each item was scored dichotomously (0-1). The total MLS score ranges from 0 to 28.

4. Discussion

This systematic review focused on 26 studies that addressed the different means of assessing the Mediterranean Lifestyle [5,10–28,31–36]. This is the first review of its kind that identifies and analyzes the strategies used in the scientific literature to examine this lifestyle.

MLS is characterized by an adherence to the MD, proper hydration, the use of locally grown and seasonal products, participation in culinary activities, physical activity, and socialization, as well as adequate rest, both at night and through daytime napping [2]. Although numerous studies have supposedly analyzed the MLS, many of them have failed to examine its components as a general construct of lifestyle [10,19–21,23–28].

All of the reviewed articles assessed the adherence to the MLS components of MD and the practice of PA. The other most frequently evaluated components include socialization, sleep, and napping. The least commonly evaluated MLS dimensions were hydration and the use of seasonal/locally grown products, which were included in the MEDLIFE questionnaire. Moreover, not all of the components making up the MLS were fully evaluated, since none of the studies assessed participation in culinary activities.

Only six articles exclusively used specific strategies to evaluate the MLS [12,16,23,28,34,36], generating the MEDiLIFE-index, MEDI-Lifestyle, Total Lifestyle Index (TLI), MedCOVID-19 Score, and MEDLIFE questionnaires.

Despite the existence of three indices and two specific questionnaires for the evaluation of the MLS, the MEDLIFE questionnaire appears to be the only tool having adequate psychometric properties. However, it has only been validated for an adult population and not for young or elderly populations. While the studies included in this review mainly used validated tools to assess different MLS components, they did so in an independent manner. Only four of the studies relied on global indices that were created through statistical processes to integrate the different evaluated dimensions and perform a global analysis of the MLS [12,23,28,34]. However, after carrying out this systematic review, we have yet to find a tool having these qualities. It has been suggested, therefore, that MEDLIFE is the best instrument for providing an assessment of adherence to the MLS. Until a new tool is developed, this questionnaire appears to be the most appropriate one for analyzing adherence, even though it does not include all the components of this lifestyle [2,5]. Once a new tool with appropriate psychometric properties has been created, it should be validated for the general and clinical population.

Data on the psychometric properties of MLS questionnaires are almost nonexistent. Measures of reliability and validity are quite scarce. Sotos-Prieto et al. [35] and Bonaccio et al. [34] have offered some evidence regarding psychometric properties. The former reported intraclass correlation coefficients and Kappa coefficients that demonstrate the reliability and validity of the MEDLIFE questionnaire, respectively. Bonaccio et al. [34] revealed adequate reliability for the MedCOVID-19 score with a Cronbach's alpha coefficient of 0.83. However, both internal consistency (via Cronbach's alpha coefficient) and test–retest reliability and equivalence reliability must be considered in order to reveal the instrument's level of accuracy with regard to the construction of an assessment [56]. Moreover, scientific papers state that convergent, concurrent, predictive, and construct validity are different gold standards to evaluate this psychometric aspect [56]. They provide information on the relationship between new and validated tools that share the same construct. Katsagoni et al. [28] show a principal component analysis and KMO values, in relation to the structure of the instruments. The Confirmatory Factor Analysis (CFA) is a powerful statistical tool for the development of measurement instruments [57]. CFA and its analytic version, the Exploratory Factor Analysis (EFA), play an essential role in measurement model validation in this regard [57].

Concerning the methods used to create questionnaires for evaluating MLS, four studies included in this systematic review have merely described how researchers have attempted to generate MLS assessment tools. One of them showed a PCA and KMO to determine the intern structure of the questionnaire [28]. Moreover, both Bonaccio et al. and

Sotos-Prieto et al. [5,34] also run psychometric analysis such as the reliability of the questionnaire they created. However, it seems extremely difficult to find studies which indicate the psychometric properties of the tools they have created to assess the MLS. As far as psychometrics is concerned, Muñiz and Fonseca-Pedrero [58,59] stated that both qualitative and quantitative methods should be included when constructing a new assessment tool. These authors have indeed suggested that reliability, convergent validity, and factor structure are needed to demonstrate the accuracy and veracity of evaluating the construct [58,60]. It goes without saying that the test construction process needs to be explained in detail, considering all the theoretical and metric principles, since these kinds of studies do not appear to be automatic or universal [58,59,61,62]. Following strictly the guidelines for creating assessment instruments written by Muñiz and Fonseca-Pedrero [58,59], the psychometric model used, the type of item response, the application form, and the assessment context should be considered for the construction of a high-quality evaluation tool.

Strengths and Limitations

This study offers considerable advances in the examination of evaluation strategies used to analyze the MLS in different populations. However, it has certain limitations that should be taken into consideration. For instance, only four relevant databases were searched. Moreover, although a wide variety of keywords were used, some specific words may not have been identified and included in the search strategies. Moreover, the fact that only articles available in full text were evaluated for inclusion in the revision could also limit the search strategy. However, in this case, all the evaluated studies were found in full text and could be fully assessed for inclusion or non-inclusion in the review. Furthermore, although many studies aim to assess the MLS, they appear to only assess MD adherence or to not explicitly state that MLS is evaluated, potentially hindering the identification of the studies that assess the MLS as a whole. Some articles evaluate two or more components of the MLS but do not name them as such, assigning all of the benefits of this LS exclusively to MD adherence. Therefore, many benefits attributed to the MD may also be derived from MLS adherence, although they are not identified as such in the studies.

Despite these limitations, an exhaustive systematic review was carried out in this study, demonstrating that the MLS is being examined in an increasing number of works. The strengths and limitations of each evaluation strategy performed in the different studies were also evaluated. This analysis provides objective and reliable data on the importance of using a tool with adequate psychometric properties that is capable of performing a comprehensive assessment of all of the dimensions that constitute the MLS.

5. Conclusions

The MLS is considered to be a healthy lifestyle in which the frequency and quantity of the consumption of certain foods play a key role. It is also a lifestyle that refers to other dimensions rooted in traditional Mediterranean life, as well as the interrelation between parameters such as socialization, physical activity, leisure activities, proper rest, and diet.

This systematic review attempted to consider all of the methods used to evaluate the MLS. A total of four indices specifically designed for assessment were obtained. However, none of the methods evaluated all of the dimensions that constitute the MLS. Although MEDLIFE may be one of the most reliable and integrating questionnaires for the assessment of the MLS, other psychometric properties of this instrument should be analyzed in depth, such as its factorial structure and functioning in both clinical and healthy populations.

A notable limitation of the current evaluation strategies is the heterogeneity of the tools used to evaluate the MLS, since different authors use distinct methods of analysis. No consensus has yet been reached on a single instrument to comprehensively and reliably measure the MLS that has proven and adequate psychometric properties. Therefore, future studies should attempt to design a tool with appropriate psychometric properties for the general population and include all of the MLS dimensions.

This would allow professionals to carry out more accurate analyses of the level of adherence to a healthy lifestyle and would lead to the identification of populations at risk of developing different pathologies. Moreover, this tool would aid in the creation of comprehensive intervention programs that are aimed at improving health by promoting adherence to a healthy lifestyle, such as the MLS.

Supplementary Materials: The following supporting information can be downloaded at: https://www.mdpi.com/article/10.3390/nu14194179/s1, Table S1. Methodological quality assessment of the cross-sectional studies included in the review; Table S2. Methodological quality assessment of the randomized controlled trials included in the review; and Table S3. Methodological quality assessment of the cohort studies included in the review.

Author Contributions: Conceptualization, E.M.-S., R.F.-C., and N.R.-R.; methodology, E.M.-S., B.C.-L., R.F.-C., and N.R.-R.; investigation, E.M.-S., R.F.-C., C.A.-B., and N.R.-R.; writing—original draft preparation, E.M.-S., C.A.-B., B.C.-L., and N.R.-R.; writing—review and editing, E.M.-S., R.F.-C., N.R.-R., N.A.-B., and B.C.-L.; supervision, R.F.-C., N.R.-R., and N.A.-B. All authors have read and agreed to the published version of the manuscript.

Funding: This research received no external funding.

Institutional Review Board Statement: Not applicable since this study is a systematic review.

Informed Consent Statement: Not applicable since this study is a systematic review.

Data Availability Statement: Data sharing not applicable. No new data were created or analyzed in this study. Data sharing is not applicable to this article.

Conflicts of Interest: The authors declare no conflict of interest.

References

1. Juanes, R.G.; Roca, M.; Gili, M.; Campayo, J.G.; Toro, M.G. Estilo de vida saludable: Un factor de protección minusvalorado frente a la depresión. *Psiquiatr. Biol.* **2017**, *24*, 97–105. [CrossRef]
2. Diolintzi, A.; Panagiotakos, D.B.; Sidossis, L.S. From Mediterranean diet to Mediterranean lifestyle: A narrative review. *Public Health Nutr.* **2019**, *22*, 2703–2713. [CrossRef]
3. Lema-Soto, L.F.; Salazar-Torres, I.C.; Varela-Arévalo, M.T.; Tamayo-Cardona, J.A.; Rubio-Sarria, A.; Botero-Polanco, A. Comportamiento y salud de los jóvenes universitarios: Satisfacción con el estilo de vida. *Pensam. Psicológico* **2009**, *5*, 71–88.
4. Yannakoulia, M.; Kontogianni, M.; Scarmeas, N. Cognitive health and Mediterranean Diet: Just diet or lifestyle pattern? *Ageing Res. Rev.* **2015**, *20*, 74–78. [CrossRef] [PubMed]
5. Sotos-Prieto, M.; Moreno-Franco, B.; Ordovás, J.M.; León, M.; Casasnovas, J.A.; Peñalvo, J.L. Design and development of an instrument to measure overall lifestyle habits for epidemiological research: The Mediterranean Lifestyle (MEDLIFE) index. *Public Health Nutr.* **2014**, *18*, 959–967. [CrossRef]
6. Del Balzo, V.; Diolordi, L.; Pinto, A.; Giusti, A.M.; Vitiello, V.; Cannella, C.; Dernini, S.; Donini, L.M.; Berry, E.M. Mediterranean diet pyramids: Towards the Italian model. *Ann. Ig* **2012**, *24*, 443–447. [PubMed]
7. Trichopoulou, A.; Vasilopoulou, E. Mediterranean Diet. In *Encyclopedia of Food and Health*; Academic Press: Cambridge, MA, USA, 2016; pp. 711–714. [CrossRef]
8. Bellisle, F. Infrequently asked questions about the Mediterranean diet. *Public Health Nutr.* **2009**, *12*, 1644–1647. [CrossRef] [PubMed]
9. Warburton, D.; Bredin, S. Health benefits of physical activity: A systematic review of current systematic reviews. *Curr. Opin. Cardiol.* **2017**, *32*, 541–556. [CrossRef]
10. Bouzas, C.; Bibiloni, M.D.M.; Julibert, A.; Ruiz-Canela, M.; Salas-Salvadó, J.; Corella, D.; Zomeño, M.D.; Romaguera, D.; Vioque, J.; Alonso-Gómez, Á.M.; et al. Adherence to the Mediterranean Lifestyle and Desired Body Weight Loss in a Mediterranean Adult Population with Overweight: A PREDIMED-Plus Study. *Nutrients* **2020**, *12*, 2114. [CrossRef]
11. Hershey, M.S.; Montero, A.F.; Prieto, M.S.; Kales, S.; Gea, A.; Estigarribia, L.R.; Villegas, A.S.; Gutiérrez, J.D.; González, M.A.M.; Canela, M.R. The Association between the Mediterranean Lifestyle Index and All-Cause Mortality in the Seguimiento Universidad de Navarra Cohort. *Am. J. Prev. Med.* **2020**, *59*, e239–e248. [CrossRef]
12. Lan, F.-Y.; Fernandez-Montero, A.; Yiannakou, I.; Marinos-Iatrides, O.; Ankeny, J.T.; Kiser, J.; Christophi, C.A.; Christiani, D.C.; Sotos-Prieto, M.; Kales, S.N. A Mediterranean Lifestyle Is Associated with Lower Hypertension Prevalence and Better Aerobic Capacity among New England Firefighter Recruits. *Occup. Environ. Med.* **2020**, *62*, 466–471. [CrossRef] [PubMed]
13. Mata-Fernández, A.; Hershey, M.S.; Pastrana-Delgado, J.C.; Sotos-Prieto, M.; Ruiz-Canela, M.; Martínez-González, M.A.; Fernandez-Montero, A. A Mediterranean Lifestyle Reduces the Risk of Cardiovascular Disease in the "Seguimiento Universidad de Navarra" (SUN) Cohort. *Nutr. Metab. Cardiovasc. Dis.* **2021**, *31*, 1728–1737. [CrossRef]

14. Sotos-Prieto, M.; Ortolá, R.; Ruiz-Canela, M.; Garcia-Esquinas, E.; Gómez, D.M.; Lopez-Garcia, E.; Martínez-González, M.Á.; Rodriguez-Artalejo, F. Association between the Mediterranean lifestyle, metabolic syndrome and mortality: A whole-country cohort in Spain. *Cardiovasc. Diabetol.* **2021**, *20*, 5. [CrossRef]
15. Pavicic-Žeželj, S.; Kenđel-Jovanovic, G.; Dragaš-Zubalj, N.; Micovic, V.; Željko, S. Associations between Adherence to the Mediterranean Diet and Lifestyle Assessed with the MEDLIFE Index among the Working Population. *Int. J. Environ. Res. Public Health* **2018**, *15*, 2126. [CrossRef]
16. Bowden, K.; Gray, N.A.; Swanepoel, E.; Wright, H.H. A Mediterranean lifestyle is associated with favourable cardiometabolic markers in people with non-dialysis dependent chronic kidney disease. *J. Nutr. Sci.* **2021**, *10*, 1–8. [CrossRef] [PubMed]
17. Hershey, M.S.; Prieto, M.S.; Canela, M.R.; Christophi, C.A.; Moffatt, S.; González, M.Á.M.; Kales, S.N. The Mediterranean lifestyle (MEDLIFE) index and metabolic syndrome in a non-Mediterranean working population. *Clin. Nutr.* **2021**, *40*, 2494–2503. [CrossRef]
18. Pérez-Ferre, N.; Del Valle, L.; Torrejón, M.J.; Barca, I.; Calvo, M.I.; Rubio, M.A.; Calle-Pascual, A.L. Diabetes mellitus and abnormal glucose tolerance development after gestational diabetes: A three-year, prospective, randomized, clinical- based, Mediterranean lifestyle interventional study with parallel groups. *Clin. Nutr.* **2015**, *34*, 579–585. [CrossRef]
19. Georgoulis, M.; Yiannakouris, N.; Kechribari, I.; Lamprou, K.; Perraki, E.; Vagiakis, E.; Kontogianni, M.D. Cardiometabolic Benefits of a Weight-Loss Mediterranean Diet/Lifestyle Intervention in Patients with Obstructive Sleep Apnea: The "MIMOSA" Randomized Clinical Trial. *Nutrients* **2020**, *12*, 1570. [CrossRef]
20. Georgoulis, M.; Yiannakouris, N.; Kechribari, I.; Lamprou, K.; Perraki, E.; Vagiakis, E.; Kontogianni, M.D. The effectiveness of a weight-loss Mediterranean diet/lifestyle intervention in the management of obstructive sleep apnea: Results of the "MIMOSA" randomized clinical trial. *Clin. Nutr.* **2020**, *40*, 850–859. [CrossRef]
21. Georgoulis, M.; Yiannakouris, N.; Tenta, R.; Fragopoulou, E.; Kechribari, I.; Lamprou, K.; Perraki, E.; Vagiakis, E.; Kontogianni, M.D. A weight-loss Mediterranean diet/lifestyle intervention ameliorates inflammation and oxidative stress in patients with obstructive sleep apnea: Results of the "MIMOSA" randomized clinical trial. *Eur. J. Nutr.* **2021**, *60*, 3799–3810. [CrossRef]
22. Sánchez-Villegas, A.; Ruíz-Canela, M.; Gea, A.; Lahortiga, F.; Martínez-González, M.A. The Association between the Mediterranean Lifestyle and Depression. *Clin. Psychol. Sci.* **2016**, *4*, 1085–1093. [CrossRef]
23. Anastasiou, C.A.; Yannakoulia, M.; Kontogianni, M.D.; Kosmidis, M.H.; Mamalaki, E.; Dardiotis, E.; Hadjigeorgiou, G.; Sakka, P.; Tsapanou, A.; Lykou, A.; et al. Mediterranean Lifestyle in Relation to Cognitive Health: Results from the HELIAD Study. *Nutrients* **2018**, *10*, 1557. [CrossRef] [PubMed]
24. Baldini, M.; Pasqui, F.; Bordoni, A.; Maranesi, M. Is the Mediterranean lifestyle still a reality? Evaluation of food consumption and energy expenditure in Italian and Spanish university students. *Public Health Nutr.* **2008**, *12*, 148–155. [CrossRef]
25. Georgousopoulou, E.N.; Mellor, D.D.; Naumovski, N.; Polychronopoulos, E.; Tyrovolas, S.; Piscopo, S.; Valacchi, G.; Anastasiou, F.; Zeimbekis, A.; Bountziouka, V.; et al. Mediterranean lifestyle and cardiovascular disease prevention. *Cardiovasc. Diagn. Ther.* **2017**, *7*, S39–S47. [CrossRef]
26. Grosso, G.; Marventano, M.; D'Urso, M.; Mistretta, A.; Galvano, F. The Mediterranean healthy eating, ageing, and lifestyle (MEAL) study: Rationale and study design. *Int. J. Food Sci. Nutr.* **2017**, *68*, 577–586. [CrossRef]
27. Katsagoni, C.N.; Papatheodoridis, G.V.; Ioannidou, P.; Deutsch, M.; Alexopoulou, A.; Papadopoulos, N.; Papageorgiou, M.-V.; Fragopoulou, E.; Kontogianni, M.D. Improvements in clinical characteristics of patients with non-alcoholic fatty liver disease, after an intervention based on the Mediterranean lifestyle: A randomised controlled clinical trial. *Br. J. Nutr.* **2018**, *120*, 164–175. [CrossRef]
28. Katsagoni, C.N.; Psarra, G.; Georgoulis, M.; Tambalis, K.; Panagiotakos, D.B.; Sidossisa, L.S. High and moderate adherence to Mediterranean lifestyle is inversely associated with overweight, general and abdominal obesity in children and adolescents: The MediLIFE-index. *Nutr. Res.* **2020**, *73*, 38–47. [CrossRef] [PubMed]
29. Moher, D.; Liberati, A.; Tetzlaff, J.; Altman, D.G.; PRISMA Group. Preferred reporting items for systematic reviews and meta-analyses: The PRISMA statement. *Int. J. Surg.* **2010**, *8*, 336–341. [CrossRef]
30. Munn, Z.; Aromataris, E.; Tufanaru, C.; Stern, C.; Porritt, K.; Farrow, J.; Lockwood, C.; Stephenson, M.; Moola, S.; Lizarondo, L.; et al. The development of software to support multiple systematic review types: The Joanna Briggs Institute System for the Unified Management, Assessment and Review of Information (JBI SUMARI). *Int. J. Evid. Based Healthc.* **2019**, *17*, 36–43. [CrossRef]
31. Toobert, D.J.; Strycker, L.A.; Glasgow, R.E.; Barrera, M.; Angell, K. Effects of the Mediterranean Lifestyle Program on Multiple Risk Behaviors and Psychosocial Outcomes among Women at Risk for Heart Disease. *Ann. Behav. Med.* **2005**, *29*, 128–137. [CrossRef]
32. Toobert, D.J.; Strycker, L.A.; Barrera, M.; Glasgow, R.E. Seven-Year Follow-Up of a Multiple-Health-Behavior Diabetes Intervention–HMC. *Am. J. Health Behav.* **2010**, *34*, 680–694. [CrossRef] [PubMed]
33. Marventano, S.; Godos, J.; Platania, A.; Galvano, F.; Mistretta, A.; Grosso, G. Mediterranean diet adherence in the Mediterranean healthy eating, aging and lifestyle (MEAL) study cohort. *Int. J. Food Sci. Nutr.* **2017**, *69*, 100–107. [CrossRef] [PubMed]
34. Bonaccio, M.; Gianfagna, F.; Stival, C.; Amerio, A.; Bosetti, C.; d'Oro, L.C.; Odone, A.; Stuckler, D.; Zucchi, A.; Gallus, S.; et al. Changes in a Mediterranean lifestyle during the COVID-19 pandemic among elderly Italians: An analysis of gender and socioeconomic inequalities in the "LOST in Lombardia" study. *Int. J. Food Sci. Nutr.* **2022**, *73*, 683–692. [CrossRef]

35. Sotos-Prieto, M.; Santos-Beneit, G.; Bodega, P.; Pocock, S.; Mattei, J.; Peñalvo, J.L. Validation of a questionnaire to measure overall Mediterranean lifestyle habits for research application: The MEDiterranean LIFEstyle index (MEDLIFE). *Nutr. Hosp.* **2015**, *32*, 1153–1163. [CrossRef]
36. Hershey, M.S.; Sanchez-Villegas, A.; Sotos-Prieto, M.; Fernandez-Montero, A.; Pano, O.; Lahortiga-Ramos, F.; Martínez-González, M.Á.; Ruiz-Canela, M. The Mediterranean Lifestyle and the Risk of Depression in Middle-Aged Adults. *J. Nutr.* **2022**, *152*, 227–234. [CrossRef] [PubMed]
37. Panagiotakos, D.B.; Pitsavos, C.; Stefanadis, C. Dietary patterns: A Mediterranean diet score and its relation to clinical and biological markers of cardiovascular disease risk. *Nutr. Metab. Cardiovasc. Dis.* **2006**, *16*, 559–568. [CrossRef]
38. Kavourasa, S.A.; Maraki, M.I.; Kollia, M.; Fernandez-Montero, A.; Jansen, L.; Sidossis, L.S. Development, reliability and validity of a physical activity questionnaire for estimating energy expenditure in Greek adults. *Sci. Sport.* **2016**, *31*, e47–e53. [CrossRef]
39. Hays, R.D.; Martin, S.A.; Sesti, A.M.; Spritzer, K.L. Psychometric properties of the Medical Outcomes Study Sleep measure. *Sleep Med.* **2005**, *6*, 41–44. [CrossRef]
40. Hays, R.D.; Sherbourne, C.D.; Mazel, R. *User's Manual for the Medical Outcomes Study (MOS) Core Measures of Health-Related Quality of Life*; Rand Corporation: Santa Mónica, CA, USA, 1995; ISBN 0-8330-1590-7.
41. Martin-Moreno, J.M.; Boyle, P.; Gorgojo, L.; Maisonneuve, P.; Fernandez-Rodriguez, J.C.; Willett, W.C. Development and validation of a food frequency questionnaire in Spain. *Int. J. Epidemiol.* **1993**, *22*, 512–519. [CrossRef]
42. Craig, C.L.; Marshall, A.L.; Sjostrom, M.; Bauman, A.E.; Ainsworth, B.E.; Pratt, M.; Ekelund, U.; Yngve, A.; Sallis, J.F.; Oja, P. International physical activity questionnaire: 12-country reliability and validity. *Med. Sci. Sport. Exerc.* **2003**, *35*, 1381–1395. [CrossRef]
43. Martínez-González, M.A.; López-Fontana, C.; Varo, J.J.; Sánchez-Villegas, A.; Martinez, J.A. Validation of the Spanish version of the physical activity questionnaire used in the Nurses' Health Study and the Health Professionals' Follow-up Study. *Public Health Nutr.* **2005**, *8*, 920–927. [CrossRef]
44. Elosua, R.; Marrugat, J.; Molina, L.; Pons, S.; Pujol, E. Validation of the Minnesota Leisure Time Physical Activity Questionnaire in Spanish men. The MARATHOM Investigators. *Am. J. Epidemiol.* **1994**, *139*, 1197–1209. [CrossRef]
45. Elosua, R.; Garcia, M.; Aguilar, A.; Molina, L.; Covas, M.I.; Marrugat, J. Validation of the Minnesota Leisure Time Physical Activity Questionnaire in Spanish Women. Investigators of the MARATDON Group. *Med. Sci. Sport. Exerc.* **2000**, *32*, 1421–1437. [CrossRef] [PubMed]
46. Buysse, D.J.; Reynolds, C.F.; Monk, T.H.; Berman, S.R.; Kupfer, D.J. The Pittsburgh Sleep Quality Index: A new instrument for psychiatric practice and research. *Psychiatry Res.* **1989**, *28*, 193–213. [CrossRef]
47. Soldatos, C.R.; Dikeos, D.G.; Paparrigopoulos, T.J. The diagnostic validity of the Athens Insomnia Scale. *J. Psychosom. Res.* **2003**, *55*, 263–267. [CrossRef]
48. Serra-Majem, L.; Ribas, L.; Ngo, J.; Ortega, R.; García, A.; Pérez-Rodrigo, C.; Aranceta, J. Food, youth and the Mediterranean diet in Spain. Development of KIDMED, Mediterranean Diet Quality Index in children and adolescents. *Public Health Nutr.* **2004**, *7*, 931–935. [CrossRef]
49. Schröder, H.; Fitó, M.; Estruch, R.; Martínez-González, M.A.; Corella, D.; Salvadó, J.S.; Raventós, R.L.; Ros, E.; Salaverría, I.; Fiol, M.; et al. A short screener is valid for assessing Mediterranean diet adherence among older Spanish men and women. *J. Nutr.* **2011**, *141*, 1140–1145. [CrossRef]
50. Durán, A.; Martín, P.; Runkle, I.; Pérez, N.; Abad, R.; Fernández, M.; Del Valle, L.; Sanz, M.F.; Calle-Pascual, A.L. Benefits of self-monitoring blood glucose in the management of new-onset Type 2 diabetes mellitus: The St Carlos Study, a prospective randomized clinic-based interventional study with parallel groups. *J. Diabetes* **2010**, *2*, 203–211. [CrossRef]
51. Taber, S.C.; Rimm, E.; Stampfer, M.; Spiegelman, D.; Colditz, G.A.; Giovannucci, E.; Ascherio, A.; Willett, W.C. Reproducibility and validity of a self-administered physical activity questionnaire for male health professionals. *Int. J. Epidemiol.* **1996**, *7*, 81–86. [CrossRef]
52. Wolf, A.M.; Hunter, D.J.; Colditz, G.A.; Manson, J.E.; Stampfer, M.J.; Corsano, K.A.; Rosner, B.; Kriska, A.; Willett, W.C. Reproducibility and Validity of a Self-Administered Physical Activity Questionnaire. *Int. J. Epidemiol.* **1994**, *23*, 991–999. [CrossRef]
53. Wareham, N.J.; Jakes, R.W.; Rennie, K.L.; Schuit, J.; Mitchell, J.; Hennings, S.; Day, N.E. Validity and repeatability of a simple index derived from the short physical activity questionnaire used in the European prospective investigation into cancer and nutrition (EPIC) study. *Public Health Nutr.* **2003**, *6*, 407–413. [CrossRef] [PubMed]
54. Stewart, A.L.; Verboncoeur, C.J.; McLellan, B.Y.; Gillis, D.E.; Rush, S.; Mills, K.M.; King, A.C.; Ritter, P.; Brown, B.W., Jr.; Bortz, W.M. Physical Activity Outcomes of CHAMPS II: A Physical Activity Promotion Program for Older Adults. *J. Gerontol. Ser. A Biol. Sci. Med. Sci.* **2001**, *56*, M465–M470. [CrossRef] [PubMed]
55. Schwarzer, R.; Dunkel-Schetter, C.; Kemeny, M. The multidimensional nature of received social support in gay men at risk of HIV infection and AIDS. *Am. J. Community Psychol.* **1994**, *22*, 319–339. [CrossRef]
56. Benítez-Arciniega, A.A.; Mendez, M.A.; Baena-Díez, J.M.; Martori, M.-A.R.; Soler, C.; Marrugat, J.; Covas, M.-I.; Sanz, H.; Llopis, A.; Schröder, H. Concurrent and construct validity of Mediterranean diet scores as assessed by an FFQ. *Public Health Nutr.* **2011**, *14*, 2015–2021. [CrossRef]
57. Jackson, D.L.; Gillaspy, J.A.; Purc-Stephenson, R. Reporting practices in confirmatory factor analysis: An overview and some recommendations. *Psychol. Methods* **2009**, *14*, 6–23. [CrossRef]

58. Muñiz, J.; Fonseca-Pedrero, E. Construcción de instrumentos de medida para la evaluación universitaria. *Rev. Investig. Educ.* **2009**, *5*, 13–25.
59. Muñiz, J.; Fonseca-Pedrero, E. Diez pasos para la construcción de un test. *Psicothema* **2019**, *31*, 7–16. [CrossRef]
60. Muñiz, J.; Bartram, D. Improving International Tests and Testing. *Eur. Psychol.* **2007**, *12*, 206–219. [CrossRef]
61. Downing, S.M. Twelve Steps for Effective Test Development. In *Handbook of Test Development*; Lawrence Erlbaum Associates Publishers: Mahwah, NJ, USA, 2006; pp. 3–25. ISBN 978-0-8058-5264-6.
62. Smith, G.T. On construct validity: Issues of method and measurement. *Psychol. Assess.* **2005**, *17*, 396–408. [CrossRef] [PubMed]

MDPI
St. Alban-Anlage 66
4052 Basel
Switzerland
www.mdpi.com

Nutrients Editorial Office
E-mail: nutrients@mdpi.com
www.mdpi.com/journal/nutrients

www.ingramcontent.com/pod-product-compliance
Lightning Source LLC
Chambersburg PA
CBHW061512210926
51850CB00008B/1892
9783036591568